The Illusion of Conscious Will

The Illusion of Conscious Will

Daniel M. Wegner

Bradford Books
The MIT Press
Cambridge, Massachusetts
London, England

This book was set in Sabon by Interactive Composition Corporation and was printed and bound in the United States of America.

Library of Congress Cataloging-in-Publication Data

Wegner, Daniel M., 1948–
    The illusion of conscious will / Daniel M. Wegner.
        p.   cm.
    "A Bradford book."
    Includes bibliographical references and index.
    ISBN 0-262-23222-7 (hc: alk. paper)
    1. Will.   2. Free will and determinism.   I. Title.

BF611 .W38   2002
153.8—dc21   2001054608

10 9 8 7 6 5 4

A leaf was riven from a tree,
"I mean to fall to earth," said he.

The west wind, rising, made him veer.
"Eastward," said he, "I now shall steer."

The east wind rose with greater force.
Said he: "'Twere wise to change my course."

With equal power they contend.
He said: "My judgment I suspend."

Down died the winds; the leaf, elate,
Cried: "I've decided to fall straight."

Ambrose Bierce, *The Devil's Dictionary* (1911)

Contents

8 Hypnosis and Will 271

In hypnosis the person experiences a loss of conscious will. This loss accompanies an apparent transfer of control to someone else, along with the creation of some exceptional forms of control over the self.

9 The Mind's Compass 317

Although the experience of conscious will is not evidence of mental causation, it does signal personal authorship of action to the individual and so influences both the sense of achievement and the acceptance of moral responsibility.

Preface

Do we consciously cause what we do, or do our actions happen to us? Most people are willing to accept that these alternatives are in fact opposites, and then they immediately become embroiled in argument. Determinism? Free will? Some middle ground? Philosophers have given us plenty of "isms" to use in describing the positions that can be taken on this question, meanwhile not really answering it in a satisfying way. Psychologists and neuroscientists, in turn, haven't helped things much by often assuming that our actions are happenings that must, of course, be caused by prior events—and thus that questions of conscious will are not answerable. Students of religion and of the law, for their part, weigh in with substantial arguments on this question as well, anchoring the problem with deep concerns about responsibility and morality.

This is a book about a different sort of answer to the question. Here it is: Yes, we feel that we consciously cause what we do; and yes, our actions happen to us. Rather than opposites, conscious will and psychological determinism can be friends. Such friendship comes from realizing that the feeling of conscious will is created by the mind and brain just as human actions themselves are created by the mind and brain. The answer to the question of conscious will, then, may involve exploring how the mechanisms of the human mind create the experience of will. And the experience of conscious will that is created in this way need not be a mere epiphenomenon. Rather than a ghost in the machine, the experience of conscious will is a feeling that helps us to appreciate and remember our authorship of the things our minds and bodies do.

Now, of course, we're getting ahead of ourselves. This is to be expected because I've already written this whole book and you're just starting to look it over. Let me just say here that as a scientific psychologist involved in research on how people think about themselves and others, I've always found it frustrating that no one seems to have thought all this through and done the proper research. So many intriguing philosophical questions have been approached in useful ways through science, and this is one that is still just begging to be addressed. If psychological and neural mechanisms are responsible for human behavior, why does it feel as though we are consciously causing the things we do? It turns out there is a world of scientific research on this question.

In these pages, this research is approached from several directions. We look at the conditions that influence illusions of the experience of will—the cases when people feel they are willing an act that they in fact are not doing, or when they feel they are not willing an act that they indeed are doing. We explore conscious will in settings such as hypnosis, Ouija board spelling, automatic writing, and facilitated communication. We examine, too, such unusual phenomena as spirit possession, dissociative identity disorder, and trance channeling, to grasp some of the extreme transformations of the experience of will. Psychological disorders—some caused by detectable brain damage and others, such as schizophrenia, by more subtle processes are examined also, to understand how the experience of conscious will is modified in these conditions. The goal of this book is to put conscious will into perspective as a topic of psychological study. To do this, we need to understand how conscious will might be an illusion, a feeling that comes and goes independent of any actual causal relationship between our thoughts and our actions.

Unlike anything I have ever studied before, the topic of conscious will excites interest and controversy. At first I didn't like the controversy—the heated, seemingly interminable question periods following my talks, during which audience members pointed out the gaping holes in my thinking and in my head. More than once I found myself closing the question period early so I could escape the interrogation. As it turned out, though, these discussions were essential for shaping this book, and I am indebted to the many people who helped in this way. I express my thanks here for their wisdom and guidance.

Specific individuals also guided this work in important ways. For reading and commenting on one or more chapters, I thank Henry Aaron, John

Bargh, Michael Bratman, Jerry Clore, Daniel Gilbert, Clark Glymour, Jon Haidt, John Kihlstrom, Angeline Lillard, Bobbie Spellman, Herman Spitz, Toni Wegner (who advised and cajoled me through four needed revisions of chapter 1), and Timothy Wilson. For valuable commentary on the entire book, I am indebted to Daniel Dennett. For extended conversations on this topic that were particularly helpful, I thank Henk Aarts, Susan Carey (an audience member whose comments were so much on target that I went off and wrote them down), Herbert Clark, Jerry Clore (the best sounding board on this work I ever encountered), Ap Dijksterhuis, John Flavell, Chris Gilbert, Daniel Gilbert, Tory Higgins, Larry Jacoby, Michael Kubovy, Benjamin Libet, Neil Macrae, Jonathan Schooler, Robin Vallacher, Henry Wellman, and Daniel Willingham.

My students have also contributed in major ways. For their reading, comments, and ideas I thank Elizabeth Dunn, Alana Feiler, Valerie Fuller, Jean Goddard, PerHenrik Hedberg, Holly Hom, Brian Malone, Abby Marsh, Carey Morewedge, Wendy Morris, Rebecca Norwick, Kelly Schoeffel, Mark Stalnaker, and Weylin Sternglanz. Special thanks go to Zita Meijer for her extensive help in collecting evidence on spirit possession across cultures. Thalia Wheatley deserves particular recognition for her key role in developing a research paradigm for the study of will, and for her contribution on this topic to chapter 3. I have enjoyed the help of outstanding research assistants, all of whom worked in valuable ways on this volume, and I thank them all: Jeanine Dick, Eva Gutierrez, Cheri Robbins, Betsy Sparrow, and Eli Ticatch. I'm grateful as well to the students in seminars on conscious will at the University of Virginia and at Harvard University for their creative and insightful contributions.

This book was started during my sabbatical year (1996–1997) at the Center for Advanced Study in the Behavioral Sciences, Palo Alto. I thank the Center, with a note of special gratitude to the staff and fellows, and I thank the University of Virginia for its sabbatical support. Some of the research described here was funded by a grant from National Institute of Mental Health (Grant MH-49127).

The Illusion of Conscious Will

1

The Illusion

It usually seems that we consciously will our voluntary actions, but this is an illusion.

All theory is against the freedom of the will; all experience is for it.
Samuel Johnson,
Boswell's *Life of Johnson*
(1791)

So, here you are reading a book on conscious will. How could this have happened? One way to explain it would be to examine the causes of your behavior. A team of scientific psychologists could study your reported thoughts, emotions, and motives, your genetics and your history of learning, experience, and development, your social situation and culture, your memories and reaction times, your physiology and neuroanatomy, and lots of other things as well. If they somehow had access to all the information they could ever want, the assumption of psychology is that they could uncover the mechanisms that give rise to all your behavior and so could certainly explain why you picked up this book at this moment.[1] However, another way to explain the fact of your reading this book is

1. This assumption is similar to a conjecture of the French astronomer and mathematician Pierre Simon Laplace (1749–1827) in his *Philosophical Essay on Probabilities* (1814): "An intellect which at any given moment knew all the forces that animate Nature and the mutual positions of the beings that comprise it, if this intellect were vast enough to submit its data to analysis, could condense into a single formula the movement of the greatest bodies of the universe and that of the lightest atom: for such an intellect nothing could be uncertain; and the future just like the past would be present before its eyes." It turns out that this "single formula" is so complex that the project of understanding the causation of even a single human action is a vast challenge to scientists, perhaps an impossible one. However, we're talking here about an ideal of science, not a practical project.

just to say that you decided to pick up the book and begin reading. You consciously willed what you are doing.

These two explanations are both appealing but in different ways. The scientific explanation accounts for behavior as a mechanism and appeals to that part of us that knows how useful science is for understanding the world. It would be wonderful if we could understand people in just the same way. The conscious will explanation, on the other hand, has a much deeper grip on our intuition. We each have a profound sense that we consciously will much of what we do, and we experience ourselves willing our actions many times a day. As William James put it, "The whole sting and excitement of our voluntary life . . . depends on our sense that in it things are *really being decided* from one moment to another, and that it is not the dull rattling off of a chain that was forged innumerable ages ago" (1890, 453). Quite apart from any resentment we might feel on being cast into the role of mechanisms or robots, we appreciate the notion of conscious will because we experience it so very acutely. We do things, and when we do them, we experience the action in such a way that it seems to flow seamlessly from our consciousness. We feel that *we cause ourselves to behave.*

The idea of conscious will and the idea of psychological mechanisms have an oil and water relationship, having never been properly reconciled. One way to put them together—the way this book explores—is to say that the mechanistic approach is the explanation preferred for scientific purposes but that the person's experience of conscious will is utterly convincing and important to the person and so must be understood scientifically as well. The mechanisms underlying the experience of will are themselves a fundamental topic of scientific study. We should be able to examine and understand what creates the experience of will and what makes it go away. This means, though, that conscious will is an illusion.[2] It is an illusion in the sense that *the experience of consciously willing an action is not a direct indication that the conscious thought has caused the action.* Conscious will, viewed this way, may be an extraordinary illusion indeed—the equivalent of a magician's producing an elephant from the

2. Calling this an illusion may be a bit strong, and it might be more appropriate to think of this as a construction or fabrication. But the term *illusion* does convey the possibility that we place an erroneously large emphasis on how will appears to us and assume that this appearance is a deep insight.

folds of his handkerchief. How could it seem so much like our wills cause our actions if this isn't actually happening? To grasp how this might be, we need to begin by examining what exactly is meant by conscious will. With any luck, we will discover a large expanse of the elephant protruding from the magician's pocket and so begin to understand how the trick works.

Conscious Will

Conscious will is usually understood in one of two major ways. It is common to talk about conscious will as something that is experienced when we perform an action—actions feel willed or not, and this feeling of voluntariness or doing a thing "on purpose" is an indication of conscious will. It is also common, however, to speak of conscious will as a force of mind, a name for the causal link between our minds and our actions. One might assume that the *experience* of consciously willing an action and the *causation* of the action by the person's conscious mind are the same thing. As it turns out, however, they are entirely distinct, and the tendency to confuse them is the source of the illusion of conscious will that this book is about. So, to begin, we'll need to look into each in turn, first examining will as an experience and then considering will as a causal force.

The Experience of Conscious Will

Will is a feeling. David Hume was sufficiently impressed by this idea so that he proposed to define the will in this way, as "nothing but *the internal impression we feel and are conscious of, when we knowingly give rise to any new motion of our body, or new perception of our mind*" (1739, 399). This definition puts the person's experience at the very center of the whole concept—the will is not some cause or force or motor in a person but rather is the personal conscious feeling of such causing, forcing, or motoring. Hume's definition makes sense because the occurrence of this conscious experience is an absolute *must* for anyone to claim they've done something that they consciously willed.

Without an experience of willing, even actions that look entirely voluntary from the outside still fall short of qualifying as truly *willed*. Intentions, plans, and other thoughts can be experienced, and still the action isn't willed if the person says it was not. If a person plans to take a shower, for example, and says that she intends to do it as she climbs into the water, spends fifteen minutes in there scrubbing up nicely, and then comes out reporting that she indeed seems to have had a shower but does not feel she had consciously willed it—who are we to say that she did will it? Consciously willing an action requires a feeling of doing (Ansfield and Wegner 1996), a kind of internal "oomph" that somehow certifies authentically that one has done the action. If she didn't get that feeling about her showering, then there's no way we could establish for sure whether she consciously willed it.

The fact that experiences of conscious will can only be established by self-reports ("I showered, yes I did") would be quite all right if the self-reports always corresponded with some other outward indication of the experience. However, this correspondence doesn't always happen. The experience of will that is so essential for the occurrence of consciously willed action does not always accompany actions that appear by other indications to be willed. Consider, for instance, the case of people who have *alien hand syndrome,* a neuropsychological disorder in which a person experiences one hand as operating with a mind of its own. One such person was the character played by Peter Sellers in *Dr. Strangelove* (fig. 1.1), who couldn't control one hand and found it alternately steering his wheelchair astray and gesturing a Nazi salute.

Alien hand patients typically experience one hand as acting autonomously. They do not experience willing its actions and may find it moving at cross-purposes with their conscious intention. This syndrome is often linked with damage to the middle of the frontal lobe on the side of the brain opposite the affected hand (Gasquoine 1993), and in some people the difficulty can come and go over time (Leiguarda et al. 1993). Banks and colleagues (1989, 456) report an alien hand patient whose "left hand would tenaciously grope for and grasp any nearby object, pick and pull at her clothes, and even grasp her throat during sleep. . . . She slept with the arm tied to prevent nocturnal misbehavior. She never denied that her left arm and hand belonged to her, although she did refer to her limb as though it were an autonomous entity."

Should the alien hand's movements be classed as willed or unwilled? On the one hand (pun couldn't be helped), the alien hand seems to do some

Figure 1.1
Dr. Strangelove. Courtesy Archive Photos.

fairly complicated things, acts we might class as willful and voluntary if we were just watching and hadn't learned of the patient's lamentable loss of control. In the case of another patient, for example, "While playing checkers on one occasion, the left hand made a move he did not wish to make, and he corrected the move with the right hand; however, the left hand, to the patient's frustration, repeated the false move. On other occasions, he turned the pages of the book with one hand while the other tried to close it; he shaved with the right hand while the left one unzipped his jacket; he tried to soap a washcloth while the left hand kept putting the soap back in the dish; and he tried to open a closet with the right hand while the left one closed it" (Banks et al. 1989, 457). By the looks of it, the alien hand is quite willful. On the other hand (as the pun drags on), however, the patient does not experience these actions as consciously willed. One patient described the experience as a feeling that "someone from the moon" was controlling her hand (Geschwind et al. 1995, 803).

Brain damage is not the only way that the experience of will can be undermined. Consider, for instance, the feelings of involuntariness that occur during hypnosis. Perhaps the most profound single effect of hypnosis is the feeling that your actions are happening to you rather than that you are doing them (Lynn, Rhue, and Weekes 1990). To produce this experience, a hypnotist might suggest, "Please hold your arm out to your side. Now, concentrate on the feelings in your arm. You will find that your arm is becoming heavy. It feels as though a great weight were pulling it down. It is so very heavy. It is being pulled down, down toward the ground. Your arm is heavy, very heavy. It is getting so heavy you can't resist. Your arm is falling, falling down toward the ground." With enough of this patter, many listeners will indeed experience the arm's becoming heavy, and some will even find their arm falling down. When quizzed on it, these individuals often report that they felt no sense of moving their arm voluntarily but rather experienced the downward movement as something that happened to them. This doesn't occur for everyone in this situation, only some proportion, but it nonetheless indicates that the experience of will can be manipulated in a voluntary action.

In the case of hypnotic involuntariness, the person has a very clear and well-rehearsed idea of the upcoming action. Admittedly, this idea of the action is really phrased more as an expectation ("My arm will fall") than as an intention ("I will lower my arm"), but it nonetheless occurs before the action when an intention normally happens, and it provides a distinct preview of the action that is to come (Kirsch and Lynn 1998; Spanos 1986). Hypnotic involuntariness thus provides an example of the lack of experience of will that is even more perplexing than alien hand syndrome. With alien hand, the person simply doesn't know what the hand will do, but with hypnosis, conscious will is lacking even when knowledge of the action is present. And without the *experience* of willing, even this foreknowledge of the action seems insufficient to move the action into the "consciously willed" category. If it doesn't feel as though you did it, then it doesn't seem that the will was operating.

Figure 1.2
A table-turning séance. From *L'Illustration* (1853).

Another case of the absence of experience of will occurs in *table turning*, a curious phenomenon discovered in the spiritualist movement in Europe and America in the mid–nineteenth century (Ansfield and Wegner 1996; Carpenter 1888; Pearsall 1972). To create this effect, a group of people sit gathered around a table, all with their hands on its surface. If they are convinced that the table might move as the result of spirit intervention (or if they are even just hoping for such an effect) and sit patiently waiting for such movement, it is often found that the table *does* start to move after some time (fig. 1.2). It might even move about the room or begin rotating so quickly that the participants can barely keep up. Carpenter (1888, 292–293) observed that "all this is done, not merely without the least consciousness on the part of the performers that they are exercising any force of their own, but for the most part under the full conviction that they are not."

In one exemplary case, the Reverend N. S. Godfrey, his wife, and a friend one evening in June 1852 placed their hands on a small mahogany table and found that after forty-five minutes it began to move. With two family servants and the local schoolmaster as witnesses, the group carried out experiments and found that the table would move in various ways, some of which seemed particularly sinister. At one point something "caused the table to revolve rapidly," yet then, as Godfrey relates, "a bible was quietly laid upon the table and it stopped! We were horror struck!" (1853, 23). Questions were asked of the table, and responses were given by a leg's rising and knocking on the floor, and interchanges ensued that convinced those assembled that there was a devil inhabiting the table and causing it to move.

The table-turning curiosity was sufficiently celebrated and controversial to attract the attention of the chemist and physicist Michael Faraday, who proceeded to test the source of the table movement. He placed force measurement devices between participants' hands and the table, and found that the source of the movement was their hands and not the table (Faraday 1853). All one needs to do, actually, is to use a dusty table and observe the direction of the streaks left by participants' slipping hands. The streaks run away from their hands in the direction opposite the table movement (as one would expect if people's fingers slipped a bit as they pushed the table) rather than toward the movement (as one would expect if the table were pulling them along and their fingers were slipping as they fell behind). Apparently, in attributing the table movement to the spirit, the participants did not have sufficient experience of will to recognize the source of their own voluntary actions. Indeed, the Reverend Godfrey disputed Faraday's findings vehemently: "[We] imparted the motion, he tells us, *which we did not.*"

Such examples of the separation of action from the experience of will suggest that it is useful to draw a distinction between them. Figure 1.3

	Feeling of Doing	No Feeling of Doing
Doing	Normal voluntary action	Automatism
Not Doing	Illusion of control	Normal inaction

Figure 1.3
Conditions of human action.

shows what might be considered four basic conditions of human action—the combinations that arise when we emphasize the distinction between action and the sense of acting willfully. The upper left quadrant shows the expected correspondence of action and the feeling of doing—the case when we do something and feel also that we are doing it. This is the noncontroversial case, or perhaps the assumed human condition. The lower right quadrant is also noncontroversial, the instance when we are not doing anything and feel we are not.

The upper right quadrant—the case of no feeling of will when there is in fact action—encompasses the examples we have looked at so far. The movement of alien hands, the hypnotic suggestion of arm heaviness, and table turning all fit in this quadrant because they involve no feeling of doing in what appear otherwise to be voluntary actions. These can be classed in general as *automatisms*.[3] More automatisms are explored in later chapters. The forms they take and the roles they play in life are something of a subtext throughout this book. We should not fail to notice here, however, the other special quadrant of the table—cases of the *illusion of control*. Ellen Langer (1975) used this term to describe instances in which people have the feeling they are doing something when they actually are not doing anything.[4]

When does this happen? The last time it happened to me was when I was shopping in a toy store with my family one Saturday. While my kids were taking a complete inventory of the stock, I eased up to a video game display and started fiddling with the joystick. A little monkey on the screen was eagerly hopping over barrels as they rolled toward him, and I got quite involved in moving him along and making him hop, until the

---

3. An automatism is not the same thing as an automatic behavior, though the terms arise from the same beginnings (first mentioned by Hartley 1749). An automatism has been defined as an apparently voluntary behavior that one does not sense as voluntary (Carpenter 1888; Janet 1889; Solomons and Stein 1896), and we retain that usage here. More generally, though, a behavior might be automatic in other senses—it could be uncontrollable, unintended, efficient, or performed without awareness, for instance (Bargh 1994; Wegner and Bargh 1998).

4. This term is not entirely fitting in our analysis because the larger point to be made here is that all of the feeling of doing is an illusion. Strictly speaking, then, the whole left side of the table should be labeled illusory. But for our purposes, it is worth noting that the illusion is particularly trenchant when there is intention and the feeling of doing but in fact no action at all.

phrase "Start Game" popped into view. I was under the distinct impression that I had started some time ago, but in fact I had been "playing" during a pre-game demo. Duped perhaps by the wobbly joystick and my unfamiliarity with the game, I had been fiddling for nothing, the victim of an illusion of control. And, indeed, when I started playing the game, I immediately noticed the difference. But for a while there, I was oblivious to my own irrelevance. I thought I was doing something that I really didn't do at all.

The illusion of control is acute in our interactions with machines, as when we don't know whether our push of an elevator button or a Coke machine selection lever has done anything yet sense that it has. The illusion is usually studied with judgments of contingency (e.g., Matute 1996) by having people try to tell whether they are causing a particular effect (for example, turning on a light) by doing something (say, pushing a button) when the button and the light are not perfectly connected and the light may flash randomly by itself. But we experience the illusion, too, when we roll dice or flip coins in a certain way, hoping that we will thus be able to influence the outcome. It even happens sometimes that we feel we have contributed to the outcome of a sporting event on TV just by our presence in the room ("Did I just jinx them by running off to the fridge?").

The illusion that one has done something that one has not really done can also be produced through brute social influence, as illustrated in a study by Kassin and Kiechel (1996). These researchers falsely accused a series of participants in a laboratory reaction time task of damaging a computer by pressing the wrong key. All the participants were truly innocent and initially denied the charge, showing that they didn't really *experience* damaging the computer. However, they were led later to remember having done it. A confederate of the experimenters claimed afterwards that she saw the participant hit the key or did not see the participant hit the key. Those whose "crime" was ostensibly witnessed became more likely to sign a confession ("I hit the ALT key and caused the program to crash. Data were lost."), internalize guilt for the event, and even confabulate details in memory consistent with that belief—but only when the reaction time task was so fast that it made their error seem likely. We are not infallible sources of knowledge about our own actions and can be duped into thinking we did things when events conspire to make us feel responsible.

Most of the things we do in everyday life seem to fall along the "normal" diagonal in figure 1.3. Action and the experience of will usually correspond, so we feel we are doing things willfully when we actually do them and feel we are not doing something when in truth we have not done it. Still, the automatisms and illusions of control that lie off this diagonal remind us that action and the feeling of doing are not locked together inevitably. They come apart often enough to make one wonder whether they may be produced by separate systems in the mind. The processes of mind that produce the experience of will may be quite distinct from the processes of mind that produce the action itself. As soon as we accept the idea that the will should be understood as an *experience* of the person who acts, we realize that conscious will is not inherent in action—there are actions that have it and actions that don't.

The definition of will as an experience means that we are very likely to appreciate conscious will in ourselves because we are, of course, privy to our own experiences and are happy to yap about them all day. We have a bit more trouble appreciating conscious will in others sometimes, and have particular difficulty imagining the experience or exercise of conscious will in creatures to whom we do not attribute a conscious mind. Some people might say there is nothing quite like a human being if you want a conscious mind, of course, but others contend that certain nonhuman beings would qualify as having conscious minds. They might see conscious minds in dogs, cats, dolphins, other animals (the cute ones), certain robots or computers, very young children, perhaps spirits or other nonexistent beings.[5] In any event, the conscious mind is the place where will happens, and there is no way to learn whether an action has been consciously willed without somehow trying to access that mind's experience of the action. We have the best evidence of an experience of conscious will in ourselves, and the second-best evidence becomes available when others communicate their experience of will to us in language ("I did it!").

5. Dennett (1996) discusses the problem of other minds very elegantly in *Kinds of Minds*.

The Force of Conscious Will

Will is not only an experience; it is also a force. Because of this, it is tempting to think that the conscious experience of will is a direct perception of the force of will. The *feeling* that one is purposefully not having a cookie, for instance, can easily be taken as an immediate perception of one's conscious mind *causing* this act of self-control. We seem to experience the force within us that keeps the cookie out of our mouths, but the force is not the same thing as the experience.[6]

When conscious will is described as a force, it can take different forms. Will can come in little dabs to produce individual acts, or it can be a more long-lasting property of a person, a kind of inner strength or resolve. Just as a dish might have hotness or an automobile might have the property of being red, a person seems to have will, a quality of power that causes his or her actions. The force may be with us. Such will can be strong or weak and so can serve to explain things such as one person's steely persistence in the attempt to dig a swimming pool in the backyard, for example, or another person's knee-buckling weakness for chocolate. The notion of strength of will has been an important intuitive explanation of human behavior since the ancients (Charleton 1988), and it has served throughout the history of psychology as the centerpiece of the psychology of will. The classic partition of the mind into three functions includes cognition, emotion, and *conation*—the will or volitional component (e.g., James 1890).

The will in this traditional way of thinking is an explanatory entity of the first order. In other words, it explains lots of things but nothing explains it. As Joseph Buchanan described it in 1812, "Volition has commonly been considered by metaphysical writers, as consisting in the exertion of an innate power, or constituent faculty of the mind, denominated will, concerning whose intrinsic nature it is fruitless and unnecessary to inquire" (298). At the extreme, of course, this view of the will makes

---

6. Wittgenstein (1974) complained about defining will in terms of experience, feeling that this by itself was incomplete. He noted that there is more to will than merely the feeling of doing: "The will can't be a phenomenon, for whatever phenomenon you take is something that *simply happens*, something we undergo, not something we *do*. . . . Look at your arm and move it and you will experience this very vividly: 'You aren't observing it moving itself, you aren't having an experience—not just an experience, anyway—you're *doing* something' " (144).

the scientific study of it entirely out of the question and suggests instead that it ought to be worshiped. Pointing to will as a force in a person that causes the person's action is the same kind of explanation as saying that God has caused an event. This is a stopper that trumps any other explanation but that still seems not to explain anything at all in a predictive sense. Just as we can't tell what God is going to do, we can't predict what the will is likely to do.[7]

The notion that will is a force residing in a person results in a further problem. Hume (1739) remarked on this problem when he described the basic difficulty that occurs whenever a person perceives causality in an object. Essentially, he pointed out that causality is not a property inhering in objects. For instance, when we see a bowling ball go scooting down the lane and smashing into the pins, it certainly *seems* as though the ball has some kind of causal force in it. The ball is the cause, and the explosive reaction of the pins is the effect. Hume pointed out, though, that you can't *see* causation in something but must only infer it from the constant relation between cause and effect. Every time the ball rolls into the pins, they bounce away. Ergo, the ball caused the pins to move. But there is no property of causality nestled somewhere in that ball, or hanging somewhere in space between the ball and pins, that somehow works this magic. Causation is an event, not a thing or a characteristic or attribute of an object.

In the same sense, causation can't be a property of a person's conscious intention. You can't *see* your conscious intention causing an action but can only infer this from the constant relation between intention and action. Normally, when you intend things, they happen. Hume remarked in *A Treatise on Human Nature* (1739) that the "constant union" and "inference of the mind" that establish causality in physical events must also give rise to causality in "actions of the mind." He said, "Some have asserted . . . that we feel an energy, or power, in our own mind. . . . But to convince us how fallacious this reasoning is, we need only consider . . . that the will being here consider'd as a cause, has no more a discoverable

---

7. The idea that the will is a property that can vary in quantity, and that it inheres in people and has some natural force that can produce actions, nonetheless remains a useful part of some theories in modern scientific psychology (Muraven, Tice, and Baumeister 1998).

connexion with its effects, than any material cause has with its proper effect. . . . In short, the actions of the mind are, in this respect, the same with those of matter. We perceive only their constant conjunction; nor can we ever reason beyond it. No internal impression has an apparent energy, more than external objects have" (400–401). Hume realized, then, that calling the will a force in a person's consciousness—even in one's own consciousness—must always overreach what we can see (or even introspect) and so should be understood as an attribution or inference.

This is not to say that the concept of will power is useless. Rather, Hume's analysis suggests that the concept of force of will, or will power, must be accompanied by careful causal inference. These ideas can be used as the basis for scientific theories of human behavior, certainly, because they serve as summaries of the degree of relationship that may exist between the mind and behavior. But we must be careful to distinguish between such *empirical will*—the causality of the person's conscious thoughts as established by a scientific analysis of their covariation with the person's behavior—and the *phenomenal will*—the person's reported experience of will. The empirical will can be measured by examining the actual degree of constant conjunction between the person's self-reported conscious thought and the person's action, and by assessing the causal role of that thought in the context of other possible causes of the action (and possible causes of the thought as well). But the precise causal understanding of the conscious will that is captured in such discussions is not something that is linked in any direct way to the person's experience of will.

The experience of will is merely a feeling that occurs to a person. It is to action as the experience of pain is to the bodily changes that result from painful stimulation, or as the experience of emotion is to the bodily changes associated with emotion. The person's feeling of pain is not the same as the degree of twist applied to a person's arm, nor is the person's feeling of fear the same as the pattern of excitation occurring in the brain. In each case, the *experience* is incommensurable with the *occurrence*. An illusory pain is still pain, in an important sense, but it may not indicate damage at the location it signals; it may not be the *effect* of an injury at the site of *apparent* injury. Similarly, a conscious willing is still a conscious willing even when it is illusory in much the same sense: it may not be the *cause* of an action of which it is the *apparent* cause. A person's feeling of will, and the associated report of this experience to others, is a key criterion commonly used for assessing whether conscious will has operated, but we must remember that this feeling is not the same as an empirically verifiable occurrence of mental causation.

The empirical will—the actual relationship between mind and action—is a central topic of scientific psychology. In psychology, clear indications of the empirical will can be found whenever causal relationships are observed between people's thoughts, beliefs, intentions, plans, or other conscious psychological states and their subsequent actions. The feeling of consciously willing our actions, in contrast, is not a direct readout of such scientifically verifiable will power. Rather, it is the result of a mental system whereby each of us *estimates* moment-to-moment the role that our minds play in our actions. If the empirical will were the measured causal influence of an automobile's engine on its speed, in other words, the phenomenal will might best be understood as the speedometer reading. And as many of us have tried to explain to at least one police officer, speedometer readings can be wrong.

Mind Perception

Why would people mistake the experience of will for an actual causal mechanism? Why is it that the phenomenal will so easily overrides any amount of preaching by scientists about the mechanisms underlying human action? Now, as a rule, when people find one particular intuition so wildly intriguing that they regularly stand by it and forsake lots of information that is technically more correct, they do so because the intuition *fits*. It is somehow part of a bigger scheme of things that they simply can't discard. So, for example, people once held tight to the Ptolemaic idea that the sun revolves around the earth, in part because this notion fit their larger religious conception of the central place of the earth in God's universe. Conscious will fits a larger conception in exactly this way—our understanding of *causal agents*. The intuitive experience of consciously willing our actions is something we return to again and again as we continue to assume that the experience of will reveals the force that creates our acts, mainly because we have a more general understanding of causal agency that allows this to make sense.

Causal Agency

Most adult humans have a very well-developed idea of a particular sort of entity—an entity that *does* things. We appreciate that a dog, for example, will often do things that are guided not by standard causal principles but rather by a teleological or purposive system. Dogs often seem to be goal-oriented; they behave in ways that seem to be understandable only in terms of goals (including some fairly goofy ones, yes, but goals nonetheless). They move toward things that they subsequently seem to have wanted (because they consume them or sniff them), and they move away from things that we can imagine they might not like (because the things are scary or loud or seem to be waving a rolled-up newspaper). Dogs, like horses and fish and crickets and even some plants, seem to be understandable through a special kind of thinking about goal-oriented entities that does not help us at all in thinking about bricks, buttons, or other inanimate objects.

The property of goal seeking is not something we attribute just to living things; we may appreciate this feature in computers or robots or even thermostats. But the important characteristic of such goal-seeking entities is that we understand them in terms of *where we think they are headed* rather than in terms of *where we think they have been.* Unlike a mere object, which moves or "acts" only when it has been caused to do so by some prior event, a causal agent moves or acts apparently on its own, in the pursuit of some future state—the achievement of a goal. Fritz Heider (1958) observed that people perceive persons as causal agents—origins of events—and that this is the primary way in which persons are understood in a manner that physical objects and events are not.

This idea was illustrated in a classic study by Heider and Simmel (1944) in which people were asked to comment on a cartoon film of the motions of geometric objects—a big triangle T, a little triangle t, and a little circle c—around a box with an opening in it (fig. 1.4). The objects moved in the film in such a way that people almost always described T as chasing t and c around a house. People did not report any of the physical

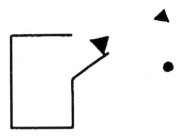

Figure 1.4
A frame from Heider and Simmel's film of the movements of a dysfunctional
family of geometric figures. From Heider and Simmel (1944). Courtesy Board of
Trustees of the University of Illinois.

forces or interactions one might expect if these items were apprehended
as physical objects. The objects weren't dropping or bumping or colliding
but rather chasing and following and seeking. Apparently, the perception of causal agency can displace the usual way we have of perceiving
physical objects, given the right circumstances.[8]

Of course, people are not simple geometric objects bouncing around a
screen, and they have a considerable advantage over dogs, too. Their
consciousness allows them the luxury of some insight into their own
causal agency. People have access to an intricate mental dashboard display of cues regarding their goals because lots of cues to their agency appear in their thoughts and words. For this reason the inner workings of
their causal agency can be interpreted in great depth. We may often learn
from people what they think in advance of their actions, and we occasionally have this information available for ourselves as well, so we
can construct elaborate understandings of likely actions and goals. The
conscious causal agency of human beings is accompanied, in particular,

8. Heider (1958) went on to analyze the features of the perception of personal
causation, which eventually gave rise to the field of attribution theory in social
psychology (Gilbert 1998; Jones et al. 1972; Taylor and Fiske 1978). Unfortunately, this analysis failed to capitalize on the idea that causal agents are perceived as goal-oriented, and instead persevered on the notion that causal agents
are perceived as performing behaviors that are themselves caused in some way
(by factors that are either internal or external to the person). This led to immense
confusion in the social psychological study of how people explain active, goal-
seeking behavior (see the helpful correctives by Gilbert 1998; Kruglanski 1975;
Malle 1999).

by relevant *intentions, beliefs, desires,* and *plans.* Let's consider each of these for a moment, even though they are rather elementary, just to remind ourselves how causal agency looks from the inside of the conscious causal agent.

Intention is normally understood as an idea of what one is going to do that appears in consciousness just before one does it. This is the thought that people usually associate most strongly with causing the action. Consider, for example, the case of watering the plants. If we actually remember to do this, the act typically seems like something we had the intention to do. In a study by Malle and Knobe (1997), people who rated the intentionality of twenty different behaviors put watering the plants at the top of the list along with such things as inviting a friend to lunch and refusing a salesman's offer. Behaviors such as sweating and yawning were rated as far less intentional. Although perceiving the causal agency of a dog might involve only figuring out what its goal might be, perceiving the causal agency of a person offers the additional prospect of considering what the person reports the goal might be—his or her professed intention. And perceiving causal agency in oneself involves coming to an understanding of one's actions in light of one's own conscious intentions.

We usually expect that a person who waters the plants has yet other conscious thoughts that are relevant to the watering. This person seems to have *beliefs* ("The plants need water," "This is water in my watering can"), for example, because it usually takes some understanding of the world and of the nature of the action to completely characterize what is going to be done. Such world knowledge seems particularly necessary for doing things that are extended or consequential (Danto 1963; Goldman 1970; Melden 1961). It doesn't take much in the way of knowledge about the world to wiggle your ears or bend a finger, but you must have a set of relevant beliefs and understandings about how your basic bodily movements will yield more distant effects if you want to do anything beyond wiggling and bending. Basic bodily actions thus seem to be nested within higher-level actions ("I bent my arm" is part of "I tilted the watering can," which is part of "I watered the plant"), even though all of them may be happening at once. We can describe an action at any of these different levels (Vallacher and Wegner 1985; 1987). However, at each higher level, more needs to be known and believed about the context in which the basic bodily movement is occurring for that action to be understood. The more we can imagine that an agent knows or believes about the world, the more extended and involved are the actions and goals we can imagine the agent pursuing.

As a rule, the perception of human causal agency also involves understanding the person's *desire* ("I'm watering these plants in hopes of winning the All Green Thumbs Award again this year"). Desires are not always the same as intentions because they are sometimes descriptive of future circumstances that cannot be fulfilled with this act alone. In desiring a gardening award, for instance, one may intend to water the plants, but getting the award will also depend on other things such as competitors' plants, judges' decisions, and so on. In other cases, however, desire and intention seem to be the same, in that a person might conceivably want to water the plants only for the sheer fact of watering those plants. Still, it doesn't make much sense to attribute agency for an action to a conscious mind that doesn't want *something,* and for this reason philosophers of action seem to agree that a mental representation of one's desire is a key feature of the conscious willing of action (Anscombe 1957; Davidson 1963).

One other category of thoughts relevant to conscious will also can be important: *plans*. In a way, a plan is simply an intention that appears in mind some significant interval before the action. Searle (1983), for example, distinguishes between "prior intention" and "intention in action," and Bratman (1984; 1987) makes a similar distinction. Such prior intentions, or plans, are not usually seen as having the same causal role in our actions that immediate intentions have. I have a good idea, for example, that I will be going to Hawaii with my family next month (Oh boy!), and barring a calamity this is probably what I will do. And it is reassuring to know in this regard that there is a large research literature showing that people often do what they plan (Ajzen 1991; Gollwitzer 1993; Miller, Galanter, and Pribram 1960; Schank and Abelson 1977). Plans go awry, however. My cautious hedging about the upcoming Hawaii trip indicates that even the best laid plans . . . well you know the rest. Conscious plans to act do not seem to *compel* behavior in the sense that once the plan is in place the behavior always occurs. Instead, plans just prepare the way. Often, they involve detailed specifications of how to act—the means or subacts of an action—and they thus make it more likely that when a situation arises in which the behavior is appropriate, the behavior can occur successfully.

Intentions that occur just prior to action, in contrast, do seem to compel the action. This is the basic phenomenon of the experience of will. In everyday language, of course, an action is often described as intended either when it is consciously planned (and we need not be conscious of it when we do it) or when we are consciously aware of doing it at the time we do it (and it might not have been planned in advance). Both are understood as acting on the basis of conscious will. However, if there is a conflict between them—as when we plan to stick to a diet at dinner but then end up (alas, all too consciously) splurging on dessert—the conscious idea of action that occurs just as the action starts is the one we will identify as our "true" intention. Prior plans that we fail to follow are then relegated to the recycling bin of false or mistaken intentions. The thoughts about the action at the time of action are the ones that prompt the strongest belief that we are causal agents who have made the act occur.

All these mental contents that seem to accompany and support causal agency in human beings need not be conscious at the moment of action. Instead, it seems that only the intention needs to appear in consciousness just as we act, whereas the beliefs, desires, and plans that may serve as the scaffolding for the intention need not be in consciousness. These other thoughts do seem to add substance to the idea that there is a conscious will that causes the action, and each of these kinds of thoughts seems to play a role in causing the action. But the conscious intention is, in a way, the mind's "call" for the action it will do, and so the intention seems to be most immediately involved in the causation of the action.

Causal agency, in sum, is an important way in which people understand action, particularly human action. In the process of understanding actions performed by oneself or others, the person will appreciate information about intentions, beliefs, desires, and plans, and will use this information in discerning just what the agent is doing. The intuitive appeal of the idea of conscious will can be traced in part to the embedding of the experience of will, and of the notion that will has a force, in the larger conception of causal agency. People appear to be goal-seeking agents who have the special ability to envision their goals consciously in advance of action. The experience of conscious will feels like being a causal agent.

Mechanisms and Minds

We all know a lot about agents and goals, desires, and intentions, and use these concepts all the time. These concepts are only useful, however, for understanding a limited range of our experience. The movements of clock hands and raindrops and electric trains, for instance, can be understood in terms of causal relations that have no consciousness or will at all. They are mechanisms. Extending the notion of causal agency to these items—to say these things have the ability to *cause themselves to behave*—doesn't fit very well with the physical causal relations we perceive all around us. Imagine a spoon, knife, and fork deciding to go for a walk to the far end of the dinner table ("We're off to see the salad"), and you can see the problem. Things don't usually will themselves to move, whereas people seem to do this all the time.

This rudimentary observation suggests that people have at hand two radically different systems of explanation, one for minds and one for everything else. Mentalistic explanation works wonders for understanding minds, but it doesn't work elsewhere unless we want to start thinking that everything from people to rocks to beer cans to the whole universe actually does what it consciously wants.[9] Mechanistic explanation, in turn, is just splendid for understanding rocks and beer cans, and the movements of the planets, but it leaves much wanting in understanding minds.

Each of us is quite comfortable with using these two very different ways of thinking about and explaining events—a physical, mechanical way and a psychological, mental way. In the mechanical explanatory system, people apply intuitive versions of physics to questions of causality, and so they think about causes and effects as events in the world. In the mental explanatory system, people apply implicit psychological theories to questions of causality, focusing on issues of conscious thoughts and the experience of will as they try to explain actions. In the mechanical way of

9. This odd possibility is the extreme consequence of attributing minds to things that can't talk. Chalmers (1996) makes the case for this theory, such as it is.

thinking, all the psychological trappings are unnecessary: A physical system such as a clock, for instance, doesn't have to intend to keep time or to experience doing so. The essence of the mental explanatory system, in contrast, is the occurrence of the relevant thoughts and feelings about the action, and in this system the objects and events of physical causality are not particularly important: A person might experience having willed the death of an enemy and become wracked with guilt, for instance, even though there was no mechanism for this to have happened.

These two explanatory systems fall into place as children develop ways of understanding both the physical and psychological worlds. The first inklings that mind perception and mechanistic explanation might develop separately in children came from the juxtaposition of two findings by Jean Piaget: Children often neglect intention in making moral judgments, and yet they sometimes overattribute intention to inanimate objects. In the case of moral judgment, Piaget (1932) found that children before the age of seven or eight who are asked to decide whether a person has done something wrong don't concern themselves very much with the person's intention and focus instead on the damage caused by the action. For instance, in deciding how bad Haley was when she pushed Kelsey into the creek, a young child (say, aged six) might focus not on whether the pushing was done on purpose but rather on whether Kelsey's shoes were ruined by mud.[10] This is a bit odd because focusing on intentions could be very useful to children, particularly when claiming good intentions might reduce their punishment ("I pushed her in the creek to prevent her from getting heatstroke"). And while children do pay a bit more regard to their own intentions than to those of others (Keasey 1977), they still focus mostly on the damage. This lack of interest in intentions in moral judgments leads one to suspect that young children also may not appreciate minds in the same way grownups do.

In looking at how children judge inanimate objects, Piaget (1929) noted that they sometimes ascribe the properties of living beings, including the property of intention, to nonliving things. Based on the discussion

---

10. Research following up Piaget's initial suggestions has pointed out some problems with his approach and has suggested that the use of intention information in moral judgment comes somewhat earlier than Piaget had suggested, but it has also generally substantiated the conclusion that young children underplay the importance of intention in moral judgment (Schultz 1980).

of animism in anthropology (the tendency to ascribe living properties to nonliving things; Lévy-Bruhl 1910; Mead 1932), Piaget discovered that children could fall prey to the same thing—overattributing mental properties to systems that are better understood as mechanical. His attribution of animism to children has turned out to be controversial because he overstated the case for older children in contemporary cultures (Looft and Bartz 1969). Still, there is compelling documentation of animistic thinking in young children around the world. An interview with one four-year-old boy about why a toy boat floats, for instance, went like this:

— *Why does it not go to the bottom?*
— Can I make it go down to the bottom?
— *Try it and you will see.*
— It comes up again!
— *Why does it not stay at the bottom?*
— Because the man who is under this [under the roof] doesn't want to go down.
— *Here's a nail.*
— It will go to the bottom.
— *Why?*
— Because there is a man in here [in the nail] and he likes to go to the bottom. (Laurendeau and Pinard 1962, 209)

At first blush, Piaget's pair of insights suggest paradoxically that children underuse intention (in moral judgment) and also overuse it (in perceiving inanimate causality). This makes sense, though, when we realize that the child's notion of a mind is under construction. Without a fully developed idea of mental processes, children can fail to attribute intent when they should (in judging human beings) and attribute it too often when they shouldn't (in judging objects). Children are faced with the problem of building a picture of their own minds and the minds of others, and of achieving an understanding of what it is *not* to have a mind as well. Early in life, they guess that things without minds might have mind-like properties of intention and that things they will later learn *have* minds might not possess such intention.

Piaget's perspective has culminated in the contemporary literature on the development of theory of mind in animals (Premack and Woodruff 1978) and in children (Astington 1993; Perner 1991b; Wellman 1990), and in work that contrasts how children develop an understanding of agency, intention, and will with how they develop an understanding of causality, motion, and the principles of physics (Astington, Harris, and Olson 1988; Carey 1996; Gelman 1990; Gelman, Durgin, and Kaufman 1995; Wellman and Gelman 1992). Neither the perception of the physical world nor the perception of the mental world is a "given" to the human newborn. Although the neonate has rudimentary abilities in both areas, both systems must be developed over time and experience as ways of understanding what is going on.

The field of psychology itself has noticed that different systems of thinking seemed to be necessary for understanding mind and matter. The main preoccupation of much of psychology in the twentieth century was translating mind talk into mechanism talk on the assumption that the two were entirely interchangeable. A telling quote from Donald Hebb (1946) on how psychologists should understand chimpanzees highlights what happened as a result:

A thoroughgoing attempt to avoid anthropomorphic description in the study of temperament was made over a two-year period at the Yerkes laboratories. . . . All that resulted was an almost endless series of specific acts in which no order or meaning could be found. On the other hand, by the use of frankly anthropomorphic concepts of emotion and attitude one could quickly and easily describe the peculiarities of individual animals, and with this information a newcomer to the staff could handle the animals as he could not safely otherwise. Whatever the anthropomorphic terminology may seem to imply about conscious states in the chimpanzee, it provides an *intelligible and practical guide to behavior.* (88)

This realization suggested to Hebb and others that the earnest project of eliminating mind entirely from the scientific explanation of behavior (Bentley 1944; Werner 1940) was misguided. You have to think about the animals' minds in order to keep from getting mugged by them. A mental system for understanding even chimp behavior seems highly preferable to a mechanical system.

Perceiving mind and causal agency is a significant human ability. It is possible that this achievement is accomplished by a fairly narrow mental module, a special-skill unit of mind that does only this, and that in different individuals this module can thus be particularly healthy, damaged, or even nonfunctional. Leslie (1994) has called this set of skills a Theory-of-Mind-Mechanism (ToMM), and Baron-Cohen (1995) has proposed that such a mechanism may be injured or missing in some forms of autism. He suggests that each of us has an "intentionality detector" that does the job of looking for actions that seem to be willed, in both self and others. The absence of this detector leaves us looking for physical or mechanistic explanations when psychological ones would really be better. Baron-Cohen has documented the "mindblindness" of autistic individuals in some detail, suggesting just how difficult life can be if one doesn't have a quick and natural ability to comprehend other people's minds. An example comes from Kanner's (1943, 232) description of an autistic child: "On a crowded beach he would walk straight toward his goal irrespective of whether this involved walking over newspapers, hands, feet, or torsos, much to the discomfiture of their owners. His mother was careful to point out that he did not intentionally deviate from his course in order to walk on others, but neither did he make the slightest attempt to avoid them. It was as if he did not distinguish people from things, or at least did not concern himself about the distinction."[11]

The idea that mind perception is variable has also been noted by philosophers. Daniel Dennett (1987; 1996) has captured this observation in suggesting that people take an "intentional stance" in perceiving minds that they do not take in perceiving most of the physical world. The degree to which we perceive mindedness in phenomena can change, so that under some circumstances we might see our pet pooch as fully conscious and masterfully deciding just where it would be good to scratch himself, whereas under other circumstances we might have difficulty extending the luxury of presumed conscious thought and human agency even to ourselves. It is probably the case, too, that the degree of mechanical causality we perceive is something that varies over time and circumstance. Viewing any particular event as mentally or mechanically caused, then, can depend on a host of factors and can influence dramatically how we go about making sense of the event. And making sense of our own

---

11. Oliver Sacks (1994) has documented the intriguing details of a life without mind perception. He recounts his interviews with Temple Grandin, an astonishing adult with autism who also holds a Ph.D. in agricultural science and works as a teacher and researcher at Colorado State University. Her attempts to understand human events—even though she lacks the natural ability to pick up the nuances of human actions, plans, and emotions—impressively illustrate the unusual skill most people have in this area yet take for granted. Grandin has cultivated this ability only through special effort and some clever tricks of observation.

minds as mentally causal systems—conscious agents—includes accepting our feelings of conscious will as authentic.

We're now getting close to a basic principle about the illusion of conscious will. Think of it in terms of lenses. If each person has two general lenses through which to view causality—a mechanical causality lens for objects and a mental causality lens for agents—it is possible that the mental one *blurs* what the person might otherwise see with the mechanical one. The illusion of conscious will may be a misapprehension of the mechanistic causal relations underlying our own behavior that comes from looking at ourselves by means of a mental explanatory system. We don't see our own gears turning because we're busy reading our minds.

The Illusion Exposed

Philosophers and psychologists have spent lifetimes thinking about how to reconcile conscious will with mechanistic causation. This problem—broached in various ways as the mind/body problem, free will vs. determinism, mental vs. physical causation, and the analysis of reasons vs. causes—has generated a literature that is immense, rich, and shocking in its inconclusiveness (Dennett 1984; Double 1991; Earman 1986; Hook 1965; MacKay 1967; Uleman 1989). What to do? The solution explored in this book involves recognizing that the distinction between mental and mechanical explanations is something that concerns everyone, not only philosophers and psychologists. The tendency to view the world in *both* ways, each as necessary, is what has created in us two largely incompatible ways of thinking. When we apply mental explanations to our own behavior-causation mechanisms, we fall prey to the impression that our conscious will causes our actions. The fact is, we find it enormously seductive to think of ourselves as having minds, and so we are drawn into an intuitive appreciation of our own conscious will.

Think for a minute about the nature of illusions. Any magician will tell you that the key to creating a successful illusion is to make "magic" the easiest, most immediate way to explain what is really a mundane event. Harold Kelley (1980) described this in his analysis of the underpinnings of magic in the perception of causality. He observed that stage magic involves a *perceived causal sequence*—the set of events that appears to have happened—and a *real causal sequence*—the set of events the magician has orchestrated behind the scenes. The perceived sequence is what makes the trick. Laws of nature are broken willy-nilly as people are sawed in half and birds, handkerchiefs, rabbits, and canes appear from nothing or disappear or turn into each other and back again.

The real sequence is often more complicated than the perceived sequence, but many of the real events are not perceived. The magician needs special pockets, props, and equipment, and develops wiles to misdirect audience attention from the real sequence. In the end, the audience observes something that seems to be simple, but in fact it may have been achieved with substantial thought, preparation, and effort on the magician's part. The lovely assistant in a gossamer gown apparently floating effortlessly on her back during the levitation illusion is in fact being held up by a 600-pound pneumatic lift hidden behind a specially rigged curtain. It is the very simplicity of the illusory sequence, the shorthand summary that hides the magician's toil, that makes the trick so compelling. The lady levitates. The illusion of conscious will occurs in much the same way.

The real causal sequence underlying human behavior involves a massively complicated set of mechanisms. Everything that psychology studies can come into play to predict and explain even the most innocuous wink of an eye. Each of our actions is really the culmination of an intricate set of physical and mental processes, including psychological mechanisms that correspond to the traditional concept of will, in that they involve linkages between our thoughts and our actions. This is the empirical will. However, we don't see this. Instead, we readily accept a far easier explanation of our behavior: We intended to do it, so we did it.

The science fiction writer Arthur C. Clarke (1973) remarked that "any sufficiently advanced technology is indistinguishable from magic" (21). Clarke was referring to the fantastic inventions we might discover in the future or in our travels to advanced civilizations. However, the insight also applies to self-perception. When we turn our attention to our own minds, we are faced with trying to understand an unimaginably advanced technology. We can't possibly know (let alone keep track of) the tremendous number of mechanical influences on our behavior because we inhabit an extraordinarily complicated machine. So we develop a shorthand, a belief in the causal efficacy of our conscious thoughts. We believe in the magic of our own causal agency.

The mind is a system that produces *appearances* for its owner. Things appear silver, for example, or they appear to have little windows, or they appear to fly, as the result of how the mind produces experience. And if the mind can make us "experience" an airplane, why couldn't it produce an experience of *itself* that leads us to think that it causes its own actions? The mind creates this continuous illusion; it really doesn't *know* what causes its own actions. Whatever empirical will there is rumbling along in the engine room—an actual relation between thought and action—might in fact be totally inscrutable to the driver of the machine (the mind). The mind has a self-explanation mechanism that produces a roughly continuous sense that what is in consciousness is the cause of action—the phenomenal will—whereas in fact the mind can't ever know itself well enough to be able to say what the causes of its actions are. To quote Spinoza in *The Ethics* (1677), "Men are mistaken in thinking themselves free; their opinion is made up of consciousness of their own actions, and ignorance of the causes by which they are determined. Their idea of freedom, therefore, is simply their ignorance of any cause for their actions" (pt. II, 105). In the more contemporary phrasing of Marvin Minsky (1985);"None of us enjoys the thought that what we do depends on processes we do not know; we prefer to attribute our choices to *volition, will,* or *self-control. . . .* Perhaps it would be more honest to say, '*My decision was determined by internal forces I do not understand*'" (306).

2

Brain and Body

Conscious will arises from processes that are psychologically and
anatomically distinct from the processes whereby mind creates action.

The feeling we call volition is not the cause of the voluntary act, but simply the
symbol in consciousness of that stage of the brain which is the immediate cause
of the act.
T. H. Huxley,
On the Hypothesis That Animals Are Automata (1874)

It is not always a simple matter to know when someone is doing something on purpose. This judgment is easy to make for animated cartoon
characters because a lightbulb usually appears over their heads at this
time and they then rear back and look quickly to each side before charg-
ing off to do their obviously intended and voluntary action. Often a cloud
of dust remains. In the case of real people, however, knowing whether
another person has done something willfully can be a detective exercise.
In some of the most important cases, these things must even be decided
by the courts or by warfare, and no one is really satisfied that the willfulness of actions judged after the fact is an accurate reflection of a person's
state at action onset. Perhaps we need a lightbulb over our head that
flashes whenever we do something on purpose.

But how would the lightbulb know? Is there someplace in the mind or
brain that lights up just as we perform a consciously willed action, a
place to which we might attach the lightbulb if we knew the proper
wiring? Certainly, it often seems that this is the case. With most voluntary
actions, we have a feeling of doing. This feeling is such a significant part
of consciously willed acts that, as we have seen, it is regarded as part of
their definition. Will is the feeling that arises at the moment when we do
something consciously—when we know what it is we are doing, and we

are in fact doing it. What is it we are feeling at this time? Is it a direct expression of a causal event actually happening somewhere in our mental or neural architecture? Or is it an inference we make about ourselves in the same way we make an inference about the cartoon character when we see the lightbulb?

We can begin to grasp some answers to such questions by examining the anatomical and temporal origins of the experience of will. Where does the experience of will come from in the brain and body? When exactly does it arrive? In this chapter we examine issues of where the will arises by considering first the anatomy of voluntary action—how it differs from involuntary action and where in the body it appears to arise. We focus next on the sensation of effort in the muscles and mind during action to learn how the perception of the body influences the experience of will, and then look directly at the brain sources of voluntary action through studies of brain stimulation. These anatomical travels are then supplemented by a temporal itinerary, an examination of the time course of events in mind and body as voluntary actions are produced. In the process of examining all this, we may learn where, when, and how we get the feeling that we're doing things.

Where There's a Will

Many modern neuroscientists localize the "executive control" portion of the mind in the frontal lobes of the brain (e.g., Stuss and Benson 1986; 1987). This consensus derives from a host of observations of what happens in human beings (Burgess 1997; Luria 1966, Shallice 1988) and animals (Passingham 1993) when portions of the frontal lobes are damaged or missing. Such damage typically leads to difficulties in the planning or initiation of activity as well as loss of memory for ongoing activity. This interlinked set of specific losses of ability has been called the frontal lobe syndrome. A person suffering from this syndrome might be unable to plan and carry out a simple act such as opening a soda can, for example, or might find it hard to remember to do things and so be unable to keep a job.[1] This widely observed phenomenon suggests that many of the

1. Antonio Damasio (1994) retells the story of one man suffering such damage, Phineas P. Gage, who survived a blasting accident that sent a metal rod up through his left cheek and out the top of his head, destroying his left frontal lobe.

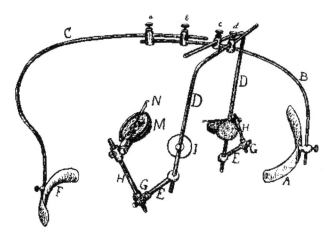

Figure 2.1
Bair's (1901) device for measuring ear wiggling. It was clamped to the forehead
(A) and the base of the neck (F), and the sensor (M) was rested on the ear.

causal sequences underlying human action may be localized in brain
structures just under the forehead. Brain-imaging studies also suggest
that voluntary actions are associated with activity in the frontal region
(Ingvar 1994; Spence et al. 1997). However, this sort of evidence tells us
little about where the *experience* of will might arise.

Voluntary and Involuntary Systems

Let's begin with the ears. Although the study of ear wiggling has never
really taken off to become a major scientific field, a number of early
experiments by Bair (1901) focused on how people learn this important
talent. He constructed an ear wiggle measurement device (fig. 2.1) to
assess the movement of the retrahens muscle behind the ear, tried it on a
number of people, and found that the majority (twelve of fourteen in his
study) couldn't move their ears using this muscle. Some could wiggle by
making exaggerated eyebrow movements, and I suppose a few were inspired to reach up and manipulate their ears with their hands. But, by
and large, this was an action beyond willful control—at least at first.

Although Gage recovered physically, and indeed appeared to have suffered no
change in his level of everyday intelligence, his life afterwards was marked by a
series of poor plans, lost jobs, and broken relationships. Damasio attributes this
to the loss of frontal lobe function.

An action that can't be consciously willed is sort of a psychological black hole. Bair noticed that when people couldn't move their ears as directed, they said they didn't even feel they were doing anything at all. One reported, "It seemed like trying to do something when you have no idea how it is done. It seemed like willing to have the door open or some other thing to happen which is beyond your control" (Bair 1901, 500). Trying to wiggle your ears when you don't know how is like trying to wiggle someone else's ears from a distance. No matter how much you think about the desired movement, or how you go about thinking of it, those movements that are beyond voluntary control simply won't happen—there seems to be *nothing to do*. This observation highlights what may be the simplest definition of voluntary or willful action, at least in people: A voluntary action is something a person can do when asked.[2]

Most of Bair's experimental participants couldn't wiggle their ears when asked, so he tried various tactics to help them along. The first was seeing whether giving a person an "idea of movement" would help. This involved sending a small electrical current through the retrahens muscle to make it contract artificially. The participant had an electrode pasted on the skin over the muscle, held another electrode in her hand (actually a big wet sponge—recall this was 1901), and then pressed a switch to complete the circuit and give the ear muscle a little shock. This created a fine wiggle, at least from Bair's point of view, but the participants reported no sense that they were voluntarily wiggling their ears, just that they were voluntarily pushing a button that made their ears jerk involuntarily.

As it turns out, voluntary and involuntary ear wiggles are not even very similar. The involuntary movements were quick jerks, whereas voluntary movements tend to be slower and more fluid and graceful, a kind of ear ballet. Moreover, providing the "idea of movement" through involuntary ear jerks was useless for helping the participants to gain voluntary control over their ears. Bair instructed his subjects to try several things—just feeling the artificial movement sometimes, or trying to move in concert with the electric contraction, or straining against the contraction to get a

2. It is also something a person can *not do* when asked not to do it. The ability to inhibit voluntary acts is so impressive that it is sometimes described as a hallmark of voluntary behavior (Kimble and Perlmuter 1970; Welch 1955). Inhibiting an involuntary act such as a hiccup is much more difficult.

sense of what it was doing—but none of this did much for their voluntary ear wiggles. Involuntary movement didn't serve as a model for voluntary movement. If this *had* worked, we could all learn Beethoven piano sonatas by plugging our hands into hi-tech milking machines that would push our fingers in all the right directions repeatedly until we, too, had the "idea of movement" (perhaps the second movement of piano sonata, op. 13, "Pathétique").

The only thing that yielded eventual success for Bair's would-be wigglers was a lengthy process of trying first to get the ears to wiggle voluntarily in *some* way—by lifting the brow violently, or by clenching the jaw. Some perhaps threw themselves to the ground. Then, over time, this movement of all the muscles in the area could be relaxed and the specific movement of the desired ear muscle could occur by itself. Although only about half the participants succeeded in the course of the experiment, those who did all followed this pattern. Bair went on to suggest that this might be how voluntary actions are developed as a rule. They seem to be winnowed from the more general movements our bodies do, selected and organized by practice.

Voluntary actions don't just spring up from nowhere, then, but are learned, sometimes with great effort. Indeed, the notion that voluntary actions are modifiable through experiencing their consequences is a key facet of the definition of action rather than mere movement. In studies of action in animals, for instance, this is the main way in which voluntariness is identified (e.g., Passingham 1993). A nonhuman primate reaching for a banana might learn to reach differently depending on whether the banana is attained or not, and this malleability is the hallmark of apparent willfulness of action in all those creatures who can't otherwise report on their sense of will. In human beings and other animals, actions that are not sensitive to rewards and punishments may be thought of as involuntary and normally are not believed to be subject to willful control.

What can be voluntary and what cannot is determined in part by the muscles, nerves, and brain systems underlying a particular behavior. A good example of this is facial expression. It is almost impossible to simulate voluntarily the involuntary facial expression associated with having someone pop a paper bag behind your head (Ekman, Friesen, and Simons 1985). To get the true "startle" expression, you just have to send someone behind you with a bag and then wait. Just as in the case of Bair's electrically stimulated ear wiggles, even a voluntary eye blink differs in form and timing from an involuntary one (Kimble 1964). And, in general, the facial expressions people make in response to real emotional stimuli (a joke, a sad movie, a piano falling from above) differ from those made in the voluntary attempt to simulate the facial expressions. The nerve pathways for involuntary facial expressions don't overlap those used for voluntary ones, and this makes the pattern and timing of facial muscle contractions for involuntary and voluntary expressions differ (Ekman and Friesen 1975; Matsumoto and Lee 1993; Rinn 1984).

The smiling muscles illustrate these effects very nicely. An involuntary smile will typically involve not only upturned corners of the mouth but also smiling eyes—the muscles in the upper face join in the action (Ekman, Davidson, and Friesen 1990). When the appropriate mouth and eye muscles are contracted together (fig. 2.2, left), observers judge the face to be truly smiling. People who are trying to fake a smile, on the other hand, often forget to scrunch their eyes in the corners and end up

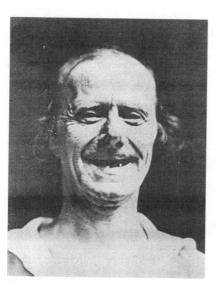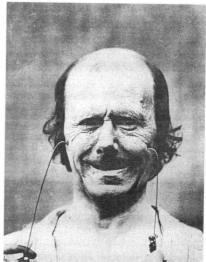

Figure 2.2
A genuine smile (*left*) is contrasted with a smile induced by electrical stimulation of the mouth muscles (*right*). From Duchenne de Boulogne (1862). Courtesy Cambridge University Press.

with a smile that looks painted on, like the smile (fig. 2.2, right) induced by electrical stimulation of just the mouth muscles.[3] Ekman (1985) reports that voluntarily faked smiles can also be more asymmetric than genuine ones (one eyebrow arched, for example) and are often much longer or shorter in duration than involuntary smiles as well. The sycophant who flashes you a grin in passing, for instance, or the beauty contestant who cements a smile in place for the whole pageant, is probably doing this voluntarily rather than having it simply happen.

Studies of people who have suffered certain kinds of nerve damage substantiate that different nerve pathways serve voluntary and involuntary facial expressions (Rinn 1984). Some patients show mimetic facial paralysis in which the facial muscles can be moved voluntarily but all spontaneous movement is lost. They don't smile at something funny unless they do it on purpose. Other patients, in contrast, show involuntary laughing or weeping (often with only slight provocation) and cannot inhibit these responses voluntarily. Anatomical studies show that voluntary movements of the face arise in a part of the outer surface of the brain—the cortical motor area—whereas involuntary facial movements arise deeper in the brain, in the extrapyramidal motor system (Rinn 1984).

The ear wiggling and facial expression research, in sum, leads us to several preliminary observations about the nature of voluntary action. Not all actions can be performed voluntarily (witness all the poor folks who've tried to wiggle their ears and failed); voluntary actions may differ in form from those that are involuntary; voluntary actions appear to occur "on command" or "at will" in that they can be started or stopped by the doer; voluntary actions are malleable over time, capable of being transformed through learning; and voluntary actions occur through specific brain and nerve pathways that are sometimes anatomically distinct from pathways that serve involuntary movements. An action must be voluntary in order to be consciously willed. But, of course, we don't

3. These photos are not particularly fetching representations of smiles, but they have some historical significance. Duchenne de Boulogne completed the first major studies of facial expression in 1862 using this man as a prime experimental participant. The man had a condition that left his face insensitive to pain, and so the muscles could be electrically stimulated to produce various expressions without creating discomfort.

know from just looking at voluntariness whether conscious will has been exerted. This still seems to be something the person needs to report.

Sensing Effort

Where does this report arise? If we look specifically at the voluntary pathways, it makes sense to try to find the will somewhere in the link between brain and muscles. Psychologists and physiologists long hoped to establish where exactly in the connection from brain to body and back again the feeling of effortful action might be found (Scheerer 1987). They presumed that the feeling of effort is the same as the sense of will, or at least that the two experiences are related (although this is certainly arguable; see Ginet 1986). Does the feeling of moving a finger, for example, arise as the brain sends an impulse along the efferent or motor nerves to the finger, or does the feeling arise when the muscle sends a return impulse along the afferent or sensory nerves back to the brain?

The basic question is, At what point in this sequence does consciousness experience the action? The premovement brain signal of action has variously been called *efference copy* (to suggest that the brain makes a copy of the instruction it sends to create the muscle effect and then delivers this to consciousness; von Holst 1954) or *corollary discharge* (to suggest that there is merely some spillover of this information; Sperry 1950), or sometimes just the *sense of effort* (Merton 1964; 1972). Studies both classic and contemporary have focused on whether we know our acts through one of these premovement brain processes, or whether we sense them through afference after they have happened by feeling our muscles move via *muscle sense*. The researchers studying this experience often seem to have believed that the sensation of effort is exactly the same thing as the experience of will, and so they examined the sensation earnestly and deeply.

Much study and thought has been devoted to the sense of effort that seems to be involved in the intriguing case of eye movement. When one moves the eyes normally, the visual world is seen as unchanged despite the fact that the image of that world on the retina is in fact moving about. However, when the eye is moved passively, the visual world seems to move. Tapping on the eyelid with your eye open, for example, makes your eye jump about a bit, and the world you see with that eye jumps about as well. This suggests that in the intentional movement of the eye, there is some sensation of the effort of eye movement that can then be used by the brain to adjust its perception of the visual world for the movement. A kind of internal feedback or cancellation of the intentional action seems to be necessary to create this phenomenon. Isolating the pathways of such feedback has preoccupied a generation of physiologists.

The issue has been sufficiently baffling, however, to inspire one researcher to have an operation performed on his own big toe to see if tension on a muscle tendon all by itself is perceptible (it is; the researcher was the senior author of McCloskey, Cross et al. 1983). Much of the research in this area is meticulously grisly because it depends on carefully ruling out a variety of sources of sensation (by the anesthetization of skin or joints, for example) before people are asked to judge their degree of effort in various tasks. This is necessary because people can get feedback about their movement not just through muscle discharges but also through nerves in the skin and bones (not to mention by looking). The issue is still not resolved, but the best guess at this time is that both kinds of sensation exist—sensation of the motor command from the brain *and* sensation of the muscle moving—and that both can contribute to the sense of effort we experience in performing muscle movement (Gandevia, 1987; Jeannerod 1997; Jones 1988; Matthews 1982; McCloskey 1978; Roland 1978).

The most striking cases relevant to muscle sense involve people with no muscle sense at all. In extremely rare instances, apparently because of unidentified viral infections, people have lost the return sensations from their muscles while at the same time retaining their ability to send commands to those muscles. Jonathan Cole (1995; Cole and Paillard 1995) reports on one such man, Ian Waterman, and his profound action problems. Struck by a mysterious illness at the age of nineteen that stopped his muscle sensations below the neck, Waterman first simply slumped into a heap, unable to control even moving an arm or sitting up. He had to watch all his actions to see what effect they were having, and if he didn't pay rapt attention at all times, the act would fail. If he looked away toward one arm he was trying to move, the other arm might flail about. Even sitting still was a challenge. If he didn't watch his hands, they could float away. And if he lost concentration as he was sitting, he could easily fall over.

Although Waterman learned to walk after prodigious effort over many months, he had to look down at his limbs all the time to guide his movements, and he remained uncomfortable walking with people or in unpredictable environments because any unanticipated bump could throw him to the ground. Without the ability to sense his movements, he also couldn't make adjustments that people make quite automatically to catch themselves before they fall. Walking in close quarters was out of the question, as any jostling could yield a spill. Even the most minor issues had to be thought out in detail—for example, he needed to remember to shift his body backward slightly whenever he extended his arm, so that the weight of his outstretched arm would not make him fall forward. Apparently, the ability to send signals to the muscles without learning anything back from them creates havoc.

Waterman still feels a sense of effort when he moves (Cole 1986), and this suggests that the loss of muscle feedback that he experienced did not eliminate this indication of his feeling of doing. So, perhaps the experience of will can come from merely having messages sent from brain to muscles. It might also be that without muscle sense, the visual perception of own movement gives sufficient feedback so that a sense of effort can be achieved. This is not an entirely telling case, though, because Cole mentions that Waterman's loss of muscle sense may not be total. There is evidence from certain cases of paralysis, though, that also supports the conclusion that the feeling of effort may be more dependent on efferent (brain to muscle) than afferent (muscle to brain) neurons. When a muscle becomes completely unmovable, the experience of effortfulness of its movement also goes away, even if the muscle's position can be sensed.

This phenomenon was illustrated graphically in an account by Ernst Mach (1906) of his own experience of suffering a stroke:

I was in a railway train, when I suddenly observed, with no consciousness of anything else being wrong, that my right arm and leg were paralyzed; the paralysis was intermittent, so that from time to time I was able to move again in an apparently normal way. After some hours [as] it became continuous and permanent, there also set in an affection of the right facial muscle, which prevented me from speaking except in a low tone and with some difficulty. I can only describe my condition during the period of complete paralysis by saying that when I formed the intention of moving my limbs I felt no effort, but that it was absolutely impossible for me to bring my will to the point of executing the movement. On the other hand, during the phases of imperfect paralysis, and during the period of convalescence, my arm and leg seemed to me enormous burdens which I could only lift with the greatest effort. . . . The paralyzed limbs retained their sensibility completely . . . and thus I was enabled to be aware of their position and of their passive movements. (174–175)

The experience of muscle effort in this case, it seems, must depend on having some movement capacity. With reduced capacity, as in fatigue or weakness or partial paralysis, the feeling of effort increased, whereas with no capacity at all the feeling of effort dropped to zero. The odd fact in Mach's case, and one that has been substantiated in other, more modern instances (Rode, Rossetti, and Boisson 1996), is that these variations in the experience of effort or heaviness can occur even when the patient has some afferent (muscle to brain) pathways intact (Gandevia 1982; 1987). Mach could feel where his paralyzed limbs were. In this sense, Mach was the opposite of Waterman, in that he lost efferent (brain to muscle) control while retaining afferent (muscle to brain) contact, and in Mach's case, the feeling of effortful movement was eclipsed entirely when he could no longer move. But without efferent control, unfortunately, there was also nothing for Mach to do (just as in the case of people who can't wiggle their ears), so it is not too surprising that no effort was experienced. This case, then, is also not entirely conclusive about the source of feelings of effort.

It is interesting to note, though, that Waterman's ability to use his visual sense to substitute for muscle sense indicates that in normal people the two senses may often be combined to allow judgments of movement. Lajoie and colleagues (1992) tested another patient who, like Waterman, had lost muscle feedback and had learned to guide her movements visually. The researchers were able to test this patient on a mirror drawing task ("Please copy these letters by watching your hand in the mirror") and found that she was notably better than neurologically normal subjects. The bizarre mirror drawings most people produce arise because they have trouble integrating the mixed signals they receive from sight and from muscle feedback. The two senses tell them different stories about where the pencil might be and they get mixed up as a result. Without muscle feedback, and after learning to control action with vision alone, this patient was able to do something that baffles everyone else.

The studies of muscle sense seem to indicate that the feeling of effort that is part of the experience of conscious will may depend on outward signals from the brain to muscles and sometimes also on muscle sense, the returning signals from muscles to brain. It would be nice if we could sum things up at this point and head home for dinner and an evening of television, but we're not done. There is a major additional mystery: The feeling of conscious will doesn't always seem to go away when body parts go away.

Phantom Limbs

That's right, people can sometimes feel they are willing movements that don't even happen. Most people who have had an arm or leg amputated continue to sense the presence of the limb thereafter, what Mitchell (1872) called a "phantom limb." Of some 300 amputees in prisoner-of-war camps during World War II studied by Henderson and Smyth (1948), for instance, fully 98 percent were found to experience a phantom limb, felt as a pleasant, tingling sensation that was not painful. Some people do experience such a limb as having pain, however, which makes it a particularly miserable burden.

Here's the intriguing part. A phantom limb can often be perceived to move, either involuntarily (as when the stump of the limb is pushed by someone else) or voluntarily (as when the amputee tries to move it). The apparent voluntary movement is not merely a gross motion of the limb, either, because the person may very well feel separate parts moving and changing position in relation to each other. Fingers may be wiggled, elbows or knees bent, arms or legs twisted—all with nothing really there (Jones 1988). As a rule, the more distal parts of the limb (fingers, toes) are felt more strongly than the proximal parts (nearer the actual stump), apparently because the distal parts are represented more fully in the brain. Movement of the phantom limb becomes more difficult with time, and eventually the ability to "move" the digits may be lost even though the limb may still be perceived to exist. As the feeling of voluntary movement subsides over a period of months or years, the limb may "telescope" toward the body such that the last sensations the person may experience are only of the digits extending from the stump.

A fascinating feature of phantom limb movement is that, at least on first analysis, it suggests that the intention to move can create the experience of conscious will *without any action at all.* For a number of researchers working in the late nineteenth century, this feature of phantom limb movement was taken as evidence that messages from the brain to the muscles could be perceived by the brain before they even left the brain to go to the muscles (Helmholtz 1867; Mitchell 1872). After all, there were no muscles out there, only a phantom. Phantom limb movements always occur consciously and are not spontaneously made (Jones 1988), and this also seems to substantiate the idea that there is some consciousness of a signal being sent to the absent limb.

Further research has found, however, that the sense of moving a phantom limb voluntarily depends on the continued functioning of sensory nerves and muscles in the stump. Henderson and Smyth (1948) observed that every voluntary movement of a phantom limb was accompanied by a contraction of the appropriate muscles in the stump, and that if the remaining muscles in the stump had lost their nerve connections, the ability to move the phantom was lost. If the brain has nowhere to send the movement commands, in other words, it no longer senses that the movement is occurring. The continued feeling of the *existence* of the phantom is not dependent on this nerve/muscle connection—just the *sensation of voluntary movement*. This finding suggests that there may be a role for information returning from the muscles in producing the sensation of phantom voluntary movement (Devor 1997; Jones 1988).

It turns out, however, that information coming from simply *looking* at a moving limb can create the sense of voluntary movement. An early hint that this might be possible appeared in a remarkable study by Nielson (1963), in which people with normal limbs were fooled into thinking that someone else's hand was their own. People in this study were asked to don a glove, insert their hand in a viewing box, and then on a signal, draw a line down a piece of paper. Unbeknownst to them, the hand they saw in the box was actually a mirror reflection of another person's hand, also gloved and holding a pen, which appeared in just the spot where they would expect their own hand to be (fig. 2.3). When the signal was given and this imposter hand started to draw a line that departed from the line the participant had been instructed to draw, participants typically adjusted their (own) arm to compensate for the observed arm's mistaken trajectory (fig. 2.4). The visual feedback from the false hand was so compelling that participants briefly lost contact with their own movement.

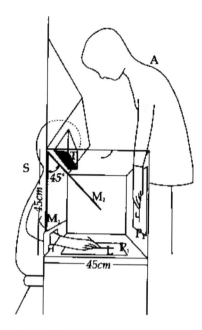

Figure 2.3
Nielson's (1963) mirror box had a subject (S) look down at a mirror (M₂),
ostensibly to see his or her hand underneath, while actually viewing the hand of
an assistant (A). Courtesy Scandinavian Psychological Association.

In a series of studies, V. S. Ramachandran and colleagues (1996;
Ramachandran and Blakeslee 1998; Ramachandran and Rogers-
Ramachandran 1996) used a different sort of mirror box to examine the
experience of phantom limb movement. In one study, an individual with
a phantom arm inserted both the phantom and his real other arm into the
mirror box. The mirror in this case was placed so that a reflection of the
person's real arm appeared in the place where the phantom would be if it
were real. The odd result of this was that when the person moved the real
arm voluntarily, he experienced the phantom as moving voluntarily as
well. The hand in the mirror seemed to extend from the person's stump
and was felt as if it were being flexed and moved on purpose. The visible
hand guided the experience of the phantom.

There is the possibility here that the person experienced the movement
through some brain pathway that produces symmetries in movements between the two hands. To check on this, in two cases, Ramachandran's group
arranged for an experimenter's arm to appear in place of the phantom.

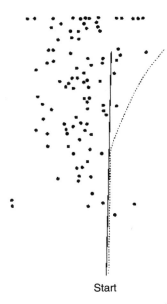

Start

Figure 2.4
Nielson's (1963) subjects each tried to trace the vertical line while the assistant's hand wandered off on the dotted path to the right. The points on this graph show the final stopping places of the subjects—most of whom seem to have tried to compensate for the apparent wandering by moving to the left. Courtesy Scandinavian Psychological Association.

They found that "the visual cue was sufficiently compelling that it created a vivid feeling of joint movements in the phantom whether or not the patient moved the contralateral hand (and even though no commands were sent to the phantom). One of the patients noted, however, that the joint sensations were less vivid when the experimenter's hand was used than when he himself moved his fingers" (Ramachandran et al. 1996, 36).[4] The point

4. The tendency for the eyes to run off with the rest of the body is something you can experiment with at home. Botvinick and Cohen (1998) reported, for example, a nice demonstration of such "tactile ventriloquism" with a rubber hand. When a person's own arm is stroked gently out of view in sync with the stroking of a rubber hand that is in view, it just takes a little while for the person to begin reporting that the rubber hand feels like their own. Ramachandran and Blakeslee (1998) report a similar example, in which a person watches a spot on the table being tapped in rhythm with taps on their own hand under the table. After a bit of this, the person reports feeling the taps on the table, and in fact, a sharp rap on the table yields a startle response that can be measured as an increase in the person's skin conductance level.

to remember, in sum, is that willful movement can be experienced merely by watching *any* body move where one's own body ought to be. This is not too surprising in view of the discovery (in monkeys) of the existence of *mirror neurons*—neurons that are activated both by own movement and by the perception of that movement in another (Rizzolatti et al. 1996).

Overall, these studies of muscle effort and of phantom limbs suggest that the experience of conscious will is not anatomically simple. There does not seem to be "will wiring" spilling from the connections between brain and body, and one begins to wonder whether the muscles are even a necessary part of the system. In a sense, it is not clear that *any* studies of the sense of effort in movement can isolate the anatomical source of the experience of conscious will. Although the hope of isolating the experience of will is certainly one of the motivations of the researchers studying muscle sense and phantom limbs, a key case of willed action is left out in this approach—the action of the mind (Feinberg 1978). We all do things consciously with our minds, even when our bodies seem perfectly still. William James (1890, 452) described the "voluntary acts of attention" that go into willful thought, and this effort of attending seems quite as palpable as the effort that goes into muscle movement.

Ask a fifth grader, for example, just how much effort she put into a long division problem despite very little muscle movement except for pencil pushing and the occasional exasperated sigh. She will describe the effort at great length, suggesting that there is something going on in her head that feels very much like work. All the effort that people put into reasoning and thinking does not arise merely because they are getting tired scratching their heads. The question of whether there is a sense of effort at the outset, as the mental act starts, or only later, when the mental act has returned some sort of mental sensation of its occurrence, begins to sound silly when all the components of this process are in the head. Rather, there is an experienced feeling of doing, a distinct sense of trying to do, but this doesn't seem to have a handy source we can identify. Certainly, it doesn't seem to be muscle sense.[5] But it also doesn't

5. Someone persevering on the muscle explanation here could reply that thoughts can involve unconscious movement of the vocal muscles, which in fact is sometimes true (Sokolov 1972; Zivin 1979). However, then it would also have to be suggested that muscles move for all conscious thoughts, and this has not been established (but see Cohen 1986).

seem to be a perception of a brain signal going out to some other part of the brain. The experience of consciously willing an action may draw in some ways upon the feeling of effort in the muscles, but it seems to be a more encompassing feeling, one that arises from a variety of sources of sensation in the body and information in the mind.

Brain Stimulation

The most direct anatomical approach to locating conscious will involves poking around in the living human brain. This approach is not for the squeamish, and nobody I know would be particularly interested in signing up to be a subject in such a study. So there is not much research to report in this area. The primary source of evidence so far is research conducted in the 1940s and 1950s—the famous "open head" studies by the neurosurgeon Wilder Penfield. Penfield mapped a variety of sensory and motor structures on the brain's surface by electrically stimulating the cortical motor area of patients during brain surgery. The surgery was conducted under local anesthetic while the patient was conscious (fig. 2.5), and this allowed Penfield to ask what happened when, for example, the stimulation caused a person's hand to move. In one such case, the patient said, "I didn't do that. You did." (Penfield 1975, 76). When further stimulation caused the patient to vocalize, he said: "I didn't make that sound. You pulled it out of me." Penfield (1975, 77) observed of the patient that "If the electrode moves his right hand, he does not say 'I wanted to move it.' He may, however, reach over with the left hand [of his own accord] and oppose the action."

Now, the movements the patient was making here were not the spasms one might associate with electrical stimulation of a muscle itself. These were not, for example, like the involuntary ear jerks that Bair (1901) prompted in his subjects when he electrified a muscle to get them to wiggle an ear. Instead, the movements Penfield stimulated in the brain were smooth movements involving coordinated sequences of the operation of multiple muscles, which looked to have the character of voluntary actions, at least from the outside (Penfield and Welch 1951; Porter and Lemon 1993). They just didn't feel consciously willed to the patient who did them. In this case, then, the stimulation appears not to have yielded any experience of conscious will and instead merely prompted the occurrence of voluntary-appearing actions.

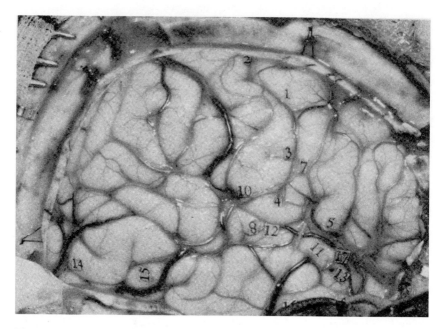

Figure 2.5
Penfield's (1975) photo of the exposed conscious brain of patient M. The numbers were added by Penfield to indicate points of stimulation, and do not indicate the discovery of the math area of the brain. Courtesy Princeton University Press.

Penfield's remarkable set of observations are strikingly in counterpoint, though, with those of another brain stimulation researcher, José Delgado (1969). Delgado's techniques also stimulated the brain to produce movement, but in this case movement that was accompanied by a feeling of doing. Delgado (1969) reported,

In one of our patients, electrical stimulation of the rostral part of the internal capsule produced head turning and slow displacement of the body to either side with a well-oriented and apparently normal sequence, as if the patient were looking for something. This stimulation was repeated six times on two different days with comparable results. The interesting fact was that the patient considered the evoked activity spontaneous and always offered a reasonable explanation for it. When asked "What are you doing?" the answers were, "I am looking for my slippers," "I heard a noise," "I am restless," and "I was looking under the bed." (115–116)

This observation suggests, at first glance, that there is indeed a part of the brain that yields consciously willed action when it is electrically stimulated. However, the patient's quick inventions of purposes sound suspiciously like confabulations, convenient stories made up to fit the moment. The development of an experience of will may even have arisen in this case from the stimulation of a whole action-producing scenario in the person's experience. In Delgado's words, "In this case it was difficult to ascertain whether the stimulation had evoked a movement which the patient tried to justify, or if an hallucination had been elicited which subsequently induced the patient to move and to explore the surroundings" (1969, 116). These complications make it impossible to point to the "feeling of doing" area of the brain, at least for now. And given the rare conditions that allow neurosurgeons ethically to tinker with brain stimulation at all, it is not clear that this particular approach is going to uncover the precise architecture of the brain areas that allow the experience of conscious will.

No matter where such an area might be, though, the comparison of Delgado's patient with the one examined by Penfield suggests that the brain structure that provides the experience of will is *separate* from the brain source of action. It appears possible to produce voluntary action through brain stimulation with or without an experience of conscious will. This, in turn, suggests the interesting possibility that conscious will is an add-on, an experience that has its own origins and consequences. The experience of will may not be very firmly connected to the processes that produce action, in that whatever creates the experience of will may function in a way that is only loosely coupled with the mechanisms that yield action itself.

This point is nicely made in another brain stimulation experiment, one that was carried out without any surgery at all. For this study, Brasil-Neto et al. (1992) simply used magnets on people's heads. They exposed participants to transcranial magnetic stimulation of the motor area of the brain (fig. 2.6). High levels of magnetic stimulation have been found to influence brain function very briefly and can have effects somewhat like that of a temporary small lesion to the area of the brain that is stimulated. (Kids, don't play with this at home.)

In this experiment, a stimulation magnet was poised above the participant's head and aimed in random alternation at the motor area on either side of the brain. Then the participant was asked to move a finger whenever a click was heard (the click of the electrical switch setting off the

Figure 2.6
Transcranial magnetic stimulation, as in the experiment by Brasil-Neto et al.
(1992). Actually, the modern TMS device looks like a doughnut on a stick and
can be waved around the head easily. The contraption in this photo is a magnet
used by Silvanus P. Thompson trying to stimulate his brain electromagnetically in
1910. This impressive machine gave him some spots in front of his eyes but little
else.

magnet). Participants were asked to choose freely whether to move their
right or left index finger on each trial. Then the magnet was moved
around while they responded. Although the stimulation led participants
to have a marked preference to move the finger contralateral to the site
stimulated, particularly at short response times, they continued to perceive that they were voluntarily choosing which finger to move. When
asked whether they had voluntarily chosen which finger to move, participants showed no inkling that something other than their will was creating their choice. This study did not include a detailed report of how the
experience of voluntariness was assessed, but it is suggestive that the

experience of will can arise independently of actual causal forces influencing behavior.

As an aside on these brain stimulation studies, we should recognize that it is not even clear that the sense of conscious will must be in any one place in the brain. Such general functions of consciousness may be at many locations in the brain, riding piggyback on other functions or being added to them at many different anatomical sites (Dennett and Kinsbourne 1992; Kinsbourne 1997). Studies of the influence of brain damage on awareness indicate that even minute differences in the location of damage can influence dramatically the degree to which a patient is aware of having a particular deficit (Milner and Rugg 1992; Prigatano and Schacter 1991; Weiskrantz 1997). There may be parts of the brain that carry "aware" signals and other parts that simply carry signals. The motor functions that create action and the structures that support the experience of conscious will could be deeply intertwined in this network and yet could be highly distinct.

The research to date on the anatomy of conscious will, taken as a whole, suggests that there are multiple sources of this feeling. It appears that a person can derive the feeling of doing from conscious thoughts about what will be done, from feedback from muscles that have carried out the action, and even from visual perception of the action in the absence of such thoughts or feedback. The research on phantom limbs in particular suggests that experience of conscious will arises from a remarkably flexible array of such indicators and can be misled by one when others are unreliable. The brain, in turn, shows evidence that the motor structures underlying action are distinct from the structures that allow the experience of will. The experience of will may be manufactured by the interconnected operation of multiple brain systems, and these do not seem to be the same as the systems that yield action.

When There's a Will

Having explored how conscious will might be localized in space (in the human body and brain), we now turn to considering the dimension of time. Exactly when does conscious will appear in the events surrounding action? Questions of "when" address the mechanism of mind in a different way than questions of "where" because they focus attention on the sequential arrangement of the cogs in the machinery that cranks out our actions. This, in turn, informs us of the structure of the machine in ways that simply looking at its unmoving parts may not.

Lifting a Finger

At some arbitrary time in the next few seconds, please move your right index finger. That's correct, please perform a consciously willed action. Now, here's an interesting question: What was your brain up to at the time? In an elaborate experiment, Kornhuber and Deecke (1965) arranged to measure this event in a number of people by assessing the electrical potentials on the scalp just before and after such voluntary finger movements. Continuous recordings were made of electrical potentials at several scalp electrodes while the experimenter waited for the subject to lift that finger. The actual point when the finger moved was measured precisely by electromyography (EMG, a sensor to detect muscle movement), and this was repeated for as many as 1,000 movements per experiment with each subject. Then, using the movement onset as a reference point, the average scalp electrical potentials could be graphed for the time period surrounding all those voluntary actions.

Et voilà—the spark of will! Brain electrical activity was found to start increasing about 0.8 seconds before the voluntary finger movement. Kornhuber and Deecke dubbed this activity the *readiness potential* (RP). As shown in figure 2.7, this RP occurs widely in the brain—in the left and right precentral regions (spots a bit above and forward of the ear, corresponding to the motor area) and in the midparietal region (top of the head), as shown in the upper three panels. This negative electrical impulse peaks about 90 milliseconds before the action and then drops a bit in the positive (downward) direction before the action. The ratio of the left to right potentials shown in the fourth panel also reveals a bit of a blip about 50 milliseconds before the action on the left side of the motor area of the brain. Just before the right finger moves, the finger and hand motor area contralateral to that finger—the area that controls the actual movement—is then activated. This blip has been called the *movement potential* (Deecke, Scheid, and Kornhuber 1969). It seems as though a general readiness for voluntary action resolves into a more localized activation of the area responsible for the specific action just as the action unfolds.

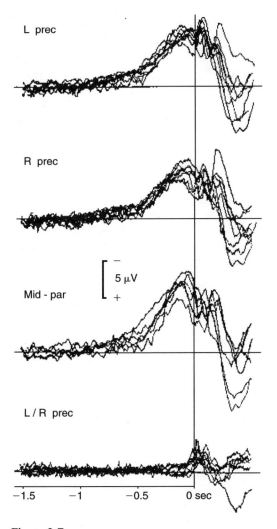

Figure 2.7
The brain potentials measured by Deecke, Grozinger, and Kornhuber (1976). Each graphic curve represents one experiment. The top three panels show the development of the readiness potential (RP) at three scalp locations, and the bottom panel shows the movement potential in the difference between left and right in the precentral motor area associated with finger movement. The RP onset is about 800 milliseconds before the voluntary finger movement, whereas the movement potential onset is only 50 milliseconds before the movement.

The discovery of the RP for voluntary action electrified a number of brains all over the world. The excitement at having found a brain correlate of conscious will was palpable, and a number of commentators exclaimed breathlessly that the science of mind had reached its Holy Grail. John Eccles (1976; 1982) applauded this research, for example, and suggested that these findings showed for the first time how the conscious self operates to produce movement. He proposed,

Regions of the brain in liaison with the conscious self can function as extremely sensitive detectors of consciously willed influences. . . . As a consequence, the willing of a movement produces the gradual evolution of neuronal responses over a wide area of frontal and parietal cortices of both sides, so giving the readiness potential. Furthermore, the mental act that we call willing must guide or mold this unimaginably complex neuronal performance of the liaison cortex so that eventually it "homes in" on to the appropriate modules of the motor cortex and brings about discharges of their motor pyramidal cells. (1976, 117)

What Eccles overlooked in his enthusiasm was that in this study the conscious self had in fact never been queried. The study simply showed that brain events occur reliably before voluntary action.

When exactly in this sequence does the person experience *conscious* will? Benjamin Libet and colleagues (1983; Libet 1985; 1993) had the bright idea of asking people just this question and invented a way to time their answers. Like participants in the prior RP experiments, participants in these studies were also asked to move a finger spontaneously while wearing EMG electrodes on the finger and scalp EEG electrodes for RP measurement. And as in the prior studies the participants were asked to move the finger at will: "Let the urge to act appear on its own any time without any preplanning or concentration on when to act" (627). In this case, however, the participant was also seated before a visible clock. On the circular screen of an oscilloscope, a spot of light revolved in a clockwise path around the circumference of the screen, starting at the twelve o'clock position and revolving each 2.65 seconds—quite a bit faster than the second hand of a real clock. A circular scale with illuminated lines marked units around the edge, each of which corresponded to 107 milliseconds of real time. The participant's task was simply to report for each finger movement where the dot was on the clock when he experienced "*conscious awareness of 'wanting' to perform* a given self-initiated movement" (627).

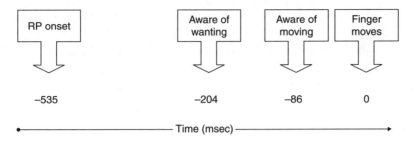

Figure 2.8
Time line of events prior to voluntary finger movement, in research by Libet et al.
(1983).

The researchers called these measurements the W series (for wanting)
and also took some other key measurements for comparison. For an M
(movement) series, instead of asking the participant to report where the
dot was when he became consciously aware of wanting to move, the participant was asked for the location of the dot when he became aware of
actually moving. And in an S (stimulation) series, the participant was
simply asked to report the clock position when a stimulus was applied to
the back of his hand.

The results were truly noteworthy, although in some sense this is
exactly what you would have to expect: The conscious willing of finger
movement occurred at a significant interval *after* the onset of the RP but
also at a significant interval *before* the actual finger movement (and also
at a significant interval before the awareness of movement). The time line
for the RP, W, M, and actual movement events is shown in figure 2.8.
These findings suggest that the brain starts doing something first (we
don't know just what that is). Then the person becomes conscious of
wanting to do the action. This would be where the conscious will kicks
in, at least, in the sense that the person first becomes conscious of trying
to act. Then, and still a bit *prior* to the movement, the person reports becoming aware of the finger actually moving.[6] Finally, the finger moves.

6. This odd finding indicates that people are aware of moving some significant
small interval before they actually move. Haggard, Newman, and Magno (1999)
and McCloskey, Colebatch et al. (1983) reported results consistent with this, and
Haggard and Magno (1999) found that the timing of this awareness of movement
can be influenced by transcranial magnetic stimulation.

Libet and colleagues suggested that the S series could be used as a guide to estimating how long any hand-to-brain activity might take. It took about 47 milliseconds for people to report being consciously aware of a stimulus to the hand, so Libet reasoned it might be useful to subtract this number from the W and M series values to adjust for this part of the process. This doesn't really change the overall conclusion; it just moves the "aware of wanting" time to −157 milliseconds and the "aware of moving" time to −39 milliseconds. One other quibble: You may have noticed that the RP in this study occurred later (−535 milliseconds) than the one in Kornhuber and Deecke's experiment (approximately −800 milliseconds). This is because Libet made a special point of asking participants to mention if they had done any preplanning of the finger movement and eliminated those instances from the analysis. In a separate study, Libet, Wright, and Gleason (1982) had learned that the RP occurred as much as a second or two earlier on trials when participants were allowed to plan for their movement, so the conscious will study avoided this by emphasizing spontaneous, unplanned movements.

The conclusion suggested by this research is that the experience of conscious will kicks in at some point *after* the brain has already started preparing for the action. Libet sums up these observations by saying that "the initiation of the voluntary act appears to be an unconscious cerebral process. Clearly, free will or free choice of whether *to act now* could not be the initiating agent, contrary to one widely held view. This is of course also contrary to each individual's own introspective feeling that he/she consciously initiates such voluntary acts; this provides an important empirical example of the possibility that the subjective experience of a mental causality need not necessarily reflect the actual causative relationship between mental and brain events" (Libet 1992, 269).

Recounting Libet's discovery has become a cottage industry among students of consciousness (Dennett 1991; Harth 1982; Nørretranders 1998; Spence 1996; Wegner and Bargh 1998), and for good reason. Although there have only been a few replications of the research itself, because this is difficult and painstaking science (Keller and Heckhausen 1990; Haggard and Eimer 1999), the basic phenomenon is so full of implications that it has aroused a wide range of comments, both supportive and critical (see the commentaries published following

Libet 1985; also, Gomes 1998). Many commentators seem to agree that it is hard to envision conscious will happening well before anything in the brain starts clicking because that would truly be a case of a ghost in the machine. The common theme in several of the critiques, however, is the nagging suspicion that somehow conscious will might at least share its temporal inception with brain events. Some still hope, as did John Eccles, that conscious will and the RP leading to voluntary action would at least be synchronous. That way, although we might not be able to preserve the causal priority of conscious will, the conscious will might still be part of the brain train, all of which leaves the station at once. Yet this is not what was observed. In what happened, the brain started first, followed by the experience of conscious will, and finally followed by action.

We don't know what specific unconscious mental processes the RP might represent.[7] These processes are likely to be relevant in some way to the ensuing events, of course, because they occur with precise regularity in advance of those events. Now, the ensuing events include both the experience of wanting to move *and* the voluntary movement. The RP could thus signal the occurrence of unconscious mental events that produce both the experience of wanting to move and the occurrence of actual movement. This possibility alerts us to the intriguing realization that conscious wanting, like voluntary action, is a mental event that is caused by prior events. It seems that conscious wanting is not the beginning of the process of making voluntary movement but rather is one of the events in a cascade that eventually yields such movement. The position of conscious will in the time line suggests perhaps that the experience of will is a link in a causal chain leading to action, but in fact it might not even be that. It might just be a loose end—one of those things, like the action, that is caused by prior brain and mental events.

7. Keller and Heckhausen (1990) found that RPs also were detectable for stray, unconscious finger movements. The technology underlying RP measurement can't distinguish, then, between the conscious and voluntary movements studied by Libet and any sort of movement, even an unconscious one. We just know that an RP occurs before actions (Brunia 1987). RPs do not occur for involuntary movements such as tics or reflex actions (e.g., Obeso, Rothwell, and Marsden 1981).

Acting Quickly

The odd sluggishness of consciousness becomes apparent in another way when people do fast things. When we react to a phone ringing, or take a swat at a fly, for example, we move so rapidly that we seem to leave consciousness behind. In fact, the consciousness of a stimulus that causes a reactive or triggered action of this kind typically *follows* much of the action, coming to mind several hundred milliseconds after the person has begun to respond to incoming signals (Rossetti 1998; Velmans 1991). Imagine, for example, being asked to press a button as soon as you feel a tap. It typically takes only about 100 milliseconds to react to such a stimulus, and sometimes much less, but it may take as much as 500 milliseconds to become conscious of having responded (Libet 1981). For example, in a study in which participants were tracking by hand an unexpectedly moving target, the change in their hand trajectory toward the target's movement happened as early as 100 milliseconds following the target jump. However, the vocal signal by which they reported their awareness of the jump (saying "Pah," which is apparently what you say in an experiment in France to signal something unexpected) did not occur on average until more than 300 milliseconds later (Castiello, Paulignan, and Jeannerod 1991).

Another illustration of the conscious delay is the finding that people can't gradually slow down their reaction times. Jensen (1979) asked people to try deliberately to lengthen their reaction time little by little and found that they could not do so. Rather, their reaction times jumped from the usual minimum values (in his study, about 250 milliseconds) to much higher values, which at a minimum were 500 to 1000 milliseconds. One cannot slow down one's reaction until one becomes conscious of the stimulus *and of having reacted,* and this takes lots of extra time. This discontinuity suggests that a response and a *conscious* response are two very different things, the first one typically far speedier than the second.

The slowness of consciousness prompted Posner and Snyder (1975) to draw a distinction between automatic processes and controlled (conscious) processes.[8] They proposed that fast responses, such as hitting the

---

8. Actually, the distinction is a far older one. The *Oxford English Dictionary* ascribes the first use of *automatic* to David Hartley, who remarked in *Observations on Man* (1749) that "the *Motions* of the body are of two kinds, *automatic* and *voluntary*." These terms were meant to describe bodily functions such as

accelerator when the light turns green, or pulling a finger away from the touch of a hot pan, could be understood as automatic. These automatic reactions take place in 200–300 milliseconds or even less and occur prior to reportable consciousness of the stimulus. They can include choices, such as picking which word to say in a given sentence or which soft drink to grab from the fridge, and they underlie the various fast and fluid skills of which people are capable. Playing tennis or reading or typing or walking are all skills that involve exceedingly fast reactions, many of which can be understood as automatic in this sense (Baars 1988; Bargh 1984; 1994; 1997; Bargh and Chartrand 2000; Wegner and Bargh 1998).

These automatic processes also are often uncontrollable in that once they have been launched, they continue until they are complete (Logan and Cowan 1984). Conscious processes are more flexible and strategic, but they also take more time—in the range of 500 milliseconds or beyond. Half a second doesn't seem like much, of course, but it can be an eternity when you're trying to do something fast. Consider that a skilled keyboarder might be able to type at the rate of 120 words per minute. That means *two words every second,* a phrase that itself would have taken me only 2 seconds to type if I were such a skilled keyboarder. So, a 500-millisecond interval would allow for the typing of an entire word. All the automatic keystrokes that go into typing that word are so fast that they are telescoped together into a sequence that takes only as long as it takes for something *once* to enter into a conscious response.

The slowness of consciousness suggests that much of what we see and do involves the operation of *preconscious* mental processes. That is, we may begin to react to a stimulus before we are aware of it. In fact, if our exposure to a target stimulus is cut short (by a masking stimulus that immediately follows the target and wipes out our visual image of it), we may have a cognitive response to the target without ever becoming aware of the target. People who are judging whether each of a series of letter strings is a word or not, for instance, are likely to judge a string correctly as a word more quickly if they have just been exposed to a related word at a very brief duration, followed by a masking stimulus (Marcel 1983).

---

breathing or lifting a finger, and so were not understood as cognitive processes. Later psychological writers, such as Carpenter (1888) and Jastrow (1906), developed the psychological distinction the way we use it today.

One might more quickly judge *wedding* to be a word, for instance, after seeing a brief flash of *bride* before it than after seeing a similar flash of *succotash*. (This might depend, of course, on one's personal opinion of marriage.) In such studies, the initial word prime never reaches consciousness, and yet it has a measurable influence on behavior.[9]

Our preconscious responses can take the form of early emotional reactions and attitudes. We may develop a quick emotional reaction to just about everything we see, even before we consciously see it (Bargh et al. 1996; Zajonc 1980). We will shrink from the enemy we see coming toward us from a distance, for instance, or get a little shiver when we see our favorite love object, and this can happen before we even know what we have seen. These fast attitudinal responses may determine our behavior when a subsequent conscious reaction to the stimulus is somehow prevented, because we are too busy or distracted, or because we must react without having the chance to spend some time thinking. As Wilson, Lindsay, and Schooler (2000) have proposed, we may have dual attitudes toward many things in our lives, one a rapid response and the other a more studied reaction that takes into account the context and our personal theory of what we ought to be feeling. The conscious attitude will only govern our responses when we have had time to consider the situation and get past the automatic reaction.

What all this means is that consciousness is kind of a slug. This slowness suggests that consciousness might not be up to some of the kind of guidance activity that seems to be needed for the production of willed action. Now, of course, many of the speeded responses we've considered here are not ones usually classified as willed. The quick push of a response key in a reaction time task is certainly not the prototypical voluntary action because it is not spontaneous and is governed by the occurrence of an outside signal. However, it is instructive indeed that consciousness seems to follow these actions rather than lead them. At the extreme,

9. There has been controversy about just how to establish that something is not conscious, as it could just be that the prime word is gaining access to a tiny bit of consciousness (once every few trials, for instance), and so achieving its effect on just a small (but significant) proportion of responses. The battle right now is leaning toward those who believe the evidence does favor preconscious processing, but stay tuned (Greenwald and Draine 1997; Holender 1986; Merikle and Joordens 1997).

it is possible to concur with Marc Jeannerod that "in conditions of normal execution [of action], there is usually no awareness of the content of the representation at any level and no image is experienced. This is explained by the fact that motor imagery and execution have different time constants. Because imagery, unlike execution, implies subjective awareness, it takes longer to appear. If imagery actually occurred in conditions of normal execution, it would be delayed with respect to the corresponding action" (1995, 1429). We may think consciously about what we are doing, turning it over and over in our minds in advance of our action, but it may be that this conscious image we develop is in fact too slow to run concurrently with many of our fast, reactive actions as they happen.

Consciousness and action seem to play a cat-and-mouse game over time. Although we may be conscious of whole vistas of action before the doings get underway, it is as though the conscious mind then slips out of touch. A microanalysis of the time interval before and after action indicates that consciousness pops in and out of the picture and doesn't really seem to do anything. The Libet research, for one, suggests that when it comes down to the actual instant of a spontaneous action, the experience of consciously willing the action occurs only after the RP signals that brain events have already begun creating the action (and probably the intention and the experience of conscious will as well). And the studies of the automaticity of fast reactions, in turn, suggest that conscious mental processes regularly follow rather than lead actions that are quick responses to environmental cues. In the case of reactive responses, knowing what we have done and what stimulated our doing is only a luxury we achieve some milliseconds after action.

The Missing Lightbulb

The search for where and when the will appears in the course of action has led us in a number of different directions. Unfortunately, none of these sorties has resulted in the discovery of the lightbulb we were looking for at the beginning of the chapter. It has taken a whole lot of scientists to try to screw in this particular lightbulb, and so far we are all still in the dark.

We do know where the lightbulb isn't. Apparently, we cannot yet trace the experience of will to any particular signal in the nervous system—from brain to body, or from body to brain. The research on the experience of muscle effort indicates that a variety of different systems can participate in the creation of the sense of effort, and the phantom limb research points to the further idea that one system may stand in for another (vision can substitute for muscle sense, for example) in creating the experience of voluntary movement. The experience of will seems to accrue from a flexible cognitive system that has not yet been isolated to one anatomical structure. The finding that people don't lose the sense of voluntary action even when their movement is being caused by transcranial magnetic stimulation lends credence to this hypothesis as well.

The brain stimulation studies offered the tempting possibility that we might finally find the will in some cranny of the brain. And indeed, some brain events yield action that occurs with an experience of will whereas others do not. However, the research supporting this idea takes the form of a few early clinical observations from different researchers, not a controlled comparison of any kind, and so leaves us with no satisfying indication that the experience of will has been localized in the brain or that it can be found if the right search is mounted. And ultimately, of course, even these studies fail to find the will per se. They indicate instead that the *experience* of willing is a variable attachment to action, and so refocus our attention on the circumstances and timing of the experience.

The timing of will, finally, seems to seal the fate of that elusive lightbulb. The detailed analytical studies of the timing of action indicate that conscious will does not precede brain events leading to spontaneous voluntary action but rather follows them. And the studies focusing on the timing of motor responses, as compared to the timing of conscious responses, indicate further that consciousness of action occurs on a different time schedule than action itself. When actions are forced to be fast, consciousness is perpetually late—the Dagwood Bumstead of the mind, running out the door in the morning and knocking down the mailman. Consciousness of responses occurs following the responses themselves whenever the person is attempting to react quickly.

The circuitous timing of consciousness combines with the difficult anatomy of the will to indicate that what we have here is no lightbulb.

Rather, it appears that the experience of will occurs through a system that presents the idea of a voluntary action to consciousness and also produces the action. The idea can occur just in advance of the action, as when people are allowed to act ad lib (as in Libet's research), or the idea may come to mind only just after the action, as when people are prompted to act rapidly (as in reaction time studies). People get the experience of will primarily when the idea of acting occurs to them before they act. In fact, this tendency to experience will when the appropriate idea precedes the act is the theme of the next chapter.

3

The Experience of Will

The experience of conscious will arises when we infer that our conscious intention has caused our voluntary action, although both intention and action are themselves caused by mental processes that do not feel willed.

While belief in the causality of the self is only an illusion, . . . there are nonetheless two phenomena which explain such a belief; the first is our ability to foresee the result before it actually takes place, the second the presence of a feeling of "activity."
Albert Michotte, *The Perception of Causality* (1954)

Imagine for a moment that by some magical process you could always know when a particular tree branch would move in the wind. Just before it moved, you would know it was going to move, in which direction, and just how it would do it. Not only would you know this, but let's assume that the same magic would guarantee that you would happen to be thinking about the branch just before each move. You'd look over, and then just as you realized it was going to move, it would do it. In this imaginary situation, you could eventually come to think that you were somehow causing the movement. You would seem to be the source of the distant branch's action, the agent that wills it to move.

If there really were such a thing as the psychokinetic powers imagined in the movies, people who had them would experience something very much like this. When Sissy Spacek in *Carrie* burned down the high school gym, for example, or when John Travolta in *Phenomenon* moved small objects into his hands from a distance, it would certainly be as easy for them to ascribe these results to their own will as would be your act of moving a tree branch at a distance. If there really were people with such occult abilities, they probably would have exactly the same kind of information that you have about your branch. They would know in advance when something was going to happen, and they would be looking in that direction and thinking about it when it did happen. The feeling that one is moving the tree branch surfaces in the same way that these folks would get the sense that they could create action at a distance. All it seems to take is the appropriate foreknowledge of the action. Indeed, with proper foreknowledge it is difficult *not* to conclude one has caused the act, and the feeling of doing may well up in direct proportion to the perception that relevant ideas had entered one's mind before the action. This is beginning to sound like a theory.

A Theory of Apparent Mental Causation

The experience of will could be a result of the same mental processes that people use in the perception of causality more generally. The theory of apparent mental causation, then, is this: *People experience conscious will when they interpret their own thought as the cause of their action* (Wegner and Wheatley 1999).[1] This means that people experience conscious will quite independently of any actual causal connection between their thoughts and their actions. Reductions in the impression that there is a link between thought and action may explain why people get a sense of involuntariness even for actions that are voluntary—for example, during motor automatisms such as table turning, or in hypnosis, or in psychologically disordered states such as dissociation. And inflated perceptions of the link between thought and action may, in turn, explain why people experience an illusion of conscious will at all.

The person experiencing will, in this view, is in the same position as someone perceiving causation as one billiard ball strikes another. As we learned from Hume, causation in bowling, billiards, and other games is inferred from the constant conjunction of ball movements. It makes sense, then, that will—an experience of one's own causal influence—is inferred from the conjunction of events that lead to action. Now, in the case of billiard balls, the players in the causal analysis are quite simple: one ball and the other ball. One rolls into the other and a causal event occurs. What are the items that seem to click together in our minds to yield the perception of will?

1. The Wegner and Wheatley (1999) paper presented this theory originally. This chapter is an expanded and revised exposition of the theory.

One view of this was provided by Ziehen (1899), who suggested that thinking of self before action yields the sense of agency. He proposed, "We finally come to regard the ego-idea as the cause of our actions because of its very frequent appearance in the series of ideas preceding each action. It is almost always represented several times among the ideas preceding the final movement. But the idea of the relation of causality is an empirical element that always appears when two successive ideas are very closely associated" (296).

And indeed there is evidence that self-attention is associated with perceived causation of action. People in an experiment by Duval and Wicklund (1973) were asked to make attributions for hypothetical events ("Imagine you are rushing down a narrow hotel hallway and bump into a housekeeper who is backing out of a room"). When asked to decide who was responsible for such events, they assigned more causality to themselves if they were making the judgments while they were self-conscious. Self-consciousness was manipulated in this study by having the participants sit facing a mirror, but other contrivances, such as showing people their own video image or having them hear their tape-recorded voice, also enhance causal attribution to self (Gibbons 1990).

This tendency to perceive oneself as causal when thinking about oneself is a global version of the more specific process that appears to underlie apparent mental causation. The specific process is the perception of a causal link not only between self and action but between one's own thought and action. We tend to see ourselves as the authors of an act primarily when we have experienced relevant thoughts about the act at an appropriate interval in advance and so can infer that our own mental processes have set the act in motion. Actions we perform that are not presaged in our minds, in turn, would appear not to be caused by our minds. The intentions we have to act may or may not *be* causes, but this doesn't matter, as it is only critical that we *perceive* them as causes if we are to experience conscious will.

In this analysis, the experience of will is not a direct readout of some psychological force that causes action from inside the head. Rather, will is experienced as a result of an interpretation of the *apparent* link between the conscious thoughts that appear in association with action and the nature of the observed action. *Will is experienced as the result of self-perceived apparent mental causation.* Thus, in line with several existing theories (Brown 1989; Claxton 1999; Harnad 1982; Hoffman 1986; Kirsch and Lynn 1997; Langer 1975; Libet 1985; Prinz 1997; Spanos 1982; Spence 1996), this theory suggests that the will is a conscious experience that is derived from interpreting one's action as willed. Also in line with these theories, the present framework suggests that the experience of will may only map rather weakly, or at times not at all, onto the actual causal relation between the person's cognition and action. The new idea introduced here is the possibility that the experience of acting develops when the person infers that his or her own *thought* (read: intention, but belief and desire are also important) was the cause of the action.

This theory makes sense as a way of seeing the will because the causal analysis of anything, not only the link from thought to action, suffers from a fundamental uncertainty. Although we may be fairly well convinced that A causes B, for instance, there is always the possibility that the regularity in their association is the result of some third variable, C, which causes both A and B. Drawing on the work of Hume, Jackson (1998) reminds us that "anything can fail to cause anything. No matter how often B follows A, and no matter how initially obvious the causality of the connection seems, the hypothesis that A causes B can be overturned by an over-arching theory which shows the two as distinct effects of a common underlying causal process" (203). Although day always precedes night, for example, it is a mistake to say that day *causes* night, because of course both are caused in this sequence by the rotation of the earth in the presence of the sun.

This uncertainty in causal inference means that no matter how much we are convinced that our thoughts cause our actions, it is still true that both thought and action could be caused by something else that remains unobserved, leaving us to draw an incorrect causal conclusion. As Searle (1983) has put it, "It is always possible that something else might actually be causing the bodily movement we think the experience [of acting] is causing. It is always possible that I might think I am raising my arm when in fact some other cause is raising it. So there is nothing in the experience of acting that actually guarantees that it is causally effective" (130). We can never be sure that our thoughts cause our actions, as there could always be causes of which we are unaware that have produced both the thoughts and the actions.

This theory of apparent mental causation depends on the idea that consciousness doesn't know how conscious mental processes work. When you multiply 3 times 6 in your head, for example, the answer just pops into mind without any indication of how you did that.[2] As Nisbett and Wilson (1977) have observed, the occurrence of a mental process does not guarantee the individual any special knowledge of the mechanism of this process. Instead, the person seeking self-insight must employ a priori causal theories to account for his or her own psychological operations. The conscious will may thus arise from the person's theory designed to account for the regular relation between thought and action. Conscious will is not a direct perception of that relation but rather a feeling based on the causal inference one makes about the data that do become available to consciousness—the thought and the observed act.

A model of a mental system for the production of an experience of conscious will based on apparent mental causation is shown in figure 3.1. The model represents the temporal flow of events (from left to right) leading up to a voluntary action. In this system, unconscious mental processes give rise to conscious thought about the action (e.g., intention, belief), and other unconscious mental processes give rise to the voluntary action. There may or may not be links between these underlying unconscious systems (as designated by the bidirectional unconscious potential path), but this is irrelevant to the perception of the *apparent* path from conscious thought to action. Any actual path here cannot be directly perceived, so there may be no actual path. Instead, it is the perception of the

---

2. If you were trying to multiply something harder, say, 18 times 3, in your head, you might have a number of steps in the computation come to mind (3 times 8 is 24, and then . . .), and so you could claim to be somewhat conscious of the mechanism because you could report the results of subparts of the process. Extended mental processes that are not fully automatic often thrust such "tips of the iceberg" into consciousness as the process unfolds and so allow for greater confidence in the inferences one might make about their course (Ericsson and Simon 1984; Vallacher and Wegner 1985). In the case of willing an action, however, there do not seem to be multiple substeps that can produce partial computational results for consciousness. Rather, we think it and do it, and that's all we have to go on. If we perform an action that we must "will" in subparts, each subpart is still inscrutable in this way.

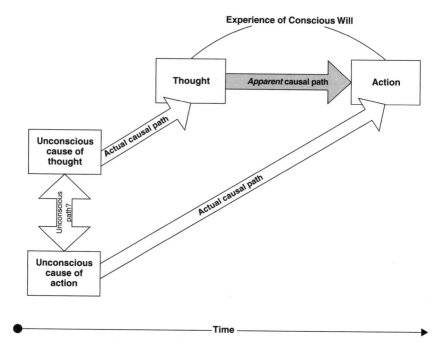

Figure 3.1
The experience of conscious will arises when a person infers an apparent causal path from thought to action. The actual causal paths are not present in the person's consciousness. The thought is caused by unconscious mental events, and the action is caused by unconscious mental events, and these unconscious mental events may also be linked to each other directly or through yet other mental or brain processes. The will is experienced as a result of what is apparent, though, not what is real.

apparent path that gives rise to the experience of will: When we think that our conscious intention has caused the voluntary action that we find ourselves doing, we feel a sense of will. We have willfully done the act.[3]

How do we go about drawing the inference that our thought has caused our action? The tree branch example yields several ideas about this. Think, for instance, of what could spoil the feeling that you have moved

3. The experience of will can happen before, during, or after the action. So, it is probably the case that the inference system we're talking about here might operate in some way throughout the process of thinking and acting. The experience of will may accrue prior to action from the anticipation that we have an intention and that the act will come. After that, apparent mental causation arrives full-blown as we perceive both the intention and the ensuing act. We can experience

the branch. If the branch moved before you thought of its moving, for instance, there would be nothing out of the ordinary, and you would experience no sense of willful action.[4] The thought of movement would be interpretable as a memory or even a perception of what had happened. If you thought of the tree limb's moving and then something quite different moved (say, a nearby chicken dropped to its knees), again there would be no experience of will. The thought would be irrelevant to what had happened, and you would see no causal connection. And if you thought of the tree limb's moving but noticed that something other than your thoughts had moved it (say, a squirrel), no will would be sensed. There would simply be the perception of an external causal event. These observations point to three key sources of the experience of conscious will—the *priority, consistency,* and *exclusivity* of the thought about the action (Wegner and Wheatley 1999). For the perception of apparent mental causation, the thought should occur before the action, be consistent with the action, and not be accompanied by other potential causes.

Studies of how people perceive external physical events (Michotte 1954) indicate that the perception of causality is highly dependent on these features of the relation between the potential cause and potential effect. The candidate for the role of cause must come first or at least at

---

the willful act of swinging a croquet mallet when our intention precedes the action, for instance, just as we might experience external causation on viewing, say, a mallet swinging through the air on a trajectory with a croquet ball, which it then hits and drives ahead. And later, on reflection, we might also be able to recall an experience of will. So the inference process that yields conscious will does its job throughout the process of actual action causation, first in anticipation, then in execution, and finally in reflection.

4. If the branch moved *regularly* just before you thought of it moving, you could get the willies. In this event, it would seem as though the branch somehow could anticipate your thoughts, and this would indeed create an odd sensation. Dennett (1991) recounted a 1963 presentation of an experiment by the British neurosurgeon W. Grey Walter in which patients had electrodes implanted in the motor cortex, from which amplified signals were used to advance a slide projector. The signals were earlier than the conscious thought to move to the next slide, so patients experienced the odd event of the slide advancing just before they wanted it to advance. Dennett swears this report is not apocryphal, but unfortunately this work was never published and seemingly has not been replicated by others since. A discovery of this kind would be absolutely stunning, and I'm thinking Grey Walter may have been pulling his colleagues' legs.

the same time as the effect, it must yield movement that is consistent with its own movement, and it must be unaccompanied by rival causal events. The absence of any of these conditions tends to undermine the perception that causation has occurred. Similar principles have been derived for the perception of causality for social and everyday events (Einhorn and Hogarth 1986; Kelley 1972; 1980; McClure 1998) and have also emerged from analyses of how people and other organisms respond to patterns of stimulus contingency when they learn (Alloy and Tabachnik 1984; Young 1995). The application of these principles to the experience of conscious will can explain phenomena of volition across a number of areas of psychology.

The Priority Principle

Causal events precede their effects, usually in a timely manner. The cue ball rolls across the table and taps into the 3 ball, touching the 3 ball just before the 3 ball moves. If they touched after the movement or a long time before it, the cue ball would not be perceived as causing the 3 ball to roll. And perhaps the most basic principle of the sense of will is that conscious thoughts of an action appearing just before an act yield a greater sense of will than conscious thoughts of an action that appear at some other time—long beforehand or, particularly, afterwards. The thoughts must appear within a particular window of time for the experience of will to develop.

The Window of Time

Albert Michotte (1954) was interested in what causation looks like, what he called the phenomenology of causality. To study this, he devised an animation machine for showing people objects that move in potentially causal patterns. The device was a disk with a horizontal slot, through which one could see lines painted on another disk behind it. When the rear disk was rotated, the lines appeared as gliding objects in the slot, and the movement of these could be varied subtly in a variety of ways with different line patterns (fig. 3.2).

Michotte's most basic observation with this device was the "launching effect." When one of the apparent objects moved along and appeared to

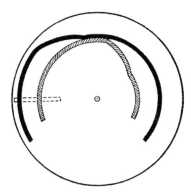

Figure 3.2
Michotte's (1954) launching disk. This disk rotated behind a covering disk through which the lines could be seen only through a slot. When the lined disk turned counterclockwise, the solid object appeared to move to the right and hit the crosshatched object, launching it to the right. Courtesy Leuven University Press.

strike another, which then immediately began to move in the same direction even while the first one stopped or slowed down, people perceived a causal event: the first object had launched the second. If the second object sat there for a bit after the first touched it, however, and only *then* began moving, the sense that this was a causal event was lost and the second object was perceived to have started moving on its own. Then again, if the second object began to move before the first even came to touch it, the perception of causation was also absent. The second object seemed to have generated its own movement or to have been launched by something unseen. The lesson, then, is that to be perceived as truly a cause, an event can't start too soon or too late; it has to occur just before the effect.

These observations suggest that the experience of will may also depend on the timely occurrence of thought prior to action. Thought that occurs too far in advance of an action is not likely to be seen as the cause of it; a person who thinks of dumping a bowl of soup on her boss's head, for example, and then never thinks about this again until suddenly doing it some days later during a quiet dinner party, is not likely to experience the action as willful. Thought that occurs well after the relevant action is also not prone to cue an experience of will. The person who discovers having done an act that was not consciously considered in advance—say, getting in the car on a day off and absently driving all the way to work—would also feel little in the way of conscious will.

Somewhere between these extreme examples exist cases in which conscious will is regularly experienced. Little is known about the parameters of timing that might maximize this experience, but it seems likely that thoughts occurring just a few seconds before an action would be most prone to support the perception of willfulness. Thoughts about an action that occur earlier than this and that do not then persist in consciousness might not be linked with the action in a perceived causal unit (Heider 1958) because thought and act were not in mind simultaneously. Slight variations in timing were all that was needed in Michotte's experiments to influence quite profoundly whether the launching effect occurred and causation was perceived.

The time it usually takes the mind to wander from one topic to another could be the basic limit for experiencing intent as causing action. The mind does wander regularly (Pöppel 1997; Wegner 1997). For example, a reversible figure such as a Necker cube (the standard doodle of a transparent cube) that is perceived from one perspective in the mind's eye will naturally tend to change to the other in about 3 seconds (Gomez et al. 1995). Such wandering suggests that a thought occurring less than 3 seconds prior to action could stay in mind and be linked to action, whereas a thought occurring before that time might shift to something else before the act (in the absence of active rehearsal, at any rate) and so undermine the experience of will (Mates et al. 1994).

Another estimate of the maximum interval from intent to action that could yield perceived will is based on short-term memory storage time. The finding of several generations of researchers is that people can hold an item in mind to recall for no longer than about 30 seconds without rehearsal, and that the practical retention time is even shorter when there are significant intervening events (Baddeley 1986). If the causal inference linking thought and act is primarily perceptual, the shorter (3-second) estimate based on reversible figures might be more apt, whereas if the causal inference can occur through paired representation of thought and act in short-term memory, the longer (30-second) estimate might be more accurate. In whatever way the maximum interval is estimated, though, it is clear that there is only a fairly small window prior to action in which relevant thoughts must appear if the action is to be felt as willed.

This brief window reminds us that even long-term planning for an action may not produce an experience of will unless the plan reappears in mind just as the action is performed. Although thinking of an action far in advance of doing it would seem to be a signal characteristic of a premeditated action (Brown 1996; Vallacher and Wegner 1985), the present analysis suggests that such distant foresight yields less will perception than does immediately prior apprehension of the act. In the absence of thought about the action that occurs just prior to its performance, even the most distant foresight would merely be premature and would do little to promote the feeling that one had willed the action. In line with this suggestion, Gollwitzer (1993) has proposed that actions that are intended far in advance to correspond with a triggering event ("I'll go when the light turns green") may then tend to occur automatically without conscious thought, and thus without a sense of volition, when the triggering event ensues.

The priority principle also indicates that thoughts coming after action will not prompt the experience of will. But, again, it is not clear just how long following action the thought would need to occur for will not to be experienced. One indication of the lower bound for willful experience is Libet's (1985) observation that in the course of a willed finger movement, conscious intention precedes action by about 200 milliseconds. Perhaps if conscious thought of an act occurs past this time, it is perceived as following the act, or at least as being too late, and so is less likely to be seen as causal. Studies of subjective simultaneity have examined the perceived timing of external events and actions (McCloskey, Colebatch et al. 1983), but research has not yet tested the precise bounds for the perception of consecutiveness of thought and action. It seems safe to say, however, that thoughts occurring some seconds or minutes after action would rarely be perceived as causal and could thus not give rise to an experience of will during the action.

There are, of course, exceptions to the priority principle. Most notably, people may sometimes claim their acts were willful even if they could only have known what they were doing after the fact. These exceptions have been widely investigated for the very reason that they depart from normal priority. These are discussed in some depth in chapter 5. In the meantime, we can note that such findings indicate that priority of intent is not the only source of the experience of will and that other sources of the experience (such as consistency and exclusivity) may come forward to suggest willfulness even when priority is not present. Now let's look at a study that creates an illusion of will through the manipulation of priority.

The I Spy Study

If will is an experience fabricated from perceiving a causal link between thought and action, it should be possible to lead people to feel that they have performed a willful action when in fact they have done nothing. Wegner and Wheatley (1999) conducted an experiment to learn whether people will feel they willfully performed an action that was actually performed by someone else when conditions suggest their own thought may have caused the action. The study focused on the role of priority of thought and action, and was inspired in part by the ordinary household Ouija board. The question was whether people would feel they had moved a Ouija-like pointer if they simply thought about where it would go just in advance of its movement, even though the movement was in fact produced by another person.

Each participant arrived for the experiment at about the same time as a confederate who was posing as another participant. The two were seated facing each other at a small table, on which lay a 12-centimeter-square board mounted atop a computer mouse. Both participant and confederate were asked to place their fingertips on the side of the board closest to them (fig. 3.3) so that they could move the mouse together. They were asked to move the mouse in slow sweeping circles and, by doing so, to move a cursor around a computer screen that was visible to both. The screen showed a "Tiny Toys" photo from the book I Spy (Marzollo and Wick 1992), picturing about fifty small objects (e.g., dinosaur, swan, car).[5]

The experimenter explained that the study was to investigate people's feelings of intention for acts and how these feelings come and go. It was explained that the pair were to stop moving the mouse every 30 seconds or so, and that they would rate each stop they made for personal intentionality.

---

5. In some early trials, we attempted to use a standard Ouija board and found enough hesitation among even our presumably enlightened college student participants ("There are evil spirits in that thing") that we subsequently avoided reference to Ouija and designed our apparatus to appear particularly harmless. No evil spirits were detected in the I Spy device.

Figure 3.3
Participant and confederate move the computer mouse together in the *I Spy* experiment by Wegner and Wheatley (1999).

That is, they each would rate how much they had intended to make each stop, independent of their partner's intentions. The participant and confederate made these ratings on scales that they kept on clipboards in their laps. Each scale consisted of a 14-centimeter line with end points "I allowed the stop to happen" and "I intended to make the stop," and marks on the line were converted to percent intended (0–100).

The participant and confederate were told that they would hear music and words through headphones during the experiment. Each trial would involve a 30-second interval of movement, after which they would hear a 10-second clip of music to indicate that they should make a stop. They were told that they would be listening to two different tracks of an audiotape, but that they would hear music at about the same times and should wait a few seconds into their music before making the stops to make sure they both were ready. Participant and confederate were also told that they would hear a word over the headphones on each trial, ostensibly to provide a mild distraction, and that the reason for the separate audio tracks was so that they would hear different words. To emphasize this point, the experimenter played a few seconds of the tape and asked the participant and confederate which word they heard in their headphones. The confederate always reported hearing a different word from the participant. Thus, participants were led to believe that the words they heard were not heard by the confederate.

The words served to prime thoughts about objects on the screen for the participant (e.g., *swan*). The confederate, on the other hand, heard neither words nor music, but instead heard instructions to make particular movements at particular times. For four of the trials, the confederate heard instructions to move to an object on the screen followed by a countdown, at which time the confederate was to stop on that object. These *forced* stops were each timed to occur midway through the participant's music. Each of the stops (e.g., to land on the swan) was timed to occur at specific intervals from when the participant heard the corresponding word (*swan*). The participant thus heard the word consistent with the stop either 30 seconds before, 5 seconds before, 1 second before, or 1 second after the confederate stopped on the object. By varying the timing, priority was thus manipulated. Each of these four stops was on a different object. The four forced stops were embedded in a series of other trials for which the confederate simply let the participant make the stops. For these *unforced* stops, the participant heard a word 2 seconds into the music whereas the confederate did not hear a word. The word corresponded to an object on the screen for about half of these trials and was something not appearing on the screen for the others.

An initial analysis of the unforced stops was made to see whether participants might naturally stop on the objects that were mentioned. The confederate would have only had a random influence on stops for these trials, as he or she was not trying to guide the movement. If the cursor did stop on items that the participant had heard mentioned, it would suggest that the participant might also have played some part in the forced stops, and it was important to assess whether he had. Distances between stops and objects on the screen were computed for all unforced stops (all trials in which the confederate heard no instruction and simply let the participant make the stop). The mean distance between the stop and an object on the screen (e.g., dinosaur) was measured separately for stops when that object was the mentioned word and for stops when the mentioned word was something not shown on the screen (e.g., *monkey*). The mean distance between stop and object when the word referred to the object was 7.60 centimeters, and this was not significantly closer than the distance of 7.83 centimeters when the word did not refer to the object. Thus, simply hearing words did not cause participants to stop on the items. The forced stops created by the confederate were thus not likely to have been abetted by movement originated by the participant.

Nonetheless, on the forced stops a pattern of perceived intention emerged as predicted by the priority principle. Although there was a tendency overall for participants to perceive the forced stops as somewhat intended (mean intentionality = 52 percent), there was a marked fluctuation in this perception depending on when the word occurred. As shown in figure 3.4, perceived intentionality was lower when the object-relevant word appeared 30 seconds before the forced stop, increased when the word occurred 5 seconds or 1 second before the stop, and then dropped again to a lower level when the word occurred 1 second following the stop. As compared to trials when thought consistent with the forced action was primed 30 seconds before or 1 second after the action, there was an increased experience of intention when the thought was primed 1 to 5 seconds before the forced action. The mean intention reported

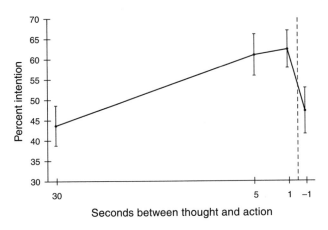

Figure 3.4
Participants in the *I Spy* experiment rated their personal intention to stop on an object as higher when they had heard the name of the object 5 seconds or 1 second before they were forced to stop on it than when they heard the name 30 seconds before or 1 second after the forced stop. From Wegner and Wheatley (1999).

on all the unforced stops—when participants were indeed free to move the cursor anywhere—was 56 percent, a level in the same range as that observed for the forced stops in the 1-second and 5-second priming trials.

In postexperimental interviews, participants reported sometimes searching for items on screen that they had heard named over their headphones. Perhaps this sense of searching for the item, combined with the subsequent forced stop on the item, was particularly helpful for prompting the experience of intending to stop on the item. It is difficult to discern from these data just what feature of having the object in mind prior to the forced stop produced the sense of will, but it is clear that the timing of the thought in relation to the action is important. When participants were reminded of an item on the screen just 1 second or 5 seconds before they were forced to move the cursor to it, they reported having performed this movement intentionally. Such reminding a full 30 seconds before the forced movement or 1 second after the movement yielded less of this sense of intentionality. The parallel observation that participants did not move toward primed objects on unforced trials suggests that participants were unlikely to have contributed to the movement on the forced trials. Apparently, the experience of will can be created by the manipulation of thought and action in accord with the principle of priority, and this experience can occur even when the person's thought cannot have created the action.

The Consistency Principle

When one billiard ball strikes another, the struck ball moves in the same general direction that the striking ball was moving. We do not perceive causality very readily if the second ball squirts off like squeezed soap in a direction that, by the laws of physics, is inconsistent with the movement of the first ball (Michotte 1962). Now, causality need not be consistent in reality. Very tiny causes (a struck match) can create very great effects (a forest in cinders), or causes of one class of event (a musical note) can create effects of some other class (a shattered goblet). It is sometimes difficult to say just what consistency might be in physical causation, for that matter, because there are so many dimensions on which a cause and effect might be compared.

Causes Should Relate to Effects

When it comes to the psychological principles that influence the *perception* of causality, however, consistency is a fundamental canon. Big causes are assumed to be necessary to create big effects, for example, and bad people are seen as more likely to have done bad things. People are far more likely to perceive causality when they can appreciate some meaningful connection between a candidate causal event and a particular effect (Einhorn and Hogarth 1986; Nisbett and Ross 1980). John Stuart Mill (1843) complained long ago that this bias, the "prejudice that the conditions of a phenomenon must *resemble* the phenomenon . . . not only reigned supreme in the ancient world, but still possesses almost undisputed dominion over many of the most cultivated minds" (765). Perceiving causality through consistency is particularly prevalent in children, in whom it even has a name—phenomenism (Piaget 1927; Laurendeau and Pinard 1962). And anthropologists have described such tendencies in other cultures in terms of "laws of sympathetic magic" (Mauss 1902; Nemeroff and Rozin 2000). Educated adults in North America, for example, are inaccurate in throwing darts at a picture when it portrays a person they like (Rozin, Millman, and Nemeroff 1986). By the principle of consistency, this would suggest that they themselves are causing harm to their loved one, and this undermines their aim.

The principle of consistency operates in apparent mental causation because the thoughts that serve as potential causes of actions typically have meaningful associations with the actions. A thought that is perceived to cause an act is often the name of the act, an image of the act, or a reference to its execution, circumstance, or consequence (Vallacher and Wegner 1985). Thoughts in the form of intentions, beliefs, or desires about the action are all likely to be semantically related to the act. Consistency of thought and act depends, then, on a cognitive process whereby the thoughts occurring prior to the act are compared to the act as subsequently perceived. When people do what they think they were going to do, there exists consistency between thought and act, and the experience of will is enhanced. ("I thought I'd have a salad for lunch, and here I am eating it.") When they think of one thing and do another—and this inconsistency is observable to them—their action does not feel as willful. ("I thought I'd have a salad for lunch, and here I am with a big plate of fries.")

The consistency phenomenon has come up a lot in studies of the perception of contingency between behavior and outcomes (Alloy and Tabachnik 1984; Jenkins and Ward 1965). These are studies in which a person presses a button repeatedly, for example, to see if it makes money come out of a slot. As anyone who has gambled will tell you, people doing things that could result in success or failure will typically envision success ("Baby needs a new pair of shoes!"). Thus, when success occurs, the consistency between the prior thought and the observed action produces an experience of will. So, for example, Langer and Roth (1975) found that people were likely to perceive that they controlled a chance event when they achieved a large number of initial successes in predicting that event. Jenkins and Ward (1965) similarly found that the perception that one is causing a successful outcome is enhanced merely by the increased frequency of that outcome. And it makes sense, then, that depressed individuals, who think less often of success ("Baby needs a new reason to cry")—are not as likely as others to overperceive control of successful outcomes (Alloy and Abramson 1979). It might even be that when people really *do* expect the worst and so think about it as they act, they might have a perverse experience of conscious will when the worst happens. The depressed person may come away from many of life's little disasters thinking, "I cause bad things to happen."

Consistency sometimes allows us to begin feeling that we are willing the actions of others. This was illustrated in a pair of experiments in which participants were given the opportunity to perceive someone else's hands in place of their own (Wegner, Winerman, and Sparrow 2001). In these studies, each participant was asked to wear a robe and stand before a mirror. Another person of the same sex (either another participant or an experimenter) standing behind the participant then placed his or her arms around the participant and out through holes in the front of the robe. The hands wore gloves, and the participant was thus given the odd experience of seeing another person's hands in place of his or her own. This setup resembles a form of pantomime sometimes called "helping hands."

The person standing in back then followed a series of some twenty five tape-recorded instructions directing the hands' actions—to clap three times, make a fist with the right hand, and so on. Participants who were asked afterward to rate the degree to which they felt they were controlling the hands under these conditions were slightly amused by the circumstance, but they didn't express much of a feeling of control (about 1.5 on a 7-point rating scale). However, when participants were played the tape of the instructions during the actions, their experience of control increased notably (to around 3 on the scale). Although they didn't claim full control, consistent previews led them to experience a distinct enhancement of the feeling that they were operating hands that belonged to another person.

In a second experiment, participants had their own right hand connected to skin conductance sensors so that their level of arousal could be measured. They then watched while, before the tape recording or action began, one hand snapped a rubber band on the wrist of the other. This gave participants a surge of arousal, as their skin conductance responses were significant. Following this, the experiment continued with the hand action sequence, again with some participants hearing the instructions while others did not. Finally, one hand again snapped the rubber band on the other wrist.

It turned out that foreknowledge of the action increased the perception of control in this study as it had in the prior experiment. It also seemed to produce an emotional attachment to the hands. Consistent foreknowledge of the action led participants to experience another strong skin conductance response to the snap, whereas those participants who didn't hear the instructions had by this time settled down and showed no significant arousal to the snap. Apparently, the experience of controlling the hands that was induced through consistent previews of action also yielded a kind of empathic ownership of the hands. When the hands hurt each other, people who felt they were controlling them because of their consistent thoughts experienced an emotional reaction.

Creative Insight

The happiest inconsistency between intention and action occurs when a great idea pops into mind. The "action" in this case is the occurrence of the idea, and our tendency to say "Eureka!" or "Aha!" is our usual acknowledgment that this particular insight was not something we were planning in advance. Although most of us are quite willing to take credit for our good ideas, it is still true that we do not experience them as voluntary. Rather, they happen to us, jumping into mind. The writer finds ideas hopping onto the page, the violinist finds musical ideas sneaking into the bow, the tennis player finds inspirations enlivening the racket. In each of these cases, the sense of willfulness of the action is curiously absent from an act that seemed eminently willed. Although one may have desperately desired to have an insight or a cool move, a fully developed thought of what it would be did not appear in mind in advance, and so there is little sense of authorship when it finally arrives.

There are repeated affidavits of the sense of effortlessness and even mindlessness that accompany creative breakthroughs and skilled productions of thought. In his essay on *Mechanism in Thought and Morals,* for instance, Oliver Wendell Holmes described this sense of everyday discovery:

The more we examine the mechanism of thought, the more we shall see that the automatic, unconscious action of the mind enters largely into all its processes. Our definite ideas are stepping stones; how we get from one to the other, we do not know: something carries us; we do not take the step. A creating and informing spirit which is with us, and not of us, is recognized everywhere in real and in storied life. It is the Zeus that kindled the rage of Achilles; it is the Muse of Homer; it is the Daimon of Socrates; it is the inspiration of the seer; . . . it comes to the least of us as a voice that will be heard; it tells us what we must believe; it frames our sentences; it lends a sudden gleam of sense or eloquence to the dullest of us all, so that . . . we wonder at ourselves, or rather not at ourselves, but at this divine visitor, who chooses our brain as his dwelling-place, and invests our naked thought with the purple of the kings of speech or song. (1877, 48–50)

The apparent involuntariness and unexpectedness of creative insights are documented nicely in a lecture of the mathematician Henri Poincaré to the *Société de Psychologie* in Paris. On his discovery of the Fuchsian functions, Poincaré remarks,

I left Caen, where I was then living, to go on a geologic excursion under the auspices of the school of mines. The changes of travel made me forget my mathematical work. Having reached Coutances, we entered an omnibus to go some place or other. At the moment when I put my foot on the step the idea came to me, without anything in my former thoughts seeming to have paved the way for it. . . . [Later, the same thing happened again.] Then I turned my attention to the study of some arithmetical questions apparently without much success and without a suspicion of any connection with my preceding searches. Disgusted with my failure, I went to spend a few days at the seaside, and thought of something else. One morning, walking on the bluff, the idea came to me, with just the same characteristics of brevity, suddenness, and immediate certainty. (Quoted in Koestler 1964, 115–116)

The transition from not knowing to knowing impresses us with its abruptness. Albert Einstein describes the seeming precipitousness of one of his ideas this way: "I was sitting in a chair in the Patent Office at Berne when all of a sudden a thought occurred to me: 'If a person falls freely he will not feel his own weight.' I was startled. This simple thought made a deep impression on me. It impelled me toward a theory of gravitation" (quoted in Highfield and Carter 1993). Creative insights differ from other problem solutions primarily in these qualities of suddenness and unexpectedness. Without a preview in thought, then, the creative leap feels more like a gift than something we have consciously willed.

When we solve a problem using a standard "grind-it-out" algorithm, such as the technique for subtraction or multiplication of lengthy numbers, we experience little in the way of an "Aha!" when we reach the solution. We know when it is coming and that it is coming, so even though the solution itself may be unknown until it pops out of the grinder, it is not particularly surprising to discover. For problems that have no such algorithm, but that have been on our minds in some way, the solution seems to arise out of nowhere and jump into mind with many of its implications already in place. Schooler and Melcher (1995) remark on the importance we all attach to such insights and the sense we typically have that we are somehow not responsible for them. Instead, we usually attribute them to our unconscious minds.

Indeed, the sense that we are somehow "not driving" our own minds is a common experience people report when they reflect on their own expert performances. As we become highly skilled at a task, it is possible for our minds to drift away from what we are doing, so that when we subsequently notice we have done something interesting, we feel almost divorced from the action. A musician might be attempting to improvise and be fully surprised at the result. The blues guitarist B. B. King described this sensation in an interview (Gelfano 1998), noting the many cases when he found his music occurring to him without conscious plans. Similarly, we may wonder at what we say when we are particularly clever, and feel that we are not really deserving of authorship for some of our best quips. We are not ready to own up to causing the action at this time because we have not experienced the prior occurrence of thoughts fully consistent with the action. We may have some vague sense of what we are up to ("I think I'll try to be clever now"), but we marvel at our good fortune when such plans do succeed.

The loss of a sense of authorship is even sought-after as a badge of skilled performance. Going "unconscious" is a good thing when you're playing basketball, and more than one postgame interview has featured a player saying, "I just waited for the game to come to me" or "the game played me." Losing oneself and one's will is a goal as well in art. Indeed, there is a contemporary art movement devoted to "automatism," the production of artistic products without the intrusion of conscious will. Dennett (2000) quotes the painter Philip Guston as saying, "When I first come into the studio to work, there is this noisy crowd which follows me there; it includes all of the important painters in history, all of my contemporaries, all the art critics, etc. As I become involved in the work, one by one, they all leave. If I'm lucky, every one of them will disappear. If I'm really lucky, I will too."

These observations suggest that people are likely to experience little willfulness for some of their most inspired actions—the peaks of their creativity and skill. These actions spring into existence with seemingly minimal conscious thought, inspired as they are by the operation of extensively developed unconscious mental expertise, and so can present to us a sense of being unwilled. It is ironic that many of the most skilled acts we can do, the actions that others enjoy or find simply marvelous because of their high level of skill, and that others may therefore ascribe uniquely to us, may not be things we experience willing. Instead, we experience will when we must plod along, thinking methodically of all the parts of an action that we are putting together. The thoughts and acts we toil over as we grind the wheels to solve problems bit by bit may seem more willful, imbued with a sense of voluntariness, because we have encountered so many thoughts about them before the desired actions have finally emerged.

Hearing Voices

The consistency principle also offers a way of understanding the experiences of involuntariness reported by people with schizophrenia. In some 65 percent of people with this disorder, the symptoms include unusual experiences that seem to emerge from inconsistency of thought and action

(Frith and Fletcher 1995; Sartorius, Shapiro, and Jablensky 1974). Certain of the person's thoughts or actions do not seem to issue voluntarily from the self, perhaps because they do not arise in the context of consistent prior thoughts.

The experience of hearing voices, for example, involves the apparent perception of voices from people who are not there. A collection of historical descriptions of such symptoms (Peterson 1982) includes this 1840 quote from one John Percival, Esq., of London: "Only a short time before I was confined to my bed I began to hear voices, at first only close to my ear, afterwards in my head, or as if one was whispering in my ear, or in various parts of the room. . . . These voices commanded me to do, and made me believe a number of false and terrible things." Now, many normal people report hearing voices from time to time—in fact, as many as 30 percent of college students in one study indicated at least one such experience (Posey and Losch 1983).[6] In the case of schizophrenia, however, the experience is often profound and disturbingly recurrent, and often leads to a preoccupation with attempts to explain the voices (Frith 1992). And in schizophrenia there may also be experiences of thought insertion (having another person's thoughts appear in one's own mind), thought echo (experiencing one's thoughts over again, sometimes in another's voice), thought broadcasting (hearing one's own thoughts spoken aloud), or alien control (experiencing one's actions as performed by someone else). Such experiences are often called Schneiderian symptoms, after the psychiatrist Kurt Schneider (1959), who described them as indicative of schizophrenia.

These symptoms usually are interpreted as originating outside the self. The voices are not, however, "like living in a cheaply built apartment where our neighbors' voices come through the walls. The voice the patient hears is directed at the patient and what the voice says has implications

6. It is also possible to extract what seem to be intelligible voices from random sounds, such as the white noise generated by the radio when it is tuned between stations. Such "electronic voice phenomena" are the result of the overeager sense-making apparatus of our language interpretation processes, and they can often produce entertaining interpretations of random sounds. A number of Web sites have audioclip examples of what seem to be particularly sensible phrases. The tendency to try to make sense of voicelike sounds is also the process that allows people to attribute satanic or other messages to rock lyrics played in reverse.

for the patient. This is the voice of an agent with the intention of altering the thought and behavior of the patient. For most patients the agent is omniscient and omnipotent" (Frith and Fletcher 1995, 74–75). The majority of a sample of patients with auditory hallucinations interviewed by Chadwick and Birchwood (1994) reported being unable to exert any influence on their voices. The voices are often interpreted as representing the patient's own conscience, although some patients understand them as coming from other people (Chapman and Chapman 1988). The standard feeling is that the voice seems alien—the voice of another—even though the patient may realize the voice is in his or her own mind.

Much of the research on auditory hallucinations has focused on the idea that they are indeed self-generated. Gould (1948) used a throat microphone to record speech from schizophrenic patients and found in some cases that whispering or other vocalizations occurred during periods for which the patients later reported having heard voices. Psychophysiological measures of muscle movement in the voice box suggest that the voices are generally self-generated (Inouye and Shimizu 1970), and brain scans in hallucinating patients have indicated activity in Broca's area, an area linked with language production (McGuire, Shah, and Murray 1993). So voices seem to arise when the patient's own inner speech is perceived to be coming from outside the self. Indeed, when patients hum or keep their mouths open, they experience the voices less frequently (Green and Kinsbourne 1989).

The intriguing aspect of schizophrenic voices is their origin in thought/ action inconsistency. Graham and Stephens (1994) have described the problem as one of "introspective alienation." The patient develops the sense that an episode occurring in the mind is attributable to someone else rather than to the self. This seems to occur primarily because the episode is inconsistent with prior thought. Thoughts that come to mind in a willful way typically do so in a format that makes sense. They follow. A person thinking this way can say, "I have a sense of deliberately directing my thinking toward a certain project or theme, such as crafting an apology, finding a solution to a problem, recollecting my trip to Berlin or Tenerife, without having some specific sequence of thoughts in mind at the outset" (Graham and Stephens 1994, 98–99). It is not that we need to know everything in advance of thinking it, but that we need to know something about where our thought may be going that then is consistent with what we think when we get there. Usually, we have a general idea of what we will think or do next. When inconsistent thought or action appears, we lose our sense that we are the ones in charge. The voices seem to belong to someone else.

The prevailing theory of auditory hallucinations is based on precisely this line of reasoning. Ralph Hoffman (1986) suggests that voices may occur when people find that their thoughts are radically mismatched with their current conscious goals for thinking. He notes that "a nervous tic feels involuntary because it does not reflect a motor plan consonant with accessible goals/beliefs. Similarly, a slip of the tongue feels involuntary because it is not consonant with the current speech goal, that is, to articulate a particular 'message'" (506). Hoffman proposed that a speaker normally generates an abstract cognitive plan that reflects the gist or intention of what he or she will say and that is sensitive to the goals and beliefs of the speaker. This plan is then transformed into actual words and syntax. In schizophrenia, this discourse planning activity breaks down and thus can lead to unexpected utterances and thoughts (Deese 1978). People with schizophrenia often experience their manifest speech as being poorly matched to what they had in mind to say (Chapman 1966). Ideas appear that don't fit the prior plan, and when this happens, perhaps it begins to seem reasonable to attribute the thoughts to a "voice."

In studies of discourse planning disturbances, Hoffman found evidence for this theory. The research developed assessments of "discourse deviations"—departures from a plan for what to say—that occur in people's answers to interview questions. Here is an example low in discourse deviation:

INTERVIEWER: Can you describe where you live?
PATIENT: Yes, I live in Connecticut. We live in a fifty-year-old Tudor house. It's a house that is very much a home. . . . ah . . . I live there with my husband and son. It's a home where people are drawn to feel comfortable, walk in, . . . let's see . . . a home that shows very much of my personality. (Hoffman 1986, 506)

And an example higher in deviation:

INTERVIEWER: Tell me about school.
PATIENT: School? Well there are schools of play and schools of fish, mostly you see fish school, people edumacating [sic] themselves, you see, sea is one thing and education is another. Fish is school in their

community, that's why the community of man stands in the way of the community of the sea, and once they see the light of the sunny sunshine then they well let it be. (Hoffman 1986, 507)

Although the first answer seems to follow from an overall plan (of explaining why the house is a home), the second seems to involve puns and plays on words with no overall goal. Hoffman found that people with schizophrenia who had verbal hallucinations had much higher scores on discourse deviation than those who did not experience verbal hallucinations. This suggests that the attribution of one's thoughts to "voices" may arise from the failure of those voices to follow a consistent plan that would help the words to seem willful.

The tendency to think that our inconsistent thoughts are not our own is not just a feature of schizophrenia. In studies of normal college students, Morris and Wegner (2000) observed the same inclination. For these experiments, the students were asked to listen to "subliminal messages" over headphones, but what they actually heard was merely a recording of garbled voices from a crowded cafeteria. As they listened, some of the participants were given a task known to produce intrusive, inconsistent thoughts: While they wrote their thoughts down on paper, they were asked to try not to think about some topic (a house, car, mountain, or child). And, of course, the suppressed thought popped into mind quite frequently, even though it had nothing to do with what the participants were trying to think about (Wegner 1989; 1992; Wenzlaff and Wegner 2000). For comparison, another group of participants was given instructions to think about one of these topics on purpose.

After doing the thinking task while listening to the audiotape, all participants were asked to judge the degree to which the "subliminal messages" influenced their thoughts. Those who had been instructed to suppress were more likely to say that the thoughts came from the messages. Apparently, thought suppression can create introspective alienation—the tendency to think that the suppressed thoughts are coming from somewhere outside oneself. Returning to mind unbidden and without specific relevance to what one wants or plans to think about, suppressed thoughts can be attributed to nonexistent outside influences, such as a bogus subliminal message. In one study, Morris and Wegner (2000) also asked people to try to imagine what kind of person might be speaking on the ostensible subliminal tape. The participants were given the chance to rate this individual's personality and style on a number of dimensions. It was found that participants instructed to suppress a thought, compared to those instructed to think about it on purpose, judged the (nonexistent) subliminal voice as commanding (rather than suggesting) and mean (rather than kind), and as the voice of someone they would want to ignore. Although these impressions of a nonexistent voice are far from the experiences of internal voices reported by people with schizophrenia, they illustrate that even in normal people the hypothesis that one's thoughts are being caused by other agents can gain a surprising level of credence.

Schizophrenia presents yet further complications that move well beyond simple misattribution of one's own thoughts. Feelings of alien control in schizophrenia might also be attributed to a specific deficit in remembering what one is intending. Perhaps it is not just that people with schizophrenia say or think things that are inconsistent with their prior thoughts; it may be that they *lose track* of their current thoughts about actions and thereby experience inconsistency in a different way.

Studies of the relation between thought and motor control, in fact, have suggested that thoughts of what one is doing are poorly represented in some forms of schizophrenia. Malenka et al. (1982) found that schizophrenic individuals have trouble correcting their own movement errors without visual feedback, perhaps because of the absence of a concurrent mental representation of the movement. They don't seem to remember what they have done, even just as they are doing it, so they can't correct an action without being able to see it. Frith and Done (1989) suggested that such problems in "central monitoring" might underlie experiences of alien control. They found that people with schizophrenia who report alien control experiences, as compared with those without such experiences, were less able to correct their movement errors on a video game in the absence of visual feedback. Without seeing what they were doing, they didn't seem to remember it long enough to correct for it.[7]

---

7. The absence of a sense of "what I'm doing now" in schizophrenia could make it possible for individuals with this disorder to misidentify their own movements as those of someone else. This has been observed by Daprati et al. (1997), who found that hallucinating schizophrenics presented with a video image of a hand were inclined to accept the hand's movements as their own, even when the hand was not theirs. It appears that this lapse in current action knowledge may be specifically traceable to hyperactivation in the parietal and cingulate cortices of the brain (Spence et al. 1997).

A deficit in the mental representation of action that occurs during the action, then, may be another way of understanding the profound disturbance in conscious will that occurs in schizophrenia. The person with schizophrenia may not just perform acts or have thoughts that are inconsistent with prior thinking but may experience inconsistency as a result of failing to recall the prior thinking as the action unfolds. Without a thought in mind that is consistent with the observed action, and presented instead with inconsistency, the schizophrenic individual may be placed in the position of feeling that the self could not have performed the action. The next step that occurs when will is not experienced may be the inference that some other agent must be responsible ("If I didn't do it, someone else must have done it"). This inference of outside agency anticipates a third rule of the experience of will—the exclusivity principle.

The Exclusivity Principle

People discount the causal influence of one potential cause if there are others available (Kelley 1972; McClure 1998). So, for instance, in the case of our friends the billiard balls, the causal influence of one ball on another can be called into question by the arrival of a third just at the time of impact. Applied to the experience of will, this principle suggests that people will be particularly sensitive to the possibility that there are other causes of an action besides their own thoughts. When their own thoughts do not appear to be the exclusive cause of their action, they experience less conscious will. And when other plausible causes are less salient, in turn, they experience more conscious will.

The causes that compete with thoughts are of two kinds—internal and external. The plausible internal causes for an action might include one's emotions, habits, reflexes, traits, or other unconscious action tendencies— psychological causes other than thoughts. The plausible external causes for an action might include real external agents, such as people or groups, or imagined outside agents in the form of spirits, voices, angels, ghosts, or other disembodied entities.

Internal Alternatives to Intention
Whenever we become aware of some cause of our action that lies inside ourselves but of which we were previously unconscious, we may lose

some of the sense of will. This may happen even though we have a prior, consistent thought of the action. Knowing that one is going to eat a large bag of potato chips, for instance, may not contribute to the sense that this is willful when one does it if one also believes that one is a habitual and compulsive chip-hound. Knowing that one is going to sneeze may also fail to prompt an experience of will when the sneeze occurs, perhaps because one has an appreciation of the uncontrollableness of sneezes that derives from a history of experiencing sneezes without prior thoughts.

People seem to know their own psychology well enough to grasp several possible alternatives to thoughts as causes of their actions. In particular, they may discount thoughts and so bypass the experience of will when they find their behavior attributable to *emotion, impulse, disposition,* or *habit*. In the case of emotion, for example, a person acting out of blind rage, profound sadness, or giddy euphoria might experience little in the way of voluntariness. This would be particularly true when relevant conscious thoughts were absent prior to the action, but it could also be that the sense of will might be undermined by the presence of strong emotions even if conscious thoughts were present. Issues of emotional justification of action are commonly broached in the law, as when people commit crimes in the "heat of passion," and the lack of the experience of will in these cases is often seen as undermining the person's responsibility for the action.

Impulse is a potential cause of action when the action regularly seems to occur without prior thought or intention. Impulsive actions seem spontaneous and may include, too, the various coughs, yawns, or other involuntary motor movements we seldom seem to think about before we do them. In people with motor disorders, such apparently involuntary actions may include tics of several kinds. A classification study by Jankovic (1997) describes two general types: "*Simple motor tics* involve only one group of muscles, causing a brief, jerk-like movement or a single, meaningless sound. *Complex motor tics* consist of coordinated, sequenced movements resembling normal motor acts or gestures that are inappropriately intense and timed. They may be seemingly nonpurposeful, such as head shaking or trunk bending, or they may seem purposeful, such as touching, throwing, hitting, jumping, and kicking" (269). People with tics sometimes feel them as voluntary or willed and sometimes perceive them as involuntary (Lang 1991), perhaps depending on the degree to which they judge their premonitions of the action as causal. When an action is of a class that usually seems to run off without prior thought, however, it would seem that people might learn to refrain from attributing that action to thought and thus come quite naturally to apprehend that action as unwilled.

It also makes sense that people might see actions that flow from their own dispositions or habits to be unwilled. If you always brush your teeth in the morning, or if you always give change to panhandlers, you might become aware that your disposition or habit is causing your behavior and so perceive it as unwilled. However, the evidence on this possibility is not clear. Kruglanski and Cohen (1973) found the opposite—that people perceived actions consistent with their dispositions to have been performed freely, whereas actions inconsistent with their dispositions were experienced as less free. In later work, though, Kruglanski (1975) observed that this finding might be an expression of a more profound tendency for people to feel they performed freely when they did things they wanted to do rather than doing things for extrinsic reasons. Perhaps people must be particularly aware of their disposition or habit to have it feel like a true cause of their behavior. Many of the things we do in a day may not feel compelled in any strong sense but rather as though we merely were carrying on as usual.

This issue is still open, then, because no one has really done a study in which the experience of will is measured when people do things with or without prior thought, and in a way that is consistent or inconsistent with their own well-entrenched habits. People do often report experiencing high levels of "will power" and self-satisfaction when they overcome unwanted habits such as overeating or smoking (Baumeister, Heatherton, and Tice 1995). In this case, thoughts of self-denial prior to the act of abstaining from a habit seem to be experienced as especially willful and efficacious (Herman and Polivy 1993).

The degree to which thoughts cause action is a common theme in the perception of self-control more generally (Bandura 1997). People often describe their "weakness of will" as a matter of succumbing to habits or impulses or demons, along with a concomitant failure to think the right thoughts at the right time that might have guided their actions in a desired direction. This conclusion makes sense if the experience of will is indeed computed in terms of the perceived exclusivity of thought as a cause of action. When internal psychological variables such as emotion, impulse, and habit vie with thought as plausible sources of behavior, will can suffer as a result. The absence of such internal causes, in turn, can bolster the attribution of action to the occurrence of appropriate action-relevant thoughts.

External Alternatives to Intention

More than once, I've started to open a door only to find that someone else is simultaneously opening it from the other side. What felt like a willed action (even if the door at first seemed to move a bit too easily) immediately became in my mind an action by someone else. The exclusivity of thought as a cause of action, quite simply, can be challenged by external causes. Plausible external causes for an action might include other people or external forces that impinge on us even when we are thinking of the action in advance. In general, when a person is engaged in a co-action with another person—such as walking hand-in-hand, kissing, dancing, arguing, wrestling, having sex, and the like (ideally, not all at once)—the proper attribution of causality to self and other can be a major puzzle. One may be thinking about some of the aspects of the co-action and not others, and may have to adjust one's notion of what is happening and what one is doing at a rapid pace as the co-action unfolds.

This puzzle of co-action turns out to be the basis of a number of common automatisms, including table turning and the Ouija board, and was an essential part of the *I Spy* study as well. But confusions about joint physical movements are just the start of the kinds of intriguing transformations of experienced will that can occur in social situations. Many things people do involve psychological rather than physical coaction. People talk together or work on projects or argue about things, and the question of who did what turns out to be open in a wide variety of these cases. Other people with whom we interact, of course, are also thinking and acting, so our perceptions of the causal relations between their thoughts and actions can enter into our interpretation of their willfulness, which may have implications for the degree to which our behavior in interaction with them is interpreted as willful.

As long as there are other possible agents around, one's own actions may at times be attributed to them, and fluctuations in the sense of one's own will may follow. Stanley Milgram (1974) brought up this possibility in the interpretation of his famous obedience experiments. His finding that most people would obey an experimenter who insisted that they deliver strong electric shocks to another person in the laboratory has long been celebrated in psychology as an extraordinary example of the apparent abdication of personal responsibility. Milgram suggested that the remarkable obedience he observed was produced by an "agentic shift," a change in the perceived source of agency for actions that occur when one obeys another. The experimental subject apparently delivering the shock does so only on guarantees from the experimenter that the subject is not responsible, and so experiences a sort of transfer of agency that eliminates the usual sense of moral accountability for action.

A further complication arising in dyads and groups is that a group level of agency may also be constructed such that things "we" do are independent of what "you" do or what "I" do (Wegner and Giuliano 1980). One might experience the will of one's group rather than that of the self, for example, as a result of knowing that the group was thinking of doing something and that group action had ensued ("We're going to the zoo"). This, then, suggests that one must keep track not only of one's own thoughts about social actions but also of other people's thoughts. If others apparently think of what the group does just before the group does it, they are more plausible willful agents of the group's enterprise than is the self. Even in just a pair of people, it is possible that each person might think or not think of what self, other, or both will do, leading to a variety of interpretations of the willfulness of the action. The computation of will in social life begins with the principle of exclusivity but then blossoms into a variety of interesting formats quite beyond the basic sense of self as agent.

The external causation of one's action is not necessarily limited to real agents or forces. What about spirits? Once the possibility of outside agency is allowed, it becomes clear that people can imagine or invent outside agents to account for actions of themselves or others (Gilbert et al. 2001). The assumption that one's actions or thoughts are being introduced by outside agents is, as we have noted, a common theme in schizophrenic thinking. However, the appeal to hypothetical outside agents is far too common an experience in human life to be attributed to schizophrenia alone. The occurrence of spirit possession or channeling, for example, is so widespread across cultures and so highly prevalent in some cultures—affecting as much as half of the population (Bourguignon 1976)—that it has become a major focus of the field of anthropology. Attribution of behavior to angels, spirits, entities, and the like is sufficiently common throughout the world that it is a mistake to assume it is limited to traditional cultures. Industrialized cultures have their share of channels, trance dancers, and people who "speak in tongues" or otherwise attribute their action to divine intervention as part of religious ceremonies. The common denominator for these phenomena is the attribution of what otherwise appears to be voluntary behavior to an imagined outside agency.

The exclusivity principle underlies the general extension of the will to others as well as the formation of the individual's own identity. In the extensive field of possible causes of a person's behavior, there exists only one self, an author that has thoughts and does actions. This self competes with internal causes and with an array of external causes of action in the individual's assessment of what he or she has willed. Whittling away all the other possible causes of actions allows the person to develop this self and so experience personal identity, and the process of finding external causes of one's own action, in turn, gives shape and attributed will to all the other actors in one's social world. Much of the discussion in later chapters (particularly chapters 6, 7, and 8) focuses on how it is that people discern their own willed actions from those of others in complicated interactions when the exclusivity of one's own thoughts as a cause of action cannot be assumed.

Perception and Reality

The processes described in this chapter rest on an important premise. They rely on the assumption that conscious will is an experience, not a cause. This means that the thoughts we attach to our actions are not necessarily the true causes of the actions, and their causal connection is something we ascribe to them. This realization gives rise to two concerns. First, how well does this causal perception process capture what is actually happening in the empirical relation between thought and action? And second, how and when do thoughts of actions get produced if they are not causal? These interrelated concerns arise if we want to understand the role of the theory of apparent mental causation in the more general psychology of human beings, so it is useful to examine some possible answers.

The real and apparent causal sequences relating thought and action probably do tend to correspond with each other some proportion of the time. After all, people are pretty good information processors when given access to the right information. The occurrence of conscious intention prior to action is often wonderful information because it provides a fine clue as to how things that are on the person's mind might pertain to what the person does. In fact, the mental system that introduces thoughts of action to mind and keeps them coordinated with the actions is itself an intriguing mechanism. However, if conscious will is an experience that arises from the interpretation of cues to cognitive causality, then apparent mental causation is generated by an interpretive process that is fundamentally separate from the mechanistic process of real mental causation. The experience of will can be an indication that mind is causing action, especially if the person is a good self-interpreter, but it is not conclusive.

The experience of will, then, is the way our minds portray their operations to us, not their actual operation. Because we have thoughts of what we will do, we can develop causal theories relating those thoughts to our actions on the basis of priority, consistency, and exclusivity. We come to think of these prior thoughts as intentions, and we develop the sense that the intentions have causal force even though they are actually just previews of what we may do. Yet in an important sense, it must be the case that *something* in our minds plays a causal role in making our actions occur. That something is, in the theory of apparent mental causation, a set of unconscious mental processes that cause the action. At the same time, that something is very much like the thoughts we have prior to the action.

One possibility here is that thought and action arise from coupled unconscious mental systems. Brown (1989) has suggested that consciousness of an action and the performance of the action are manifestations of the same "deep structure." In the same sense that the thought of being angry might reflect the same underlying process as the experience of facial flushing, the thought and performance of a voluntary action might be different expressions of a single underlying system. The coupling of thought and action over time in human adults is really quite remarkable if the thought is *not* causing the action, so there must be some way in which the two are in fact often connected.

The co-occurrence of thought and action may happen because thoughts are normally thrust into mind as *previews* of what will be done. The ability to know what one will do, and particularly to communicate this to others verbally, would seem to be an important human asset, something that promotes far more effective social interaction than might be the case if we all had no idea of what to expect of ourselves or of anyone around us. The thoughts we find coming to our minds in frequent coordination with what we do may thus be produced by a special system whose job it is to provide us with ongoing verbalizable previews of action. This preview function could be fundamentally important for the facilitation of social interaction.

We must remember that this analysis suggests that the real causal mechanisms underlying behavior are never present in consciousness. Rather, the engines of causation operate without revealing themselves to us and so may be unconscious mechanisms of mind. Much of the recent research suggesting a fundamental role for automatic processes in everyday behavior (Bargh 1997) can be understood in this light. The real causes of human action are unconscious, so it is not surprising that behavior could often arise—as in automaticity experiments—without the person's having conscious insight into its causation. Conscious will itself arises from a set of processes that are not the same processes as those that cause the behavior to which the experience of will pertains, however. So even processes that are not automatic—mental processes described as "controlled" (Posner and Snyder 1975) or "conscious" (Wegner and Bargh 1998)—have no direct expression in a person's experience of will. Such "controlled" processes may be less efficient than automatic processes and require more cognitive resources, but even if they occur along with an experience of control or conscious will, this experience is not a direct indication of their real causal influence (Wegner, in press). The experience of conscious will is just more likely to accompany inefficient processes than efficient ones because there is more time available prior to action for inefficient thoughts to become conscious, thus to prompt the formation of causal inferences linking thought and action. This might explain why controlled/conscious processes are often linked with feelings of will, whereas automatic processes are not. Controlled and conscious processes are simply those that lumber along so inefficiently that there is plenty of time for previews of their associated actions to come to mind and allow us to infer the operation of conscious will.

The unique human convenience of conscious thoughts that preview our actions gives us the privilege of feeling we willfully cause what we do. In fact, however, unconscious and inscrutable mechanisms create both conscious thought about action and the action, and also produce the sense of will we experience by perceiving the thought as cause of the action. So, while our thoughts may have deep, important, and unconscious causal connections to our actions, the experience of conscious will arises from a process that interprets these connections, not from the connections themselves.

4

An Analysis of Automatism

The experience of will can be reduced to very low levels under certain conditions, even for actions that are voluntary, purposive, and complex—and what remains is automatism.

Although it has been usual to designate by the term *voluntary* all those muscular movements which take place as the result of mental operations, . . . a careful analysis of the sources from which many of even our ordinary actions proceed, will show that the Will has no direct participation in producing them.

William B. Carpenter, *Principles of Mental Physiology* (1888)

Our sense that we consciously cause what we do ebbs and flows through the day and even changes by the moment. We feel ourselves willing our actions almost the way we use the accelerator pedal in an automobile: Once in a while we floor it; more normally we give it a little punch from time to time; but for long periods we just have a foot on it and maintain speed, experiencing little sense at all that we are pushing on the pedal. Either because we are very good at what we are doing, because we have simply lost interest, or for yet other reasons, there are intervals when we lose the experience of agency even while we are performing voluntary actions.

Automatisms involve this lack of the feeling of doing an action but may even go beyond this to include a distinct feeling that we are *not* doing. The absence of conscious will in automatism, then, is particularly profound. It is more than those little recognitions we have that we seem to have let up on the mental gas pedal. The loss of perceived voluntariness is so remarkable during an automatism that the person may vehemently resist describing the action as consciously or personally caused. It seems to come from somewhere else or at least not from oneself. This experience is so curious that automatisms often are noteworthy events in themselves rather than just unnoticed lapses in conscious willing.

This chapter applies the theory of apparent mental causation to automatisms. We begin by exploring the classic automatisms—actions that under certain circumstances yield such curious and jarring absence of the feeling of doing that they have been celebrated for many years. To add to the earlier discussion of table turning, we look at automatic writing, Ouija board spelling, the Chevreul pendulum, dowsing, and the phenomenon of ideomotor action. The chapter then examines the key features of behavior settings that promote the occurrence of automatisms, and so points to the ways in which the lack of perceptions of priority, consistency, and exclusivity underlie lapses in the experience of conscious will.

The Classic Automatisms

A standard college library has few books on automatisms except for books of the nineteenth century. The amount of literature on automatisms generated then by the spiritualist fad in America and Europe is astounding. There are stacks on stacks of dusty books, each describing in detail spooky experiences at a séance of some family or group. People caught up in this movement took seriously the idea that when humans behave without conscious will, their behavior is instead caused by spirits of the dead. And this, of course, is great fun. With no television, an evening's entertainment for the family in that era often involved yet another séance to attempt to communicate with dead Aunt Bessie, her cat, or a spirit who knew them.

The spiritualist movement attracted extraordinary popular attention and focused in the early years (1848–1860) on the automatisms—particularly table turning, tilting, and rapping—and on spirit mediumship, the ability to experience automatisms regularly and easily. According to a *Scientific American* article of that time, "A peculiar class of phenomena have manifested themselves within the last quarter century, which seem to indicate that the human body may become the medium for the transmission of force . . . in such a way that those through whom or from whom it emanates, are totally unconscious of any exercise of volition, or of any muscular movement, as acts of their own wills" ("What Is Planchette?" 1868, 17). Demonstrations of such unconscious actions

Figure 4.1
French Victorian salon games included hat turning (at the table on the left), table turning (center), and pendulum divining (right). From *L'Illustration* (1853).

piqued public interest, and the popularity of the automatisms helped to fuel the spiritualist fad (fig. 4.1).

The genuine experience of automatism, unfortunately, was not the only phenomenon underlying the interest in spirits. There was also trickery. People were unusually ready to accept spurious evidence of spirits offered by charlatans, and several widely known cases, which only later were traced to trickery, became celebrated at the beginning of the movement. Brandon (1983) points in particular to the early influence of the "spirit rappings" heard by many people in the presence of two young girls, Katherine and Margaretta Fox, in the spring of 1848. Large crowds gathered to witness these phenomena, which were publicized via the popular press. Confessions by the girls, given much later, indicated that they were making the noises by cracking their toe joints against tables or other sound-conducting surfaces. But by then the movement was well underway.

The demand to satisfy popular appetites led mediums and their managers to resort to an ever-expanding range of trickery to produce evidence of spirits. Séance phenomena eventually grew to include disembodied voices, dancing trumpets, apparitions of limbs, faces, or bodies, levitation, rapping on walls or tables, chalk writing on sealed slates, materialization of ectoplasm, and so on (Grasset 1910; Jastrow 1935; Podmore 1902; Washington 1995). My personal favorite is the ectoplasm, a gooey substance that for some reason emerged from a spirit medium's mouth on occasion (always in the dark, and usually later to disappear) and that was taken as a physical embodiment of the spirit world. Why would *this* particular odd thing happen, and not something else? Why not the sudden appearance of jars of mustard in everyone's pockets? If you're an otherworldly spirit, why limit yourself to the equivalent of silly putty? At any rate, it seems that simple parlor automatisms such as table turning couldn't compete with all the dramatic stunts produced by chicanery, so the entire spiritualist movement slowly devolved into something of a circus sideshow. With the inevitable exposure of the deceptions underlying these theatrics, the movement died in the early part of the twentieth century. Aside from a few anachronisms (e.g., a group in the 1960s that met to conjure up a table-rapping spirit called Philip; Owen 1976), the major course of spiritualism appears to be over.

This checkered past left many scientists suspicious of the genuineness of automatisms in general, and whatever valid observations were made in that era have largely languished as curiosities rather than serving to spur scientific inquiry. Any new approach to the automatisms therefore must retain a large measure of scientific skepticism. To that end, the phenomena discussed here have been reduced to a specified relevant few. Reports of events that sound so exaggeratedly supernatural as to suggest deception are not addressed. The focus on classic automatisms here is limited to motor movements that are accompanied by accounts indicating that the movement occurs without the feeling of doing, and that have been reported by enough different people so that the effect appears replicable. Even with these limitations, we are still left with a number of fascinating phenomena.

Automatic Writing

Consider, for example, the case of automatic writing. It is not clear who discovered it or when, but reports of automatic writing appeared often in the spiritualist literature.[1] Mattison (1855, 63) quotes one such individual: "My hand was frequently used, by some power and intelligence entirely foreign to my own, to write upon subjects of which I was uninformed, and in which I felt little or no interest." Another said: "I found my pen moved from some power beyond my own, either physical or mental, and [believed] it to be the spirits." James (1889, 556) quotes yet another: "The writing is in my own hand, but the dictation is not of my own mind and will, but that of another . . . and I, myself, consciously criticize the thought, fact, and mode of expressing it, etc., while the hand is recording the subject-matter."

Some automatic writers claim to remain unaware of what their hands are writing, only grasping what has been written when they later read it. Others have ideas of what they are writing but report little sense that they are authoring the writing because the ideas "surge apparently from nowhere without logical associative relation into the mind" (Prince 1907, 73). The "automatic" part of automatic writing thus has two definitions, depending on which automatic writer we ask. The experience for some is a lack of consciousness of the written content, whereas for others it is more along the line of a lack of the experience of will even when there is consciousness of what is written. Unfortunately, both kinds of automatic writing seem perfectly easy to fake, so we depend on the good faith of the people who report the effect. An example appears in figure 4.2.

The process itself usually involves writing while intentionally attending elsewhere. Automatic writing can be accomplished with pen and paper but is also sometimes performed with devices designed to enhance the effect—a sling supporting the arm above the writing surface (Muhl 1930) or, more commonly, a planchette (figure 4.3). This device, recognizable also in the design of the Ouija board pointer, is a heart-shaped or triangular piece of board mounted on three supports, often two casters and a pencil (Sargent 1869; "What Is Planchette?" 1868).

1. Hilgard (1986), Koutstaal (1992), and Spitz (1997) give useful reviews of the historical and modern study of automatic writing.

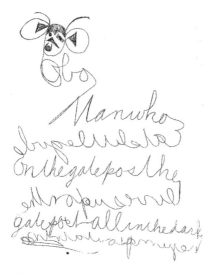

Figure 4.2
The Oboman who scared little girls. A particularly fanciful example of automatic writing, featuring both an introductory doodle and reversing flow. From Mühl (1930). Courtesy Steinkopff Verlag.

Figure 4.3
An automatic writer with planchette and (optional) blindfold. Courtesy of Harry Price Library, University of London.

The use of special devices to reduce friction highlights an interesting feature of many automatic writings: Writers may well feel that they consciously intend to move but not that they consciously intend to move in a particular meaningful pattern. Solomons and Stein (1896) and Stein (1898) report getting started by making loops or other rhythmic motions in hopes that eventually this start would develop into writing.[2] Automatic writing, then, is not a movement that arises from a dead stop without any conscious initiation; the specifics of the movement just are either not consciously anticipated or are not sensed as voluntary.

With or without slings or planchettes, automatic writing gained great popularity as a pastime, and some people claimed that they wrote whole books this way. One spiritualist leader, the Rev. W. Stainton Moses, for instance, introduced his *Spirit Teachings* (in 1883, under the pseudonym M. A. Oxon) as having been "received by the process known as automatic or passive writing" (2). It is tempting on first hearing about automatic writing to run out and try it. I've given it my best shot, and nothing happened. Most people fail, like me; only about one in twenty will produce the full-blown phenomenon: sensible messages written without the experience of conscious will (Harriman 1942). This limit suggests that there may be something special about those who are susceptible to the effect, and indeed most of the early commentators on automatic writing sought out just such special, unusually florid cases for their studies. A regular Who's Who of early psychologists—Binet (1896), James (1889), Janet (1889), and Prince (1890)—each published reports of automatic writing virtuosos.

One whimsical example of such an extreme should suffice. A gentleman, William L. Smith, who had amused himself with occasional planchette writing over a period of some two years, was observed by William James on January 24, 1889. Smith's right hand was placed on a planchette while he sat with his face averted and buried in the hollow of his left arm. The planchette made illegible scrawling, and after ten minutes, James pricked the back of the right hand with a pin but got no indication

2. This is Gertrude Stein, who subsequently wrote *The Autobiography of Alice B. Toklas* (1933) and many other works. Her writings are not noted for their content but rather for the use of sounds and rhythms of words, and it is possible that she may have produced them automatically.

of feeling from Smith. Two pricks to the left hand prompted withdrawal and the question "What did you do that for?" to which James replied, "To find whether you were going to sleep." The first legible words from the planchette after this were *You hurt me.* A pencil was then substituted for the planchette, and now the first legible words were *No use in trying to spel when you hurt me so.* Later on, testing the anesthesia of the hand again, James pricked the right wrist and fingers with no sign of reaction from Smith. However, after an interval the pencil wrote, *Don't you prick me any more.* When this last sentence was read aloud to him, Smith laughed and, apparently having been conscious only of the pricks on his left hand, said "It's working those two pin-pricks for all they are worth."

This case resembles alien hand syndrome and could indeed have a neuropsychological basis (e.g., Joseph 1986). After all, the automatism in Smith's hand included not only unconsciousness of action and loss of the feeling of doing but also anesthesia. Then again, it was au courant in Smith's day for people to experience limb anesthesia, often as a symptom of hysteria, the psychiatric disorder frequent in the nineteenth century that has largely disappeared (Veith 1970). Given this cultural fashion, such anesthesia may have been Smith's response to a strong belief that anesthesia could happen in automatic writing. Although it is tempting to speculate on remarkable cases like Smith's, the still more remarkable fact is that thousands of other people working their pencils or planchettes have also experienced some degree of automatic writing, albeit less dramatically. How should we understand these more commonplace experiences?

One possibility is that awareness of action dims in automatic writing, just as it seems to subside with practiced or habitual actions in general. When we can do something well, distractions can happen and we can lose track of our action even while it carries on.[3] The few laboratory

3. This was observed even in the heyday of automatic writing, for example, in studies of skilled telegraphers (Bryan and Harter 1899). As formulated by Jastrow (1906, 42), this broad principle of action states, "At the outset each step of the performance is separately and distinctly the object of attention and effort; and as practice proceeds and expertness is gained . . . the separate portions thereof become fused into larger units, which in turn make a constantly diminishing demand upon consciousness."

studies of automatic writing in normal individuals attempted to produce the effect by giving people distracting tasks (such as reading or arithmetic) and then having them practice writing during such a task (Downey and Anderson 1915; Solomons and Stein 1896; Stein 1898). These endeavors met with mixed success because even extended practice does not entirely erase the consciousness of action. If anything, with practice or distraction, the consciousness of action becomes elective or optional rather than necessary. More modern experiments along this line by Spelke, Hirst, and Neisser (1976) revealed that "the introspections offered by the subjects . . . were chaotic and inconsistent: Sometimes they knew exactly what they were writing, sometimes they were not aware of having written at all" (Neisser 1976, 104). Under laboratory conditions with normal participants, then, the consciousness of writing comes and goes.

Automatic writing is facilitated by confusion about the source of one's movement. Alfred Binet (1896) described a method for producing automatic writing that involves such *movement confusion* and that also qualifies as a cute trick to play on the gullible. What you do is ask a person to think of a name and then tell her that you will make her write the name. Have the person look away while you grasp her hand lightly, "as one teaches a child to write" (228). Then, saying, "I will write it," you begin simply to move your hand, slightly jiggling the person's hand. Binet claimed frequent success in stimulating a person to write the name even while the person claimed that Binet was producing the movement. I've tried this a few times with people I've thought might be willing to accept the claim that I could read their minds, and have found in this informal sampling that the technique produces the imagined name about one third of the time. This seems particularly effective with children. Some of my victims do believe that I've made them write the name, whereas others correctly perceive that they wrote it while I just served as their personal jiggler.

These curious effects are, unfortunately, still more in the nature of parlor games than sturdy, reproducible scientific phenomena. There is simply not enough systematic research on automatic writing to allow a full understanding of its nature and causes. What we have at present is a collection of observations that point to the possibility that some people can lose either conscious awareness of what is written, or the feeling of doing, or both when they try to do so as they write. We don't have enough collected observations of the effect to have a strong conception of when and why it happens.

Some of the murkiness surrounding the topic of automatic writing must be the conceptual difficulty surrounding the *perception of a lack of consciousness*. How can people tell that they are not conscious of something? How can they tell if they've written automatically? This puzzle is nicely described by Julian Jaynes (1976): "Consciousness is a much smaller part of our mental life than we are conscious of, because we cannot be conscious of what we are not conscious of. . . . How simple that is to say; how difficult to appreciate! It is like asking a flashlight in a dark room to search around for something that does not have any light shining upon it. The flashlight, since there is light in whatever direction it turns, would have to conclude that there is light everywhere. And so consciousness can seem to pervade all mentality when it actually does not" (23). Jaynes rightly observes that, by definition, we cannot know what lies beyond our consciousness.

In the case of automatic writing, people can really only report a lack of consciousness of their action of writing after they have finished, when they are ostensibly conscious once again. They might then base their report of lack of consciousness during the writing on several different after-the-fact cues. They might notice that they don't recall what was said; they might notice that they don't recognize what was said when they read it; they might notice that things were written that they don't believe they would write or that they don't believe are true; or perhaps, even if they were conscious of the content before or during the writing, they might notice that while they recall or recognize the writing, they don't recall the experience of consciously willing their act of writing. The scientific study of this phenomenon could begin in earnest if it focused on the nature and interplay of these various cues people may use to judge the automaticity of their writing.

Ouija Board

The face of the Ouija board is as familiar to many people as the face of a Monopoly board, and it is fitting that both are copyrighted by Hasbro,

Figure 4.4
A modern Ouija board. © Hasbro, Inc.

Incorporated (fig. 4.4). The name is often attributed to a conjunction of the French *oui* and German *ja,* making it a yes-yes board (although if it were spelled Wee-Jah, it could be a pairing of Scottish with Jamaican patois, meaning "little God"). The use of an alphabet or symbol board for divining is traced by some to antiquity, with versions attributed to early Greek, Roman, Chinese, and Native American societies (Hunt 1985). One origin story involves the use of a "little table marked with the letters of the alphabet," which in A.D. 371 apparently got one unlucky Roman named Hilarius tortured on a charge of magical operations against the Emperor (Jastrow 1935). Apparently the Emperor didn't think it was so funny.

The version of the Ouija board in use these days, complete with a three-legged planchette, was initially manufactured in 1890 by Charles Kennard, and then soon after by William Fuld and the Baltimore Talking

Figure 4.5
Norman Rockwell's painting of this Ouija board graced the cover of the *Saturday Evening Post* on May 1, 1920. A young couple in love, conjuring up a demon. Courtesy of Dr. Donald Stoltz.

Board Company.[4] The instruction calls for the users (usually two, as in fig. 4.5), but more are allowed) to concentrate on a question as they place fingertips on the planchette and then to wait for movement (fig. 4.6). What people usually do, however, is to start moving in a circular or random pattern around the board quite on purpose, waiting then for unintended direction or relevant pauses of the movement. The experience of people who have tried this is that it may or may not work, but that when it does, the sense of involuntariness regarding the planchette's moves can be quite stunning.

4. A Web site by Eugene Orlando, *The Museum of Talking Boards,* features photos of a variety of boards and planchettes. My thanks to Orlando for a personal tour of his board collection and for his insights on the history and operation of the talking board.

Directions on How to Use the Ouija Board

Place the board upon the knees of two persons, lady and gentleman preferred, with the small table upon the board. Place the fingers lightly but firmly, without pressure, upon the table so as to allow it to move easily and freely. In from one to five minutes the tablet will commence to move, at first slowly, then faster, and will be then able to talk or answer questions, which it will do rapidly by touching the printed words or the letters necessary to form words and sentences with the foreleg or pointer.

2nd--Care should be taken that one person only should ask questions at a time, so as to avoid confusion, and the questions should be put plainly and accurately.

3rd--To obtain the best results it is important that the persons present should concentrate their minds upon the matter in question and avoid other topics. Have no one at the table who will not sit seriously and respectfully. If you use it in a frivolous spirit, asking ridiculous questions, laughing over it, you naturally get undeveloped influences around you.

4th--The Ouija is a great mystery, and we do not claim to give exact directions for its management, neither do we claim that at all times and under all circumstances it will work equally well. But we do claim and guarantee that with reasonable patience and judgment it will more than satisfy your greatest expectation.

WM. FULD
INVENTOR AND MANUFACTURER
GAMES-PARLOR POOL TABLES-COLLAPSIBLE KITES
THE MYSTIFYING "ORACLE" TALKING BOARD, Etc
Factory and Show Rooms, 1226-1228-1306 N. Central Avenue
BALTIMORE, MD., U.S.A.

Figure 4.6
These instructions were printed on the back of a board manufactured in 1902.

Of course, the first option for an explanation here is deception. One mystified person might experience involuntariness while another is in fact mischievously moving the planchette around on purpose. It is impossible, of course, to sense whether part of the movement coming from the other person is intended. Some people report planchette spelling and answering that occurs even when they are performing solo, however, much as in automatic writing, and this suggests that there can be an experience of automatism with the Ouija that transcends mere deception.[5]

The fact that Ouija board automatism is more likely with groups than with individuals is significant by itself. Even if we assume that some proportion of the people in groups are actually cheating, there still seems to be a much greater likelihood of successful automatism in these social settings. James (1889, 555) observed that in the case of automatic writing, "two persons can often make a planchette or bare pencils write automatically when neither can succeed alone." This is, of course, a usual feature of the experience of table turning and tilting as well (Carpenter 1888). The standard Ouija procedure takes advantage of this social effect, and it is interesting to consider the possible mechanisms for this social magnification of automatism.

One possibility is that in groups, people become confused about the origins of their own movement. We've already seen this happening in the Binet "mind-reading" effect, when one person jiggles the hand of another and so prompts automatic writing. James (1889, 555) remarked that "when two persons work together, each thinks the other is the source of movement, and lets his own hand freely go." The presence of others may introduce variability or unpredictability into the relation between one's own intentions and actions. The exclusivity principle of apparent mental causation would suggest that co-actions reduce the individual's tendency to assume a relation between his thoughts and the observed movements because these movements may have been produced by the other person. The consistency principle, in turn, would also predict ambiguities or reductions in the experience of will because the other person's contributions could introduce trajectories to the group movement that are not consistent with the individual's initial thought about the movement. Difficulty in tracking the relation between intentions and observed actions—what we have called movement confusion—is likely to reduce the experience of will.

5. One planchette speller, Pearl Curran, began experimenting alone with a Ouija board in 1912. After a year of practice and increasing involvement, she began to receive communications from a personality calling herself Patience Worth, allegedly a woman who had lived in the seventeenth century. Worth "dictated" an enormous quantity of literary compositions, including poems, essays, and novels, a number of which were subsequently published. The works were written in varieties of old English dialects that had never been spoken (Yost 1916).

Another possibility is that the presence of others makes the individual less likely to rehearse conscious intentions. Knowing that others are at least partly responsible, the person may lend his own intentions less than the usual amount of attention. So the action may seem to arise without prior thought. It may even be that when a nonself source is in view, this neglect of preview thoughts leads the individual to become less inclined to monitor whether the action indeed implements his own conscious thoughts. There may be a kind of social loafing (Latané, Williams, and Harkins 1979) in the generation and use of consciousness of action plans. Such a tendency to ignore or even suppress one's own conscious contribution to a group product may be part of the production of social behaviors other than automatisms as well.

We should note one further aspect of the Ouija phenomenon that is perhaps its most remarkable characteristic. People using the board seem irresistibly drawn to the conclusion that some sort of unseen agent—beyond any of the actual people at the board—is guiding the planchette movement. Not only is there a breakdown in the perception of one's own contribution to the talking board effect but a theory immediately arises to account for this breakdown: the theory of outside agency. In addition to spirits of the dead, people seem willing at times to adduce the influence of demons, angels, and even entities from the future or from outer space, depending on their personal contact with cultural theories about such effects. Even quite skeptical people can still be spooked by the idea of working with the board, worried that they might be dealing with unfathomable and potentially sinister forces. Hunt's (1985) book about Ouija is subtitled *The Most Dangerous Game,* exemplifying exactly this kind of alarm. The board clearly has a bad reputation, abetted in large part by cultural myths and religious ideologies that have created scary ways of constructing and interpreting forms of outside agency. The head-spinning, frost-breathing demon possession in *The Exorcist* started with a seemingly innocent talking board.

Chevreul Pendulum

The hand-held pendulum has long been used for divining, ostensibly obtaining messages from the gods. The pendulum is usually a crystal or other fob on a string or chain and is held without any intentional swinging (fig. 4.7). Its movement is read in various ways. A popular current

Figure 4.7
Chevreul pendulum. This one seems to be moving very vigorously, so it may be an intentional movement posed for the camera. Unintentional pendulum movements are typically more subtle. Courtesy Eduardo Fuss.

notion is that it will move in a circle over the belly of a woman pregnant with a girl but in a straight line when the infant is a boy, apparently as a result of its extensive knowledge of phallic symbolism. Carpenter (1888) and James (1904) both remarked that when a person is thinking about the hour of the day and swings a ring by a thread inside a glass, it often strikes the hour, like the chime of a clock, even while the person has no conscious sense of doing this on purpose. And our fourth-century Roman friend Hilarius, mentioned earlier, was actually using a pendulum along with his letter board when he tested the Emperor's sense of humor (Chevreul 1833). The use of the pendulum for answering questions or testing properties of objects, sometimes called radiesthesia, has traditionally attracted a small following of adherents (Zuzne and Jones 1989).

The French chemist Michel Chevreul did such a lovely job of debunking the occult interpretation of pendulum movement that he ended up lending his name to the phenomenon—the Chevreul pendulum. It seems that chemists of his time had been using pendulums to assay the metal content of ores and had developed intricate theories of just how the pendulum would move in response to various metals. Chevreul (1833) observed that this movement only occurred if the operator was holding the pendulum in hand and, further, looking at it. There seemed to be nothing special about the pendulum itself or its relation to the ore. Rather, the pendulum moved in response to the unconscious responses of the operator, directed in some unknown way by the operator's perception of its movement.

Pendulum movement qualifies as an automatism because of the strong sense most operators express that they are not moving the pendulum on purpose. Well over half the population of individuals I've seen try the pendulum do get clearly unintentional movements. All you need to do is hold the pendulum, watch it carefully, and think about a particular pattern of movement (e.g., back and forth toward you, or in a circle). Without any intention on your part, the pendulum will often move just as you've anticipated. The effect is strong enough to make one understand how people may feel compelled to invent theories of supernatural forces or spirits responsible for the swing. Without a sense of conscious will to account for the movement, other agents become potential sources.

Modern research on Chevreul pendulum effects (Easton and Shor 1975; 1976; 1977) substantiates the basic characteristics of this phenomenon. It seems to happen particularly when one is looking at the pendulum and imagining a course of movement but trying not to move. This effect may be the simplest and most vivid demonstration we have of the translation of thought into movement without the feeling of doing. Carpenter (1888) summed it up as "a singularly complete and satisfactory example of the general principle, that, in certain individuals, and in a certain state of mental concentration, the *expectation* of a result is sufficient to determine—without any voluntary effort, and even in opposition to the Will (for this may be honestly exerted in the attempt to keep the hand perfectly unmoved)—the Muscular movements by which it is produced" (287).

On toying with the pendulum for a while, it is difficult to escape the idea that the pendulum is simply hard to operate. The perceived involuntariness

of the movement seems to derive from thought/action inconsistency arising in the sheer unwieldiness of the pendulum. Moving one's hand in one
direction produces an impulse to the pendulum in the opposite direction,
so the control of the movement is like trying to write while looking at
one's hand in a mirror. And once a movement gets started, it seems difficult to know just what needs to be done to dampen it. How do you stop
a pendulum that is swinging in an oval? Even slight errors of timing can
cause one's attempts to stop the pendulum to start it instead, and in just
the wrong direction. The lack of consistency between intention and action of the pendulum promotes the sense that the pendulum's movement
is not controlled by the will.

The other intuition that is hard to dispel once one has played with a
pendulum is that it often seems to do the opposite of what one desires.
Trying to keep it from swinging to and fro, for example, seems to be a
good way to nudge it toward just such movement. In studies in my laboratory (Wegner, Ansfield, and Pilloff 1998), this possibility has been observed in detail. Participants were specifically admonished *not* to move
the pendulum in a particular direction, and the pendulum's movement
was observed by a video camera. The repeated finding was that this suggestion not to move in a certain direction yielded significant movement in
exactly the forbidden direction, and that this tendency was amplified if
the person was given a mental load (counting backward from 1,000 by
3s) or a physical task (holding a brick at arm's length with the other arm).
These observations illustrate the possibility that the desire not to perform
an action can ironically yield that action. Given that a person is consciously intending not to perform the action, ironic effects like this one
opposing the intention are particularly apt cases of automatism.

Dowsing

The use of a dowsing or divining rod to find water or other underground
treasures also qualifies as an automatism. To do this, a person usually
grasps the two branches of a forked twig, one in each hand, with the neck
(or bottom of the Y) pointing upward at about a 45° angle. The forked
twig is placed under tension as a result, such that certain slight movements of the wrists or forearms will cause the stick to rotate toward the
ground. When this happens, the automatism is usually interpreted as a

sign of water below. This interpretation turns out to be superstitious, however, because controlled investigations reveal that there is no reliable association of the stick's movement with water, minerals, or anything else under the ground beyond what might be expected on the basis of the dowser's personal judgment (Barrett and Besterman 1926; Foster 1923; Randi 1982; Vogt and Hyman 1959). Although the dowser clearly moves the stick, and uses knowledge about when and where this should be done, he or she professes a lack of the feeling of doing this (fig. 4.8).

Figure 4.8
Clarence V. Elliott, of Los Angeles, demonstrates dowsing equipment of his own design. The forked metal rod has a detachable top into which can be fitted samples of the substance sought; the containers are carried, ready to use, in a cartridge belt. From Vogt and Hyman (1959).

The psychological interpretation of this effect involves several parts, as detailed by Vogt and Hyman (1959).[6] First, the person who gets started dowsing usually has an experienced dowser as a guide and gets drawn in initially by imitating the master's activities. Second, there are various cues to the presence of water underground (e.g., green areas, gravel washes) that anyone who has thought about this very much might pick up. Third, the dowser undoubtedly does experience some unexpected and involuntary movement, largely because the rod is unwieldy and leads to confusion about what role the dowser is playing in moving it. With his muscles straining slightly against the rod, an awkward tension is set up that indeed induces involuntary action, in the same way that one's leg braced at an uncomfortable angle underneath an airline tray table will sometimes suddenly straighten out, usually during a meal. (Although why anyone would actually want to locate airline food is a mystery.) And finally, dowsers like all people are good at overestimating the success of their activities, and often take credit for performance that is actually no better than random. In 1982 the renowned skeptic ("the Amazing") James Randi tested several professional dowsers with an elaborate underground plumbing system that could reroute the flow of water through pipes without their knowledge, and though they located the flow at no better than a chance level, they nonetheless left the experiment proclaiming triumph. Automatism plays a role in dowsing, then, but is really only part of the psychological show.

Another dowsing device is the L-rod or swing rod (fig. 4.9). This is an L-shaped wire or metal rod held in the hand like a pistol, sometimes with a tube as a handle that allows the long end to swivel in different directions. The beauty of this device is that it points not down or up but left and right, so one can follow it around to find things. Normally, the dowser holds two, one in each hand, and they may signal that it is time to stop by crossing. (If they both suddenly stick into the ground and stay there, it may mean that the dowser has fallen down and can't get up.)

6. Vogt and Hyman (1959) describe this in a clever fictional passage about how a naive observer, Jim Brooks (of course), gets involved in dowsing. Vogt and Hyman's is by far the best account anywhere of why dowsing doesn't work and of why some people are so convinced that it does. This book is perhaps the best model in existence of the careful scientific analysis of supernatural claims.

Figure 4.9
A selection of brass, chrome, and steel L-rods, available from the American Society of Dowsers.

Like the dowsing rod, the L-rod seems to operate on the principle of movement confusion, in that variations in the upright posture of the tube in the dowser's hand translate into rotary movements of the wire perpendicular to the tube. As in the case of pendulum movement, the relation between what is thought about before the action and what happens becomes difficult to grasp intuitively or quickly, and the result is that the movements of the pointer often seem to the dowser to be unrelated to conscious thoughts and intentions. Ultimately, though, the movements of L-rods and Y-rods may follow from the same kinds of processes that lead beginning drivers inadvertently to steer in the direction they are looking ("Keep your eyes on the road!"). Unconscious sources of movement can be particularly powerful when one is unskilled in tracking the relation between one's thought and action.

The apparent involuntariness of the rod's movement seems to mask the role of the person's thoughts in causing the movement. In a class of mine, for instance, a student performed a dowsing demonstration by placing a shot glass of water under one of five overturned opaque plastic cups while an experimental subject was outside the room. When the subject returned, she was given a small Y-rod and asked to find the water by dowsing for it. She picked the wrong cup, and said that the rod didn't seem to move much. Then, after she was aware of where the water had been hidden, almost as an afterthought she was asked to try dowsing again. This time, the rod rapidly dipped over the correct cup, and the experimental dowser remarked that the rod really did seem to move of its own accord. The knowledge of the water's location clearly informed her movement but was not interpreted as an intention that caused her movement. She reported feeling instead that the rod had moved.

As in the other automatisms, the experience of the involuntary dowsing movement often leads to an attribution of agency outside the self. Early dowsers ascribed their movements variously to water spirits, supernatural earth forces, and other gods of moisture, whereas more contemporary dowsers have added the possibilities of electrical fields, magnetism, and more scientific-seeming forces (e.g., Maby and Franklin 1939). The possibility that dowsing taps the dowser's own unconscious ideas has also been suggested, and dowsing devices have been used as mind-reading devices, both by supposed mind readers and by people seeking self-knowledge of their own unconsciously held proclivities. Pendulums and L-rods can answer questions like those posed to the Ouija board. Much of the amazement at the responses occurs because the answers appear to be involuntary as the result of circumstances that reduce the perception of apparent mental causation.

Ideomotor Action

The clamor of interest in the spirits in the nineteenth century did not escape the attention of scientific psychologists. William Carpenter (1888) was intrigued by automatisms and yet was highly skeptical of the spiritualist interpretation of such things that was so popular in his time. As a response to the spiritualist agenda, he proposed a general theory of automatisms that still remains useful and convincing. According to his ideomotor action theory, "The Idea of the *thing to be done* . . . may, indeed, be so decided and forcible, when once fully adopted, as of itself to produce a degree of Nervous tension that serves to call forth respondent

Muscular movements" (424). With one sweep, Carpenter proposed a central mechanism underlying table turning, pendulum movement, dowsing, automatic writing, and talking board spelling. In essence, he said the idea of an action can make us perform the action, without any special influence of the will. This ideomotor action theory depended on the possibility that ideas of action could cause action but that this causal relation might not surface in the individual's experience of will. Thoughts of action that precede action could prompt the action without being intentions.

Now, the first question that arises is, Why do all thoughts of actions not yield immediate action? Why, when I think of walking like a duck, don't I just do it? And given that you are also now thinking about it, why are you also not waddling around? (Are you?) James (1890) proposed an important addendum for the ideomotor theory to solve this problem, that *"every representation of a movement awakens in some degree the actual movement which is its object; and awakens it in a maximum degree whenever it is not kept from so doing by an antagonistic representation present simultaneously to the mind"* (Vol. 2, 526). I don't do the duck thing on thinking about it, in other words, because I'm also (fortunately) thinking about not doing it. In this theory, we normally do whatever we think of, and it is only by thinking not to do it that we successfully hold still. For ideomotor theory, the will becomes a counterforce, a holding back of the natural tendency for thought to yield action.

Absentmindedness tends to produce ideomotor movements. James (1890) proposed that when we are not thinking very intently about what we are doing, we don't tend to develop "antagonistic representations." He gives examples: "Whilst talking, I become conscious of a pin on the floor, or some dust on my sleeve. Without interrupting the conversation I brush away the dust or pick up the pin. I make no express resolve, but the mere perception of the object and the fleeting notion of the act seem of themselves to bring the latter about. Similarly, I sit at table after dinner and find myself from time to time taking nuts or raisins out of the dish and eating them. My dinner properly is over, and in the heat of the conversation I am hardly aware of what I do, but the perception of the fruit and the fleeting notion that I may eat it seem fatally to bring the act about. . . . In all this the determining condition of the unhesitating and resistless sequence of the act seems to be *the absence of any conflicting notion in the mind*" (Vol. 2, 522–523). This theory explains why one may loll around in bed in the morning thinking of all kinds of acts yet still lie there like a lump. According to James, such lumpishness is caused by a balancing or conflicting notion in the mind that keeps these acts from happening: besides thinking of the acts, one is also thinking of staying in bed.

People who have experienced certain forms of damage to their frontal lobes seem to be highly susceptible to ideas of action in just this way. Patients with such damage may exhibit what Lhermitte (1983; 1986) has called "utilization behavior," a tendency to perform actions using objects or props that are instigated (often inappropriately) by the mere presence of those objects or props. An examiner sits with the patient, for example, and at no time makes any suggestion or encouragement for the patient to act. Instead, the examiner touches the patient's hands with a glass and carafe of water. Normal individuals in this situation typically sit there and do nothing, but the frontal-damage patients may grasp the glass and pour it full from the carafe. Touching the patient's hand with pack of cigarettes and a lighter prompts lighting a cigarette, and a variety of other objects may prompt their associated actions. One patient given three pairs of eyeglasses donned them in sequence and ended up wearing all three. It is as though, in these individuals, the Jamesian "conflicting notion" does not arise to stop the action, and the idea of the act that is suggested by the object is enough to instigate the action.

Experiments designed to overcome these "conflicting notions" in normal individuals have supported the ideomotor theory. One early laboratory demonstration was conducted by Jastrow and West (1892), for example, with the aid of a device they called an automatograph (fig. 4.10). This contraption consisted of a piece of plate glass resting in a wooden frame, topped by three brass balls, upon which rested another glass plate—kind of a super-planchette. The participant's hand was placed on the upper plate, and recordings of movement were made with a pen attached to a rod extending from the plate while the participant tried to hold still. The investigators remarked that "it is almost impossible to keep the plate from all motion for more than a few seconds; the slightest movement of the hand slides the upper plate upon the balls" (399). A large screen inserted to prevent the participant from seeing the recording

Figure 4.10
The automatograph. From Jastrow and West (1892).

completed the apparatus. With such a sensitive surface, and an inability to tell just what one has done, there seems to be less possibility for a "conflicting notion" to arise and squelch automatic actions.

The automatograph revealed a variety of interesting movement tendencies. Beyond all the drifting and wobbling one might expect from such movements, there were some remarkable regularities in how people moved in response to certain mental tasks. Asked to count the clicks of a metronome, for example, one person showed small hand movements to and fro in time with the rhythm. Another person was asked to think of a building to his left and slowly moved his hand in that direction. Yet another participant was asked to hide an object in the room (a knife) and then was asked to think about it. Over the course of some 30 seconds, his hand moved in the direction in which the knife was hidden.

It turned out that these movements followed not from thinking about a direction per se but more specifically from thinking about moving one's hand in that direction. Further automatograph studies by Tucker (1897) revealed that the thought of movement itself was a helpful ingredient for the effect.[7] People who were thinking of movement showed directional

7. In related studies, Arnold (1946) found that the more vividly a person imagined the movement, the more it occurred. So, for instance, standing still and imagining falling over—by thinking about both what it would look like and what it would feel like—produces more teetering than does thinking about either the look or the feel alone.

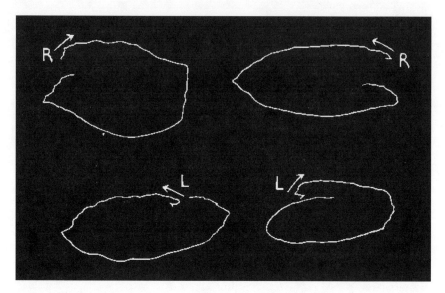

Figure 4.11
Automatograph tracing by a person watching an object being moved in circles around the room. From Tucker (1897).

movement effects more strongly than did people who were just thinking of a place. Tucker also found that a person who is intently watching a person or object move will sometimes show automatic hand movement. In figure 4.11, for example, we see an automatograph tracing for a person watching an object being moved around the room in closed curves. A tendency toward unconscious mimicry of movement may help translate the mere perception of movement into the thought of one's own movement and thus into the occurrence of ideomotor automatism.

Ideomotor action has also been observed with equipment designed to measure electrically what would otherwise be imperceptible muscle movements. These electromyograph (EMG) readings were first used for this purpose by Edmund Jacobson, the inventor of modern relaxation therapy techniques. While a male participant was relaxed in a darkened room, Jacobson (1932) asked him to imagine bending his right arm without actually bending it. An electrode on the right arm's biceps-brachial muscles showed a deflection, an indication of electrical activity in the muscle. Asking the participant to think about bending his left arm or right foot created no such effect in the right arm, and requests to imagine the right arm perfectly relaxed or to imagine the right arm paralyzed also produced no indication of fine movement. Less direct suggestions to flex the arm, such as calling for the man to imagine himself rowing a boat, scratching his chin, or plucking a flower from a bush, however, again produced the indication of movement. All this served as a basis for Jacobson to propose that thinking about actions is what makes our muscles tense and that to relax we need to think about relaxing and not acting. These demonstrations suggest that thinking about acting can produce movement quite without the feeling of doing.

The use of these sensitive devices to detect ideomotor movements suggests that the movements are quite meager. The notion that ideomotor phenomena are relatively weak doesn't seem to square, though, with the finding that people can sometimes read the ideomotor muscle movements of others. Without benefit of special equipment, a variety of stage performers have exhibited muscle reading that appears to involve communication through ideomotor action. One such performer is the mentalist ("the Amazing") Kreskin. He often asked a sponsor of his performance to hide his paycheck in the auditorium. Then, as part of the act, he grasped that person's hand and, after marching around the place a bit, uncovered the paycheck somewhere in the seats—amidst protestations from the sponsor that he had not tried to give the location away.[8] Early muscle-reading performers were described by Beard (1877; 1882) and Baldwin (1902).

In some cases, the muscle reader might not even be aware of the source of the input and could react to the target person's movements entirely unconsciously. In "The control of another person by obscure signs," Stratton (1921) described the case of Eugen de Rubini. This performer would read muscles by holding the end of a watch-chain held by the subject. He could sometimes dispense with the chain entirely and just observe the person, yet locate places or objects the person was thinking about. Rubini often didn't even seem to look at the person and professed little awareness of the precise cues he used to do this. Beard (1882)

---

8 Kreskin (1991) tells his secrets in a book that recounts this and dozens of other tricks that indeed are at least moderately amazing. He also takes credit for the Chevreul pendulum, however, calling it the Kreskin pendulum, an amazing bit of self-aggrandizement. A box containing one of his fobs along with instructions and an answer board was marketed as *Kreskin's ESP* by Milton-Bradley.

described another muscle reader: "Mr. Bishop is guided by the indications unconsciously given through the muscles of his subject—differential
pressure playing the part of 'hot' and 'cold' in the childish game which
these words signify. Mr. Bishop is not himself averse to this hypothesis,
but insists that if it is the true one he does not act upon it consciously. He
described his own feelings as those of dreamy abstraction or 'reverie,' and
his finding a concealed object, etc., as due to 'an impression borne in'
upon him" (33).

The elevation of muscle reading into stage performance suggests that it
is a special talent, but this may not be the case at all. Muscle reading of
some kind may well occur in many normal people and in normal situations, leading generally to our ability to coordinate our movements with
others without having to think about it. James (1904) mentioned muscle
reading not as a skilled performance, for example, but as a parlor amuse-
ment called "the willing game" in which even a naive participant could
often discern another's secret thoughts about a place or object and find it
in this way. It seems fair to say at this point, then, that ideomotor actions
can be detected in a variety of ways, from delicate instrumentation to the
relatively unsophisticated expedient of holding hands.

A clear ideomotor effect was shown in experiments Clark Hull (1933)
conducted on what he called "unconscious mimicry." He asked a young
man to see how still he could stand with his eyes closed. Then, "under the
pretext of placing him in the right position, a pin with a tiny hook at its
end was deftly caught into the collar of his coat at the back. From this pin
a black thread ran backward through a black screen to a sensitive recording apparatus. This apparatus traced faithfully on smoked paper . . .
the subject's forward and backward movements, but quite without his
knowledge [fig. 4.12]. After he had been standing thus for about four
minutes an assistant came apologetically into the room and inquired of
the experimenter whether she could take her 'test' at once, as she had an
appointment" (43).

The subject consented for her to go first and was permitted to open his
eyes but cautioned not to move from his position. Hull recounted, "The
assistant then took up a position in clear view of the subject, and just far
enough from the wall so that she could not possibly touch it. She then
proceeded to reach for the wall with all her might, giving free expression
to her efforts by facial grimaces and otherwise. Meanwhile, the uncon-

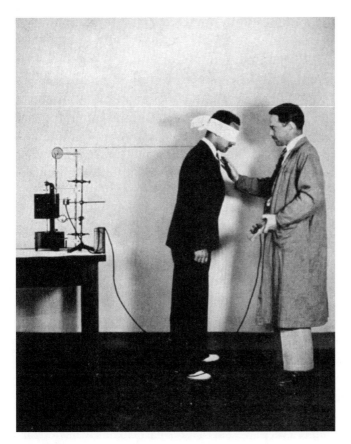

Figure 4.12
Body sway measurement device in Clark Hull's laboratory. From Hull (1933). Courtesy Irvington Publishers.

sciously mimetic postural movements of the unsuspecting subject were being recorded in detail. Sometimes subjects see through this ruse and then it commonly loses much of its effectiveness. But with a naive and unsuspicious subject there can usually be seen in the tracings evidence of a tendency to reproduce in his own body the gross postural movements of the person under observation. If the assistant reaches far forward, the subject sways forward slightly; if the assistant bends backward, the subject unconsciously sways backward" (43).

Perhaps this kind of mimicry underlies a lot of unintentional coordination of action in everyday life. The unintended communication of movements may be involved in the way loving couples walk together, the way soldiers march, the way crowds swarm, and the way gestures and postures guide every social interaction. The young man with the hook on his collar seems to have been put into a position where his fleeting consciousness of the assistant's movements influenced his own movements quite measurably, perhaps in a way that could have led to intentional movement later on. Had she been walking by his side and made a start toward the ice cream shop across the street, he could well have followed. The initial ideomotor action could launch him on a trajectory that his conscious intention might only overtake some moments later.

In fact, there is evidence that merely thinking about a *kind of person* can induce ideomotor mimicry of that person's behavior. Bargh, Chen, and Burrows (1996) had college student participants fill out a scrambled-sentence test that for some repeatedly introduced the idea of aging (with sentences that included words such as *wrinkled, grey, retired, wise,* and *old*). These people were thus primed with the stereotype of an old person, whereas other participants in the study did not receive this version of the test. As each participant left the experiment room, the person's gait was measured surreptitiously. The individuals who been led to think about senior citizens *walked more slowly* than did those not primed with this thought. The idea of the action arose from the stereotype and so influenced the behavior directly, apparently without conscious will. Extensive postexperimental interviews suggested that the participants were not particularly conscious of the aged stereotype after the experiment. And even if they were, they were certainly not aware that this might suggest they should walk at a different speed, or for that matter that their walking speed was being assessed. Yet merely thinking of the kind of person who walks slowly seemed to be sufficient to induce shuffling.

Needless to say, this experiment has been quite controversial and has been followed by a number of further tests of this effect. In general, the phenomenon holds up very well (e.g., Dijksterhuis, Bargh, and Miedema 2001). Intriguing observations of this type have been made by Dijksterhuis and van Knippenberg (1998), for example, in experiments in which participants were asked to think about professors. When these individuals were then given a series of questions from a *Trivial Pursuit* game, they answered more items correctly than did participants given no professor prime. And, in turn, participants asked to think about soccer hooligans (who are stereotypically less than intelligent, particularly in the Netherlands, where this research was done) showed decreased performance on the trivia items. Dijksterhuis, Bargh, and Miedema (2001) also found that thinking of old age can prompt memory loss. And in studies of the tendency to be helpful, Macrae and Johnston (1998) observed that unscrambling sentences about helpfulness made people more likely to pick up dropped objects for an experimenter.

In these modern ideomotor studies, the idea that leads to an ideomotor action may or may not be conscious. The person may be asked to think about the idea for a while, may be exposed to the idea surreptitiously via a scrambled sentence task, or may be primed with the idea through brief subliminal exposures (Bargh and Chartrand 2000; Dijksterhuis, Bargh, and Miedema 2001). In the historical literature, this feature of ideomotor action also varies. In some of the examples (e.g., the person imagining an action in Jacobson's experiments), the idea is perfectly conscious. In others (e.g., the participant in Jastrow and West's automatograph study who is just listening to a metronome), the idea seems unlikely to be conscious. And in yet others (e.g., the person whose muscles are being read), the idea may be conscious but is probably accompanied by another conscious idea to the effect that the behavior should be inhibited ("I mustn't give away the location"). All this suggests that the ideomotor influence of thoughts on actions may proceed whether the thoughts appear in consciousness or not—the thoughts merely need to be primed in some way.[9] The common thread through all the ideomotor phenomena, then, is not the influence of unconscious thoughts.

What ideomotor effects have in common is the apparent lack of conscious intention. In all these various observations, it is difficult to maintain that the person had a conscious intention to behave as he or she was seen to behave. Rather, the action appeared to come from thoughts directly without translation into an "I will do this" stage. People are not

9. Conscious primes don't lead to ideomotor effects if people are told that the primes are expected by the experimenters to influence their behavior. This draws the person's attention to the priming event and the behavior, and introduces a process of adjustment that eliminates the usual effect (Dijksterhuis, Bargh, and Miedema 2001). This effect harks back to James' hypothesis that "conflicting notions" would block the occurrence of ideomotor effects.

trying to clench their arms, walk slowly, keep rhythm, be especially helpful, guide the muscle reader, retrieve trivia, or the like. Rather, it appears
that these actions seem to roll off in a way that skips the intention.
Because of this, most people who have thought seriously about ideomotor effects have been led to propose that such effects are caused by a system that is distinct from the intentional system of behavior causation
(Arnold 1946; Bargh and Chartrand 2000; Prinz 1987). If ideomotor
action "must be under the *immediate* control of ideas that *refer to the
action itself* " (Prinz 1987, 48), it can't be under the person's control and
thus must be caused by something other than the will.

Viewed in terms of the theory of apparent mental causation, however,
ideomotor action takes on a different light. Rather than needing a special
theory to explain ideomotor action, *we may only need to explain why
ideomotor actions and automatisms have eluded the mechanism that
produces the experience of will.* In this way of thinking, ideomotor action
could occur by precisely the same kinds of processes that create intentional action but in such a way that the person's usual inference linking
the thought and action in a causal unit is obstructed. The surprising thing
about ideomotor action, then, is not that the behavior occurs—behavior
occurs with conscious and unconscious prior thoughts all the time—but
rather that the behavior occurs without the experience of conscious will.
Automatisms could flow from the same sources as voluntary action and
yet have achieved renown as oddities because each one has some special
quirk that makes it difficult to imbue with the usual illusion of conscious
will. Automatism and ideomotor action may be windows on true mental
causation as it occurs without apparent mental causation.

Conditions of Automatism

Now that we have a nice collection of automatisms, it is time to start
collecting our wits. We need to examine the commonalities among the
various automatisms to learn how and why they happen. To do this, we
consider in turn each of several *conditions of automatism*—variables or
circumstances that enhance the occurrence of automatism by clouding
the perception of will. In what follows, we explore characteristics of the
people who perform automatisms and, more to the point, the situations

that generate automatisms in anyone, to see how the principles of priority, consistency, or exclusivity are breached in each case.

Dissociative Personality

The most common explanation for automatisms is the idea that they only happen to certain people—an explanation that might be called the *odd person theory*. Because the automatisms involve strange behaviors, and because people who perform strange behaviors are quickly assigned personal qualities consistent with those behaviors by the rest of us, by far the most frequent explanation of automatisms is that the person who does them is odd or abnormal. (This is why I was so relieved that I didn't have to start walking like a duck.) Certainly, there are people who do seem unusually susceptible to certain automatisms—the spirit mediums, for example, or talented automatic writers. And, beyond this, there are cases of automatisms associated with serious mental disorders or brain damage that have gained great notoriety in the history of abnormal psychology.

Pierre Janet (1889) was a great collector of such cases. He established the study of abnormal automatisms in terms of the concept of *dissociation*—the idea that the conscious executive part of the mind can become cut off from unconscious parts of the mind that produce behavior. This line of thinking about automatisms goes back far earlier among many investigators of hysteria and hypnosis and must also include Sigmund Freud and William James.[10] Janet collected and presented a variety of unusual cases as forms of dissociation—people who experienced blindness, deafness, anesthesia of various parts of the body, convulsions, possession, odd voices or sudden new habits, physical illness, and other remarkable symptoms. Intertwined with this history is the use and study of hypnosis, which has also long traded on the idea that there are special people who are particularly good at accepting suggestions to behave involuntarily (e.g., Hilgard 1965). People prone to experience dissociation were commonly believed to be especially susceptible to hypnosis, and vice versa. Taken together, these historical traditions suggest that there may be

10. Histories of the psychiatric and psychological analysis and treatment of automatisms and related phenomena have been written by Ellenberger (1970), Gauld (1992), and Whyte (1960), and there is an excellent account of James's interest in these topics by Eugene Taylor (1983).

people who are prone to dissociate and thus lose conscious control of their actions.

If such dissociative individuals exist, they might be identified by the frequency with which they have dissociative experiences. This is the approach taken with a personality scale called the *Dissociative Experiences Scale* (Bernstein and Putnam 1986; Carlson and Putnam 1993). The scale asks questions about experiences of the loss of agency and lapses of memory and attention. For example, it asks about the experience of finding yourself in a place and not knowing how you got there, the experience of listening to someone talk and realizing that you did not hear what was said, or the experience of noticing new belongings you did not remember buying. These aren't quite prototypical experiences of loss of conscious will, but they're in the ballpark. There are other items on the scale that are only vaguely related to automatism, however, including experiences of hearing voices, sometimes not recognizing family members, and being able to ignore pain, so that the overall score seems to involve the general tendency to admit to odd symptoms. People who report more such experiences on the scale are inclined to be diagnosed with certain mental disorders, including dissociative identity disorder (multiple personalities), so the scale does seem to be linked with an important pathology of the will. The evidence that this is a unitary personality trait or syndrome is not clear (e.g., Sanders and Green 1994) because the various experiences are not all commonly reported by the same people. All told, this particular scale measures both more and less than what we might want to include in a test of whether people regularly fail to have the experience of conscious will.

The odd person theory fails because it is too simple. If there are dissociative individuals who fail to experience apparent mental causation, they are not all likely to do this in the same way. There are lots of avenues by which a person might bypass an experience of will. Some people might have a tendency to forget their intentions, for example, such that when they do act, they can't grasp where the action might be coming from. Other people might have a tendency not to notice when they've completed actions and so fail to draw the experience of will from what they do. Yet others might experience preoccupation with certain kinds of thoughts and so draw inferences of will with great frequency to whatever behaviors they perform that are consistent with those thoughts. Another set of people might specifically ignore or suppress certain areas of thinking and thus fail to infer that any of their behaviors relevant to those areas might be willed. There may even be people who regularly fail to grasp the consistency between their thoughts and actions and thus experience the actions as less than willed.

A full analysis of the individual differences underlying automatism could yield a broad and complex range of deficits in the ability to process information about one's own apparent causal influence. For this reason, it is important as a first step to establish the conditions under which various such deficits occur even in people with normal processing capacities. Suffice it to say at this point that the search for a general dissociation-prone personality is likely instead to unearth many individual differences that can contribute to such effects. There may not be such a thing as one type of odd person, in other words, so it may be easier to attack the problem of classifying the causes of dissociation by focusing on odd situations.

Expectant Attention
One common ingredient in several automatisms is the simple expectation that the automatism will happen. This was part of Carpenter's (1888) analysis of automatisms; he frequently used the term *expectant attention* to describe the mind-set of people who were prone to a certain automatism. The table turner expects the table to move; the dowser anticipates the rod will dip; the Ouija board speller thinks something will be learned from the board. In the cases of automatic writing, the individuals who have tried to produce this effect seem to have devoted inordinate amounts of time to sitting around, pen or planchette in hand, waiting and hoping and scribbling. A bit of expectation seems to occur with Chevreul pendulum movement, too, because even while the person holding the pendulum is trying not to move it, there may be the sense that it will move. However, ideomotor action as measured with Jastrow's automatograph and the Jacobson EMG technique doesn't really require any expectancy of movement, just the idea of movement. And the Bargh, Chen, and Burrows (1996) slow walking study in fact dispenses with expectant attention to the action entirely.

Expectant attention may work in several ways to produce automatisms. First, in the process of waiting to see whether a movement will occur, the usual operation of the priority principle gets undermined and obscured. When we wait for an effect of a thought, expecting that at some time the action will happen, we separate the cause and effect in time by some variable interval. This variability cannot support a causal inference, then, as there is no constant connection in time between the thought and action. You don't get the idea that a cat caused your sneeze, for example, if one time you sneeze immediately after a cat jumps into your lap, whereas another time you sneeze only after three days of intense cat petting. By the same token, people waiting for the Ouija board to move or for the table to turn, or who are trying not to think of something as they begin automatic writing, are undermining any regularity in the timing of the relation between thought and action, and in this way are reducing the degree to which they are likely to experience the action as caused by the thought.

Another effect of expectant attention is that it leads to a kind of "trolling" for consistent action. A fishing expedition of sorts is undertaken, as actions are sought over time that are consistent with the thought. If you think about coughing for a long, long time, for example, and manage to keep attentive to this possibility, in a long enough interval you may eventually cough, clear your throat, feel a tickle in your chest, or the like, at which moment you are then prone to note the consistency between the idea and the action. However, you won't feel that you caused the action, again because of the failure to perceive an appropriate experience of priority. The thought of coughing was far too early. Waiting for table movement or Ouija planchette movement may operate in this way. The person sits for a long while looking for something to happen in line with some idea of what could happen. In the process of looking for a particular kind of action, the person may find actions that are at least partially consistent from time to time—and so draw attention back to the fact that the action was initially thought about—but have such low levels of priority that the sense of causation is not strong. The use of expectant attention to create automatisms creates actions that don't happen on time just as we think of them, so we don't feel we've done them on purpose.

Expectant attention does orient us toward an action that is relevant to our initial thought, however, and in this way it promotes the experience of automatism as well. It allows us to be looking in the right direction so we can know when we have done what we thought. In the several ideomotor action demonstrations that do not draw the person's attention to the action—Jacobson's EMG studies, Jastrow's automatograph, or any of the priming studies by Bargh or Dijksterhuis—the person does not experience an automatism per se. The experience of conscious will was not assessed in these studies, but it is not likely that any reduction in this experience actually occurred. In these settings, the person is not attentive to the behavior at all, so the person doesn't even note or remark on its occurrence. The behavior qualifies as an automatism merely because it happens even when the person doesn't know it exists. With expectant attention, however, the person is specifically oriented to look for the behavior and so when it happens, the lack of conscious will is likely to be salient. It is only by comparing thought and behavior that a lapse in intention may be detected. Then, the person is likely not only to perform an automatism but also to recognize it as such.

Movement Confusion

Several automatisms depend on circumstances that obscure the nature or source of the person's movement. If you can't tell what you're doing, it is hard to gauge whether you're doing it on purpose. Movement confusion creates difficulties in the application of the consistency principle because the relation between thought and action is clouded. Comparing what we think we will do with what we have done must depend, of course, on clarity in knowing the thought, the action, and their meaningful interrelation. Consistency can be rendered ambiguous by at least three forms of movement confusion: *misdirection, amplification,* and *obscured monitoring.*

Movement confusion occurs through *misdirection* in the case of dowsing (with both Y-rods and L-rods) and also with pendulum movement. The action is redirected such that it becomes unclear how one's initially conceptualized movement has translated into the observed automatism. With the Y-rod, for example, it seems that moving one's wrists together or apart (a movement limited to one direction, from side to side) can yield pressure on the rod that results in rotation of the dowsing rod point up or down (a movement of rotation in a different plane). This is confusing. Similarly, pushing the pendulum in one direction becomes pulling it the opposite way. These items are simply unwieldy, and this makes it hard to tell whether one's actions are what one initially thought they might be.

There is also an *amplification* of movement with some of these devices. Slight tilts of the L-rods become major direction swings of the pointers. Vogt and Hyman (1959) note this with the standard Y-rod: "Two ways to produce the rod's movements are to pull the hands slightly apart or to push them slightly together. Either of these movements creates greater tension in the rod than the force of the grip. When the balance is so upset, the rod acts like a coiled spring and may straighten out with such force that the bark may literally come off in the hands of the diviner" (128–129). Gravity probably makes the rod move down more than up when it springs in this way because otherwise we would have heard of more instances of people poking an eye out while looking for water. The pendulum also amplifies slight movements, as do the slippery surfaces of the wheeled writing planchette, the Ouija planchette, and Jastrow's automatograph. And of course, the EMG amplifiers used by Jacobson were specifically designed to amplify movement. When the person can see the result of the amplified movement, it becomes difficult to apply the consistency principle because the action seems out of proportion and inconsistent in direction with the initial idea of what to do.

Obscured monitoring can explain the automatisms produced by circumstances that make it difficult to see what one has done. When the monitoring of action is made difficult or impossible—as with the curtained-off automatograph, for instance, Jacobson's EMG tracings visible only to the polygraph operator, or Hull's surreptitious thread attached to the collar—it seems that automatisms become more likely. Similarly, automatic writing may be enhanced when people look away or have their attention diverted to other tasks. It may be that when action is hard to perceive, the consistency of thought and action becomes less evident and conscious will thus diminishes. Monitoring is entirely impossible, of course, in the case of the various modern ideomotor effects we have reviewed (such as slow walking or *Trivial Pursuit* performance) because in these cases only the experimenter notices and measures the changes in behavior that occur as a result of ideomotor effects. In all likelihood, participants in these studies thus experienced no particular sense of involuntariness in their action, even though the actions arose automatically in response to the primed ideas. With no sense of what to monitor, a person is likely to experience no special feeling of automatism even though the action may well ensue from the prime.

The social magnification of automatisms occurs through all three sources of movement confusion—misdirection, amplification, and obscured monitoring. When people work the Ouija planchette together, for instance, or sit at a table to make the table turn, they may find that their slight movements combine with the other person's movements, sometimes producing stillness but other times yielding new misdirected movements or amplifications as well. This is compounded when, as the co-actors make these minute and unconscious adjustments for each other, they don't know just what part of the action they personally have created. With this obscured monitoring, the group performs a mystery dance,[11] a collective automatism that occurs when no one has conscious and specific knowledge of what self or others are doing.

Desire for Automatism

Automatisms happen in part because we want them to happen. When people perform automatisms for the entertainment of themselves or others, with the Ouija board, for instance, it would be pretty disappointing to get only gibberish. The desire to do something unwilled can be responsible for a variety of ways in which people might avoid, deny, or reinterpret the usual features of willed action to recast it as unwilled.

Consider, for example, the cases of the complex or lengthy performance of automatism produced by automatic writers. If one desperately wanted to engage in automatic writing, one way to do this would be to just start trying it and then to look at what has happened and try to find evidence of automatism. In this way, it might be possible to find some hints of the desired involuntariness, particularly if one could take one or a few instances of apparent involuntariness as evidence that the whole production was an automatism. One might write a few loops and slip

11. Thanks, Elvis Costello.

into a word, or a few letters and then finish up with another few letters that made sense. This episode as a whole might seem sort of involuntary. Given enough desire to produce the effect, it might be the beginning of a fine self-delusion.

Ouija board spelling may work the same way. On moving the planchette around with a friend, one might include some movements that seem quite conscious and intentional (say, the first letter in a word) and others that seem less so (as when the planchette stops on a letter that one suddenly recognizes will make a sensible word from what has gone before). With a strong desire to produce an automatism, the speller could easily overlook the conscious choice of some or many letters and thereby overemphasize the role of involuntariness in the whole sequence, especially when the final letter is one that pops up to "make sense" of the sequence.

This happened when a group of students I had coaxed into a Ouija exercise one afternoon reported on what had made them write the word *Jew* on the letter board. Although they reported feeling that they had picked "j" randomly, one mentioned then "kind of wanting" the next letter to be "e" so as to make a sensible word of some kind. No one reported consciously anticipating the "w" that was chosen next, and in fact all expressed surprise. But they also went on to report that they felt the whole word *Jew* had occurred involuntarily—whereas this really happened clearly only for the last letter. The curious feature of all this was that the word was spelled right after one of the students, who happened to be Jewish, made fun of the Ouija session and left the room. Everyone's recognition of the word and its reference to the absent student added greatly to the sense that the spelling was involuntary yet intelligent. More generally, it may be that enthusiasm and desire to believe in occult effects can contribute to complex automatisms of all kinds by leading automatism wanna-bes to gloss over intentional or accidental occurrences and to judge the whole agglomeration of subacts as involuntary merely on the basis of a few. The potential blindness created by the desire to believe is a danger in the interpretation of all these effects, both for the people who experience them and for the scientists who study them.

Another way that motivation for automatisms might work is by leading people to the strategy of consciously suppressing thinking about their intentions. In those automatisms that involve sustained performance rather than brief movements, and that also are supported by the individual's strong motivation to behave involuntarily, a conscious attempt to suppress or neglect subsequent conscious intentions might be operative. If people can indeed rid their minds, even for a while, of the thoughts that they would normally associate with an action, they might be able to overcome the experience of will. Perhaps consciousness of an ongoing action such as writing can be suppressed, or in Hilgard's (1986) terms, "intentionally excluded."

Can people suppress their conscious intentions? There is a fair amount of evidence that people find it unusually difficult to suppress thoughts, at least for short periods of time in the laboratory (e.g., Wegner 1989; 1994; Wenzlaff and Wegner 2000). So at one level, the answer would seem to be no. Yet there are times when, at least for a while, it works. Right when you try to stop thinking of a white bear, for instance, it may come back in a flurry, or should I say a furry. But then if you keep it up, there may be a moment or even moments of peace—islands of time that are not populated by conscious thoughts or images of the bear. It may be that people trying to produce automatic writing, Ouija spelling, or similar automatisms are sometimes actively drawing their own attention away from the conscious intentions that come to mind, either by direct suppression or by other mental control techniques. They may be purposefully avoiding the conscious representation of their purposes, at least for a while until the thought returns. This could then yield a temporary reduction in the experience of will.

Resistance to Action

Curiously, a number of automatisms hold in common the attempt *not* to produce the target behavior. In these cases, the person who experiences the automatism seems to create it by *trying not to do it*. A distinct resistance to table turning, for instance, was noted by Carpenter (1888) as common among people who in fact produced this automatism. Similarly for dowsing, Vogt and Hyman (1959) observe, "The diviner typically will assert that he was trying to prevent the rod from moving at the moment of its action" (121). And the series of pendulum experiments conducted by Wegner, Ansfield, and Pilloff (1998) showed that counterintentional automatism is likely to occur and is particularly evident when people are given a simultaneous mental load, as when they are asked to count backward from 1,000 by 3s. The desire to resist the movement creates a tendency to perform that movement, and this tendency becomes functional primarily when the normal mental effort at resistance is subverted by a distracting mental task.

You may have noticed that the tendency to experience small automatisms in daily life follows this rule. When you stand looking down from a height, for example, it is only natural to resist any movement toward the edge. But this resistance sometimes prompts a bit of teetering, and you should be particularly careful at this time not to count backward from 1000 by 3s. The odd impulse you might experience to veer into oncoming traffic, to ride your bike into a rut, or in sports to make precisely the error you have been desperately hoping to overcome count as further examples of this perverse motion tendency. These instances suggest that resisting an action serves to induce what we know as ideomotor movement but, in this case, movement that follows from the unfortunately compelling idea of what *not* to do.

The analysis of this perversity of automatisms involves two ideas. First, we can point to the application of the consistency principle that must happen when a person tries not to do something. The thought the person has is *about* the action but it is entirely inconsistent with it. The thought is not to do the act. Thus, any performance of the action would seem not to have been caused by this thought. How could the thought not to do it be the cause? Actions that do occur under conditions of resistance are also, however, the focus of considerable expectant attention in that the person is primed to look for their occurrence. This means that the resistance produces conditions in which the resisted action will surely be interpreted as unwilled if it indeed occurs. In essence, resistance produces a circumstance that is ripe for the experience of automatism in that the individual is deeply focused on both the thought and action but at the same time is precisely opposed to the notion that the thought is the cause of the action.

As it happens, then, the resistance also actually enhances the likelihood that the action will occur because of the priming and ideomotor effect that accrue from thinking about what not to do. Attending to and remembering what shouldn't be done are powerful primes for the behavior.

The reason resistance works in this way can be understood more completely through the theory of *ironic processes of mental control* (Wegner 1994; 1997). This theory was prompted initially by the observation that people have great difficulty suppressing an unwanted thought—that darned white bear.

In trying to understand what kind of mental system would make a suppressed thought come back to mind again and again, my colleagues and I did a series of experiments in which people were asked not to think about white bears, sex, and a variety of other things (Wegner 1989; 1992; 1994; Wegner et al. 1987). As it turned out, this research revealed a general principle: The mind appears to search, unconsciously and automatically, for whatever thought, action, or emotion the person is trying to control. A part of the mind, in other words, is looking surreptitiously for the white bear even as we are trying not to think about it. The theory goes on to suggest that this *ironic monitoring process* can actually create the mental contents for which it is searching. This is why the unwanted thought comes back to mind.

The ironic process theory turns out to explain a lot of otherwise perplexing effects: why we get depressed when we're trying to be happy (Wegner, Erber, and Zanakos 1993), why we stay awake when we're trying desperately to sleep (Ansfield, Wegner, and Bowser 1996), why we get anxious when we're trying to relax (Wegner, Broome, and Blumberg 1997), and why we get distracted when we're trying to concentrate (Wegner 1997), to name a few. What seems to be happening in these cases is that mental loads or stresses can come forward to undermine our normal mental control efforts. The automatic process whereby we monitor control failures is not as distractible as these conscious efforts, and so such distractions unleash it to yield the ironic opposite of what we are trying to create. In the case of action, this ironic, automatic process is the equivalent of a prime that enhances the production of ideomotor action. There is no new counterthought (in William James's sense) to stop the action that is produced through suppression because the person is *already* engaged in trying to stop the action. So, ideomotor effects occur quite often for things we are trying to resist thinking or doing.

Taken together, the consistency principle and the ironic process theory provide a useful way of understanding many of the automatisms (see

Ansfield and Wegner 1996). When people try not to do things, they very likely perceive those things as unwilled because such action is inconsistent with their avowed thought and yet they are prone to do the forbidden act nonetheless because of ironic processes. When mental load or distraction or stress arise, these ironic effects are particularly evident, and apparent automatisms abound.

Potential Outside Agency

Many automatisms seem to be accompanied by attributions of agency or will outside the self. James remarked in this regard, "The great *theoretic* interest of these automatic performances, whether speech or writing, consists in the questions they awaken as to the boundaries of our individuality. One of their most constant peculiarities is that the writing and speech announce themselves as from a personality other than the natural one of the writer, and often convince *him,* at any rate, that his organs are played upon by someone not himself" (1889, 45). The notion of spirit causation or outside agency has been an underlying integrative theme for most of the automatisms. In fact, the only automatisms we've considered that are not associated with such an attribution are those such as automatograph movement that produce effects invisible to the participant. Whenever people produce actions of which they are aware but that they don't ascribe to their own mental causation, they seem to look elsewhere to attribute the action to an outside agent of some kind.

Does the perception of outside agency follow the occurrence of automatism or precede it? This is like asking, Do we think there are ghosts because of the noises in the attic, or do we hear noises in the attic because we think there are ghosts? In the first case, it could be that a person who observes a personal automatism looks for an explanation and, finding no feeling of doing in the self, then turns elsewhere to look for an outside agent. Alternatively, it may be that the theory of outside agency is an aid to the creation of the automatism. Given a strong belief in an outside agent, it might take far less convincing experiences of automatism for a person to decide that indeed the feeling of doing was gone. Both of these possibilities follow from the exclusivity principle. It makes sense that people might look for nonself causes of their own action if they are led by considerations of nonpriority or inconsistency to doubt their own agency. And in complementary fashion, people might begin to doubt their own causal agency when they have embraced an alternative theory of their action that suggests some other agent is its cause.

The remarkably strong link between automatism and the attribution of outside agency suggests that when we see an action, we immediately require that *someone* did it. If we cannot trace the origin of the action to our own mind because we have no recollection of conscious intention, because the priority of the intention is incorrect, or because the intention is inconsistent with the action, we nevertheless insist on the origination of the movement in *some* mind. This fundamental looseness in the connection between our behaviors and their author gives rise to a variety of fascinating phenomena that we take up later in the book—clever animals, trance channeling, and dissociative identity disorders. For now, it is important to recognize just the basic fact that actions cry out for explanation in terms of an agent. That agent can be found in the self when there is an illusion of conscious will, and elsewhere when the illusion breaks down. And the presence of any potential agent other than self can relieve us of the illusion that we consciously willed our action.

The Rule and the Exception

The central idea of this chapter has been to explore the automatisms and study why and when they occur. The automatisms have a special place in the analysis of apparent mental causation, of course, because they represent a class of instances in which apparent mental causation fails. This means that if conscious will is illusory, automatisms are somehow the "real thing," fundamental mechanisms of mind that are left over once the illusion has been stripped away. Rather than conscious will being the rule and automatism the exception, the opposite may be true: Automatism is the rule, and the illusion of conscious will is the exception.

The problem of explaining anomalies exists whether we assume conscious will or deny it. If we begin with "voluntary behavior can occur without conscious will" and so accept that people construct an experience of will for much of their voluntary action, we must then explain the common co-occurrence of intention and action. Where does intention come from, and why does it predict action so nicely so much of the time? On the other hand, if we begin with "all voluntary behavior is consciously willed," then we must explain the many counterexamples— anomalies such as the automatisms and ideomotor cases when apparently voluntary behavior occurs without signs of conscious will. In either event, we must work to explain the exceptions.

And, unfortunately, it has to be one way or the other. Either the automatisms are oddities against the general backdrop of conscious behavior causation in everyday life, or we must turn everything around quite radically and begin to think that behavior that occurs *with* a sense of will is somehow the odd case, an add-on to a more basic underlying system. Now, people have been treating automatisms as exceptions for many years and relegating them to the status of mere oddity. And at the same time, conscious will has been elevated to the status of truism. The theory of apparent mental causation suggests it may be time for a reversal. If we transpose the assumptions completely and take the approach that voluntariness is what must be explained, we immediately begin to see some light. The automatisms and ideomotor effects become models of how thought can cause action in all those moments in everyday life when we don't seem to be in conscious control. Knowing this, we can then focus on how the experience of conscious will is wrapped around our voluntary actions in normal behavior causation and stripped away from some few acts by conditions that reveal them in their nakedness as unwilled.

5

Protecting the Illusion

The illusion of will is so compelling that it can prompt the belief that acts were intended when they could not have been. It is as though people aspire to be ideal agents who know all their actions in advance.

My drawings have been described as pre-intentionalist, meaning that they were finished before the ideas for them had occurred to me. I shall not argue the point.
James Thurber (1960)

By some rules in the game of pool, you have to call your shots. You have to say where the ball is going to go, and sometimes even how it will get there ("Thirteen in the corner pocket off the nine"). This prevents you from claiming you meant to do that when half a dozen balls drop into pockets on a lucky shot. Life, however, is not always played by this rule. For some amount of what we do every day, our conscious intentions are vague, inchoate, unstudied, or just plain absent. We just don't think consciously in advance about everything we do, although we try to maintain appearances that this is the case. The murkiness of our intentions doesn't seem to bother us much, though, as we typically go right along doing things and learning only at the time or later what it is we are doing. And, quite remarkably, we may then feel a sense of conscious will for actions we did not truly anticipate and even go on to insist that we had intended them all along.

The fact is, each of us acts in response to an unwieldy assortment of mental events, only a few of which may be easily brought to mind and understood as conscious intentions that cause our action. We may find ourselves at some point in life taking off a shoe and throwing it out the window, or at another point being sickeningly polite to someone we detest. At these junctures, we may ask ourselves, What am I doing? or perhaps sound no alarms at all and instead putter blithely along assuming that we must have meant to do this for some reason. We perform many unintended behaviors that then require some artful interpretation to fit them into our view of ourselves as conscious agents. Even when we didn't know what we were doing in advance, we may trust our theory that we consciously will our actions and so find ourselves forced to imagine or confabulate memories of "prior" consistent thoughts. These inventions become rewritings of history, protestations that "I meant to knock down all those balls," when we truly had not called the shot at all.

This chapter examines how people protect the illusion of conscious will. People do this, it seems, because they have an *ideal of conscious agency* that guides their inferences about what they must have known and willed even when they perform actions that they did not intend. The chapter focuses first on this ideal agent. We examine the basic features of agency and then look at how people fill in these features based on their conception of the ideal. The expectancy that intention must be there, even when the action is wholly inscrutable, can lead people to infer that they intended even the most bizarre of actions. As a starting point, we look at the explanations people give for the odd acts they can be led to perform through posthypnotic suggestion. The ability to discern what might have been intended is something that people gain as they develop, so we look next at the development of the idea of intention. Then, we turn to the circumstance that first prompts the protection of the idea of will: unconscious action. When people's actions are caused unconsciously, they depend on their ideal of agency to determine what they have done. Several theories in psychology—cognitive dissonance, self-perception, and the left brain interpreter theory—have focused on the way in which people fill in what might have been consciously intended even after one of these unconsciously caused actions is over.

The Ideal Agent

We perceive minds by using the idea of an agent to guide our perception. In the case of human agency, we typically do this by assuming that there is an agent that pursues goals and that the agent is conscious of the goals and will find it useful to achieve them. All this is a fabrication, of course, a way of making sense of behavior. It works much better, at least as a shorthand, than does perceiving only mechanistic causation. As in the case of any constructed entity (such as the idea of justice or the idea of the perfect fudge), the ideal can serve as a guide to the perception of the real that allows us to fill in parts of the real that we can't see. We come to expect that human agents will have goals and that they know consciously what the goals are before they pursue them. This idealization of agency serves as the basis for going back and filling in such goal and intention knowledge even when it doesn't exist. Eventually, however, this strategy leads us to the odd pass of assuming that we must have been consciously aware of what we wanted to do in performing actions we don't understand or perhaps even remember—just to keep up the appearance that we ourselves are agents with conscious will.

The Architecture of Agency

An agent is anything that perceives its environment and acts on that environment. This means that an agent is not just someone who sells you life insurance or real estate. True, these people perceive things and act on them, and they are human beings, but humanness is not necessary for agency. Animals, plants, and many robots can be agents, too, as can some processes that take place in computers. Software agents are commonplace in several kinds of programming, and the essentials of agency are nicely set out in the study of artificial intelligence (AI). Whole textbooks on AI focus on the concept of rational agency, on programs that get things done (e.g., Russell and Norvig 1995). It turns out that when you want to build an agent that does things, you need merely have three basic parts—a *sensor*, a *processor*, and an *effector*. In the hoary marmot, for example, these might be the nose, the brain, and the legs; in a robotic AI agent, they might be a light-sensitive diode, a processing circuit, and a motor attached to a flag. The marmot's action might be to sniff something and approach it; the AI agent's action might be to run the flag up the pole at dawn.

There are good and bad agents. Consider, for example, the thermostat in the typical hotel room. This is usually a dial on a window unit that you twist one way for "cooler" and the other way for "warmer." With luck, there might also be a "low fan"/"high fan" switch. In order to get the temperature of the room right, you basically need to stay up all night fiddling with the controls. Unlike the normal home thermostat that takes a setting of 72° F and keeps the temperature there, the hotel unit can only be set for *different from now*. This thermostat is a bad agent. It can't be aimed at a desired goal and instead can only be set to avoid what is at present undesired. It does have a goal: it will shut off when it has gotten to the point on its dial that it discerns is "cooler" or "warmer," but it is very coy about this. It cannot even tell you where it is going. If I were a thermostat, I'd want to be the house, not the hotel, variety (Powers 1973; 1990).

When we make comparisons between agents, we imply that there is some sort of standard or ideal agent by which all of them are measured. This ideal agent does things in an ideal way, and it is this ideal to which we compare our own agency—and often come up wanting. What is an ideal agent like? The simple answer is that it is God. After all, God can do anything, and most religious people are ready to claim that God does things in the best way. So the traditional Judeo-Christian view of God, who is omniscient, omnipotent, and benevolent, captures the image of an ideal agent very well. This agent knows all (so it has perfect sensors), can do all (so it has perfect effectors), and always acts correctly (so it has a perfect processor). No wonder people pray. Getting an agent like this on your side certainly seems worth the effort. Meanwhile, though, even if we can't always get God to talk back, we can aspire to be God-like. We can hope to be ideal agents and compare ourselves to this standard. Just as God has a will, we are ideal agents to the extent that we have wills as well. In his fourth *Meditation,* Descartes (1647) reflects on this: "It is chiefly my will which leads me to discern that I bear a certain image and similitude of Deity."

Other than acting perfectly, what does an ideal agent do? As it happens, there are a variety of characteristics that agents might look for in themselves, or in each other, as indications of an approach toward the ideal agent. In an analysis of *How to Build a Conscious Machine,* Angel (1989) suggests that agents look for a variety of qualities in themselves and others as a way of learning whether or not an agent is even present. He calls these "basic interagency attributions," and suggests that they may include indications of *agentive presence* ("That is an agent"), an *agent's focus of attention* ("That agent is looking toward the kitchen"), *belief* ("That agent believes there is food in the kitchen"), *desire* ("That agent is hungry"), *plan* ("That agent plans to go to the kitchen and open the refrigerator"), and *agent's movement* ("That agent walked to the kitchen and opened the refrigerator").

An ideal agent should probably have all of these things and more. To be sure, however, it must have intention and conscious will. Just like a thermostat that doesn't know what temperature it is set for, a person who doesn't know what he or she is intending to do can't be much of an agent. This is particularly true if the person is doing something. People who can't answer the question What are you doing? are generally considered asleep, drugged, or crazy. Knowing what it is doing is a highly valued characteristic in an agent, and the aspiration to be an ideal agent must drive people to claim such knowledge a great deal of the time. It may, in fact, push them to claim they did things intentionally when this is provably false.

Posthypnotic Suggestions

A fine example of such filling in of intentions occurs in some responses to posthypnotic suggestion. People who have been hypnotized can be asked to follow some instruction later, when they have awakened (When I touch my nose, you will stand up, pinch your cheeks, and say "I feel pretty, oh so pretty"). And in some instances, such posthypnotic suggestions will be followed with remarkable faithfulness.[1] In one example, Moll (1889, 152) recounted saying to a hypnotized woman, "After you wake you will take a book from the table and put it on the bookshelf." She awoke and did what he had told her. He asked her what she was doing when this happened, and she answered, "I do not like to see things so untidy; the shelf is the place for the book, and that is why I put it there." Moll remarked that this subject specifically did not recall that she had been given a posthypnotic suggestion. So, embarking on a behavior for which no ready explanation came to mind, she freely invented one in the form of a prior intention.

1. Of course, only about 10 to 20 percent of the population can be said to be highly susceptible to hypnosis (Hilgard 1965), and even within this group the susceptibility to posthypnotic suggestion varies. But such suggestions can work. Several historic reports announced this phenomenon (Bernheim 1889; Moll 1889; Richet 1884), and more modern assessments of posthypnotic responses concur with the early research (Edwards 1965; Erickson and Erickson 1941; Sheehan and Orne 1968).

How extreme can this effect become? Would people invent prior intentions for entirely preposterous actions? In another example, Moll recounts just this:

I tell a hypnotized subject that when he wakes he is to take a flower-pot from the window, wrap it in a cloth, put it on the sofa, and bow to it three times. All which he does. When he is asked for his reasons he answers, "You know, when I woke and saw the flower-pot there I thought that as it was rather cold the flower-pot had better be warmed a little, or else the plant would die. So I wrapped it in the cloth, and then I thought that as the sofa was near the fire I would put the flower-pot on it; and I bowed because I was pleased with myself for having such a bright idea." He added that he did not consider the proceeding foolish, [because] he had told me his reasons for so acting. (153–154)

Such postaction invention of intention for hypnotically suggested actions does not always happen. Sometimes, the suggested behavior is performed but then immediately denied. Moll reported one subject who followed the suggestion to laugh but then explicitly disavowed having done it ("I did not laugh") (145). At other times, the suggested behavior is performed and no explanation emerges. Moll gave a posthypnotic suggestion, for example, that a man use an insulting expression to him on awakening. The man awakened and then paused for a few seconds, during which his face expressed some inward struggle, and then he called out "Donkey!" Asked why he would do this, the man explained only that "I felt as if I must say 'Donkey!'" (153). The man apparently wasn't quite ready to invent some prior wrong for which he was reciprocating, or to assert that Moll in fact resembled a donkey, and so was marooned with no explanation.

It would be very useful to know just when it is that people feel they can or must provide such invented reports of intention or when they can just throw up their hands and say they don't know why they did something. Part of the explanation, as Moll noted, must focus on whether there are any glimmerings in consciousness of the real (hypnotic) cause of the behavior. He mentioned that in his subjects, if the original source of the suggestion was forgotten, he was more likely to observe the invention of explanations and intentions following suggested actions. Certainly, too, there must be circumstances that cry out for intentional explanation and others that are perhaps too surprising or odd to allow a fanciful construction.

The case of posthypnotic suggestion attracted the attention of Freud and gave rise to his concept of "defensive rationalization." Freud pointed out that each of us can, at times, be like the person who carries out a posthypnotic suggestion. Almost anyone, on being "asked why he is acting this way, instead of saying that he has no idea . . . feels compelled to invent some obviously unsatisfactory reason" (Freud, 1900, 230). The psychoanalytic theory proposes that such invention of impossible intentions occurs in everyday life chiefly when prior intentions are troubling. In this theory, the reasons people offer for their behaviors after the fact may be invented to distort or cover up the true causes, which could be left out because they are unconscious, unbearable, or perhaps just unseemly.

It is more likely, however, that people invent intentions merely because they expect them. The notion of conscious agency is so easy and handy for understanding others and oneself that it is overextended to cases when it doesn't apply. Rather than a Freudian expression of human nature's darker side, then, the filling in of impossible intentions may merely reflect human nature's stupider side trying to be ideal. And, ironically, it takes human adults considerable cognitive growth and development to get smart enough to be this stupid.

Developing the Idea of Intention

We humans begin life as creatures who can't reasonably claim to have conscious will, mainly because we can't stop drooling, let alone make a "claim" of some kind (fig. 5.1). But we blossom into beings who do claim

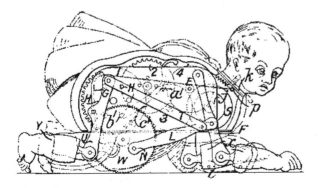

Figure 5.1
A nineteenth-century artist's rendition of an automaton baby doll, which seems somehow relevant here.

a will. How does this happen? Is it just that when we're babies and not yet verbal, we can't say what we intend? The developmental research on intention suggests that there is quite a bit more to it than this, in that children develop not only the ability to act but also the ability to preview or know about what it is they will do. Beyond learning to perform voluntary actions of all sorts, children must develop a quite separate range of capacities to think about those actions, reason about their actions' causes, and experience their prior thoughts of action as intentions. Figuring out what minds are like has been called the development of theory of mind.[2] This is, of course, the central task of *mind perception,* which was discussed in chapter 1. A big part of mind perception for any child must include developing notions of intention, conscious will, and their interrelation (Astington 1991; Zelazo, Astington, and Olson 1999).

To say that intention is part of a child's developing "theory" is not to say that a child has no plans or goals prior to the theory's development. Children do lots of voluntary actions pretty much from birth. There is evidence, for instance, that newborn infants who appear to be reaching for objects indeed are doing this, not just flailing their arms. When infants reach toward "virtual objects" seen through special glasses, and thus do not actually get to touch anything, they cry, whereas when they reach out to real objects and touch them, they don't fuss as much (Bower, Broughton, and Moore 1970). True, their disappointing inability to talk makes it impossible for us to verify the occurrence of conscious intentions in very young infants. But it is clear that as soon as language develops, very young children (2 years old or so) say and do things that suggest the operation of mental goals, planning, and forms of self-prediction (Poulin-Dubois and Schultz 1988). They report, "Gonna go now" and then they leave, or they say "Wanna banana" and then reach for one (Brown 1973). Toddlers describe their actions in advance on occasion, and so appear to have the ability to think about their actions in advance—even in words. The moral judgment and animism findings,

2. Premack and Woodruff (1978) coined this term to refer to the tendency to impute mental states to oneself and others; their interest was in whether chimps do this. For overviews of the developmental theory of mind literature, see Astington (1993); Flavell, Green, and Flavell (1995); Perner (1991a; 1991b); Wellman (1990); and Wellman and Gelman (1992).

however, suggest that very young children are not yet up to reasoning about these ideas in the way that adults often do and that the thoughts of their actions serve primarily as signals to other people of their upcoming actions.

It seems that as children develop, their speech about their actions only gradually comes to preview what they do. The Russian psychologists Vygotsky (1934) and Luria (1961) observed this in children as the development of nonsocial speech—speech used for the guidance of one's own action. These observers described the tendency in very young children to say what they were doing after they had done it. A two-year-old might say, "I throw bunny," just after throwing a stuffed animal across the room. Later the child might say "throw bunny" while throwing it, and at a yet later stage, "I've got a good mind to throw this bunny" just before doing so. This sequence would suggest that language and thought might serve merely to describe or label action after the fact in very young children but could surface as a preview to action over the course of development. The theory suggested by Vygotsky and by Luria is that the verbal representation of the action comes to have a guiding or mediating function, helping the child think about goals and determine what to do in advance.

Although the evidence on the speech mediation theory is mixed, there is a fair amount of research indicating that conscious previews of action do occur more frequently as children get older (Zivin 1979). Thus, it would seem that the occurrence of intentions and the use of intentions to compute the experience of will might make quite a bit more sense to older than to younger children. For youngsters, after all, thoughts about action may not occur very often before their actions occur and may instead perform a kind of postmortem function. Like impulsive adults, children often do things first and think afterward.

Young children don't seem to understand that intentions should occur *prior to* action. This was illustrated in a study by Abbott and Flavell (1996) in which children were asked to consider stories about another child. Each story had the following structure: The child in the story likes A and dislikes B; at his mother's urging, however, he intends to and tries to attain B; by accident he actually attains A instead. For instance, he says that he likes going to a friend's house (desired goal) and not to the skating rink, but then when mom says to go to the rink he dutifully decides to gets on a bus going there. Going to the rink, then, is apparently what he intends. However, the bus driver gets lost and, gosh, ends up at the friend's house. The question of interest is whether this child will be judged to have *intended* going to the friend's house.

The study dealt with very young children, and of course this creates vocabulary issues. You can't really expect three-year-olds to understand a word like *intention*. But it does make sense that they would understand the question Where did he try to go? When three-year-olds were asked this, their usual response was to indicate that the story character tried to go, and thought he would go, to the place he preferred and to which, by a fortunate error, he actually did go. In the sample story, they said, the child tried to go to the friend's house (where the bus driver had accidentally delivered him). By so responding, they gave no evidence of distinguishing between intention and desire. Older children made this distinction and so noted that the protagonist tried to go to the place he did not want to go (the rink). Apparently, three-year-olds set aside any sense of prior intention and accepted the lucky outcome of the action as having been just what the person "tried" to do.

This effect is not limited to perceptions of others, as children will also fill in their own intentions after action. Schult (1997) set up a situation to observe this in which children tossed a beanbag toward three colored buckets. They were asked to name in advance which color bucket they wanted to hit, and they were given a color chip to remind them of their choice. Hidden at the bottom of one bucket was a prize—a picture signaling that they had "won" (and that they could mark on a score sheet). After each time they hit a bucket, the children were asked, "Which one were you trying to hit?" The interesting case here, of course, is when the child "wins" by hitting a bucket other than the color they had said they wanted. And, indeed, when the intended bucket was missed but a picture was found, the three-year-olds answered incorrectly more often than the four- and five-year-olds. The youngest children often claimed that they had been "trying to hit" the winner all along.[3]

---

3. It turns out that adolescents with autism also have difficulty distinguishing their own intended actions from actions they perform that just happen to create desirable outcomes (Phillips, Baron-Cohen, and Rutter 1998).

This finding fits nicely with the more general observation that young children often misremember their immediately past mental states. Notable examples of this can be found in studies of false belief—experiments in which children are asked to evaluate the current status of things they previously understood in a different way.[4] In one version of this study, Perner, Leekam, and Wimmer (1987) showed children a candy box, which on examination turned out to be disappointingly full of pencils. The child was then asked what someone else will think when they first see the box. Three-year-old children often said that the other person will think there are pencils in the box, even though this box is closed and has pictures of candy on the outside. Apparently, they do not understand that the other person's beliefs will be false and instead somehow overextend their own current knowledge (of the pencils) in making their prediction.

You would think that children would recall that they themselves had once thought there was candy in the box and so perhaps appreciate the fact that this new child would think the same thing. But children at this age don't even seem to grasp that their own prior mental states were different. Gopnik and Astington (1988) found that children in the false belief situation even make errors about their own immediately past beliefs. That is, after the children had been allowed to play with a candy box and learn that it contains pencils, the experimenters asked, "When you first saw the box, before we opened it, what did you think was inside it?" More than half of the three-year-olds questioned in this study said they had originally thought there were pencils in the box. This answer shows what seems to be a profound lapse in immediate memory. Whatever delight or anticipation the child may have felt in expecting candy was somehow entirely erased by the reality of the pencils.

To explain this and other such effects, developmental theorists speak of a tendency for what is currently in the young child's perceptual experience to outweigh other information in judgments of the mind—a kind of tyranny of present perception. The curious operating rule for very young children, then, seems to be that newly learned information is assumed always to have been known. In other words, although they may well be

4. The first such study was by Wimmer and Perner (1983). Reviews of this literature can be found in Gopnik (1993), Perner (1991b), and Wellman (1990).

cute, children are lousy historians. Even when four- and five-year-olds are taught new facts about animals, for example, or are taught new names for colors, they often later insist that they knew these things from the outset (Taylor, Esbensen, and Bennett 1994). They make little distinction between the novel and the familiar and so become prey to a "knew it all along" effect.[5]

By this principle, any presently perceived situation permeates backward into estimates of the past mind. It makes sense, then, that young children make mistakes about their own mental previews with great regularity. Their view of what they had intended to do in a particular instance is based profoundly on what they found out they did. It is only with the eventual development of a representation of one's own mind, and how that mind might differ from one time to the next (Ingvar 1985), that the individual becomes capable of understanding that prior intentions might differ from currently understood consequences of action. The fact that adults can sort out prior intentions from the observed effects of their actions means that they must have constructed a representation of their own minds that has separate pockets for these things—a mind past and a mind present. Very young children seem to have just one big pocket.

Human adults, of course, start out as kids. This means that every one of us begins our lives with this odd tendency to invent false intentions after the fact. It wouldn't be surprising if we slipped back into this habit from time to time or perhaps even did it quite regularly when we knew no other grownups were looking. Still, we know it is incorrect. The development of the idea of an agent gives adults a perspective with which we can see that intentions must have at least one special characteristic: They can't occur for the first time after the action is over. To adhere to our notion of the ideal human agent, we presume that conscious intentions must occur prior to the action they apparently cause.

Unconscious Action

Not all human actions begin with conscious intentions. Much of what we do seems to surface from unconscious causes, and such causation provides a major challenge to our ideal of conscious agency. The unconscious

5. Adults do this a bit as well but not nearly as much (Begg et al. 1996).

causation of action is the fly in the ideal agent's ointment, the blemish on what would otherwise be a well-formed conscious goal seeker. So, even after children develop the idea of intention and apply it effectively to much of what they do, they encounter regular instances in which they don't seem to have intended their action. These instances prompt a fix-up routine, an attempt to return to the ideal. To get a sense of how this happens, it is useful to consider unconscious action itself in detail.

How would you know if you were doing something unconsciously? If you do something consciously, of course, knowing seems to come with doing. But if you do something unconsciously, you are by definition out of the loop, perhaps only to become aware of what you are doing after the fact. You could be doing a bunch of different things unconsciously this minute, perhaps to find out later, or more likely, never to know at all. Right now, are you ignoring that it's time to phone someone you promised to call? Are you sitting with poor posture? Damaging your eyesight by reading in low light? Making the person you borrowed this book from mad that it hasn't been returned? Twiddling with your hair or clothes in an absentminded way? Failing to get the exercise you promised yourself to get today? Obviously, you can't be conscious of everything you're doing—even holding perfectly still can be a variety of acts, not all of which you may know or understand. It is inevitable that you are doing many things unconsciously.

With this in mind, the odd example of a person responding to posthypnotic suggestion may not seem so odd at all. Each of us does many things throughout our lives that we might as well have been hypnotized into doing because we will never know we did them. This ghost army of unconscious actions provides a serious challenge to the notion of an ideal human agent. The greatest contradictions to our ideal of conscious agency occur when we find ourselves behaving with no conscious thought of what we are doing. When life creates all the inevitable situations in which we find ourselves acting without appropriate prior conscious thoughts, we must protect the illusion of conscious will by trying to make sense of our action. We invent relevant thoughts according to the template that conscious agency suggests. We may rue that we did not have the appropriate thought beforehand, or even without evidence that the thought was absent, we may simply assume that it was fully in place all along.

Unconscious action is possible because actions and our knowledge of them are different things. Action and knowledge of action stand in the relation of object and representation. This means that while actually hugging a puppy is an action, anything at all that reminds us of hugging a puppy which is not itself hugging a puppy can qualify as a representation of the action.[6] This separability of action and its mental representation means that acts can be done that we never knew (because we never encountered or thought about what they were); acts can be done that we weren't thinking about (because we didn't have our existing knowledge of them in consciousness); and acts can be done that we can't think about (because we can't remember what we may have intended or meant by them). Unconscious action results from problems, then, in *action identification,* in *thoughts of action,* and in *memory for intention.* It is important to examine each of these processes to see just how it is that unconscious actions can arise. These are what our ideal of conscious agency must be protected from.

6. There are two immediate complications here. The first complication is that actions can themselves be representations. Bruner (1964) called this *enactive representation* and pointed out that sometimes when we don't have words or images for something we may act it out, perhaps not even for communicative purposes. So there could be cases when doing something serves as a representation of doing something else. This need not worry us much because the act that serves to represent another act serves most of the functions of a thought and is usually quite distinguishable from it. When I grimace as a way of thinking about lifting something heavy, for example, the grimacing is easy to distinguish temporally and functionally from the lifting.

The second complication is that thoughts often have the features of actions. When you purposefully study a poem to memorize it, for example, you perform a series of mental actions—looking at the poem repeatedly, saying it to yourself, putting it down and trying to see whether you can say it again, and so on. This thinking and rethinking certainly seems to qualify as voluntary action by several criteria. Thus, it is possible to suggest that a thought about thought could sometimes look just like a thought about action. In the case of the thought about thought, of course, the first is a representation of the second. Having the desire to think about going to the beach, for example, involves a representational thought and an "active" thought.

All this is to say that the distinction we need to make here between thought and action is better understood as a distinction between either physical or mental representation and either physical or mental behavior—but thought and action are nicer words.

Action Identification

Most human actions are open to multiple identifications or descriptions. An action one might call "sunning on the beach" could perhaps also be described as "vacationing" or "getting a tan" or "lying down" or "relaxing" or even "exposing oneself to harmful cancer-causing ultraviolet rays"; the list continues indefinitely. It is not just that different identifications of actions are synonyms because each identification can suggest a unique meaning of the action. "Walking into a party," for instance, is not a synonym for "winning a door prize," even though both may identify the same action under the right circumstances. This indeterminacy of action has interested philosophers for some time (Anscombe 1957; Goldman 1970), and it suggests a variety of psychological observations that Robin Vallacher and I have studied under the rubric of *action identification theory* (Vallacher and Wegner 1985; 1987; Wegner and Vallacher 1986).

The central idea of this theory is that whereas people may think about any action in many ways, they typically think about an action in just one way. Although the person could be said to know the action through all its various descriptions, the theory proposes that the person's effective knowledge of the action at any one moment is limited to one identity— usually the identity that the person has in consciousness or has most recently held in consciousness. The person's conscious identification of the action can range, then, along a dimension from low-level identifications that indicate how the action is done ("I'm waving my hand") to higher-level, more encompassing identifications that indicate why or with what effect the action is done ("I'm signaling the waiter to bring on the cheese dip"). This flexibility in the naming of actions suggests that they might be undertaken under one identity and later recognized under others.

Consider the case of the action of "shooting a person." A burglar might go to an empty home with the conscious plan of stealing a TV and be carrying a gun in case he might need to protect himself. Hearing noises in the next room, he pulls out the gun. At this moment, if the homeowner steps into the room, the burglar might think of the next action in many ways. He might "protect himself," "aim at the sound," "squeeze the trigger," "commit a felony," "take a human life," "shoot someone," "make a mess," "keep from getting caught," or yet more things—all in the same action. Now, it is widely believed, and rightly so, that *"to the extent that someone is paying attention to their behavior,* they do not normally allow themselves to perform actions without reason" (Marcel 1988, 146–147). Yet the burglar in this case might merely be attending to the behavior of "aiming" or "squeezing" and so pretty much miss the point of what the action is all about. The action could well be murder, and in this sense, it is committed without reason.

A moral observer might be inclined at this moment in the burglar's life to shout out, "For God's sake, you idiot, you're about to kill someone." But this particular facet of the action's meaning might be quite in the background for a nervous burglar in a dark room fumbling with the trigger of an unwieldy pistol. Thus, an action that started out in the early planning stages as "protecting myself" might be achieved in the heat of the moment merely as "pulling the trigger" and understood only at some point later in terms of its larger meaning and moral overtones as "taking a life." Although the burglar may have done all the things that would allow his behavior subsequently to be viewed as intended, the explicit intention corresponding to the most important identification of his action—at least to someone reading the lurid story in the paper later on— may not have been in his mind beforehand or as the action was done.

In a number of experiments, it has been found that people do change their identifications of actions over time in just this way. Wegner, Vallacher, and Kelly (1983) found, for example, that people who are getting married will commonly identify what they are doing—if asked far in advance of the ceremony—in a romantic sense such as "showing my love." Yet if they are asked to describe the act of getting married a day or two before the wedding, love is no longer in mind and instead they mention all the details ("getting flowers," "finding the proper outfit," "walking down the aisle," etc.). And if they are queried some weeks after the wedding, they see it differently again, usually as "getting in-laws" or "becoming a member of a family." The identification of action seems to change over time, often following this very pattern—from a meaningful identification, through a morass of details, and back to a meaningful identification that may or may not be the same as the original one.[7] People in

7. This process of identification change is illustrated in several studies, for example, Wegner et al. (1984).

advance of getting married might not want to think that they are merely getting in-laws, and those who are sadder and wiser afterwards might no longer adhere to their initial romantic idea of the act as showing love. However, the transition from one meaning to the other can occur through a kind of deconstruction of the act's meaning that happens on becoming immersed in all the thoughts of how (rather than why) it is done.

The job of discerning intentions, in this light, can be excruciatingly difficult. The particular identity of an act can shimmer and fluctuate over time, touching on different meanings at a rapid rate.[8] Intentions may only hold still to be named and catalogued in those special moments when we are called upon to produce publicly reportable meanings for action. This might happen when we are specifically asked to explain why we did something or when we self-consciously pause to introspect on the meaning of what we have done. Or intentions might come to mind at the right point just before action and so fuel the inference that they caused the action as it was identified. In essence, the fact that there are different identities for any action suggests that people will inevitably be doing some things unconsciously no matter what. Unless they act very, very slowly and think about it so much their heads hurt, people are doomed to do many things they don't consciously consider, and they will do this every single time they act.[9]

Thoughts of Action

Unconscious action can also be understood in terms of what a person is thinking consciously and unconsciously at the time of action. It is possible that both kinds of representation of action might contribute to the causation of an action, and in either event we would say that real mental causation had taken place. Although the notion of the ideal conscious agent only allows for causation by conscious thoughts, we must consider

8. Vallacher et al. (1998) explore the idea that action identifications vary over time.

9. There is a whole lot more I could say about action identification, but since much of it has already been said, it seems silly to repeat it here. After all, this is only a footnote. The fuller story is in Vallacher and Wegner (1985). In essence, we tried to develop an operating system for a human agent based on the premise that people always have some idea of what they are doing.

as well the whole range of thoughts or mental states that might influence action without consciousness.

What sorts of unconscious thoughts could cause action? Certainly, Freud's notion of the unconscious mind tapped a broad definition of unconscious mental causation. His postaction interpretations often presumed whole complexes of unconscious mental material influencing the simplest action. A woman calling her husband by her father's name, for example, could provide grist for a lengthy interpretive exercise invoking unconscious thoughts of her childhood, her sexuality, and all the usual psychoanalytic gremlins. This view of the unconscious is far too sweeping, allowing unconscious thoughts to be the length of novels. It is probably the case that the unconscious thoughts powering action are more rudimentary.

A contemporary version of the theory of unconscious mental causation was voiced by Jerome Bruner (1957) in terms of the idea of *readiness*. Unconscious thought can be understood as a kind of readiness to think of something consciously. Bruner suggested that some limited array of mental states guiding perception and action could be active yet not conscious. The unconscious readiness to think of food could make us notice it is time for lunch, just as a readiness to think of competition could make us punch the accelerator and speed past another driver. Such readiness has been described in terms of thoughts that are *accessible* at the time of action (Bargh and Chartrand 1999; Higgins and King 1981; Wegner and Smart 1997). An accessible thought is one that the person may or may not be able to report as conscious but that has some measurable influence on the person's conscious thoughts or observable actions.

Thoughts can become accessible in several different ways. In some cases, thoughts are chronically accessible for a person (Bargh and Pratto 1986), as when a depressed person regularly tends to think about failure (Gotlib and McCann 1984; Wenzlaff and Bates 1998) or a person with a phobia finds thoughts of the phobic object always easy to bring to mind (Watts et al. 1986). At other times, a thought may be accessible as a consequence of the person's contact with some cue in the environment. African American students who take a test that they are told is diagnostic of intellectual ability, for instance, show temporarily increased accessibility of thoughts about the racial stereotype of African Americans; in a word completion task, they become more likely to respond to the prompt "LA _ _" by filling in LAZY (Steele and Aronson 1995). People who try to concentrate on a thought can also increase its accessibility intentionally for a while, but paradoxically people who attempt not to think about a thought also will increase its accessibility briefly as well (Wegner and Erber 1992). However the thought is made accessible, though, the point is that it can then produce further thought or behavior even though it is technically unconscious.

Conscious thoughts are in mind and can be reported *now*, whereas accessible thoughts are not there yet and must be understood instead as having a potential to rise into consciousness. Distinguishing between conscious thought and accessible thought suggests that there are three ways in which a thought could be activated in mind prior to action (Wegner and Smart 1997). First, a thought might be conscious but not accessible. Such *surface activation* of the thought could occur, for example, when a person is trying to concentrate (without much luck) on studying for a test. Thoughts of the study materials might well be conscious, but thoughts of other things might be so accessible as to jump to mind at every turn and distract the person from the study topic. The thought of the test, then, would be conscious but not for long, because it was not simultaneously accessible.

A second way in which a thought could be present in mind prior to action would be if it were both conscious and accessible. Such *full activation* often happens for things we find deeply interesting or compelling, as when we are wallowing in some favorite thought of a splendid vacation, a fine restaurant, a great love, or a delicious revenge. Life's greatest preoccupations often take the form of thoughts that are both in consciousness and also next in line to enter consciousness. We think of these things and, at the same time, have a high level of readiness to think of them some more. With full activation, moreover, we are seldom surprised with what our minds do, because with the thought already in consciousness, we know all along on what path the accessibility of this thought will continue to lead us.

The third form of cognitive activation suggested by this analysis concerns a thought that is accessible but not conscious. Such *deep activation* describes the nature of much of our mental life, but it is the mental life of the unconscious. Deep activation occurs, for example, when we have a conscious desire to have a thought—when we have a memory on the tip of the tongue, or are on the verge of a the solution to a problem we've not yet achieved. These thoughts are not yet in mind, but we are searching for them and they are thus likely to pop up at any moment. Deep activation also happens when we have a thought we have actively suppressed from consciousness.

When we try not to think about something, we may find we can indeed get away from it for a while. We achieve a kind of uneasy mental state in which, while the thought is not in consciousness, it is somehow very ready to jump back to mind. In these instances of deep activation, we may typically be surprised, and sometimes amazed or dismayed, when the accessible thought does have some influence. It may simply intrude into consciousness, popping into mind, or it may influence other things, such as our word choice, our focus of attention, our interpretation of events, or our observable action. These intrusions can sometimes alert us to the state of deep activation, but of course when they happen, the state no longer exists and is replaced by full activation. The thought is now conscious, and if it remains accessible, the characteristics of full activation have been met.

We can speak of thoughts influencing action from any of these states of activation—surface, deep, or full activation (Wegner and Smart 1997). The interesting point here is that a person will only know something about this causation if the thought is in surface or full activation (fig. 5.2), that is, when the thought is conscious. When deeply activated thoughts (accessible but not conscious) cause action, they can do so without the person's experiencing any will at all. It is only when a thought is conscious prior to action that it can enter into the person's interpretation of personal agency and so influence the person's experience of will. When a thought is not conscious prior to action yet is accessible, it may influence action and leave the person with no clue about how the action came about. In this event, the person will normally experience a reduced sense of conscious will and perhaps begin looking elsewhere for the action's causation. This is how we can explain the automatisms—cases when people do things influenced by nonconscious behavior priming (Bargh and Chartrand 1999; Dijksterhuis and van Knippenberg 1998).

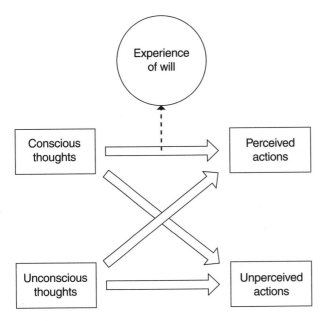

Figure 5.2
The experience of conscious will occurs only when conscious thoughts are seen as causing perceived actions. If unconscious thoughts cause actions, will is not experienced; and if actions are unperceived, will is not experienced either.

The experience of will is not likely to occur when action is caused by unconscious thoughts.

The experience of will is also unlikely when the action itself goes unnoticed. When actions are subtle, when they involve only small changes or variations in movements already underway, or when they occur in the context of other actions or events that demand more attention, the actions may not be noticed enough to start an explanatory exercise. The process of assessing apparent mental causation, then, may never be undertaken. It is only in the special case when conscious thoughts precede easily perceived action that a causal attribution of action to thought may be made. People may invent false intentions after the fact of the action, then, when they have been led to perform an action by unconscious thoughts, or when they fail to notice the action until some later time and subsequently find they do not recall the thoughts that may have preceded it.

Intention Memory

Actions and their meanings are stored separately in memory. Otherwise, we would always know exactly what we intend and never suffer the embarrassment of walking into a room and wondering what it was we wanted there. Just as there is a system of mind (and body) that remembers the actions themselves, there must be an *intention memory system* that encodes, stores, and retrieves our thoughts about what we intend. There are three types of intention memory, each corresponding to a point in time at which a person may retrieve the intended meaning or identity of an action. These include *prospective memory* for intention (remembering what one will do), *synchronous memory* for intention (remembering what one is doing), and *retrospective memory* for intention (remembering after acting what one thought one would do).

Prospective memory is involved in remembering plans for action (Brandimonte, Einstein, and McDaniel 1996; Morris 1992). When we devise plans, it is nice to remember them at least long enough to arrive at the time for the action with the plans still in mind. Otherwise, we will simply forget to do what we have intended. In some cases, prospective memory is short-term memory; a person may just think of or rehearse the action for a few moments before it is time to do it. A common example of this is when we are trying to remember the brilliant thing we've just thought of to say while some windbag at the other end of the conversation finishes holding forth. Another form of prospective memory covers longer periods (Kvavilashvili 1992), as when we must remember to do something later in the day or week or month (e.g., remember to take medicine), or after some triggering event (e.g., remember to wipe feet after walking in mud).

These preaction ideas of what will be done are often quite easily remembered. In fact, Kurt Lewin (1951) proposed that the things we get in mind to do will each create their own tension systems, packages of psychological discomfort that ride along with them until their associated action is complete and the tension is discharged. He suggested that this is why we often become obsessed with incomplete tasks, coming back to them again and again while we forget things that are completed. The tendency to remember incomplete tasks better than complete ones is the *Zeigarnik effect,* named after Lewin's student who first tested the idea (Zeigarnik 1927). There is a great deal of research on the phenomenon, and while some of it calls the effect into question, the current view is that memory for unfinished tasks is indeed enhanced compared to memory for those that are finished (Goschke and Kuhl 1993; Marsh, Hicks, and Bink 1998; Martin and Tesser 1989; Wicklund and Gollwitzer 1982).

Enhanced memory for unfinished acts implies a comparative reduction in memory for acts that are finished. In short, performing an action itself tends to erase the memory of the act's intention. If people will often forget tasks for the simple reason that the tasks have been completed, this signals a loss of contact with their initial intentions once actions are over—and thus a susceptibility to revised intentions. Moreover, people may forget their own intended action as soon as *anyone* completes the act (Lewis and Franklin 1944). The intentions we form and do not yet enact may be quickly forgotten if we believe that other people in our group have done them. All this reveals a remarkable fluidity in our moment-to-moment memory for actions. Initial ideas of what to do can fade rapidly when the action appears to have been done. And this, of course, leaves room for the later invention of what might have been intended.

Synchronous memory for intention is the next type of intention memory. This simply involves remembering the action's meaning when we are in the process of performing the action. This is convenient for answering the person who asks, "What are you doing?" when we are part way through doing something really strange. But synchronous intention memory is more deeply useful for remembering parts of the action if they are not well-integrated and fluid, for confirming in the course of action whether we're doing a decent job, and for knowing when we're done and can go on to the next thing. For that matter, ongoing act memory is also useful for determining whether, when a certain action involves our bodies, we are the ones to whom it can be attributed (e.g., Barresi and Moore 1996). To perform these important services, it is useful to think of intention during action as filling a *current act register,* a memory storage area devoted to the symbolic representation of what we are now doing. Without such a register, we would not be able to communicate or think about actions unfolding and might lose track of them in mid-course. Meacham (1979) has called this function a matter of "memory for the present."

We don't normally think of memory for the present as a big problem. The present is here and now, and if we forget what it is, we can just look around us and, yes, gosh, there it is. However, the loss of synchronous act memory can have some interesting and even tragic repercussions. When does this happen? The lack of awareness of an intention that is observed in some of the classic automatisms appears to signal a failure of current act memory. A person may be engaged in an action and have forgotten what was being done. As a result, the action seems to be occurring without awareness. This possibility was specifically noted in one study of automatic writing: "As the experiment progressed we came to realize more and more the extent to which a reported lapse of awareness might be a lapse of memory instead" (Downey and Anderson 1915, 193). The determination that a particular moment of writing is automatic depends on the person's current memory for what is being done. Not remembering what was intended as it is being done counts quite clearly as unawareness of action. This inability to remember what one is doing during the action can translate into a failure to recall the nature of the action afterwards as well. So the absence of an intention in the current act register pretty much dooms the person to postaction interpretation of intention.

Without a memory of what the self is currently doing, a person is left with some fairly odd options for postaction interpretation. As we saw in the case of posthypnotic suggestion, the person could deny that any action took place or could simply declare the source of the action unknown and the action inexplicable. Another clear alternative would be inventing intentions. These options hold in common the assumption that the person continues to view the body's behaviors as emanating from the self and that explanations therefore will be made in terms of that actor.

Ongoing behavior for which there is no entry in the current act register could also be accounted for in a very different way—as the doing of an agent other than the self. This possibility seems highly unlikely for normal people under normal conditions, but it does occur in certain cases of schizophrenia. Christopher Frith (1987; 1992; 1994) has proposed that there is an impairment of memory for current action in some people with schizophrenia. He has suggested that such impairment is responsible for the phenomena of alien control that they experience when they hear voices or experience their thoughts or actions as those of someone else. We have already discussed some of the evidence regarding auditory hallucinations, but it is instructive to examine, too, the research on synchronous intent memory in schizophrenia.

In one study, Frith and Done (1989) arranged for schizophrenic patients suffering from alien control, and other patients without this experience, to play a video game that measured memory for current action. The player used a joystick to shoot at birds coming from the left or the right, and the video bullet took a long time to reach the target (2.8 seconds). At any time, the player could correct an error by changing aim to shoot the bird coming from the other direction. Although all players did equally well under these conditions, the alien control patients experienced a noteworthy failure when a small variation was made in the game: Barriers were placed to hide the trajectory of their bullet for the first 2 seconds after the shot, leaving them with only a brief interval in which to see where they had shot and to correct any wrong moves. Under these conditions, the patients with alien control symptoms performed far less well than did the comparison group. Mlakar, Jensterle, and Frith (1994) observed much the same thing among alien control patients who were asked to make drawings without immediate visual feedback on their performance. They had great difficulty keeping track of what they were doing.

This characteristic of schizophrenia suggests that people with this problem might be deeply distractible because they constantly fail to remember what they're doing. In fact, this is a common observation. Back in the heyday of research on the Zeigarnik effect, a set of studies by Rickers-Ovsiankina (1937) focused specifically on the degree to which people with schizophrenia showed the magnified memory for incomplete tasks that is common in normal individuals. She observed that people with schizophrenia "tend towards undirected playful activities, which do not lead to any definite outcome. Striking on a xylophone without attempting to produce a melody is an example" (179). And, indeed, she found a clear tendency in normal individuals to resume tasks that were interrupted, whereas this did not occur nearly as often for people with schizophrenia. The lack of a continued memory of current action, as suggested by Frith's hypothesis, could account for such findings. This conclusion depends on the idea that the same psychological cause may underlie different symptoms simply because they co-occur in this disorder, of course, and this interpretation is tempting but not beyond doubt. The analysis of a wider range of disorders in terms of this model, as undertaken by Frith, Blakemore, and Wolpert (1999), holds promise for understanding how breakdowns in current act memory might influence a variety of human abilities.

Taken together, these observations suggest that the current act register is a piece of mental architecture that allows us to produce action with the illusion of conscious will. Without a well-functioning memory of what one is doing now, any actions which ensue that are hard to predict from past thoughts might seem instead to come from elsewhere, perhaps even outside the self. Actions that are not known as they are being produced— that is, that are not coded in the current register—might be entirely disowned and experienced as alien or perhaps simply disregarded. Knowing that our actions are our own seems so entirely natural and automatic that it is startling to realize that such ownership only occurs as a result of a finely tuned system that adheres the knowledge of action to the action itself. Breaks in this system can range from the profound in schizophrenia to the minor lapses that occur in absentminded behavior among normal individuals (Reason 1984). Just as people with schizophrenia may hear voices, the rest of us may wonder who rearranged our sock drawer or moved the teapot when we don't recall doing these things ourselves.

The final type of intention memory is retrospective memory for intention—knowing what we did after the action is done. Presumably, of course, we all expect that our retrospective memory of intention will correspond nicely with our prospective and synchronous memories. We presume that the same intention will be remembered after action that we anticipated beforehand and that we embraced as the action occurred. As it happens, however, a number of observations indicate that what we think afterwards about what we were doing can diverge quite dramatically from what we thought we were doing before or during the action. The matter of retrospective memory for intention is the focus of the rest of this chapter.

Our discussion of unconscious thought can be summed up simply: We don't always know what we are doing. Whether our thoughts of action are unconscious because of shifting action identification, because of action instigation through thoughts that are only accessible and not conscious, or because of lapses in memory for intention, these cases provide serious challenges to our conception of ourselves as pretenders to ideal agency. We can't be ideal agents if we didn't consciously intend *each and every action we come to understand we have performed.* This means that we must respond to the challenge of unconscious action creatively—by finding, inventing, or constructing notions of what our intentions must have been whenever we find ourselves falling short as ideal agents.

The Confabulation of Intentions

Aesop knew that people, or foxes who act like them, may change what they say about their intentions (fig. 5.3). The fox whose dearly desired snack turned into "sour grapes" reminds us that initial intentions ("I'd

Figure 5.3
The fox in Aesop's fable wanted the grapes but couldn't reach them, so she decided that they were sour and not worth having. This revision of her initial intention suggests that it was easily clouded in her mind. Marcus Gheerhaerts' 1674 engraving for L'Estrange's translation of the fables.

love some grapes") can be readily overwritten by replacements ("These grapes are no doubt sour, and I didn't want them in the first place"). As it turns out, such intention invention stands at the center of several psychological theories. Studies of cognitive dissonance suggest that intention confabulation occurs from conflict between old and new intentions; self-perception theory alerts us to the confabulation of intention that may flow from the apparent absence of old intentions. Finally, the most unusual circumstances of invented intention occur when brain damage leaves the left side of the brain interpreting what the right side is doing.[10] Each of these perspectives illustrates the confabulation of intention through a different conceptual lens, but together they have provided a consistent array of evidence to show that people often revise what they think they intended to do after their action is complete. This confabulation protects the ideal of conscious agency from the fact that actions are caused by unconscious processes.

Cognitive Dissonance

With the theory of cognitive dissonance, Leon Festinger (1957) proposed that people will revise their attitudes to justify their action. In a nutshell, the theory says this happens because people are motivated to avoid having their thoughts in a dissonant relationship, and they feel uncomfortable when dissonance occurs. The strongest dissonance arises when a person does something that is inconsistent with a preexisting attitude or desire. So, for instance, buying a house that has an aging, decrepit furnace would create cognitive dissonance. The person goes ahead and buys the house knowing full well that there will be a big furnace problem. The theory proposes that when this happens, the person will change his or her attitude to make it consonant with the behavior. The attitude (in this case, of neutrality toward the house) is relatively changeable because it exists only in the person's private thoughts, whereas the behavior of buying the house (with its broken heating plant) is typically public and much more difficult to undo. The person comes to like the house that was purchased,

---

10. In *Altered Egos*, the neurologist Todd Feinberg (2001) has woven a variety of case studies of brain-damaged patients into a lucid account of the maintenance of a sense of self through confabulation. This book is a key piece in the puzzle of how the agent self is constructed.

strangely enough, for the very reason that the furnace is faulty. The furnace remains unloved, but the house is seen as desirable because it was purchased in spite of that furnace.

In everyday parlance, the theory merely says that people justify the things they do. This much had been observed in research that predated Festinger's theory. For instance, in studies of laboratory role playing by Janis and King (1954), participants who agreed to make a speech for which they played the role of someone who believed strongly in an issue were found afterwards to have come to believe in the issue themselves, especially in comparison to those who had simply to listen to a speech on the topic by someone else. The role players' attitudes moved in the direction of the speech and so became consistent with their behavior. Imagine: You might get someone to pretend to be an opera lover (no one actually starts out life that way) and the person would come to like opera more as a result. Festinger's theory took such observations a step further by noting that such changes are particularly likely to occur *the more the person feels in advance that there were good reasons not to perform the behavior,* and *the more the person feels he or she chose the behavior and was responsible for it.*[11]

These principles are illustrated nicely in an experiment on a kind of role playing by Linder, Cooper, and Jones (1967). Participants for this study were students who were asked to write essays praising a ban on speakers at their college—a silly position that all disagreed with in advance. For some of them, the pay for writing the essay was announced as 50 cents, whereas for others it was $2.50 (at that time, although the latter sum was actually a fair wage for writing an essay, 50 cents was still cheap). A further variation in the experiment manipulated the perception of choice: Some participants were led to believe that they had considerable personal choice on whether to write an essay—the experimenter explained at the outset that after he had described the study they could decide for themselves whether or not to write the essay. For others, this emphasis on choice was not made.

11. Festinger (1957) didn't say precisely these things about dissonance, but this gloss on his theory follows the understanding of these processes that follows from current research. For reviews of this literature, see Cooper and Fazio (1984), Eagly and Chaiken (1993), and Wicklund and Brehm (1976).

Everyone did write an essay, probably because of the subtle social pressure to finish something one has started for an experiment. But, as compared to participants who were not given the sense of choice (an illusory sense, because everyone did write the essay), those who perceived choice showed a classic cognitive dissonance effect. The ones who wrote the essay against their own attitudes for 50 cents believed it more afterwards than did those who wrote for the larger sum of $2.50. Performing a dissonant act under conditions designed to arouse a feeling of choice made people become more positive toward the topic they were paid less to espouse. These results suggest that people will become more positive toward their action, the more negative the consequences of it that they knew in advance of choosing to do it. This curious turn of events—in which people come to like something more the *less* rewarding it is—is the hallmark of dissonance phenomena and is surely the reason that many psychologists have studied dissonance over the years. It is always interesting to learn about seemingly irrational behavior, and liking things precisely because they are unrewarding seems irrational indeed.

Now, although cognitive dissonance theory is usually understood to be about attitudes and attitude change, it can also be understood to characterize a process of the revision of intention.[12] This is because dissonance always arises in the context of action or the choice to act. The change that occurs after the person has written a counterattitudinal essay, for instance, can be understood as a change in conceptualizing what was intended. From an initial state in which the intention to write the essay is weak or contrary (as marked by the negative attitude on the topic), the person moves to perform the action in response to complex pressures that are not fully represented in terms of any intentions. But having now done the act, and recalling having been told both that it was "your choice" and that a paltry 50 cents would be the pay, the person develops a positive attitude toward the act. This new attitude, in turn, suggests that there must have been a prior conscious intention that would predict

12. Researchers studying dissonance have not made a practice of asking people their intentions, but when they do, it typically turns out that attitudes do predict intentions in this way (e.g., Aronson, Fried, and Stone 1991). The relation between attitudes and behavioral intentions outside cognitive dissonance theory has been well-established (e.g., Ajzen 1985; 1991).

writing that essay for only 50 cents. Following the action of essay writing, in other words, the person may develop the idea that there was a prior intention that would predict the action ("I wanted to write an essay on what I believe").

The key process underlying this transformation, at least for dissonance theory, is the resolution of conflict between the person's old intention (which wouldn't be sufficient to motivate the act or might even cause its opposite) and the action itself. In this sense, the theory suggests that actions can "sneak by" without sufficient intention, but that once having sneaked, they can become unpleasantly inconsistent with those contrary prior intentions and prompt the revision that creates a new intention. At some level of mind, then, the person knows that there is an insufficient old intention. The theory suggests that the conflict of the action with the old intention is what motivates the creation of the new intention.

The circumstances that create dissonance effects say some important things about how the confabulation of intention comes about. Apparently, the circumstances in which the action occurs must suggest to the person that the action was freely chosen and must also allow the person to believe that the consequences of the action were known or at least foreseeable (Wicklund and Brehm 1976). People do not commonly resolve dissonance for *fait accompli* consequences of action. So, for instance, dissonance forces might lead one to become particularly happy with an automobile one had purchased while knowing that it needed an engine overhaul ("It must be a marvelous car indeed if I bought it even with that engine problem"). But learning about the overhaul after the choice would do nothing to enhance one's love of the car and instead would probably undermine it. *Fait accompli* consequences of action do not entail conscious will, and so do not lead through dissonance to the confabulation of intention.

Self-Perception

A different way to explain the confabulation of intention is to say that we have no attitudes at all before action and instead often compute our attitudes and the associated intentions *only* after we have acted. If this is true, then intentions are often matters of self-perception following action, not of self-knowledge prior to action or of any conflict between action and prior intents or attitudes. In fact, this was suggested before cognitive dissonance theory was born. Bertrand Russell (1921, 31) said it this way: "I believe that the discovery of our own motives can only be made by the same process by which we discover other people's, namely, the process of observing our actions and inferring the desire which could prompt them." Subsequently, this idea was expressed yet more fully by Gilbert Ryle in *The Concept of Mind* (1949), a volume that served as a guide for the behaviorist philosophy of mind. Ryle proposed that the various reasons we invent to account for our behavior might all be an exercise in creative interpretation, no matter whether we invent them before or after we act.

Ryle's insight was to compare the perspective of a person performing an action with that of an observer of the action—for example, a speaker and a listener. Although we normally think that the speaker knows everything about what is being said while the listener knows nothing, the difference between them may not be that great. Ryle granted that "the listener may be frequently surprised to find the speaker saying something, while the speaker is only seldom surprised," and he also noted that "while the speaker intends to say certain fairly specific things, his hearer can anticipate only roughly what sorts of topics are going to be discussed." He went on to argue, however, that "the differences are differences of degree, not of kind. The superiority of the speaker's knowledge over that of the listener does not indicate that he has Privileged Access to facts of a type inevitably inaccessible to the listener, but only that he is in a very good position to know what the listener is in a very poor position to know" (179). Ryle reasoned that the internal states such as attitudes or intentions that we often attribute to a person's "Privileged Access" to some repository of his or her own mind could well be no more than the result of the person's self-perceptions, derived from processes like those that might be applied by outside observers. Perhaps people don't just *know* their own attitudes or intentions but instead *discern* them because they are in a particularly good position to figure them out.

In a clever theoretical advance, Daryl Bem (1967; 1972) applied this analysis to the cognitive dissonance studies. He reasoned that one might not need to propose an internal tension resulting from dissonant behavior if, when people behave, they simply observe themselves and draw inferences about their attitudes and intentions from what they find they have done and the circumstances in which they did it. So, when a person chooses Thai food over German food, for example, and does this despite the fact that the German meal is nearby and the Thai restaurant is across town through traffic, any observer would probably infer that the person prefers noodle to strudel. In fact, the person might make this same inference. It could be that the person simply infers a positive attitude toward Thai food after making this choice and so actually embraces that attitude. The "changed" attitude does not come from dissonance between the chosen behavior and some prior preference for German food. Rather, the person just self-perceived. In this analysis, the behavior itself comes from subtle situational cues of which the person is unaware (perhaps the person was unconsciously primed to recall a pleasant flirtation that once happened over satay at a Thai restaurant?). Prior conscious intention is simply not a factor. Instead, intention is invented after the fact in the process of self-perception.

This logic suggests that people who merely *observe* a participant in a dissonance experiment should estimate the participant's attitudes quite correctly. And indeed, this is just what happens. Bem (1967) tested this by having two groups of observers each learn of a participant in a dissonance study. One group heard of a participant who wrote an essay for $5, whereas another group learned that a participant wrote an essay for 50 cents. In an original dissonance study exactly like this (Cohen 1962), of course, the essay topic had been assumed to be something that countered participants' initial attitudes. And in the original dissonance study, it was found that participants in the 50 cent condition changed more in the direction of the essay than did those in the $5 condition, presumably because of the dissonance between their initial attitudes and the attitudes they espoused in the essay. In Bem's observer study, no one made any mention of initial attitudes. Still, the groups of observers of people in each of these conditions were found to make estimates of the person's attitude that corresponded precisely to the dissonance prediction: they thought that the 50 cent person believed the essay more than did the $5 person. It seems the observers asked themselves, "What sort of person would write an essay in favor of this position for this amount of money?"

When the money was less, they inferred that the person had a stronger intention to write the essay because he must have believed it.

This finding suggests that conflict with an initial attitude may not be critical for the occurrence of dissonance-type effects. Observers didn't know anything about such initial attitudes and still were able to guess postbehavior attitudes quite nicely. Perhaps, then, this is just the same position that the original participants were in when they wrote essays for money. Their attitudes or intentions may have been quite obscure to begin with and may only have become clear after they perceived what they had done and the circumstances in which they had done it. Seeing that they had written an essay in circumstances that would not justify this—there was very little money—they perceived themselves as believers in the essay. Just as Ryle had suggested, people seemed to be observers of themselves. Even without "Privileged Access" to their own attitudes, they nonetheless figured out what their attitudes ought to be by using the same information available to any observer of their behavior.

Self-perception was highlighted in a different way in a further study by Bem and McConnell (1970). They asked people who had written counterattitudinal essays to report not their final (postessay) opinion on the issue but their *prior* opinion. People couldn't do this. Instead, these reports of prior attitudes mirrored faithfully the standard dissonance effect: Participants led to believe that they had a high degree of choice in whether to write the essay reported that they had agreed with the essay *all along,* whereas those led to believe they had low choice reported no such agreement. What happened, apparently, was that people looking back after they had written the essay had no conscious memory of their pre-essay attitudes. It is as though the confabulation of intention erases its tracks, leaving people with no memory of ever having wanted other than what they currently see as their intention.

One way to interpret this finding is to say that it undermines the idea that people in the high-choice condition experienced dissonance. Bem and McConnell said just this, arguing that the participants' failure to remember their previously conflicting thoughts indicated that there really was no mental conflict of the kind that dissonance theory suggests. At the same time, one might also argue that such failure is in fact evidence of a successful conflict resolution process and so supports a dissonance theory interpretation. A number of experiments subsequently focused on this problem, and it is probably safe to say that neither theory is clear enough about what happens to prior attitudes following the action to allow us to decide between them on this point (Greenwald 1975; Ross and Schulman 1973; Snyder and Ebbesen 1972).

The question of whether dissonance or self-perception theory offers a better account of these effects turns out to hinge on a different issue— the occurrence of the actual bodily tension created by dissonance. Self-perception theory holds that there is no conflict and that there should be no experience or sign of an emotional tension state when people behave in a way that counters their attitudes. Dissonance theory, on the other hand, portrays the process as driven by the unpleasant emotional state created when one behaves in a way that clashes with one's convictions.

Lots of clever studies have been aimed at this distinction, and the conclusion they reach is simple: When people behave in a way that doesn't conflict very strongly with their prior attitudes or intentions, no measurable tension state is created, so self-perception theory is all that is needed to understand their self-justification behavior. When people are led to behave in a way that does conflict strongly with their prior attitudes, however, measurable tension is created, and thus, dissonance theory is more clearly applicable (Cooper and Fazio 1984; Fazio 1987; Fazio, Zanna, and Cooper 1977). In the end, then, both theories meld into a kind of supertheory that allows us to understand how people justify their behavior in general.

The picture we are left with emphasizes the impromptu nature of reports of intentions. Intentions do not seem to persist in some pristine, timeless format, etched in mind permanently as they guide behavior. Rather, some fair amount of human behavior seems to occur without much influence by intentions, especially when the behavior is not particularly discrepant from prior beliefs and so can slip by without producing dissonance. But regardless of whether behaviors merely produce self-perception or actually cause dissonance, they come to be understood afterward as having accrued from certain intentions that make them seem sensible. These intentions, however, may not have existed in advance of the behavior, and in many of these studies, we know that the intentions surely did not predate the behavior. They are created post hoc as a way of protecting the illusion that we are conscious agents.

A telling example of this postbehavioral intention construction process was provided in a study by Kruglanski, Alon, and Lewis (1972). For this research, elementary school students were asked to play a series of group games, and the winners were either given a prize afterwards or were not. Normally, if the students had known about the prize in advance, this would have been expected to introduce a reduction in reported enjoyment of the games. Both dissonance and self-perception theories would predict that doing something for a known prize would lead the students to say that they liked the activity itself somewhat less. However, in this experiment, there was no actual mention of the prize in advance of the games. Instead, the experimenters told the prize group after they had won the games, "As we said before, members of the winning team will be awarded special prizes as tokens of their victory." In essence, then, although the prize was a *fait accompli,* an unexpected consequence of the action, the prize winners were given to believe that this surprise was something they might have known all along. And under this misapprehension, students in the prize group indeed showed a reduction in their reported enjoyment of the games. The revision of intention ("I didn't really want to play those games") took place when people were hoodwinked into thinking that they had known the consequences of their action in advance.

The processes that operate during the confabulation of intention are fallible, then, just like most human judgment. When people learn that they might have known or ought to have known of a consequence of their action, they go about revising their attitudes and intentions as though they actually did know this beforehand. The process of intention revision, in short, is a process of fabrication that depends on an *image* of ourselves as responsible agents who choose our actions with foreknowledge and in accord with our conscious intentions. Although such an agent may not actually animate our intention and action, an idealized image of this agent certainly serves as a guide for our invented intention. When we look back at our behavior and believe that the circumstances surrounding it are compatible with seeing ourselves acting as agents, we construct—in view of what we have done—the intention that such an agent must have had. Then we assume that we must have had that intention all along.

The post hoc invention of intentions can lead us away from accurate self-understanding. In the process of confabulating intentions, we may concoct ideas of what we were trying to do that then actually cloud whatever insight we do have into the causes of our action (Wilson 1985; Wilson and Stone 1985). Normally, for instance, the ratings people make of how much they like each of five puzzles they have done are strongly related to the amount of time they spent playing with each one. However, when people are asked to write down the reasons they like or dislike each of the puzzles, their later ratings of liking are far less related to actual playing time (Wilson et al. 1984). The process of analyzing reasons—or what Wilson (1985) calls "priming the explanatory system"—can even bend preferences awry and lead people to make bad decisions. In research by Wilson and Schooler (1991), for example, students who analyzed why they liked or disliked a series of different strawberry jams were found to make ratings that agreed less with experts' opinions of the jams than did those who reported their likes and dislikes without giving reasons. It is as though reflecting on the reasons for our actions can prompt us to include stray, misleading, and nonoptimal information in our postaction assessments of why we have done things. We become less true to ourselves and also to the unconscious realities that led to our behavior in the first place. The process of self-perception is by no means a perfect one; the intentions we confabulate can depart radically from any truth about the mechanisms that caused our behavior.

Left Brain Interpreter

Much of the evidence we have seen on the confabulation of intention in adults comes from normal people who are led by circumstance into periods of clouded intention. With behavior caused by unconscious processes, they don't have good mental previews of what they have done, so they then appear to offer reports of pre-act intentions they could not have had in advance. The role of the brain in this process is brought into relief by the very telling lapses of this kind found in people who have experienced brain damage—in particular, damage that separates the brain sources of behavior causation from the brain sources of behavior interpretation. This work by Michael Gazzaniga (Gazzaniga 1983; 1988; 1995; Gazzaniga and LeDoux 1978) suggests that the left brain interprets behavior in normal adults.

These studies began as investigations of the abilities of people who have had their left and right brains surgically severed by partial or complete section of the corpus callosum as a treatment for severe seizures. Such treatment leaves mid and lower brain structures joining the two sides intact but creates a "split brain" at the cortex. Animal research had shown that this yields a lateralization of certain abilities—the capacity to do something with one side of the body but not the other (e.g., Sperry 1961). The analysis of the separate talents of the sides of the brain can be achieved in human beings, then, by taking advantage of the fact that inputs can be made and responses observed for each side of the brain separately. For inputs, tactile material presented to one hand or visual material shown quickly on one side of the visual field (too fast to allow eye movement), stimulates the opposite or contralateral brain hemisphere. Responses then made by that hand are generated by the contralateral hemisphere as well. With these separate lines of communication to the two hemispheres, it was soon learned that verbal responses are generated exclusively by the left hemisphere in most patients studied. Material presented to the right brain does not usually stimulate speech.

The few exceptions to this rule provide the key cases for observations of left brain involvement in intention plasticity. A patient identified as J. W., for instance, had sufficient verbal ability in the right hemisphere to be able to understand and follow simple instructions. When the word *laugh* was flashed to the left visual field, and so to the right brain, he would often laugh. Prior study had determined, however, that his right brain was not sufficiently verbal to be able to process and understand sentences or even make simple categorizations. Thus, when he was asked by the investigator why he had laughed, it was clear that any response to this sophisticated query would necessarily have to come from the left brain. What J. W. said was, "You guys come up and test us every month. What a way to make a living." Apparently, the left brain developed an on-the-fly interpretation of the laughter by finding something funny in the situation and claiming that this was the cause of his behavior. In another example, the instruction "walk" presented to the right brain resulted in the patient's getting up to leave the testing van. On being asked where he was going, the patient's left brain quickly improvised, "I'm going into the house to get a Coke" (Gazzaniga 1983).

Similar observations were made of P. S., another patient with a modest but suitable level of verbal ability in the right brain. The patient was

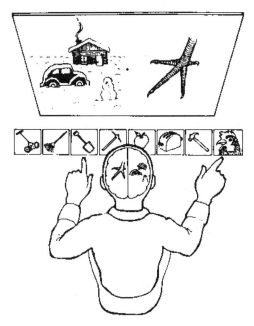

Figure 5.4
The upper images were flashed on the screen and so were channeled to the contralateral brain hemispheres. The patient P. S. was then asked to choose from the array of pictures below, the ones associated with those that were flashed. From Gazzaniga and LeDoux (1978). Courtesy Plenum Publishing.

shown two pictures, one exclusively to the left brain and one exclusively to the right, and was asked to choose from another array of pictures in full view any ones that were associated with the pictures that had been flashed to each side of the brain. In the test shown in figure 5.4, a picture of a chicken claw was flashed to the right visual field, and so to the left brain. A picture of a snow scene was flashed to the left visual field and so to the right brain. Of the array of pictures in view, the best choices are the chicken for the chicken claw and the shovel for the snow scene. P. S. responded by choosing the shovel with the left hand (right brain) and the chicken with the right hand (left brain).

When he was asked why he chose these things, P. S. was in something of a dilemma. The chicken choice was obvious enough to the left brain, as it had in fact engineered that choice. The chicken clearly went with the claw. But the shovel? Here was a choice made by the right brain, and the left brain had not played any part in making it. The left brain interpreter was up to the task, however, as P. S. responded, "Oh, that's simple. The chicken claw goes with the chicken, and you need a shovel to clean out the chicken shed." The left brain interpreted the right brain's response according to a context consistent with its own sphere of knowledge and did so without being informed by the right brain's knowledge of the snow scene.

To account for this and similar neuropsychological findings, Gazzaniga (1988) has suggested a brain-based theory of plasticity of intention:

Human brain architecture is organized in terms of functional modules capable of working both cooperatively and independently. These modules can carry out their functions in parallel and outside of the realm of conscious experience. The modules can effect internal and external behaviors, and do this at regular intervals. Monitoring all of this is a left-brain-based system called the interpreter. The interpreter considers all the outputs of the functional modules as soon as they are made and immediately constructs a hypothesis as to why particular actions occurred. In fact the interpreter need not be privy to why a particular module responded. Nonetheless, it will take the behavior at face value and fit the event into the large ongoing mental schema (belief system) that it has already constructed. (219)

This theory locates the invention of intention on the left side of the brain. It goes on to propose that the function of constructing postaction intentions is conducted on a regular basis by that side of the brain. It is interesting to wonder whether, when people do get their intentions clear in advance of acting, it is the same set of structures in the left brain that are involved. The split brain studies do not address the brain structures involved in producing the predictive awareness of action people enjoy when they do experience such awareness. The interpreter isolated by Gazzaniga does appear, however, to be a fine candidate for carrying out this function. The implication of the left brain interpreter theory is that whenever the interpreting happens, the interpretations are just narrations of the actions taken by other modules of the brain—both right and left—and are not causal of the actions at all.

The Three-Piece Puzzle

Will, intention, and action snap together like puzzle pieces. Consciousness of will derives from consciousness of intending and consciousness of acting, but this is not the only order in which the puzzle can be put together. Indeed, evidence of any two of these yields a presumption of the other.

In this chapter, we have seen a number of examples of action and the sense of conscious will leading to a postaction confabulation of intention. This is perhaps the best-researched relation among these variables, probably because it is so odd when people do it. We can't help but notice and sometimes chuckle when people insist, "I meant to do that and wanted to all along" when we know full well they just happened into the action. Politicians, for example, seem to be under some of the most intense public pressure to maintain the image of being conscious agents, and their machinations in service of looking as though they had wanted something all along that later came out well are famous indeed. Vice President Al Gore's 1999 claim in a CNN interview, "I took the initiative in creating the Internet," for example, is exactly the sort of thing we all might like to do if we could get away with it. Gore's comment went too far, of course, but such confabulated intentions often have the potential to make us look good—like conscious human agents, people who have willed what we do.

The equation can be worked in other directions as well. The perception that we have had a thought that is prior to, consistent with, and exclusively likely to be the cause of an action gives rise to experiences of conscious will. And perhaps when we experience a sense of conscious will or choice, and also have in mind a clear conscious intention, we may begin to fill in the third segment of the equation in another direction—by imagining, overperceiving, or confabulating a memory of the action itself. Consider what happens, for instance, when you are highly involved in playing or watching a game. It seems to be excruciatingly easy to misperceive the action of the game in accord with what you want to have happen. The tennis ball looks to be outside the line when you want it to be out, and inside when you want it to be in. The basketball player looks to be fouled in the act of shooting when you want the player's team to win but not when you want the team to lose. A classic social psychological study called "They Saw a Game" by Hastorf and Cantril (1954) recounted the wholesale misperception of the number of infractions on each side of a football game between Princeton and Dartmouth. Fans saw more infractions on the other side and blamed the other team for a dirty game. When we really want to do something, or even want to have our team do something, it seems easy to perceive that it was done. The ideal of conscious agency leads us not only to fabricate an experience of conscious will and to confabulate intentions consistent with that will, it also can blind us to our very actions, making us see them as far more effective than they actually are. After all, the actions must fit with the intention and the will.

When we see a person perpetrating one or the other of these blatant distortions, it is tempting to assume that the person is motivated by self-aggrandizement. We all know the soul who brags whenever something good comes of his or her action but who looks quickly to excuses or the meddling of others when the action falls short. The overgrown ego we attribute to this person seems to be a grasping, cloying, demanding entity, and the notion that the person is powered by selfish motives is a natural explanation (Miller and Ross 1975; Snyder, Stephan, and Rosenfield 1978). However, when we realize this person is assuming the self to be an ideal conscious agent, the striving seems understandable. The person who views actions as plausibly caused by the conscious will must necessarily complete the puzzle whenever parts are missing. Imagining oneself as a conscious agent means that conscious intention, action, and will must each be in place for every action. Intention and action imply will; intention and will imply action; and action and will imply intention. An ideal agent has all three. Putting these parts in place, it seems, involves constructing all the distortion of reality required to accommodate the birth of an ego.

6

Action Projection

The authorship of one's own action can be lost, projected away from self to other people or groups or even animals.

Give the automaton a soul which contemplates its movements, which believes itself to be the author of them, which has different volitions on the occasion of the different movements, and you will on this hypothesis construct a man.

Charles Bonnet, *Essai de Psychologie* (1755)

When you do something, how do you know that you are the one who did it? And when someone else does something, how do you know that you *weren't* the one who did it? These questions seldom arise in everyday conversation because the answer is usually obvious: Everybody *knows* that they are the authors of their own actions and *not* the authors of other people's actions. If people got this sort of thing mixed up on a regular basis, right now you might think that you are the one who is writing this sentence and I might think that I am reading it. With such a breakdown of the notion of personal identity, we might soon be wearing each other's underclothing as well.

The fact that we seldom discover that we have confused our actions with those of others does not indicate, however, that this is impossible. Perhaps it happens all the time, but mostly we just don't notice. The theory of apparent mental causation suggests that breakdowns in the sense of authorship do happen and in fact are quite likely under certain conditions. According to the theory, the actions our bodies perform are never self-evidently our own. We are merely guided in interpreting them as consciously willed by our "selves" because of our general human tendency to try to understand behavior in terms of the consciously willed action of specific minds—along with evidence that, in this particular case, the mind driving the action seems to be ours. The causal agent we perceive at our own core—the "I" to which we refer when we say we are acting—is only one of the possible authors to whom we may attribute what we do. We may easily be led into thinking there are others.

This chapter focuses on the inclination we have in certain circumstances to project actions we have caused onto plausible agents outside ourselves. These outside agents can be imaginary, as when people attribute their actions to spirits or other entities, and we turn to this possibility in chapter 7. The focus in this chapter is the more observable case of action projection to agents who are real—individual persons, groups of people, or sometimes animals. When we impute our actions to such agents, we engage in a curious charade in which we behave on behalf of others or groups without knowing we are actually causing what we see them doing. It is important to understand how this can happen—how things we have done can escape our accounting efforts and seem to us to be authored by others outside ourselves. If this is possible, our selves too, may, be merely *virtual* authors of action, apparent sources of the things our bodies and minds do.

The Loss of Authorship

How could normal people become convinced that something they are doing is actually being done by someone else? We have seen glimpses of this odd transformation in the case of automatisms; there is a fundamental uncertainty about the authorship of each person's actions that becomes apparent in exercises such as table turning and Ouija spelling. People who do these things may make contributions to the movement of the table or the planchette that they attribute to others—either to the real people who are cooperating in the activity or to some imaginary agent or spirit invoked to explain the movement. These are not, however, the only circumstances in which action projection has been observed. There are a variety of cases in which errors in perceiving apparent mental causation lead people to misunderstand what it is they have consciously willed.

Perhaps the most elementary case is the *autokinetic effect*. This is the tendency to see an object, such as a point of light in a darkened room, moving when in fact the object is stationary and it is one's eyes and body that are moving. Muzafer Sherif (1935) took advantage of this phenomenon in his studies of conformity. He told individuals that a light was going to be moved by an assistant in a darkened room, and he asked them judge how far it was moving. In some cases, the individuals were asked to make these judgments after hearing others describe what they saw, and it turned out that these estimates were influenced, often drastically, by what they heard others say. People would describe the light gyrating in circles, for example, if others before them said that this was what they saw. All the while, however, the light was perfectly stationary. The fact is, sometimes it's very difficult to discern that we are doing an action, and this is the starting point of many interesting errors—cases in which we project our own actions to the world around us.

Clever Hans

Some of the most famous examples of action projection involve the attribution of exceptional skills to animals. Clever Hans, a horse renowned in Berlin in 1904 for his astounding mental abilities, is a particularly well-documented case. Under the tutelage of the trainer Wilhelm von Osten, Hans could add, subtract, multiply, and divide, read, spell, and identify musical tones—giving his answers by tapping his hoof or with the occasional shake of his head for "no." So, for example, on an occasion of being asked the sum of 2/5 and 1/2, Hans answered 9/10 (by first tapping the numerator, then the denominator). To the question, What are the factors of 28? Hans tapped consecutively 2, 4, 7, 14, 28. (He left out 1 by horsing around.) Von Osten made a letter board that enabled Hans to spell out answers to questions (fig. 6.1). Hans could recognize people and spell their names after having met them once. He could also tell time to the minute by a watch, and answer such questions as, How many minutes does the big hand travel between seven minutes after a quarter past the hour, and three quarters past? There were little things, too, that made the horse really convincing—for instance, when tapping out higher numbers, Hans went faster, as though he was trying to speed along.

The truly astonishing thing about Hans was his ability to answer questions offered by different people, even in the absence of trainer von Osten. This immediately voided any suspicion of purposive deception by his trainer. Even people who dearly wanted to debunk Hans's abilities found the darned horse could answer their questions all alone in a barn. Hans

Figure 6.1
Trainer Wilhelm von Osten and his horse, Clever Hans, facing the letter board with which Hans spelled out answers to questions. From Fernald (1984). Courtesy Dodge Fernald.

was debated in the newspapers of Germany for months, leading to a "Hans Commission" report by thirteen expert investigators in September 1904, which certified that the horse was in fact clever. But Hans's feats were the topic of continued investigation by Oskar Pfungst (1911), a student of the psychologist (and commission member) Carl Stumpf. Pfungst carried out a series of studies of Hans that finally clarified the causes of the horse's amazing behavior.

The principal observation that made Pfungst suspicious was the fact that Hans could not answer when he couldn't see. A blinder wrapped around Hans's head quickly put a stop to his cleverness (fig. 6.2). Having one's head wrapped in a big bag might leave some of us humans unwilling to answer hard questions as well, but suspicions about Hans did not stop there. Pfungst went on to find that Hans also could not answer questions when the answer was unknown to a person. So in one experiment

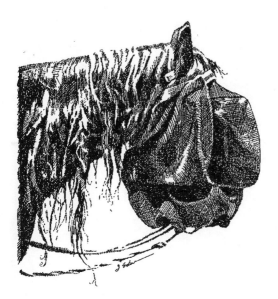

Figure 6.2
Clever Hans with a blindfold bag over his head. From Fernald (1984). Courtesy
Dodge Fernald.

Pfungst spoke a number directly into the horse's ear and then von Osten
did so as well. When they called on the horse to report the sum of the two
numbers, he was not able to do it, even though he could calculate sums
given him by one person all day.

Eventually, Pfungst discovered a subtle mannerism in von Osten that
also appeared quite unconsciously in most of Hans's questioners. On asking Hans something, questioners would slightly incline their heads forward at the end of the question so as to see Hans's hoof tapping. When a
questioner did this, Hans began to tap out the answer. (Pfungst found that
leaning forward would get Hans started tapping even without any question at all.) When Hans was tapping and the correct answer finally was
reached, von Osten and most other questioners tended to straighten up,
ever so slightly. Hans, sans the head-wrap, could time his tapping to start
and stop by attending to these very delicate movements and so answer
pretty much any question to which the questioner knew the answer. In
a detailed test of this idea, Pfungst took the part of Hans tapping out
answers and answered correctly the *unspoken* questions proffered by
twenty-three of twenty-five questioners. Admittedly, attending to such tiny

unconscious movements is fairly clever all by itself and must have been mastered by the horse only after considerable (inadvertent) training by von Osten. Indeed, Hans's tendency to go fast for large numbers indicated that he was even attending to the degree of tilt of the questioner's body because most people lean further forward the longer they expect to wait for the answer. However, even this keen perceptiveness doesn't measure up to the feats of math, memory, and pure horse sense that everyone had imagined.

After Pfungst pointed all this out, von Osten was not the least bit convinced. He was adamant that Hans was not merely reading the inclinations of his body. Pfungst explained in detail what he had discovered, and the trainer countered by saying that Hans was merely "distracted" when von Osten straightened up. On one occasion von Osten even made a test by saying to Hans, "You are to count to 7; I will stand erect at 5." He repeated the test five times, and each time Hans stopped tapping when von Osten straightened up. Despite this evidence, von Osten claimed that this was just one of Hans's little foibles—the horse was often tricky and stubborn—and maintained that with further training the problem could be eliminated. It never was.

There have been many other clever animals. My personal favorite is Toby the Sapient Pig (fig. 6.3), but the menagerie includes Rosa the Mare of Berlin, Lady the Wonder Horse, Kepler (an English Bulldog), the Reading Pig of London, Don the Talking Dog, and lots more (Jay 1986; Rosenthal 1974; Spitz 1997). Clever Hans has a special place in the history of psychology, however, because of Pfungst's meticulous research and the well-documented blindness of von Osten and other questioners to their influence on the horse. The Hans incident has become a byword in the psychological study of *self-fulfilling prophecy,* the tendency of people unconsciously to create what they expect of other people in social interaction (Merton 1948; Rosenthal 1974; Snyder 1981).

It is quite possible that in daily life each of us cues others to behave in the ways we hope or expect or even guess they will behave while we also then overlook our causal contribution and attribute the behavior to them. This is particularly likely when the behavior we are performing is subtle and difficult to observe in ourselves. In the tradition of von Osten, we may miss our own fleeting smiles or anxious looks, pay no heed to our tendency to stand near one person or far from another, or not notice

TOBY

THE
SAPIENT PIG,

From the Royal Rooms, Spring Gardens,

The only Scholar of his Race in the World.

THIS MOST EXTRAORDINARY CREATURE

Will Spell and Read, Cast Accounts,

PLAY AT CARDS;

Tell any Person what o'Clock it is to a Minute

BY THEIR OWN WATCH;

ALSO TELL THE AGE OF ANY ONE IN COMPANY,

And what is more Astonishing he will

Discover a Person's Thoughts

A Performance beyond all others the most Incredible.

Mr. HOARE having spent a number of Years in accomplishing this great un-
dertaking, leaves it to a discerning Public, to judge of the laborious task he has
had in bringing the above Animal before them, as of all others in Nature, none
are so obstinate as his species, and it is only by unremitted assiduity and attention,
that he has finally brought to such great perfection what Man never did before.

He is in Colour the most beautiful of his Race, in Symmetry the most Perfect,
in Temper the most Docile; his Nature is so far from being offensive, that he
is pleasing to all who honor him with their presence.

> The silken rob'd peer, and the delicate *belle,*
> Are unsulled by filth, unoffended by smell:
> Toby turns all disdainful from deeds of offence,
> For what would so blast his pretensions to sense.

He EXHIBITS every day at the

Temple Rooms, Fleet-street,

Near TEMPLE BAR, opposite CHANCERY LANE,

At the Hours of **1** and **3**, precisely,

And again in the Evening at **7** and **9** o'Clock.

ADMITTANCE ONE SHILLING.

Just Published, The Life & Adventures of TOBY the SAPIENT PIG,
With his Opinion on Men and Manners,
May be had at the Exhibition Rooms, Price One Shilling.

Printed by H. LYON, John Street, Edgware Road.

Figure 6.3
A flyer advertising the feats of one Toby the Sapient Pig, London, 1817. From Jay (1986).

when we guide others with our eyes or unconscious gestures to where they should sit or what they should do. Beyond horses or other pets, we could be making many people around us "clever"—in the sense that they seem to know how to behave around us—because we are subtly cuing them to do just what we think they should. In fact, thinking that students are clever tends to make them smart, even in our absence. Rosenthal and Jacobson (1968) found that teachers who were led to expect that certain of their students would soon "bloom" came to treat the students differently (in subtle ways) and so helped the students to learn. This created improvements in the students' actual test scores, even though the students designated as bloomers were randomly chosen by the experimenters.

The most noteworthy and insidious process of self-fulfilling prophecy occurs when we expect others to be hostile and unpleasant. We may then launch our interaction with them in such a way as to prompt the very behavior we expect. Snyder and Swann (1978) produced an illustration of this in their laboratory by giving people "noise weapons" to use in an experimental game, to be deployed if it was necessary to threaten an opponent. These weapons were no more than compressed-air boat horns, but they blasted home the point. When participants in the study were led to believe their opponent might be hostile, they used their weapons more readily. Although the opponents in this circumstance were not actually selected for hostility and instead had been randomly picked for the session, they responded to their cacophonous welcome by honking more in return. Perceived as likely to be hostile, they then actually became more hostile in the course of the game. The participants, meanwhile, were oblivious to their own roles in this transformation and merely chalked the noise up to a cranky opponent. The implications of this finding for social interaction across boundaries of race, ethnicity, or other group memberships are painfully clear. People who expect others to be hostile (merely by virtue of knowing the other's group identification) may well produce precisely the hostility they expect through a process of action projection. Tendencies to stereotype people according to their group membership can create evidence in favor of the stereotype, quite without any preexisting truth to the stereotype.

This possibility, of course, is something of which we are sometimes aware. We know that our expectancies for an unpleasant interaction may fuel our own unpleasantness, and we thus may try to compensate for this possibility. We go overboard trying to be nice, stepping gingerly around the minefield when we expect an explosive interaction. As a result, we may have a pleasant interaction with people we expected to dislike. Research by Ickes et al. (1982) uncovered precisely this response to expectations of unpleasantness: People got along quite well in conversations with interaction partners they expected to be abrasive. The research also yielded a further result: When the interaction was over, the person who expected it to go poorly—and who therefore had worked hard to make it go well—was likely to continue to believe that the other person (who was originally thought to be unpleasant) remained unpleasant at heart. The pleasantness of *this* interaction is attributed to the self rather than to the partner, and thus nothing is learned about the partner's true inclination one way or the other. When people go to extra lengths to compensate for the expected behavior of others, they appreciate their own influence on what others have done. Without such compensation, they often seem oblivious of the degree to which they cause the very actions they attribute to the people with whom they interact.

Clever Hands

The projection of action to Clever Hans seems to have occurred because the trainer's actions themselves were unconsciously produced. Hans's master overlooked his own contribution to the horse's behavior because of its very subtlety. You have to wonder whether this level of action projection would still occur if people were conscious of their own behavior. But you don't have to wonder for long. An extraordinary example of just such action projection has been observed all over the world—the phenomenon of *facilitated communication* (FC). This form of action projection was introduced when, in the mid-seventies, the Australian teacher Rosemary Crossley started using a manual procedure in the hope of communicating with people with autism, cerebral palsy, or other disorders that hamper speech.

The idea was for a trained facilitator to sit with the impaired client and hold his or her hand at a computer keyboard or letter board. The facilitator would keep the client "on task" and help to support the pointing or typing finger and guide the retraction of the arm. The facilitator was not to guide the client's responses explicitly or implicitly, and facilitators were cautioned not to influence the client's responses themselves. The result? With such facilitation, it was often found that individuals who had never said a word in their lives were quickly able to communicate, typing out meaningful sentences and even lengthy reports (Crossley 1992; Crossley and McDonald 1980). An early article on this phenomenon was even entitled with a facilitated quote: "I AM NOT A UTISTIC OH THJE TYP" [I am not autistic on the typewriter] (Biklen et al. 1991).

Many FC clients have little or no speech at all. There may be some with *echolalia* (repeating what others say), or with the ability to give stereotypical greetings or farewells. Most for whom the technique is used have had no training in any aspect of written language. They may type at the keyboard during facilitation without even looking at it. The level of language ability observed in some facilitated communications, nonetheless, is simply astounding. Beyond simple letters to parents or requests or questions to the facilitator, communications are often correctly spelled, grammatical, intelligent, and even touching. In one case, a fourteen-year-old boy who does not speak, and who often paces back and forth, slaps tables, bites at the base of his thumbs, flicks his fingers, and does not attend to people who talk to him, communicated the following with facilitation as part of a poetry workshop (Biklen et al. 1992, 16):

DO YOU HEATR NOISE IN YOUR HEAD?
IT PONDS AND SCREECHES
LIKEA TRAIN RUMBINGF THROJGH YOUR EARS
DO YUOU HEAR NOIXSE IN YOUR HEAD?
DO YOU SEE COLORS
SSWILING TWIXSTIBNG STABBING AT YOUJ
LIKE CUTS ON A MOVIE SCREEN HURLING AT YOU
DO YOU SEE CO,LORS?
DO YOU FEEL PAIN
IIT INVADES EVERHY CELL
LIKE AN ENEMY UNWANTED
DO YOU FEEL PAIN?

Such communications seem utterly miraculous. And, accordingly, there were skeptics from the start who wondered just how this kind of material could arise from the authors to whom it is attributed. The focus of suspicion, of course, was on the facilitators. The possible parallel with Ouija board spelling is not easy to overlook (Dillon 1993). But the facilitators have been among the strongest advocates of the technique and as a group have not only dismissed the idea that they might be the source of the communication but even argued heatedly against this possibility. Indeed, it doesn't take much experience with facilitation for a person to become quite thoroughly convinced of the effectiveness of the technique (Burgess et al. 1998; Twachtman-Cullen 1997), and in one case we even find a facilitated message that addresses the doubters: "I AM REALLY DOING IT MYSELF. YOU HAVE TO TELL THE WORLD SO MORE AUY. AUTIASTIC PEOPLE CAN COMMUNICATE" (Biklen et al. 1992, 14).

The scientific examination of FC was prompted when legal challenges arose to the use of FC as a technique for delivering testimony in court (Gorman 1999). Otherwise uncommunicative clients made accusations of sexual abuse against their family members, for example, and did so only through FC (e.g., Siegel 1995). Subjected to intense scrutiny, the clever hands of facilitated communication were found to operate by much the same process as Clever Hans. There is now extensive evidence that the "communicative" responses actually originate with the facilitators themselves (Felce 1994; Jacobson, Mulick, and Schwartz 1995).

One telling study, for example, issued separate questions to facilitators and clients (by means of headphones), and all the resulting answers were found to match the questions given the facilitators, not the clients (Wheeler et al. 1993). In other studies, communicator clients were given messages or shown pictures or objects with their facilitators absent; during subsequent facilitated communication, clients were not able to describe these items (Crewes et al. 1995; Hirshoren and Gregory 1995; Klewe 1993; Montee, Miltenberger, and Wittrock 1995; Regal, Rooney, and Wandas 1994; Szempruch and Jacobson 1993). Yet other research has found that personal information about the client unknown to the facilitator was not discerned through facilitated communication (Siegel 1995; Simpson and Myles 1995) and that factual information unknown to the facilitator was also unavailable through facilitated communication (Cabay 1994). Although some proponents of facilitated communication continue to attest to its effectiveness even in the face of such evidence (e.g., Biklen and Cardinal 1997), the overwhelming balance of research evidence at this time indicates that facilitated communication consists solely of communication from the facilitator.[1]

1. The recommendations on facilitated communication made by a variety of professional organizations can be found at <http://www.autism-society.org/>.

All of this has been very hard to bear for the families and supporters of people with communication disorders. The curtain drew open for a short time; just briefly it seemed that it was possible to communicate with loved ones who before this had been inert, mere shadows of people. But then the curtain drew shut again as the scientific evidence accrued to show that facilitation was in fact communicating nothing. This was a personal tragedy for the victims of communication disorders and for those around them. Yet at the same time, this movement and its denouement have brought to light a fascinating psychological question: Why would a person serving as the facilitator in this situation fail to recognize his or her own active contribution? This is an example of action projection *par excellence*.

It seems remarkable indeed that someone can perform a complex, lengthy, and highly meaningful action—one that is far more conscious and intentional than the unconscious nods of von Osten to Hans—and yet mistake this performance for the action of someone else. Yet this is the convincing impression reported by hundreds of people who have served as facilitators, and it seems unlikely that such a large population would be feigning this effect. Facilitators with only a modicum of training, and with little apparently to gain from the production of bogus communications, have nonetheless become completely persuaded that their own extended keyboard performances are in fact emerging from the silent person on whose behalf they are attempting to communicate. How does such action projection occur?

There seem to be two required elements for the effect. First, action projection could only occur if people had an essential inability to perceive directly personal causation of their own actions. If we always knew everything we did—because the thought of what we did was so fundamental to the causation of the action that it simply could not be unknown—then action projection would be impossible. The effect depends on the fact that people attempting facilitation are not *intrinsically informed* about the authorship of their own action. The second element needed for action projection is the inclination to attribute such orphaned action to another plausible source, for instance, the person on whose behalf we are trying to act. Because of the basic sense in which we do know what we are doing, our behaviors are unanchored, available for ascription to others who might plausibly be their sources. The general tendency to ascribe actions to agents leads us, then, to find agency in others for actions we have performed when the origins of those actions in ourselves are too obscure to discern. The two parts of action projection, in sum, can be described as *conscious will loss* and *attribution to outside agency*.

Several of the major causes of a loss of conscious will have been the topic of our prior discussions. We've looked in particular at how reduced perceptions of the priority, consistency, and exclusivity of thought about action can undermine the experience of will, and it follows that these factors are important here as well. People may lose the sense of conscious will when they fail to notice the apparent causal role of their thoughts. This can happen because the thoughts are not salient in mind just prior to the action, when the consistency of the thoughts with the action goes unnoticed, or if there are other competing causes that suggest the thoughts are not the exclusive cause of the action.

It seems particularly likely that this latter factor—lack of exclusivity—is of special importance in the case of action projection during facilitated communication. After all, the whole reason for doing facilitated communication is to allow the other person to act. The stage is thus set for the interpretation of one's own action as due to causes other than one's own thoughts. In most cases, people probably do have thoughts about the action that quite nicely satisfy the principles of priority and consistency. They may think, "It would make sense here to type an F," for example, and they have the thought indeed just before the F is typed. But because the assumption of nonexclusivity is so overwhelming in this setting, such causal candidate thoughts may be ignored or discounted, written off as mere perceptions of the other's actions, for example, or understood as predictions or anticipations of what the other will do ("He ought to type an F"). The potential causal role of one's own thoughts is thus unappreciated, and the experience of will does not surface.

This analysis suggests that the simple *belief* that the action can come from the other person is the main basis of action projection. It is the attribution to outside agency, in other words, that helps to fuel the loss of conscious will. Once the belief in outside agency is in place, the processes for interpreting one's own action are rocked at the base. A fundamental assumption changes as the person switches modes from "my will" to "other's will."[2] The usual interpretive scheme, in which one looks for causes of an action in one's own thoughts, is bypassed because the causes of the action are presumed to be the other person's thoughts. This then may lead to a failure to interpret even the most obvious causal candidates among one's own thoughts as intentions and instead change the focus to guessing what might be on the other person's mind.

Part of the reason these changes take place so readily in FC must be that facilitators are strongly motivated to achieve communication. They are inclined to be sympathetic with the client, of course, and beyond this there are also pressures of circumstance that arise as soon as they agree to try to facilitate a communication. Holding the client's hand and dearly hoping for something to come through ("Why else would I be doing this?"), one is now in a position in which a "communication" is a success and anything else is failure. Rapt attention is focused on the keyboard, and in fact facilitators often may ignore or stifle the client's other communicative signs. Facial expressions, body language, and even moaning or crying can be entirely inconsistent with what is happening at the keyboard, and the keyboard is assumed to convey the true message (Twachtman-Cullen 1997).

Beyond this immediate motivation and situational pressure, the actual practice of facilitation has a certain shoot-from-the-hip haphazardness that further promotes action projection. In practice, facilitated communication is almost never pure or simple. Facilitators report that when they work with a client, sometimes they will guess what the client would say and try to "get them started" by typing the first letters of words. Facilitators also report that they sometimes will "finish" a word or phrase once they understand the gist of what the client is trying to say. In fact, in a fine-grained examination of a series of facilitation sessions, Twachtman-Cullen (1997) discovered that facilitation involves a startling amount of overt helping. A facilitator in one session remarked "OK, to give you a start, let's type

2. Or to "God's will." A group of ultraorthodox caregivers in Israel developed facilitated communication with autistic individuals as a means of divining communications from God. The autistic clients were housed in a group home and given daily lessons in the Talmud, and then were asked theological questions during FC. Based partly on the Talmudic tenet that God selects fools and children to be prophets (after the destruction of the Temple), the communications secured in this fashion were interpreted as having mystical significance. The technique has been highly controversial in the Jewish community (Gross 1998).

the word *to*" (90). Another facilitator, instructing Twachtman-Cullen on how to apply the technique, said *"You might want to lead him to the letters when you first start"* (100) and *"You should sort of go to the area of the board where he should be going"* (101). These hints at how to proceed are echoed, albeit subtly, in FC training manuals (e.g., Crossley and Remington-Gurney 1992).

In the turmoil and awkwardness of attempted FC, then, there is much room for interpretation. Facilitation often involves a long series of effortful fits and starts, with hinting, helping, erasing and starting over, waiting, guessing, and even cajoling and scolding—interposed with occasional actions, sometimes of only a letter or two, that are felt by the facilitator to be "true" communications. The facilitator's decision of whether a whole communication was produced by self or by the client is thus a summary judgment of literally hundreds of smaller episodes that might have been "helping" or might have been "acting" as each letter was typed. The result of this curiously syncopated interaction is an overall sense that the client must have communicated, derived largely from the initial belief that such communication would take place in combination with a consequent series of errors of interpretation of one's own thoughts about the action.

Ventwilloquism

If belief in outside agency is the central element in action projection, it should be possible to produce action projection simply by leading people to believe that their actions are being produced by someone else. Such "throwing of the will" to another person was the focus of a series of studies by Wegner and Fuller (2000). In this research, individual college student participants were asked to attempt to read the unconscious muscle movements of another person. This situation borrowed some features of the facilitated communication setting but changed things as well. Instead of asking people to support a person's hand and finger to spell out answers at a whole keyboard, for instance, we limited responses to two keys for yes or no answers. The participant was asked to place middle and index fingers on these keys, and then an experimental confederate serving as the "client" in this situation rested the complementary fingers of the opposite hand atop the participant's fingers (fig. 6.4). This yes/no format kept us from having to interpret extended typed responses.

Figure 6.4
In the studies of Wegner and Fuller (2000) the participant placed his or her fingers on two keys marked "yes" and "no," and the confederate/communicator rested his or her fingers on top during the questions.

Our idea was to ask the participant to try to "read the muscle movements" of the confederate as the confederate was ostensibly asked a series of questions. The confederate was introduced as a fellow college student, so no communication impairment was suggested. However, at the outset and in the presence of the participant, the confederate was admonished not to respond overtly to any questions. Rather, it was explained that both the "communicator" (our confederate) and the "facilitator" (the participant) would hear a series of yes/no questions over headphones, and that the facilitator's job was to try to "read the communicator's unconscious finger muscle movements" and press the key that the communicator would have pressed for each question. The facilitator was told that these movements could be very subtle and might not even be consciously perceptible, but that he or she should go ahead and respond on behalf of the communicator because "you might be tapping into something of which you are unaware."

Now, because muscle reading is quite possible, the situation was arranged to preclude this. The questions were not even transmitted to the communicator at all. Thus, each facilitator was in the position of trying to discern answers that were ostensibly conveyed through unconscious muscle movements from someone who was, in reality, entirely blank on what was being asked. The communicator's fingers could just as well have been hot dogs, for all the relevant muscle movement they would be making. The questions transmitted to the facilitator, fifty in all, included twenty very easy factual questions (e.g., "Is the capital of the United States Washington, D.C.?"). The first main measure of interest in our experiments, then, was the proportion of correct answers produced for these easy questions. If the proportion correct was significantly greater than that expected by chance (50 percent for yes/no questions), the facilitator was contributing to the answers. We found across six experiments that participants answered these items correctly for the confederate 87 percent of the time.

This performance wouldn't really count as action projection if the participants judged that they were answering the questions on their own. The second key measure in these studies was of the participants' subjective sense of how much influence (on a scale from 0 to 100) the communicator had on the answers that were generated during the session. Given that the communicator heard no questions and was moving randomly if at all, zero would be the technically correct answer. Overall, however, participants acting as facilitators attributed 37 percent of the influence for the answers to the confederate communicator. This means that, on balance, facilitators correctly attributed the action more to themselves than to the communicator. However, they did not leave the communicator out of it entirely—as was actually the case—and instead attributed over a third of the influence to this inert outside agent.[3]

How did this degree of action projection occur in our simple laboratory experiments? This question should rightly be answered in two parts: First, how did people get so many answers correct, and second, how did they come to attribute this to the communicator? The first question is difficult to answer at this time because in our experiments a variety of conditions were tested to see whether this tendency to answer correctly could

---

3. People who gave more correct answers to the easy questions did not necessarily tend to attribute the answers to the communicator. In fact, the correlation between the number correct and the attribution of the answers to the communicator was near zero across the studies.

be changed—and very few had a significant influence. The number correct hovered around 87 percent (from 83 percent to 98 percent across studies) with all sorts of different variations, including when, in one study, we even asked participants not to touch the communicator and instead merely to "empathize" with the communicator and discern his or her answers from a distance.

It turns out that people even give a large proportion of correct answers to the easy questions *when they are told to respond randomly.* In one study, we dispensed with the communicator entirely and just asked our participants to respond yes or no in a random pattern, one answer following each question they heard. Even then, some 82 percent of answers to the questions were correct. A few participants seemed to react against the right answers, giving mostly wrong answers under this circumstance. But this number was far smaller (about 15 percent) than the majority who met the questions with correct answers even when admonished to behave spontaneously and with no discernible pattern. Apparently, there is an automatic tendency to follow questions with the right answers, and this tendency may be largely responsible for the correct answering that occurs in FC when the facilitator answers on behalf of the communicator.

One change we made in the muscle reading situation had a significant influence, enhancing this automatic correctness yet further. We noticed that in many of the instructional materials about facilitated communication, people learning to facilitate were strongly admonished not to help the client press particular keys. Instead, they were regularly instructed to provide an opposing pressure, pulling back the client's hand at all times and thereby depending on the client for the downward motion. In the words of Schubert and Biklen (1993, 12), "When supporting the hand or arm, give constant backward pressure. Push away gently from the keyboard to reduce the possibility of accidentally directing the individual toward specific letters." Commenting in a related vein on one FC client, Biklen et al. (1992, 11) observed, "Mary, a twelve-year-old student who does not speak words, requires support under her hand or at the wrist to slow her down. If her pointing is not slowed, she will type seemingly unrelated series of letters."

This theme in the FC literature suggests that the resistance or upward pressure might give rise to ironic, impulsive actions in the downward

direction. As we observed in our earlier discussion of the role of resistance in automatisms, people who are trying hard not to do something
may at times end up doing that very thing because of ironic processes.
Unconscious search processes may target the resisted behavior and,
during conditions of mental load, can actually prompt that behavior
(Ansfield and Wegner 1996; Wegner 1994; Wegner, Ansfield, and Pilloff
1998). A facilitator's tendency to produce upward pressure as part of FC
could, then, provide a fertile setting for the growth of automatic downward strokes.

This was exactly what Wegner and Fuller (2000) found in the muscle reading investigation. Participants in an experiment who were instructed to apply upward pressure for the entire muscle-reading session—
presumably pushing up against the fingers of the confederate that were
resting atop their own—went beyond the usual 87 percent level of accuracy to achieve 94 percent correct, a significantly higher rate. It may be,
then, that part of the process whereby correct answers are provided on
behalf of the communicator involves the production of an ironic automatic behavior. The facilitator's attempt *not* to put words into the communicator's mouth ends up doing exactly that.[4]

This experiment also tested how participants reacted when they were
told to go ahead and answer the questions for the communicator. A blatant instruction to "do it for them" led to an even higher level of correct
answering on the easy questions—an increase to 96 percent correct. And,
indeed, when these participants were asked whether they followed the

4. This is not the whole story on how this automatism is caused, of course, and
more research is needed to uncover the process precisely. It makes sense, for example, to think that in the case of normal college students who are "facilitating"
for other normal college students, there is a strong suspicion by the facilitator
that the communicator does indeed know the answers to the easy questions.
In fact, this suspicion could make it somewhat strange and embarrassing not to
answer correctly on behalf of the communicator, especially when one's answers
are known to the communicator. This is not the entire solution to the problem of
how the correct answers are given either, however. Wegner and Fuller (2000)
conducted a series of tests that appear to undermine the likelihood of this interpretation. In their studies, people who were asked to read muscle movements of
someone who was ostensibly given questions *subliminally*, and who thus could
not know whether the facilitator was answering correctly on their behalf, nonetheless gave a high proportion of correct answers to easy questions.

instructions to make the responses for the communicator, they were more inclined than participants given the usual muscle-reading instructions to agree that they had taken over and made the responses. Yet their level of attribution of the responses to the communicator persisted essentially unchanged (39 percent). Through the rigmarole of touching the other person's fingers and waiting for their possible (but imaginary) muscle movements, participants became convinced that the communicator must have had some effect on the answer even when they themselves were admonished to provide it.

How is it that participants come to attribute a substantial proportion of their correct answers to the communicator? All that seems to be necessary for such attribution is the belief that it is possible. In our experiments, we regularly measured belief by asking people to indicate whether they believed that they could discern another person's preferences by reading the person's muscle movements. Such belief was very strongly predictive of attribution of the answers to the communicator in all the studies. Of course, it is unclear when there is a correlation of this kind what is causing what. Although it might be that belief in muscle reading causes the attribution of action to the communicator, it could also be that the attribution of action to the communicator causes belief in muscle reading.

To ascertain whether belief was indeed causal, in one study we directly manipulated belief. For this experiment, the parallel between facilitated communication and our muscle-reading task was emphasized to participants. Then participants watched a video of a segment of a PBS *Frontline* program entitled "Prisoners of Silence" (Palfreman 1993). This program began with the history and apparent promise of FC and concluded with a review of the more recent findings indicating that the technique is invalid. For our study, some participants saw the breathless buildup of FC only, whereas others saw the entire episode, complete with debunking. We found that these groups then differed in their impressions of what had happened in their own muscle-reading sessions. Both groups showed similar levels of correct answers to the easy questions, but the pro-FC video group attributed their performance more strongly to the communicator (38 percent influence) than did the anti-FC video group (24 percent influence). It is interesting that even this latter group did not give up on the idea of muscle reading entirely, as they maintained a tendency toward action projection even after having seen a strong argument against it. However, it is clear that undermining belief in the possibility of outside agency indeed hampered action projection in this situation.

These findings suggest that people might conceivably project actions to others whenever they believe that others are potential sources of those actions. When else does this happen? Consider any instance of helping. A parent helps a child get dressed and may easily come away thinking the child put on the mittens successfully and will be able to do it again. Next time, though, the parent is struck with the child's apparent lapse in memory. It seemed as though the child was perfectly capable of doing this independently but now can't do it. Perhaps the parent was projecting the action in the initial session and ended up attributing to the child what the parent had actually accomplished.

And what about a teacher helping a student with fractions? The student is trying to figure out what 1/3 of 5/12 might be. The teacher produces an elegant explanation of the problem, the student correctly answers all the subquestions the teacher volunteers during the solution ("And how much is 3 times 12?"), and the final answer pops up just as it should. The teacher may well feel that the student has done the problem and should now be able to do others. Time to drift off to the teachers' lounge? The real test comes, though, if the teacher remembers to say "now you try one." All too often the student turns directly into stone or some other dense material. The action of solving the problem was projected by the teacher onto the student in the first place, and the assumption that the student had learned turned out to be too optimistic.

Yet other examples of action projection arise not with children or students but in the pursuit of sexual partners. One person romancing another, for example, may become very ready to presume that the interaction is proceeding as hoped. The person who is the target of these advances may be perceived to have reciprocated, or even to have originated them, largely through a process of action projection. The finding that men tend to read sexual meanings into women's behavior (Abbey and Melby 1986) suggests that action projection could occur in such situations, with the result that men might come away from romantic interactions believing that women had acted far more provocatively and sexually than was actually the case. This process could lead to a striking conflict of perceptions, in which the male self-righteously claims how much the female "wanted it," while the female validly reports that the male overstepped her clearly indicated bounds.

Action projection is a process in which one person operates another almost like a puppet and then attributes life to the puppet. Each of us is potentially a Geppetto with our own band of Pinocchios. The process of action projection is exceedingly difficult to notice, however, so the act of puppetry will not easily be detected. People who make horses do math and who procure messages from victims of autism when those victims can't even talk seemingly do all this without much clue that their own actions are creating the exhibition. Action projection may well operate pervasively in many situations, but it is unlikely when we are watching this show that we will concurrently be keen enough self-observers to realize that we are the ones pulling the strings.

The Whodunit Problem

It appears that people can get pretty bollixed up in their understanding of who did what in a social interaction. In a way, this is inevitable. Even with the computational tools of the average rocket scientist, for instance, it could be a sizable task to figure out who did what in just half an hour of a typical facilitated communication interaction. There are all kinds of behaviors going on, as well as hints about who was thinking about what, not to mention information about the priority, consistency, and exclusivity of every potential pairwise thought-action combination in both partners. Imagine what this would look like if we were to try figuring out who willed what actions by whom in the course of a few hours of court proceedings or in the snappy repartee of a good romantic comedy. Whew.

You or Me?

People must necessarily use a shorthand approach, a way of estimating who is willing what in the heat of social interactions. One such approach is simply to assume that the predominant willing is coming from one of the people and then to sort things out from there. Which person gets picked for this role could be largely a matter of basic principles of attention (Taylor and Fiske 1978). The person who is louder or taller or moving faster or wearing the brighter clothing could draw the viewer's attention and so could become the default source of the perceived will in the interaction. In fact, there is evidence that such standout people are often perceived to be running the show, even if they are not actually in charge (McArthur and Post 1977). If this salient person is oneself, for some reason (if one is particularly self-conscious, for example), then the focus on oneself will promote a tendency to default to self when questions of who did what arise (Duval and Wicklund 1972; Storms 1973).

The attribution of action to oneself can be enhanced unconsciously by the presence of subliminal stimuli that direct attention to self. Participants in experiments by Dijksterhuis, Wegner, and Aarts (2001) were asked to react to letter strings on a computer screen by judging them to be words or not and to do this as quickly as possible in a race with the computer. On each trial, the screen showing the letters went blank either when the person pressed the response button, or automatically at a short interval after the presentation (about 400–650 milliseconds). This made it unclear whether the person had answered correctly and turned off the display or whether the computer did it, and on each trial the person was asked to guess who did it. In addition, however, and without participants' prior knowledge, the word *I* or *me* or some other word was very briefly presented on each trial. This presentation lasted only 17 milliseconds and was both preceded and followed by random letter masks such that participants reported no awareness of these presentations.

The subliminal presentations influenced judgments of authorship. On trials with the subliminal priming of a self-relevant pronoun, participants more often judged that they had beaten the computer. They were influenced by the unconscious priming of self to attribute an ambiguous action to their own will. In a related study, participants were subliminally primed on some trials with the thought of an agent that was not the self— God. Among those participants who professed a personal belief in God, this prime reduced the attribution of the action to self. Apparently, the decision of whether self is the cause of an action is heavily influenced by the unconscious accessibility of self versus nonself agents. This suggests that even when we are not thinking consciously about ourselves or others, we may be influenced by circumstances we can't discern to judge the predominant authorship in one direction or the other.

One such nonobvious influence on the computation of self's versus other's will is the psychological *punctuation* of the interaction. We all remember examples from grammar class in which punctuation can change or even reverse meaning (compare "John said Mary is oversexed" with "John, said Mary, is oversexed"). A typical social interaction involves a series of actions by two or more persons that are interleaved over time and that therefore may present different meanings depending on a sort of punctuation as well (Whorf 1956). With repunctuation of the interaction, for example, a bright young lab rat might reflect, "I have got my experimenter trained. Each time I press the lever he gives me food" (Bateson and Jackson 1964, 273). More generally, any interaction in which persons A and B alternate their behaviors in sequence might be punctuated as "A causes B's act" or "B causes A's act," and it may be difficult or impossible to tell from the sequence itself which punctuation is more apt.

A classic example of this phenomenon is the viciously circular marital problem recounted by Watzlawick, Beavin, and Jackson (1967). A couple is engaged in a constant relationship struggle in which he passively withdraws while she nags and criticizes. In explaining the situation, the husband is likely to describe his withdrawal as a *response* to her nagging, whereas the wife is inclined to describe her nagging as a *response* to his withdrawal. Their fights thus consist of a monotonous exchange of "I withdraw because you nag" and "I nag because you withdraw." In fact, both things are happening, but it is difficult for either partner to recognize the whole sequence or its repetitive self-sustaining quality. Instead, each believes that his or her own behavior is quite involuntary, occurring largely because of the other's prior behavior.

Such gridlocked interactions have been explored in laboratory experiments by Swann, Pelham, and Roberts (1987). For these studies, college students were paired for interactions in which they played roles of world leaders during the Cold War. Each "leader" was given a series of statements about nuclear weaponry from which to choose, and the two exchanged statements six times over a phone hot line. The statements varied from warlike ("We will not tolerate any threats to our national security") to conciliatory ("Our goal is to establish a climate of mutual trust"). Some of the participants were instructed to adopt an "offensive" set for the exchange in that they were to convince their partners that they were very powerful leaders who would initiate a first strike with nuclear weapons if conditions made it necessary. Other participants were given a "defensive" set and asked to decide whether they would be willing to initiate a nuclear first-strike against their partners based on the statements their partners made during the interaction.

When the leaders got off the hot line, they were given the task of retrieving the interaction from memory by recalling what statement was made before and after each of several cue statements. Memory for the interaction was influenced by the set each "leader" had been given. Those prompted to think defensively remembered their own statements that *followed* the statements of their partner but not their own statements that *preceded* the statements of their partner. As compared to a control group given no instructional set, these defensive-set participants apparently punctuated the interaction in such a way as to see the other person as causal. The participants given an offensive set, however, showed no memory punctuation effect compared with the participants given no special set. The experimenters concluded that it may be difficult to enhance the degree to which people remember themselves as causal in an interaction by means of an instructional set. Recalling self as the initiator might already be the default setting, as it were.

For the defensive-set people in this study, there is something quite like action projection going on. As in the cases of Clever Hans and FC, people in this situation are not accepting authorship of the behavior that their bodies are nevertheless causing. The attribution of one's action to the other person—seeing one's action as a response rather than as an initiation—has the same formal properties as the attribution of one's action to a horse or to a person who cannot communicate at all. When people are set to think of their behavior as a reaction to the behavior of others—whether as a defensive set, as a matter of facilitation, or as some other form of helpful sensitivity to the other's actions—they can become oblivious to their own causal role in prompting the other to behave and instead perceive the other as the willful agent of the behaviors the other has been forced or obligated to perform.

Projecting one's own action to others is not, it turns out, a rare or abnormal event. People can mistake their own actions for those of others in a variety of contexts and with a fairly high degree of regularity. The main ingredient that gets this started is the simple belief that the other may be the agent of the action. Because the task of attributing authorship is dauntingly difficult even in some of the most apparently straightforward social settings, the moment-to-moment assignment of authorship can veer quite far away from reality. We can pin "whodunit" on anyone, even the butler who is locked in the cellar. The presence of other social agents makes available an important source of nonexclusivity and thus undermines the perception of own conscious will for one's actions. The tendency to project action to others, in this light, is produced by our inclination to focus on the causal properties of the other people. When we focus on another mind in great depth, we neglect to consider the causal status of our own thoughts. Instead, we may read most everything that happens in an interaction in terms of what it says about the other's mental state, inclinations, and desires. In a way, we lose ourselves in the other person. The tendency to simplify the computation of will by focusing on another person while ignoring the self can oversimplify and blind us to what we are doing.

And We Makes Three

Assuming that one person is in control is not the only way to solve the whodunit of will in interactions. There is yet another wrinkle in will computation that is introduced by the human proclivity to think of groups as agents. When you and I go to the beach for an afternoon, for instance, it is often true that each of us will think about what *we* are going to do rather than what I am going to do or what you are going to do. The reclassification of the two individuals into a co-acting entity serves to reduce the overall concern with just who is influencing whom within the group and focuses instead on our joint venture. We do things, stuff happens to us, and then we come home all sandy. The beach trip will always be ours.

This invention of the group agent can reduce the number of authorships each person needs to think about and remember. Keeping track of which person did what becomes unnecessary, and indeed somewhat divisive and insulting, when people are joined in a co-acting group. Families, couples, school classes, office co-workers, political liaisons, and many other groups become "we," occasionally just for moments but at other times in a rhythm that recurs throughout life. This we-feeling was noted early in the history of the social sciences by C. H. Cooley (1902), who described some of the circumstances that can give rise to this transformation in the individual's state of mind. He remarked that although there are many bases for categorizing people into groups (Campbell 1958; Heider 1958), the most dramatic changes in perception seem to happen when people come to understand that they are part of a group attempting to reach a common goal.

The change to "we" as the accounting unit for action and will is marked quite clearly by the use of the word in everyday language. People say "we went to the park" to indicate not only the motion of more than one body but also that a group goal was formed and achieved. The "we" becomes an agent, coalescing from individuals at least once to select and attain the group goal, and at this time the individuals all refer to their (individual) action as something "we" did. The "we" is a convenient ghost, a creature born just briefly for the purpose of accounting for the action of this collective, which may pass away just as quickly if no more group goals are set (Wegner and Giuliano 1980).

The quicksilver formation and dissipation of the "we" can be tracked over time in the stories people tell about what they have done with their friends and intimates. In a study of such intimate episodes, Wegner (1982) asked college students to write accounts of a series of different events, such as when they first met their partner, a time when their partner went away for a while, and so on. Participants were to write about each episode in five segments: beforehand, when it started, during the episode, as it ended, and after it was over. The pronouns people used throughout the narratives were counted, and the births and deaths of many a "we" were thus rendered in statistical detail.

Watch what happens to the pronouns in this, a typical story of a first encounter: "I was going to the dance just to hang out and saw him a couple of times early in the evening. I liked his smile, and he seemed to be looking at me whenever I looked over there. Then he was gone for a long time and I worried that I would never meet him. But he showed up and asked me to dance. We danced once and it was really short before the band took a break, and then he asked if we could dance together a whole lot more, and I couldn't help but giggle at him. We stood and talked and

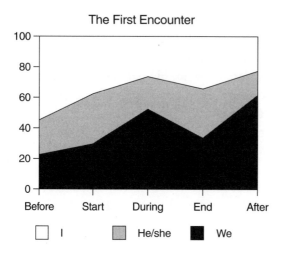

Figure 6.5
Proportions of personal pronouns at five points in narratives of a first encounter with a person who subsequently became a close friend. From Wegner (1982).

then kept on dancing later, and my friends were pointing at us and waving at me. We went in the hall and talked and then walked home together. Since then we've been seeing each other pretty much every day."

The transition from *I* and *he* early in this episode to the predominance of *we* later mirrors the overall trend for many stories of such episodes (fig. 6.5). Other episodes, in turn, revealed different patterns. When the partner goes away for a while, *we* begins the episode, wanes in the middle, and then returns at the end. The same thing happens when self and partner go through a fight (fig. 6.6). When the person meets a friend by chance on the street, *we* appears only at the meeting and then dissipates when the person returns to individual activities. When one person helps another, *we* forms during the incident as well. However, when a person happens to meet an enemy, there is very little mention of *we* at any point in the description of the episode.

The formation of the "we" can reduce the awareness of self and other as individual social entities. There is a decrease in the use of the pronoun *I* by individuals in a group, for example, as the size of their group increases (Mullen, Chapman, and Peaugh 1989). This process has been called *deindividuation* (Festinger, Schacter, and Back 1950; Zimbardo 1970) and has been implicated in the reduction of personal responsibility and morality

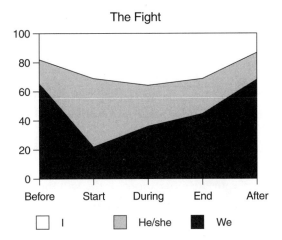

Figure 6.6
Proportions of personal pronouns at five points in narratives of a fight with a close friend. From Wegner (1982).

that comes with the immersion of individuals in crowds and active groups. Children who trick-or-treat in large groups, for example, are more likely to snitch extra candy from an untended bowl than are children who do so in smaller groups (Diener, et al. 1976). Such snitching is but a minor example of the kinds of mayhem that accrue when people get together in groups—from suicide-baiting crowds ("Jump! Jump!") to rioting rock concert audiences to angry mobs and warring clans. The loss of self-awareness in such groups makes individuals less inclined to focus on themselves as responsible agents and so yields disinhibition of immoral impulses (Diener 1979; Wegner and Schaefer 1978).

In a way, it seems as though the conscious will of the self is replaced by the conscious will of the group. Perhaps the will of the group is experienced by each person through a process much like the one whereby individual conscious will is experienced. The thoughts that are attributed in common to the *group* are understood as potentially causing the *group's* actions. The group negotiates what its intentions are and observes itself acting, and individuals link these intents and acts through the principles of priority, consistency, and exclusivity to constitute their experience of a group will. Members of a couple who are planning to go out to dinner, for instance, might achieve a group intention that is not easily attributable to either individual. Thus, the couple may do something that it (the "we") alone has willed. He suggests seafood, she mentions the Mexican place, and "we" eventually settle on a candle-lit dinner at the Cabbage Hut. This is uniquely a group choice, in part because it was not the first choice for either individual, and so can be something that helps to define the "we" and set it in motion as an independent agent (Wegner, Giuliano, and Hertel 1985).

The "we" can also turn company into a crowd. When people encounter situations in which intention and will are difficult to discern, the existence of this further entity creates new partitions of the will that can complicate further any understanding of who caused what. Consider this exercise in pronouns: When "he" accuses "her" of not doing the right thing for "us," and "she" says that "we" have never acted so distant from each "other" before, and "they" then go to separate rooms and sulk even though "he" wants to make up with "her"—the skein of wills is difficult indeed to unravel. A person may feel one conscious will identified with the self and yet a different one identified with the group of which self is a member. Serious internal conflicts and mixed feelings can result. The basketball player who wants her team to win but wants her rival on the same team to fall into a hole, for example, is likely to experience an ambivalent sense of accomplishment with either the winning or the falling.

Does group will count as action projection? In the cases of individual action projection we have reviewed, one person does something and perceives that action as having emanated from another person (or animal). It may be that similarly, in performing group actions, the individual in a group may well do something and yet perceive that action as having emanated from the group. In some cases, of course, the individual's intent may clearly coincide with the group's intent, and it may thus be quite reasonable for the individual to claim that the self's action was actually that of the group. In other cases, however, the individual may intend and do something that the group does not intend or do. Yet, if the individual simply misperceives the intention as belonging to the group, then anything the individual does can be ascribed to the group. The formation of a "we," then, can be a basis for doing acts on behalf of the remainder of the group that are in fact generated solely by the self.

There are many examples of acting "on behalf" of one's group when the group couldn't care less about or even disapproves of one's action. The husband who buys tickets for the couple to go to the Monster Truck Noise Derby may be thinking this is something his wife would actually want them to attend. And the wife who buys tickets for them to see the Vegetarian Ballet may also be laboring under the false assumption that this is the group will. People do things in pursuit of group goals all the time, often without even checking on whether the intentions they have formulated for the group correspond with what the group would want. When a white supremacist acts on behalf of the "white race," when a religious politician acts on behalf of moral individuals everywhere, when a feminist acts on behalf of all women—when any individual acts as a group member rather than as an individual—there is the ever-present possibility that the intentions of the self may unknowingly be substituted for those of the group. Individuals may project actions to the groups to which they belong, causing the group to act but failing to recognize that the action may be solely their own.

Fictions of Action Projection

People are profoundly interested in maintaining the fiction that they have conscious will. Indeed, the lengths to which they will go to uphold this illusion are amazing, particularly when they get caught up in trying to be ideal agents. But here we have run into a phenomenon that is the exact opposite of such illusion making. Action projection involves frittering away one's precious action, squandering its authorship on other people who really have not willed it at all. To produce such projection, there must be some powerful forces at work, forces strong enough to dispel the quite normal human tendency to grasp every loose action we find lying in the shadows and to hold it up to the light to claim "I did it!"

Action projection must involve errors that are so befuddling that they can counteract the fundamental illusion of will. Although there are no doubt a number of these, it is possible to summarize much of what we've explored in this chapter in terms of just four such errors or fictions—the fictions of inaction, reaction, stimulation, and collaboration—a quartet of mistakes people make that seem to underlie many of the cases of action projection. These mistakes are possible because of the basic obscurity of the source of our own action—the fact that we are not intrinsically informed of our own authorship and instead must build it up virtually out of perceptions of the thoughts and actions we witness in consciousness. Starting in this essential muddle, we can become confused and fall into action projection as a result of the following fictions.

The Inaction Fiction

Many cases of action projection arise simply because people are not conscious of everything they do. They think that they are inactive, when in truth they are doing something. This was the basis of the autokinetic effect—when the unnoticed movements of one's own body and eyes are attributed to a stationary light source. By the same token, believing in his own inaction was the underlying factor in von Osten's attribution of cleverness to Hans the horse. The trainer was performing an unconscious action—an action with no preview in the form of conscious thought and no subsequent evidence of its occurrence in the form of an attention-drawing bodily movement. The actions we don't notice ourselves doing may not escape the attention of others, however, particularly if the others are as clever as Hans. The responses these others make to what they see us doing may end up being clever, interesting, unusual, hostile, loving, or otherwise meaningful. We will fail to appreciate that we have actually produced that meaning, however, as long as we continue to believe we have done nothing. Because we can never know all the little quirks of our faces and bodies, all the yawns and grimaces and quivers and sideways looks and random nervous glances our bodies give off, we will forever be reading more into our social world than is there to begin with. People are destined by the lack of consciousness of much of their own behavior to attribute to others the impetus for what they themselves have set in motion.

The Reaction Fiction

People abdicate action to others by assuming that they themselves are simply reacting to what the other has done. This basis of action projection is important in how facilitated communication operates. Facilitators typically assume that the communicator is acting sensibly and that their own behavior at the keyboard is merely a matter of finishing, polishing, or bringing out the meaning that was already there in the message that was started. The reaction fiction operates acutely when people punctuate their interaction in a way that interprets their own behavior as a response to the other person's behavior rather than as a cause of the other person's behavior. Because behaviors of people are interleaved in interaction, the assumption of a *purely reactive stance* is inevitably false in almost every case. Actions are both causes and effects in the cycle of interaction, and a set to assume that one's actions are only effects will fail to acknowledge whatever causal features they may have. In thinking that we are merely reacting to others, we can create (in our minds) other people who are fantastically effective—communicating beyond their abilities (as in FC) or dominating the interaction with superhuman competence (as in the wife/husband vicious circle of interaction). Such curiously strong will from others should be a clue.

The Stimulation Fiction

Another way action projection comes about is through the mistaken idea that one is merely stimulating, helping, or prompting the other person to act. When one interprets one's own behavior as merely getting the other person started, the power of these prompts can be seriously underestimated. Many of the behaviors that facilitators did to stimulate communicators in FC were the beginnings of words or sentences that eventually became whole communications. And the interpretation of one's behavior as "helping" is similarly likely to produce the projection of action to the person being helped. This fiction is particularly likely to arise in interactions with beloved animals or babies, when we are radically disposed to give them the benefit of the doubt at every turn. When we desperately want baby to take a first step, or the pet to survive an hour on the carpet with no mistakes, we can give our own contributions so little regard that we merrily project success to our charges. We believe, certainly, that we have stimulated them to behave. But we regard this stimulation less as causal and more as helping to provide the proper conditions for the other to be causal. Thus, we project our action onto them. Next time when we're not there, they will fall down or wet the carpet, depending on who's who.

The Collaboration Fiction

Action projection is also likely to ensue when people become involved in what they believe to be collaborative action. In the process of acting together, the individuals may often find it useful to assume that their own intentions are those of the group. In many co-action situations, this is probably a very realistic and efficient assumption. Yet there may be individual intentions that depart notably from what the group might decide were it polled, and the assumption of agreement could thus be wrong. The fiction of co-action in this case would result in individual action that issues from the individual but that is incorrectly believed to be emanating from the group. The projection of action to close partners or to groups with whom one frequently collaborates would seem to be particularly likely because the assumption of agreement in these instances would be most pervasive.

Despite all we have explored in this chapter, the projection of action to others is still not well understood in current scientific psychology. For this reason, the four fictions outlined here should be taken as guides to potentially important sources of action projection, not as bedrock principles. The phenomena of action projection do seem to have common features, but much new research will need to be done on these before we can begin to know when and how action projection is most likely to occur.

7

Virtual Agency

When people project action to imaginary agents, they create virtual
agents, apparent sources of their own action. This process underlies
spirit possession and dissociative identity disorder as well as the
formation of the agent self.

A device should not be described as being a rational agent . . . unless there are
specific grounds for attributing to the device the understanding (or apparent understanding, since the illusion is all we are interested in at this stage) that it *is* a
rational agent.

Leonard Angel, *How to Build a Conscious Machine* (1989)

The ventriloquist Edgar Bergen became famous in the 1930s with his
dummy Charlie McCarthy (fig. 7.1). His act was immensely popular on
radio, and there were many news items on Bergen's colorful life and times.
One account goes like this:

One day, a visitor came into Bergen's room and found him talking—not
rehearsing—with Charlie. Bergen was asking Charlie a number of philosophical
questions about the nature of life, virtue, and love. Charlie was responding with
brilliant Socratic answers. When Bergen noticed that he had a visitor, he turned
red and said he was talking with Charlie, the wisest person he knew. The visitor
pointed out that it was Bergen's own mind and voice coming through the wooden
dummy. Bergen replied, "Well, I guess ultimately it is, but I ask Charlie these
questions and he answers, and I haven't the faintest idea of what he's going to say
and I'm astounded by his brilliance." (Siegel 1992, 163)[1]

The experience of losing the authorship of one's action to an imagined
agent is the topic of this chapter. This transformation is sufficiently
bizarre that it has been something of an obsession in both the popular
press and in scientific literature. Much of the liveliness of the field of anthropology, for instance, has to do with the documentation of intriguing

1. Unfortunately, the source of this story is not documented by Siegel. I've
not been able to verify it from other sources, so the account may be a bit of
Hollywood mythology. The experience it suggests does occur verifiably in related
circumstances, however, so I include it here for its entertainment value.

Figure 7.1
Edgar Bergen with dummy Charlie McCarthy and their friend Marilyn Monroe.
From Bergen (1984).

practices of spirit possession in various cultures around the world. Cases of spirit mediumship and channeling in this culture, meanwhile, as well as manifestations of the Holy Spirit such as glossolalia (speaking in tongues), are ever-popular topics of press coverage and cable TV documentaries. And the phenomena of dissociative identity disorder (DID; known earlier as multiple personality) have been the focus of novels and films, not to mention a matter of ongoing active debate in scientific psychology (Acocella 1999; Gleaves 1996; Putnam 1989; Ross 1988; Spanos 1994).

Most people faced with accounts of these anomalies of conscious agency have great difficulty imagining something like this happening to them. What would it be like to have a spirit take over your body? Where would "you" go at that time? If you had multiple personalities, what would it be like to switch between them? And if you leave one "self" and become another, what was the new one doing for your whole life until it just now popped into being? There are skeptics who reject these phenomena as faked (e.g., Aldridge-Morris 1989; Spanos 1994), perhaps in part because it seems so difficult to understand what it would be like to have this happen. Indeed, Aristotle's theory of spirit possession in ancient Greece involved suspicion that the possessed were merely pretending, play-acting the role of a spirit as in the theater (Stoller 1995). We can't appreciate how a subjective self might go away or how another might be created because we *are* such selves and can't imagine going out of existence and coming back as something else. To confront the topic of virtual authorship, then, is to try to understand how the very seat of human agency can be transformed (Matthews 1998; Wilkes 1988). The standard one person/one agent equation is seriously challenged, and we are vexed by the question of what it is like to be the person who changes subjective senses of self in this way. How could Bergen play the dummy and yet think that the dummy was someone else?

Our explorations in prior chapters have given us some helpful tools for thinking about these puzzling phenomena. In essence, these curiosities of agency can be understood as forms of action projection and are likely to follow the principles of apparent mental causation. However, they do so with an important twist. To this point, the examples of action projection we have examined are errors in the partitioning of causation among real agents—errors in which the person perceives that some other agent is causing action that is really attributable to the self. In these cases, there are no necessary implications of action projection for the identity of the first person—the one who is doing the projecting—in that this person can certainly continue to exist and be the author of other actions even as the action projection is going on. It is just that some of the self's actions are lost, transferred to an other's authorship. What happens, though, when there is in fact *no other real agent* present? When a person attributes agency for the self's actions to a spirit, to God, to another personality, to a wooden dummy, or to some agent or entity only the person has imagined, where do the actions go? And more important—what remains? In particular, what is left when all one's actions are projected away from self to some imaginary agent that is not self? Is anything left over that one could experience as self?

The prospect of this radical transformation is what makes the study of action projection to imaginary agents particularly exciting and at the same time strange, verging on the surreal. Although some kinds of action projection to imaginary agents seem entirely commonplace, others take off directly to Mars. Unlike projection to real agents, which involves the misperception of a real situation, action projection to imaginary agents can be understood as a glitch of an action accounting scheme inside the actor's own head. There is no one else really there to have done the action except for some imaginary agent. This glitch, however, has profound effects on the person's consciousness. At the extreme, the attribution of agency to imaginary minds other than the self seems to annihilate the self and thus wreaks havoc on our intuitions about personal identity and the continuity of conscious life.

In this chapter, then, we walk on the wild side. We examine action projection to imaginary agents of all kinds, beginning with ordinary forms of pretend play and role enactment, and proceeding to cases of channeling and mediumship, spirit possession, and dissociative identity disorder. With luck, we will emerge knowing more about how our own agent selves are constituted.

Imaginary Agents

There are two essential steps in the process of creating a new agent inside one's head. First, the agent must be imagined. Second, the imagination must be mistaken for real. Once this has happened, the processes that create action projection can start churning to produce all kinds of new actions attributable to the imaginary agent. Several key circumstances can promote the occurrence of these steps and thus yield active agents in the person.

Imagining an Agent

It is easy enough to imagine a conscious agent. Children do it all the time. Marjorie Taylor (1999) has made a detailed study of one such phenomenon in her book on imaginary companions. She reports that a substantial proportion of children in her samples of preschoolers report having imaginary companions, who may be other children, adults, puppies, aliens, clowns, robots, fairies, or oddities such as talking cotton balls, and who may appear singly or in groups. Children interviewed about their imaginary companions had stable descriptions of them over the course of seven months, although some were forgotten even in this short time. The children usually express attachment to and fondness for these companions, and also report playing with them frequently. They freely call them imaginary, however, and in most cases are quite happy to relegate the companions to a status distinct from that of real agents. Children with and without such companions do not differ in their ability to distinguish fantasy and reality, and Taylor reports that having such companions is not at all an unhealthy sign. Instead, it seems to be associated with a facility for creativity and an ability to pretend. Children with imaginary companions were more likely, for example, to hold an imaginary object instead of substituting a body part when performing a pretend action, as when they pretended to use a toothbrush rather than extending a finger to indicate the brush (Taylor, Cartwright, and Carlson 1993).

Eventually, of course, children with imaginary playmates abandon them and join other children, and they all then graduate to become adults with seemingly less active imaginations. Children sort out many of the magical and wishful entities from real ones, and learn, too, which entities—such as the Tooth Fairy, angels, or the devil—might still be okay to talk about even though they can't be authenticated by the usual means (Woolley 2000). Adults and children alike continue to perceive an amazing array of people, animals, or spirits in their everyday worlds. In *Faces in the Clouds,* Guthrie (1993) displays a wealth of examples of such anthropomorphism (fig. 7.2) in art, humor, philosophy, advertising, literature, engineering, science, and religion. The theme of his book is that the thoroughgoing human tendency to see agents all around us in the form of ourselves culminates naturally in the perception of a God who is also

Figure 7.2
Anthropomorphism takes many forms. In this seventeenth-century etching by
Michel Maier, the sun is a man and the moon is a woman. The parts of the
chickens are played by themselves. From Roob (1997).

quite human in temperament and psychology.[2] The proclivity to believe
that there is a God, or more than one god, is consistent with our willy-
nilly perception of agents everywhere, although in this case the agent is
writ large as an ideal agent, a best possible mind. God may be the ultimate imaginary friend.

2. It is interesting that the conception of God held by North Americans, at
any rate, is highly anthropomorphic in that people can't seem to conceive of a
Deity that is unlike a person. In a clever study, Barrett and Keil (1996) presented
people with stories of various agents who were called on to help one person
while they were already helping another. The researchers found that when the
agent was described as a person, participants recalled that the agent had to stop

Social psychologists have long appreciated the person's ability to understand and create roles and dramas, playing one position against the other—all inside the head (Goffman 1959; Sarbin and Allen 1968). The fact is, we have a well-developed sense of the other person in our own minds. In routine situations such as at a restaurant, for example, we have self and other so well rehearsed that we know when anyone has fouled up in even the most minor way (Schank and Abelson 1977). Patrons know almost instantly if the waitperson doesn't follow the script ("Why did he not ask to take my order?"). Waitpersons are similarly alert to unscripted patron behaviors ("When I asked if she wanted fries with that, she just said 'perhaps'"). In nonroutine situations the interplay of self and other that can happen in our own heads is often so innovative that it can be informative and downright entertaining. Witness the times you've thought through the various ways that some tricky interaction might unfold and have worked out in your mind how it might go if you asked the boss for a favor or tried to make friends with that interesting stranger.

The mental invention of other people is paralleled by a similar kind of imagining about ourselves. We can invent people or agents whom we *imagine ourselves being* and so create selves that may be quite different from the ones we usually inhabit. We can imagine not only how we might react to the waitperson in that restaurant, for example, we can also imagine how we might react *as* the waitperson. The ability to imagine people's visual perspectives, goals, and likely behaviors and perceptions in a situation gives us the ammunition to pretend to be those people. People seem to have the ability to take roles—to assume certain physical or social perspectives—that consist of general mental transformations of world knowledge. We can switch mentally between the viewpoint of a person standing outside a car facing it and a person sitting inside a car facing

---

attending to the first person in order to help the other; when the agent was described as a supercomputer, however, participants recalled the computer's helping both people simultaneously. However, when the agent was described as God, the participants remembered the Deity in a very human way, as having to stop attending to one person in order to help the other. Like the absurdity of a Santa Claus who must sequentially climb down billions of chimneys in one night, anthropomorphism leads people to intuit a difficult theology in which God cannot multitask.

out, for example, and then make rapid judgments of specific changes (e.g., the steering wheel will now be on the left) based on this global change. We can similarly switch perspectives from waitperson to diner, from patient to doctor, or from parent to child, at least to a degree. This ability develops as children interact with the world and each other (Flavell et al. 1968; Piaget and Inhelder 1948) and is only available in a most rudimentary form among even our most accomplished chimpanzee and monkey friends (Povinelli 1994; 1999).

Taking on the perspectives or roles of others is not merely play; it can become deeply involving and may manifest many of the properties of real interaction. Consider the invention of own and other identities that occurs in theater. The first role you take in a high school play, for example, involves not just learning lines and figuring out where to stand. You may suspect that this is the whole project when you first volunteer, but you soon realize there is much more to it. There is a sense in which you must imagine a whole person and put that person on like a glove or a suit of clothes. In the desire to act more authentically, some students of acting adopt the "method" approach (Stanislavski 1936). This involves attempting to experience the emotions of the character one is playing. Although we don't know whether this enhances the actor's experience or imagining of the character, there is some evidence that it does improve the quality of the role enactment (Bloch, Orthous, and Santibañez-H. 1995).

Treating imaginary agents as though they are real can eventually lead to a strong sense of involvement with the agents and concern about their pursuits. The world of interactive role-play gaming depends on this kind of appeal. Games such as *Dungeons and Dragons* have entranced enough people in the last generation to create an entire subculture (Fine 1983). And interactive fantasy has jumped to whole new levels in computer-based environments such as chat rooms and other MUDs (multiuser domains). Sherry Turkle (1995) recounts the rich and detailed stories and identities that people have created in the process of playing roles and forming interactive fantasies. When the individual adopts an avatar or virtual identity and begins to interact in such a community, he or she can invent whole people—not just as imaginary others but instead as imaginary selves. The process of imagining people can grow through role-playing to become a process of creating a new identity, complete with wings, a floppy hat, red shoes, and a big purple nose.[3]

In most of these cases of imaginary agents—be they childhood companions or characters in plays or games—we are quite conscious that they are imaginary. We know, at least at the outset, that we are embarking on an imaginary exercise, and though the world we've created may seem quite real in the heat of the action, we still have that sense that it was all imagined when it is over. These various forms of imagining have in common a kind of "as if" quality, a background recognition that they are not real, that demarcates them sharply from the kind of experience reported by people who have dissociative identity events. In normal garden-variety imagining, we *know that the imagined persons are imaginary.* As long as this knowledge is retained, we do not actually become the persons we imagine being, nor do we presume actually to interact with the persons we imagine meeting. What, then, pushes people over the edge? When does the imagining turn real?

Cues to Reality

People decide that imaginary persons are real in the same way they decide that anything is real. There are reality cues, various hints that can be used to distinguish the real from the unreal (Brickman 1978; Gorassini 1999; Johnson and Raye 1981; Johnson, Hashtroudi, and Lindsay 1993; Schooler, Gerhard, and Loftus 1986). It is just that in the case of imaginary agents we mistake for real, the cues *falsely* point to reality. Consider the case of a completely unreal experience that often seems resoundingly real—a dream. When we're in the middle of a dream, it may be difficult to distinguish the dream world from the real world.[4] No matter how fantastic or strange, the dream world is real at the time we are in it. All the

3. Hans Suler (1999) has created an interesting and detailed Web page on this.

4. Some people insist that they have dreams in which they know that they are dreaming. This has been called lucid dreaming, and there is a fair amount of descriptive material suggesting that many people share this sense at times (e.g., Kahan and LaBerge 1994). However, it is also possible that such dreams occur primarily when people are just waking up or falling asleep and become aware of the fact that they are dreaming through the juxtaposition of the dream with the waking state.

cues are there: Everything *seems* real in that we have rich and detailed input to the mind's eye, the mind's ears, and the mind's other senses (although curiously, we don't get smell in dreams; Hobson 1988). Everything also *feels* real; we can get tremendously worked up about what is happening. We react with emotion—becoming afraid, angry, embarrassed, tickled, or overjoyed, and sometimes having orgasms or heart attacks as well. And everything *acts* real; things behave in ways we cannot anticipate or control. In short, things seem real when they have *perceptual detail,* feel real when they have *emotional impact,* and act real when they are *uncontrollable.* Just as in a dream, when we imagine agents in waking life in ways that create these same three cues, we are more likely to judge the agents as real.

Perceptual detail is a particularly good cue to reality in the case of our own memories. People believe that their recollections represent real events rather than imaginings when they are able to recall more perceptual detail about the events (Johnson and Raye 1981). In Marcia Johnson's words, "Memories arising in perception should have more perceptual information (e.g., color, sound), time and place information, and more meaningful detail, while memories originating in thought should have more information about the cognitive operations (such as reasoning, search, decision, and organizational processes) that took place when the memory was established" (Johnson 1988, 41). A mental image of an angel, for example, may be amorphous and incompletely detailed. Even if you study the image for a while, your subsequent memory for it will probably include fewer specifics (Was the angel wearing a belt? shoes or sandals? What color was its harp?) than if you studied a painting of an angel for the same length of time. Also, reflecting back on that imagined angel, you might also be able to judge that it had been imagined and not real because you remember thinking about the Archangel Gabriel after hearing a religious song on the radio. Memories of how you came to image the angel would predominate over memories of perceptual detail.

Detail cues are likely to be available during perception itself, not just in memory. A tree in the mind's eye may have many of the properties of the perception of a real tree, of course, and the number of details available in each case might help us to determine which is real. The details we have available in a waking image may not be as rich as the details we can get from perception, perhaps, and this allows us to distinguish the image from a perception. The perceptual details in an image could be rich enough to support an inference of reality only under certain conditions, as when, for example, the reality we are imagining is itself sufficiently undetailed (as at dusk, for instance) so that images do not differ much from the real. Dreams may seem real even with relatively little detail, however, perhaps because at the time of dreaming there are no perceptions with which the dream image can be compared.

False perceptual details could prompt us to judge imagined agents to be real. Finding out that we know lots of details about a person, for example, might make that person—even if imaginary—seem real. An example of this can be found in the story of the reincarnation of Bridey Murphy (Gardner 1957).

This odd story began when Virginia Tighe, a housewife in Pueblo, Colorado, was hypnotized by Morey Bernstein. She started speaking in an Irish brogue and reported that in a previous life she was Bridey Murphy from Cork, Ireland. In further hypnotic sessions, she reported many bits of Irish lore, even breaking into Irish songs and dancing an Irish jig. Recordings of the sessions were made and sold widely. With the help of a local reporter, Bernstein published a book in 1956, *The Search for Bridey Murphy,* that became a best-seller and started a sensation. The boom in reincarnation had juke boxes blaring *Bridey Murphy Rock and Roll.* Costume parties featured "Come as you were" themes and stage hypnotists were suddenly called upon to help subjects find their past lives.

The inevitable search for the real Bridey Murphy in Irish records revealed nothing, but reporters in Chicago uncovered a Bridie Murphy Corkell who had lived in the house across the street from where Virginia grew up. It was further discovered that in high school drama classes, Virginia had been known for her particularly convincing Irish brogue, and that Virginia had an Irish aunt (no longer living) of whom she was very fond and who used to tell her about the old country. The memories Virginia reported in hypnosis were not her memories of a previous life but an admixture of her own childhood memories with those of her aunt and her early childhood friend.

This example points up the importance of *source memory* (Johnson, Hashtroudi, and Lindsay 1993), and more generally of *source perception,* in the creation of imaginary agents. Virginia Tighe failed to remember the source of her detailed memories of Bridey Murphy and so came to attribute them to her own memory and experience. Although it might seem strange that someone would make this mistake, it is actually quite possible for anyone. In one experiment, for example, participants imagined themselves saying words and heard another person saying other words. Later, the participants were fairly accurate at discriminating the words they had thought from those they had heard the other person say. This was not true, however, among people who had been instructed to imagine saying the words *in the other person's voice* (Johnson, Foley, and Leach 1988). This latter group confused the words they heard the person say with the words they themselves thought of in the other's voice. The perceptual details people use to judge whether experiences are real may come from unremembered or unperceived sources and thus can lead people to confuse imagination with reality.

Anything that increases the perceptual detail we experience about a particular agent will make that agent seem more real. In the case of virtual agents outside ourselves, this means that multiple perceptual hints of an agent's existence (such as a whole night's worth of creaking sounds in the attic) will be more convincing than one such hint (a single creak). In the case of virtual agents that we become, the same rule applies. More detail means more reality, but in this case the detail can arise from our own thoughts and behaviors. So, if we can think of lots of memories that could belong to the virtual agent, or if we notice that our voices or faces or gestures resemble those of some other agent, we may assemble these perceptual details into an overall judgment that we have indeed become someone else. What starts out merely as acting, in other words, may look so good to us that we convince ourselves of the reality of the characters we play.

The tendency to mistake imagined agents for real ones is likely to be further enhanced when the imagined agents have *emotional impact*. Although we may often know that we are pretending, at least at first, our emotional reactions to events in imaginary social worlds can be so compelling that we may drift into deep absorption (Brickman 1978). We can become involved in the experience, and as a result we seem to lose interest in continuing to remind ourselves that it is not real. The knowledge that we are in fact pretending might be quite salient at the start—when we begin to play a role, to act like someone, or to pretend we see someone who really is not there—but this knowledge does not keep surfacing into consciousness during the experience because of the emotions that arise to distract us from this pursuit.

Anyone who has ever wept at a movie knows this: We imagine agents most effectively when we experience the agents through gripping emotions (Hodges and Wegner 1997; Stotland 1969). This happens if we start empathizing with the agent and feel the emotions the agent might feel (such as when we feel sorrow for Bambi when his mother is killed). It also happens if we start reacting to an agent and have emotional responses to what the agent does (such as when we become angry at the hunter who so cruelly gunned her down). We can experience imaginary agents from the inside (when we role-play or empathize) or from the outside (when we conjure them up or think about what they are like), but we seem to get particularly involved and carried away with such imagining when it impinges on our bodies to create emotional experience.

There are cases of brain damage that can hamper the emotional authentication of the experience of agents. In Capgras' syndrome, for instance, bilateral frontal and right hemisphere damage may lead patients to experience the delusion that people they know well are actually "doubles," stand-ins who merely look or act like these individuals (Alexander, Stuss, and Benson 1979; Berson 1983). The usual sense of familiarity experienced on encountering a friend or relative may be replaced by a sense of strangeness—the wrong emotional reaction—and the conclusion the patient reaches after such repeated lack of familiarity is that the friend is not the same person the patient once knew. There is also evidence for an opposite phenomenon, the Frégoli syndrome (De Pauw, Szulecka, and Poltock 1987), in which a patient comes to identify many different people as the same familiar person (who is usually thought, therefore, to be stalking and persecuting them). In this case, there appears to be an overreliance on a sense of emotional familiarity without sufficient attention to the details of the other people.

A further related syndrome, as yet unnamed, occurs in rare cases when brain damage leads people to fail to recognize themselves in mirrors (Breen 1999; Feinberg 2001). The absence of the usual sense of familiarity may help fuel the delusion that the reflection in the mirror is really some-one else looking back from the other side ("That's old Tom over there, not me"). Cases of such misidentification syndromes are rare, of course, and are complicated by what may be associated brain damage that makes the person have difficulty in many life tasks. A lack of emotional familiarity of self or others might not influence a person who is otherwise normal to reach the radical conclusion that doubles are all around or that the self has gone missing. Still, it seems reasonable to conclude that there are at least two "layers" of the perception and imagination of agents: a surface identification of the person and a deeper emotional familiarity (Ellis and Young 1990). Part of what can make imagined people seem real is the enhanced emotional response we achieve when we become familiar with the characters.[5]

The perception of detail and the experience of emotion both help to transform imagined agents into seemingly real ones, but there is a third source of this transformation: the perception that the imagined agent does things that are *uncontrollable*. Johnson (1988) observed that the realm of the mental and the realm of the real can often be distinguished by their controllability. A real car, for example, might be broken down on a de-serted street in the middle of the night. It might steam and shake and even burst into flame. And no matter how much we wish or hope it to be fixed, it will just sit there. When we imagine a car, however, we can imagine it to be running. For that matter, we can imagine it to be a fine new limousine with a smiling driver, a wet bar, and bud vases in the doors. The fact that we cannot create these changes in reality is tragic, true, but it is also a fine cue to help us discern what is real and what is not.

5. This dual aspect of experience—the surface recognition of details and the deeper sense of familiarity—is echoed in another neurological disorder in which the two are dissociated because of traumatic brain injury (TBI). Stuss (1991, 77) recounts that "three of our TBI patients with moderate head injuries described al-terations in their recall of remote memories from various periods of their lives. Memories were not lost, but the recalled facts had lost their personal reference, i.e., although the patients could remember the facts, the memories did not belong to them. There was a loss of warmth and immediacy to these memories. . . . Although biographical, the memories were no longer truly self- or autobiograph-ical. . . . This detached, impersonal memory disrupts at least in part the feeling of continuity, the community of self."

The observation that an imaginary agent does not respond to our conscious will, then, is a cue that the agent is real. It is also a cue, however, that the agent is not the self. Control is only a cue to reality relative to an agent, a particular subjective perspective. One's current subjective self seems real if the thoughts and behaviors attributed to this virtual agent appear controllable, whereas virtual agents other than one's current subjective self seem real if their thoughts and behaviors are *not* controllable by one's current subjective self.[6] So, for example, from the perspective of a person whose body is taken over by a spirit, the body's actions may seem uncontrollable during the possession. To the person the spirit is real because the body inhabited by the spirit can't be controlled by the person. But from the perspective of the spirit, in turn, all of this must be reversed. When the spirit takes over, any actions of the self will now be viewed as uncontrollable by the spirit and so will have reality from the spirit's point of view.

In the creation of new subjective perspectives, then, the judgment of what is real and what is only in the mind must make a revolutionary reversal. Can this happen? Such trading of imagination for reality as people change virtual authorship is concretely illustrated in the phenomena of spirit possession.

The Spirit Is Willing

How can a person become possessed by a spirit? The transformation from a normal self to possession by a spirit or entity is one that many of us have not experienced, at least not in its most extreme form. Admittedly, we may have noticed ourselves becoming pretty darn strange at a drunken late-night party, overwrought by emotion at a funeral or in church, loudly

6. The uncontrollable self is often a motivation for developing a further perspective on the self from outside—an outside view that is itself more controllable. *Alice in Wonderland* does just this: "'Come, there's no use in crying like that!' said Alice to herself, rather sharply; 'I advise you to leave off this minute!' She generally gave herself very good advice, (though she very seldom followed it), and sometimes she scolded herself so severely as to bring tears into her eyes; and once she remembered trying to box her own ears for having cheated herself in a game of croquet she was playing against herself, for this curious child was very fond of pretending to be two people" (Carroll 1882, 22).

boorish at a sporting event, or possessed one evening by some sex-crazed impulse that seemed to override politeness. The ancients often spoke of these different versions of self as though they were distinct agents, each causing its own range of relevant behavior, and they often believed these agents were gods (Jaynes 1976).[7] Indeed, there is a sense in which our different moods and desires create different states of mind that might be understood as different selves or spirits (Bower 1994). But in contemporary culture we use the idea of "self" to refer to a wide range of such flavors of being, and reserve talk of spirits or possession for phenomena that are radically unlike our usual sense of subjective agency.

Yet people do experience these radical changes, and it is important to understand how this happens. It is essential to get a grasp on how such a transformation occurs in order to see whether this might fit into the notion of virtual agency. So we examine some of the major features of the psychology of spirit mediumship and channeling as practiced in this culture, and of the psychology and ethnopsychology of spirit possession worldwide.

Mediums and Channels

The traditions of channeling and mediumship in Western cultures represent widespread experiences of the transfer of virtual agency from self to a nonself agent. In these cases, an individual experiences a partial or total reduction in the usual sense of self as the author of consciously willed action. A spirit or entity replaces self as the agent. This unreal agent does not exist physically, of course, and is thus brought into being entirely in the experience and behavior of the person. It is possible to chalk such cases up to the fantastic delusions of a few unusual people—channeling does seem to happen mostly in California, and why are mediums in old films always wearing headwraps and speaking with bad accents? It turns out, however, that there are many historical case accounts of mediums (e.g., Brandon 1983) and widespread contemporary accounts of channels (e.g., Brown 1997), suggesting by sheer numbers that this experience may not be entirely explicable by the "odd person" theory. There

7. Kirkpatrick (1985) reports that in the Marquesan society it is common to credit certain body parts with a kind of autonomous agency. Sex organs, in particular, are said to lead the person around. This happens all over the world.

are commonalities in the experiences and behavior of such people that are worth examining.

Spirit mediumship was associated primarily with the spiritualist movement of the nineteenth century. Although most of the historical mediums who became famous at the peak of the movement were charlatans (fig. 7.3)—indeed, their great fame came from the outrageous tricks they performed as "evidence" of their spirit contact—there were also many who merely produced the basic phenomena of possession without added tricks. Typically, this involved some ritual of induction to produce the possession—a transitory change in body position or facial expression,

Figure 7.3
Cover illustration for an 1891 book debunking charlatan spirit mediums. From Farrington (1922).

temporary eye closure or blinking, an apparent trance state (eyes closed, sometimes head down or tilted back)—followed by the production of messages, perhaps with a change in vocal quality or pitch, ostensibly from some entity other than the medium. The entity was usually a spirit of the dead returning to communicate from the "other side." The medium professed that the experience of possession was involuntary and that the will of the spirit entity would determine what was done during the trance.[8]

Modern channeling is the descendant of this practice, and it appears to take two forms: one more like mediumship and another that is not so dramatic. In *trance channeling,* the practitioner, like a spirit medium, loses consciousness of self during the session and afterward usually cannot recall the experience. So, for instance, one popular channel, Kevin Ryerson, who does "workshops" rather than séances, describes his state while he channels as "benign amnesia." He says he recovers the experience only by listening to tapes made during his trance (Brown 1997). This oblivious state can be contrasted with *conscious channeling,* in which practitioners remain aware of what happens around them from their own subjective perspective and yet speak and behave in the manner of their channeled entity. The experience of conscious channeling has been described as "blending with an other" (Hughes 1991). Brown (1997, 25) quotes one conscious channel saying, "When I channel, it's like being at a party and overhearing another conversation. At the same time, the entity uses my mind, my vernacular, perhaps my memory." Various degrees of trance versus consciousness are experienced by different practitioners, and occasionally one practitioner may alternate between these formats on different occasions.

8. The term *trance* seems to be controversial in this context and in others, as it is difficult to define when a person is in a trance. Some commentators have taken issue with the term on the grounds that a trance is merely a descriptive term for outer appearances but is often taken to be an explanation of the unusual behaviors that it often accompanies (Iglis 1989; Spanos 1986). Because people who exhibit such trance states often describe them afterwards as having been associated with unusual states of consciousness, and may also be amnesic for the experience of trance, it seems a worthwhile term to keep in our psychological lexicon despite the quibbles. We should merely remember that calling the person's state a trance doesn't explain the state or the behaviors that occur during it.

Channeling seems like well-developed play-acting because channelers often produce what seem to be caricature-like impersonations of known individuals. Paula Farmer (1998), for example, is among the several people who claim to channel Elvis Presley. Her channeled book, *Elvis Aaron Presley: His Growth and Development as a Soul Spirit Within the Universe,* claims to offer "an emotional and inspirational account of Elvis's past life that gives you insight to the man behind the music. . . . Elvis shares his innermost thoughts with us on life, sex, drugs and religion, [and] reveals his experience with death, his understanding of his life on Earth, his meeting with God and his aspirations for his next incarnation." So, unlike the many people who impersonate Elvis in song, Farmer channels Elvis in print, producing the book he apparently needed to give the world. There are also reports of people channeling Barbie (Baskin 1994) and Babe Ruth (Polley 1995). However, the far more common case involves channeling of individuals who are not known but who have distinctive vocal characteristics, such as high, deep, or droning voices, or accents ranging from the recognizable (Irish, Scottish, English, German, old English) to the bizarre (ancient Babylonian, Etruscan, space alien, a future being from New Jersey). There is cross-sex channeling and channeling of children as well as channeling of the younger self (Brown 1997; Hughes 1991).

Although some of these characterizations are so skillful as to be uncanny, there are often flaws in the role-play. Linguistic analyses indicate that accents produced by channels are often erroneous (when claimed to capture a known dialect) and are marked by unusual syntax and hybrids of different dialects. The channeling of archaic speech may sound potentially archaic to the untrained ear, but it is often strangely anachronistic, peppered with modern idioms (Roberts 1989; Thomason 1989). In channeling Atun-Re, a Nubian priest who lived around 1300 B.C., for example, Kevin Ryerson "joyfully plagiarized the punch line of a popular country-western song by referring to Cleopatra as the 'Queen of Denial'" (Brown 1997, 29). Channels rationalize such lapses by saying that the entities must necessarily work through them, using their memories and vocal apparatus. Ryerson explained that Atun-Re speaks English rather than Nubian, for example, saying that the "spirit must use the neuromotor responses that I'm conditioned with" (Brown 1997, 29). And, indeed, if channelers are blending with another person, it makes sense that their

speech might be an odd admixture. This explanation is not very satisfying, however, to those who hear a channel's accent break down over the
course of a lengthy session from a fairly convincing Scottish brogue, for
instance, to something more like a whiny Canadian.

The literature on "how to channel" also has the suspicious ring of instruction on how to pretend. In *Opening to Channel*, Roman and Packer
(1987) give a detailed set of instructions (which they channeled, of
course) for conscious channeling. You should set up a tape recorder, have
questions ready to ask the "guide," put on special music, surround yourself with the image of a bubble of white light, imagine energy and light
flowing through your throat, feel the presence of your guide growing
stronger, and so on. In the midst of this, instruction number 8 is, "If your
mind is saying, 'I wonder if it is just me' or asking 'Have I really connected with a guide?' let that thought go, and for now believe that you
have indeed connected with a high-level guide, even if you cannot sense
or prove the reality of it" (85).

In Kathryn Ridall's (1988) manual, *Channeling: How to Reach Out to
Your Spirit Guides,* we learn that "as people begin to channel, they almost inevitably feel as if they are making it up. . . . When my students
complain that they're just making it up, I tell them, 'Good. Continue to
make it up.' Allow your imagination to roam freely. . . . Don't allow your
rational mind to rule at that time. Push its thoughts aside; soon enough
it will be back in control" (113–114). In fact, in a four-step instruction on
how to channel, Ridall's fourth step is, "Pretend that you are your guide.
Speak to yourself aloud as if you were sitting a few feet away. Begin to
offer yourself guidance on the topic you want to address. . . . Refer to
yourself in the second person. For instance, 'You feel nervous about our
current interaction. You are afraid you are making it up'" (109). All this
sounds like a kind of ventriloquism school.

It makes sense that, at least in the case of conscious channeling, practitioners are developing rather detailed and careful plans for how to imagine themselves as another person. This serves as the first step, creating
an imagined virtual agent that the individual can then proceed to mistake
for real. The actions of the channel's body are not informative about
authorship, of course, because either self or the virtual agent could be
causing them. Rather, it is the perceived source of the person's thoughts
that determines the allocation of action authorship. The body's actions,

although play-acted, may reveal surprising levels of perceptual detail about the virtual agent ("I didn't know I could do that accent") and may have unexpected emotional impact ("These jokes are actually funny"). This could promote the inference that the virtual agent is real.

With the development of the virtual agent comes a transition in the locus of the *control experience,* as the agent's thoughts begin to predict the body's action better than the self's thoughts do. Successful channeling seems to follow from the continued observation that the body's acts are previewed by thoughts that are being (actively) attributed to the virtual agent. The acts seem uncontrollable by self, not necessarily because the self is even trying to control them but because the virtual agent's thoughts seem to have this control. Thoughts coming to mind in the virtual agent's accent, for example, may preview the body's actions again and again. The misattribution of actions to the virtual agent continually deflates the sense of the self's conscious will for the body's actions. When the person is "in" the agent, the body's actions seem controllable by that agent, and the person's normal self seems less in control because thoughts attributed to self are simply not occurring as often.

The theory that imagination becomes real is a potential way to understand many conscious channelers. Consider one of the best known early channelers, Jane Roberts, who consciously channeled the entity Seth and wrote several widely read books. She had been an author of fiction and had been planning to write a do-it-yourself book on ESP. She reported starting off with her husband at a Ouija board and having sessions in which they became convinced they were getting messages from Seth. Then she recounts that two sessions "were much the same, except for one bewildering element: I began to anticipate the board's replies. . . . I heard the words in my head at a faster and faster rate, and not only sentences but whole paragraphs before they were spelled out" (Roberts 1970, 18). Soon she dropped the board, and with it her husband's help, and began to speak as Seth (in a somewhat lower-pitched voice than her usual one). Seth's new-age pronouncements were very popular, and this early example was one of the starting points of the current channeling fad.[9]

9. It is interesting that since then Seth has been speaking through other channels; Frances Morse of Connecticut began channeling Seth in 1975 and reports that counseling clients of hers who are familiar with Jane Roberts's Seth have generally been satisfied with her version of Seth as well (Brown 1997, 157).

Jane Roberts clearly had strong motivation to channel—she was hoping to write a book—and she had a strong ability to imagine, as evidenced by her past work as a fiction author. Perhaps in her case, a deep desire to believe that her virtual agent was real helped to fuel her performance and her commitment to the reality of Seth.

The idea that imagination becomes real is more difficult to apply to the case of unconscious channels. If the self is totally gone, submerged in a netherworld of mind and not even available to direct or execute the performance of the role-play, how could the pretending be done? *Who exactly* is doing the pretending? This question presupposes that there must always be a self, a subjective seat of consciousness, for the performance of a role or the creation of any virtual agent. But of course, this can't be true. If there is always a self beneath any character we imagine and become, there should by extension also always be a self beneath the self. This suggests an infinite regress, a serious homunculus problem. To escape this conundrum, it is necessary to suppose that the person can perform actions without a self and that these can then be perceived as emanating from any virtual agent at all, including the self. In this view, the conscious will of a self is not necessary for creating voluntary action.

The transition from self to entity control that occurs in unconscious channelers seems to be a brief period when the person *assigns no author to action*. This transition appears quite unlike a normal waking state of consciousness and instead resembles sleep. It is useful to examine the phenomena of unconscious channeling of virtual agents in more depth, and it turns out much of the best descriptive evidence comes from studies of possession and trance states.

Possession and Trance

Many people have experienced spirit possession throughout history and around the world. To begin with, there is evidence for forms of possession and trance in the Hebrew and Greek roots of Western society. In 1 Samuel 10, for instance, God sent possessed prophets to Samuel who told him he too would be "overcome with the spirit of the Lord . . . and be turned into another man." And in Greece the priestess Pythia at the Delphic oracle of Apollo went into trance to deliver her divinations. In medieval Europe, of course, there are many accounts of possession by devils, not to mention plenty of witchcraft (Bourguignon 1973; Oesterreich 1922). The stereotype of spirit possession in Western cultures stems largely from these archaic European examples viewed through the lens of a Christian account of possession. We can all bring to mind images of diabolical possession and exorcism from horror movies. But this is a stilted and unrepresentative stereotype.[10] In a sample of 488 societies, Bourguignon (1973) found that 90 percent exhibit institutionalized forms of altered states of consciousness, and 52 percent exhibit the specific case of trance with spirit possession. Most such possession occurs in religious contexts in which the spirit is benevolent and desirable, so the notion that such activity is satanic turns out worldwide to be a minority view (Lewis 1989).

The incidence of spirit possession has always been low in North America and Europe. Early groups such as the Shakers and the Quakers practiced forms of possession (by the Holy Spirit) as part of their worship (Garrett 1987), and there still exist significant minority religions (such as Pentecostal and Charismatic Catholic churches) that carry on such practices. But membership in such groups is small. The incidence of spirit possession is dramatically higher in certain societies of Africa, South America, and Asia. For example, spirit possession during trance is estimated to occur in 25 percent of the population of Malagasy speakers on the island of Mayotte off Southern Africa (Lambek 1988), in 50 percent of the !Kung bushmen of South Africa (Lee 1966), and in 47 percent of adult females among the Maasai of Tanzania, East Africa (Hurskainen 1989). Adherents of Vodoun ("voodoo") in Haiti and of Santeria in Cuba include substantial proportions of the population, and the Afro-Brazilian religions Umbanda and Candomblé have upwards of 10 million adherents in Brazil (Brown 1986; Wafer 1991). In these religions, significant proportions of worshipers experience spirit possession as part of regular ceremonies. Any inclination we might have to write possession off as individual madness is seriously undermined by the sheer frequency of this phenomenon in some cultures. Seemingly, with the proper cultural support, almost anyone can become possessed.

10. The stereotype of possession also usually suggests that people become possessed permanently or at least for lengthy bouts. Long-term possession is very rare, however, unlike possession trance, and is usually understood to be a form of mental disorder (Bourguignon 1976).

A typical example is the possession ritual in an Umbanda Pura ceremony in urban Brazil (described by Brown 1986). Meetings in the Umbanda church take place on Monday, Wednesday, and Friday evenings at 8 o'clock. At first, the ceremony involves singing and hand-clapping that celebrates the Caboclo spirits (spirits of Amazonian Indians), and invites them to "come down and work." The congregation moves around the small meeting hall in slow circle in a samba step. This may go on for half an hour or more, and then, "Mediums, as they become possessed, stop dancing, begin to perspire and often look slightly ill, sway, and then, bending over and giving a series of rapid jerks, receive their spirits. Upon straightening up, they have taken on the facial expressions, demeanor, and body motions characteristic of the particular spirit they have received. Caboclos wear stern, even fierce expressions and utter loud, piercing cries. They move vigorously around the dance floor in a kind of two-step, often dropping to one knee to draw an imaginary bow, and smoke large cigars, whose smoke will be blown over their clients as a form of ritual cleansing and curing" (Brown 1986, 81). Possessed mediums give *consultas,* consultations in which the members of the congregation seek the advice of the spirits for their problems. Ritual servants supply the Caboclos with fresh cigars and copy down recipes for herbal baths or other ritual preparations recommended to clients. These servants also help to interpret the advice of the spirits, which is often delivered in a ritual code language that is hard to understand. Later in the ceremony, possessions may occur by other classes of spirits, such as "old Blacks" (the wise and kindly spirits of slaves) or the spirits of children.

The behavior of the possessed has commonalities across cultures. The behavior depends, as in the Umbanda religion, on the particular spirit agent that is said to possess the host. There can be different classes of spirits possessing only certain people; in Northwest Madagascar, for instance, mass possession of school children during classes is blamed on "reckless and dangerous" *Njarinintsy* spirits, whereas older women experience possession by the more sedate *tromba* spirits (Sharp 1990). But, by and large, the possession involves a sequence much like that of trance channeling, in which the host may go limp or silent for a while or perhaps experience a period of convulsions or agitated movement. Brown (1986) notes in the Umbanda case that "in contrast to the extremely controlled possession states achieved by experienced mediums, possession, when it occurs among those inexperienced in controlling it, is often violent, and clients must be protected from injury to themselves or others" (83). When the spirit "gains control" of the host, some change in the host's behavioral style typically signals the arrival of the new virtual agent (fig. 7.4). The possession may be fleeting or, in some cultures, may last many hours.

The induction of possession in the case of Umbanda also shares common features with induction in other cultures. Four such features are

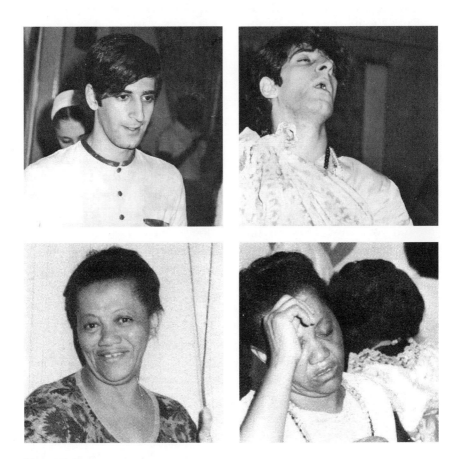

Figure 7.4
Before/after pictures of people being possessed by Coboclo spirits at an Umbanda ceremony. From Pressel (1973). Courtesy Esther Pressel.

particularly worthy of note. They include a prior *belief* in the reality of the spirits, a socially sanctioned *ritual* in which one or more people are possessed in the presence of others, the use of a driving *rhythm* in the ritual, and the *interaction* of the spirit-possessed with other group members. Although different cultures add all sorts of twists to possession induction—some merely inducing trance without possession, others focusing on the induction in one person who is the spirit-master and healer of the group (in the practice of shamanism)—the characteristics of belief, ritual, rhythm, and interaction seem to be shared by many if not most spirit possession inductions (Boddy 1994; Goodman 1988; Lewis 1989; Locke and Kelly 1985; Price-Williams and Hughes 1994).

The finding that people must have belief in the spirits comes as no surprise. We have already seen the importance of belief in action projection and the importance of transforming imagined agents into ones that are believed to be real for the creation of virtual agents. Belief in spirits is not just fanciful, but as emphasized by many anthropological commentators, it is strongly motivated. During possession, people suddenly have an ability to say and do things courtesy of the spirit that might otherwise be forbidden. Studying the Shango religion of Trinidad, Mischel and Mischel (1958) proposed that possession is widely learned because such release can be rewarding, allowing the expression of taboo impulses ("I spit on you and your cow"). Several anthropologists have suggested that this "alibi" theory might account for the finding that spirit possession occurs most often among people who are oppressed in their culture—usually, the women (Bourguignon 1976; Lewis 1989). The belief in spirits is not just the sharing of a fairy story, then, but instead is a useful fiction. Just as people might get drunk to excuse actions they are motivated to perform, they may urgently (yet perhaps unconsciously) want to believe in spirits to allow an avenue for the expression of thoughts and actions they might never be able to express otherwise.

The form of the possession ritual is remarkably similar in many cultures. A group gathers, usually with some religious significance attached to their meeting and fully expecting that spirits will appear through some of those present. Dancing, singing, chanting, or listening to a speaker usually begin the ritual in a kind of group entrainment or co-action. This may last from a few minutes to many hours before the possessions begin,

Figure 7.5
A possessed priestess at an Akwambo festival in Ghana. From Cole and Ross (1977). Courtesy Herbert Cole.

and then there may be simultaneous or sequential possessions in the group. The ritual may involve the use of alcohol, tobacco, or other drugs and in different societies can include such features as preparatory rituals (e.g., fasting), special costumes (fig. 7.5), group rites of passage (e.g., marriage), and feats of bravery among the possessed or in preparation for possession (e.g., snake-handling, fire-walking).

Rhythm, in the form of music, drums, dancing, or chanting, is curiously customary in the production of trance. It is not absolutely essential, but it is a frequent accompaniment. A good example occurs in the "filling with the Holy Spirit" among Pentecostal church members in Southern Appalachia, a ritual that often culminates with many of the congregation performing glossolalia (speaking in tongues).[11] Abell (1982, 128–130) describes one such event:

[The Evangelist] begins to preach. As he speaks quietly and clearly, he begins to rock forward and then backward. . . . As his voice grows louder, it also becomes more rhythmic, corresponding to the shifting of his weight from one foot to the other. Gradually he begins to lift each foot as he shifts his weight and slams it down as his voice grows to the limits of human vocal intensity. . . . Many persons in the congregation begin to sway side by side or front to back, keeping time with his driving behavior. As the driving becomes more intense, persons close their eyes and begin to manifest rapid quivering of the head from side to side as they continue their backward and forward movement. Some people clap their hands or stomp their feet to the rhythm and semi-audibly praise God. Faces turn red and blue as jerks and quivers become manifest. . . . As [the Evangelist's] driving behavior approaches its climax, a person may begin to speak in tongues, stand up and dance in the spirit, jerk and shiver, or stand up and shout. After a few minutes of acting out, [the Evangelist] starts again in his quiet, forceful voice. Each cycle from the quiet beginning to the thundering climax lasts from five to fifteen minutes.

One theory of the role of rhythm is that it creates a unique brain condition that yields an altered state of consciousness and that this promotes trance and possession (Locke and Kelly 1985; Rouget 1985). Auditory rhythm may stimulate corresponding rhythmic activity in the brain that contributes to trance. Although there is evidence that rhythmic auditory stimulation can cause changes in EEG patterns and other behavioral effects (e.g., Neher 1961; 1962), the rhythmic driving hypothesis of possession trance has little independent evidence other than the frequent co-occurrence of trance with music. The ecstatic movements of dancers and musicians at rock concerts and raves in this culture suggest that rhythm has a disinhibiting influence even when it occurs outside the context of a belief in the spiritual meaning of rhythm-induced states of mind. However, rhythm is clearly not sufficient by itself to produce spirit possession. If it were, everyone with a loud stereo in the apartment upstairs would soon glaze over and be taken by a spirit.

11. Glossolalia is the production of vocalization that sounds like language but isn't (Goodman 1972). Like the "scatting" of jazz singers (shoobedoowopwop), the sounds made in glossolalia seem interesting and potentially intelligible, and there are unskeptical reports of actual production of languages unknown to the speaker. There is no scientific evidence for this, however (Samarin 1972), and the actual production of glossolalia is something most people seem to be able to do with only a bit of coaching (Spanos et al. 1986; Spanos and Hewitt 1979).

The social interaction between possessed and nonpossessed group members is a further common feature of spirit possession in many cultures. In general, people don't seem to become possessed alone. Rather, this is something people do in groups who share the belief that it can happen, for special socially oriented purposes, and with important social consequences. The spirits are often seen as guides, and their advice is sought in matters of love, health, work, or social discord. Shamanism (once known as witch doctoring or spirit healing) is common in many societies worldwide, and individuals in this role often experience trance and possession on the way toward offering their healing nostrums (e.g., Eliade 1972).

The interaction between individual believers and the spirit-possessed goes beyond such advice-giving, however, and in some societies the spirits appear to have as complex and multilayered a social life as do the real people. Lambeck (1988) recounts how, in Malagasy speakers of Mayotte, individual spirits with unique identities visit each of several people in an assembled group in turn, taking care not to possess different hosts at the same time but offering consistent demeanor, stories, and advice from one host to the next. None of this is particularly magical, of course, as the people present conduct their interaction in public and everyone knows when a particular spirit has taken over a particular host. Certain spirits possess some people and not others, and each member of the community not only has an appreciation of the social life of the people but also knows all the spirits, who they like and dislike, and who they will inhabit and who they will not. In a society that shares belief in spirits, the individual spirits can take on the role of members of the society, albeit fairly special ones. Observing these clearly social features of possession, many theorists have remarked on the apparently crucial role of culture and social expectations in shaping the phenomenon.

What is it like to be possessed? Reports people offer after the experience recount a mixture of consciousness and nonconsciousness. Describing the experience of speaking in tongues in their Pentecostal church, for example, Abell's (1982) respondents talk about it in various ways:

When I got the Holy Ghost, it took a while before I came back. I was off in another world. (134)

I was over on one side of the church on my knees. When I came to myself later, I was on the other side of the church, still on my knees. (134)

I was just playing the piano one time in church. I felt the power of God and the next thing I knew, I was underneath the piano bench speaking in tongues. . . . There is no way I forced it. There is no way I tried to make myself do that. (135)

I've had the Spirit just nearly cover me up . . . and I just nearly lost sight of the world. I've not done that often . . . the Spirit is so strong that you lose sight of everything. (137)

In these and a variety of cases from other cultures, it appears that the frequent response of hosts after the spirit possession is over is to report some degree of amnesia for events and for their thoughts and actions during the experience. This reported lack of consciousness of the experience may be complete or, as observed in the Shango religion of Trinidad, may suggest "a halfway state between full possession and normal behavior, [in which] a high degree of consciousness is retained" (Mischel and Mischel 1958, 439). More often, however, lack of consciousness seems to be partial or sporadic at best (Samarin 1972). Spirit possession, like channeling, then, seems to have both trance and conscious varieties. Unlike channeling, however, which generally seems to be anticipated by the channel, spirit possession may be unexpected, involuntary, and even dreaded in some cases. The *Njarininsty* possession of school children in Madagascar, for instance, is generally undesired by the children and their teachers ("How will I ever get her to clap erasers now?") and is thus credited to bad or evil spirits rather than to the desired spirits that populate spirit religions (Sharp 1990). Even possession by desired spirits, however, is often described as happening involuntarily to the host despite all the preparation and ritual that seems to precede it (Besnier 1996). What appears to be a highly intentional, complicated, and almost theatrical performance is nevertheless experienced as involuntary and unwilled (Lee 1989).

There is reason to doubt the validity of some of these claims of unconscious, unwilled possession. Among believers in unconscious possession, there is likely to be great pressure for any who express the outward appearance of possession to report inward experiences of going unconscious. This pressure can create a tendency to report unconsciousness as the rule when it more often may be the exception. In a telling set of interviews, Halperin (1995) used the technique of *praising* conscious mediumship in talks with a number of "unconscious" mediums to see if he could prompt them to admit consciousness. These were people practicing

Tambor de Mina in Northern Brazil, an Afro-Brazilian possession religion related to Umbanda, and they were normally quite reticent to discuss the degree of consciousness in their trances.

Although the general expectation in these mediums was that conscious possession was less desirable and a poorer reflection of spirit involvement than unconscious possession, this interview strategy allowed respondents to admit that much of their experience involved conscious possession. One such medium remarked that his possessions are usually of short duration and that in these brief intervals he "goes in and out of consciousness." He reported, "In some moments, I lose all control and blank out. . . . It is like a dream, I remember some things but the rest is blurry or forgotten" (11). He reported that at other times he remains aware of what he sees, hears, and does while possessed. The doubts of this medium were sufficient so that he noted he might not be alone in his worship group because most of his compatriots "always seem to come out of trance just in time to catch the last bus home" (12). Although there may be strong enough pressure so that most people in a possession group report unconscious mediumship, their individual experience may more often amount to an "ebb and flow of awareness, with the medium sometimes in contact with the events around him and sometimes aware only of internal sensations" (Leacock and Leacock 1972, 210). The experience of possession seems not to imply a total oblivion and loss of self as much as it does the "total or partial loss of control of the body and the feeling that someone else is moving and talking through the possessed individual" (Frigerio 1989, 7).

Reports of the possession experience that are collected *during* the possession, of course, may come from the spirit and are difficult to collect or assess. Spirits are notoriously recalcitrant virtual agents who may not make a lot of sense even when they're not speaking in tongues. Their references to their hosts may range from indicating no knowledge of the host at all to full knowledge of the host's thoughts and concerns (e.g., Lambeck 1981). Any knowledge the spirit reports of the host suggests an incomplete amnesia for the host's memories, of course, so knowledgeable spirits also fuel doubts of the degree to which real partitions of consciousness and memory characterize the transition from self to spirit in possession.

Taken together, the evidence on spirit possession is not easy to put in a simple theoretical package. The usual simple packages that suggest themselves are two: trance and faking. A trance theory suggests that possession involves a major change of mental state (which perhaps could be measured in the brain), during which time people may be unconscious of their prior selves and are entirely operated by some new executive system corresponding to an imagined spirit (Lewis 1971; Locke and Kelly 1985; Price-Williams and Hughes 1994; Winkleman 1986). The faking theory suggests that people are always conscious of themselves and are simply overwhelmed by the social pressure to report trance phenomena (such as unconsciousness) while they are pretending to be a spirit, and so report such things falsely (Lee 1989; Spanos and Hewitt 1979). The widespread self-reports of unconsciousness, the dramatic behavioral changes in possession (such as convulsions), and a smattering of brain activity studies (Lex 1976; Winkleman 1986) support the trance theory. In contrast, the strongly social character of trance, the widespread self-reports of consciousness, and some reports of feigned unconsciousness during possession support the faking theory.

There is not enough evidence at this time to decide between trance and faking, but a better approach than deciding may be to suggest a middle position—a *self-induction* theory. Maybe people generally get into possession by faking or, to put it less pejoratively, through a process of pretending to be spirit-possessed. Then, during this process of social deception, a kind of self-deception develops (Gilbert and Cooper 1985; Gorassini 1999). The process of imagination becoming real intervenes to make the person experience progressively less action as willed by the self and more action as willed by the spirit. Processes creating perceptual detail, emotional experience, and feelings of uncontrollableness support the acceptance of the imagined virtual agent as real. In this process of action projection, the person becomes so deeply involved in performing the spiritlike behaviors and enacting the spirit role that consciousness of self is intermittently lost. Just as one might lose self-consciousness in driving a car and not "come to" very often with an awareness of driving, the person driving a spirit might not "come to" during the pretense. The person could forget, for a time at least, that there is a self that started this process.

In essence, self-induction would occur as a result of the failure of continuous identity rehearsal during the possession trance. The person is privy to much behavioral and mental evidence—feigned and self-produced though it may be—in favor of the idea that a spirit is running things, and might thus have to make a special effort to rehearse the idea that the self is still there in order to maintain awareness of this throughout the performance. This effort, then, is simply not made for some interval. In addition, alterations in mental state might accompany this transition. These trance states might be understood as sleeplike, altered states of consciousness (e.g., Barrett 1994), but they would not necessarily have causal role in the possession. Rather, the self-induction explanation would suggest that pretending generally precedes any such state changes. Just as people go to sleep, for example, by following a regimen (lying down, head on pillow, closing eyes), they may induce various alterations in brain states by following the spirit possession induction rituals. The self-induction theory, in short, says that people might fake themselves into a trance.

A self-induction theory is consistent with some evidence on both ends of the trance/faking dimension. The observations that people differ in their degree of consciousness and amnesia, and that they differ in their enactment of the spirit, for instance, can be understood in terms of variations in the ability to pretend and in the degree to which the imagination becomes real for each person. Those individuals who become professional channels or mediums may self-induce quickly and easily. This ability may be related to the ability to be hypnotized. But, also, important conditions in the person's situation could account for stronger or weaker self-inductions. Imagination could seem real because of emotion, perceptual detail, or lack of control. If a person is particularly emotional one evening (for reasons unrelated to the spiritual ritual), this emotion could fuel higher levels of self-induction. A person might have recently experienced something that could give rise to greater perceptual detail in the imagined experience of the spirit (e.g., hearing someone else give items of information about the spirit, or watching someone else become possessed), and this could fuel greater self-induction. And experiences of lack of control of own thoughts or actions could fuel this transformation as well, authenticating the person's progress into possession and prompting further self-induction.

Where does the self go during the possession? The self-induction theory would suggest that the conscious self is simply not being rehearsed or used during such a thorough and deeply felt imagining of another agent. Indeed, there are a number of cultures in which the loss of self is reported as a symptom by itself, without any spirit possession that replaces the self. This phenomenon of Susto, or spirit loss, for example, involves just such an absence of self, along with protracted illness, lethargy, and wasting away (Logan 1993). Victims of Susto report symptoms like those of *depersonalization,* a mental disorder (*Diagnostic and Statistical Manual of Mental Disorders, IV* 1994) characterized by a vague sense of self and by difficulty in understanding boundaries between self and nonself (Simeon et al. 1997). The person may feel like an automaton or as if he or she is inhabiting a movie or a dream. There can also be sensations of being an outside observer of one's own mental processes and of lacking control over one's actions. People with depersonalization disorder, like those who experience Susto, realize that these feelings are just feelings— they do not believe they are automatons. However, the feelings are deep and very disturbing. The sense of being an agent seems to be an important organizing scheme for the mind, one that provides a constant source of orientation and understanding, whether one is oneself or a visitor from the spirit world.

Identity and the Subjective Self

One way of appreciating identity is to note the continuity of subjective experience over time, the sense we have that we are agents who do things and experience things, and who in some regard are the same from one time to another. This sense of identity is inherent in the aspect of self that William James (1890) called the "knower," the self that is the seat of experience, the self that is doing all our thinking and living. Another way of conceptualizing identity is to speak of the self as an object one can think about, the aspect of the self that James called "known." People who speak of "self-concept" often are referring to this latter definition of identity, and in fact there are many theories of how people think about themselves (Baumeister 1998; Swann 1999; Wegner and Vallacher 1980). These theories examine the properties people attribute to themselves, how they evaluate themselves, and how these judgments of self influence behavior. There are very few accounts, however, of how the subjective self—the knower—is constituted. The notion of virtual agency is all about this and so opens up a new way of theorizing about an aspect of self that has previously been something of a mystery.

If it weren't for strange things like spirit possession and channeling, we might never have noticed that the subjective self can fluctuate and change over time. It is only by virtue of the ways in which people step outside themselves—to see the world from new perspectives, as different agents, with radically different points of view—that it becomes possible to recognize what an exciting and odd thing it is to have a subjective self at all. The subjective self each of us inhabits, in this light, is just one virtual agent of many possible virtual agents. Admittedly, the normal person's point of view is pretty stable; it takes a lot of drumming and believing and channeling lessons and who knows what else to get people to switch identities through the methods we've investigated so far. Yet such switching makes it possible to imagine that the self is not too different from a spirit—an imagined agent that is treated as real and that has real consequences for the person's behavior and experience.[12]

We now look into the very center of this fabrication of the subjective self—first by examining the topic of dissociative identity disorder, in which transformations of self and identity are endemic, and then by focusing on how the sense of virtual agency is constructed so as to give rise to the experience of being an agent.

Multiple Personalities

People who seem to have more than one personality have been noted from time to time in history. Perhaps the best-known instance is fictional, *The Strange Case of Dr. Jekyll and Mr. Hyde* by Robert Louis Stevenson (1886; fig. 7.6). The earliest nonfictional accounts of multiple personalities involved people who split into two, like Jekyll and Hyde, but later cases came to light in which people adopted many different identities, including, for example, the widely read case of "Miss Christine Beauchamp," described by Morton Prince (1906). Reports of cases

12. Dennett (1992) proposes a similar concept of the agent "self as the center of narrative gravity."

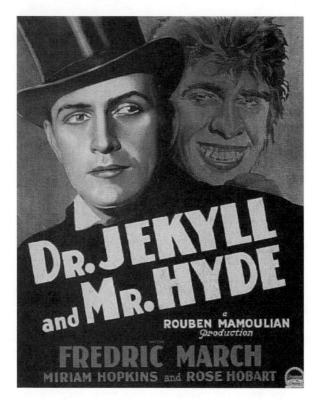

Figure 7.6
One of the movie versions of Robert Louis Stevenson's *The Strange Case of Dr. Jekyll and Mr. Hyde.*

continued through the 1920s until a period in which almost no cases were reported for forty years.

Perhaps because of confusion between multiple personality disorder and the far more prevalent diagnosis of schizophrenia, few cases were observed, and there were several pronouncements that multiple personality disorder might not exist (Taylor and Martin 1944; Sutcliffe and Jones 1962).[13] Then, however, a best-selling book, *The Three Faces of Eve*

13. Putnam (1989) provides a balanced and thorough account of this history. Still, it is interesting to note that the question of whether dissociative identity disorder exists remains a matter of some debate (Acocella 1999). Humphreys and Dennett (1989) offer an illuminating outsiders' view of the continued scrapping among the insiders.

(Thigpen and Cleckley 1957), and a movie of the same name starring Joanne Woodward, drew popular attention and scientific interest to the disorder. The book *Sybil* (Schreiber 1974), and its TV movie (with Sally Field as the victim and Joanne Woodward as the therapist) had further impact. The incidence of a syndrome once so rare that its existence was in doubt has since grown to thousands of documented cases, and the disorder has been accorded formal diagnostic status as dissociative identity disorder (DID) in the *DSM-IV* (1994).

In this disorder, an individual experiences two or more distinct personalities or personality states, each of which recurs and takes control of the person's behavior. There is usually a main personality, which is often dull, depressive, and quiet. As a rule, the other personalities seem to develop to express particular emotions or to fit certain situations that the central personality does not handle well. So there may be a lively, extroverted personality, a childlike personality, personalities of the opposite sex, personalities that express extreme anger or fear, or personalities that have witnessed traumatic events the main personality knows nothing about. There may be an "internal self-helper" personality that tries to make peace among the others, or an "internal persecutor" personality that badgers the main personality (Putnam 1989). The number of personalities emerging from one individual may number from a few to hundreds, and the trend in recent cases has been for more personalities to be observed. Far more women than men suffer from the disorder.

Some of the central features of the disorder can be seen in Morton Prince's (1906) analysis of Miss Beauchamp. In this case, the main personality was one that Prince came to call "the saint." She was morbidly conscientious, prudish, patient, and deeply religious, and consulted Prince because of her headaches, insomnia, nervousness, fatigue, and depression. He undertook a program of therapy and hypnosis with her, and one day under hypnosis she referred to herself not as "I" but as "she." Asked why, she explained "because she is stupid; she goes around mooning, half asleep, with her head buried in a book" (Prince 1906, 28). This new personality called herself Sally. The original personality (which Prince later labeled B1) knew nothing of Sally, but Sally was co-conscious with B1—knowing B1's thoughts and being able to influence her behaviors even without B1's knowledge. Sally deeply disliked B1 and would play tricks—she would tear up her letters, conceal money and stamps, and even sew up the sleeves of B1's clothes. She sent through the mail to B1 packages containing spiders, spent money lavishly on unsuitable clothes, broke B1's appointments, and walked out on jobs B1 had worked to keep (Wilkes 1988).

Later on, other personalities came forward, and Prince noted and labeled them although not all named themselves. He identified each personality's hypnotized state as another personality (for example, B1a was the hypnotized B1), and he noted differences in style and memory access between them. These personalities were generally unknown to B1, and some were also unknown to each other. A personality Prince called B4 emerged during their conversations (not during hypnosis), of which B1 knew nothing. Sally was conscious of B4's actions but not of her thoughts, and B4 knew nothing directly of either B1 or Sally. Sally continued to play the persecutor and was able "by a technique she described as 'willing,' to induce positive and negative hallucinations in both B1 and B4; she could induce aboulia (failure of will) or apraxia (inability to act), especially if the primary personality was, as she put it, 'rattled'; she could tease B1 by making her transpose letters of words she was writing . . ." (Wilkes 1988, 126). In this case and others, the personalities have differing levels of awareness of each other and control of the body.

The process of changing from one personality to another doesn't take very long. Putnam (1994) made observations of the switching process in DID patients and concluded that it takes about one to five minutes for a switch. He observed that "most, but not all, patients exhibit either a burst of rapid blinking or one or more upward eye rolls at the beginning of the switch . . . [which] may be followed by a transient 'blank' or vacant gaze. . . . [There] is a disturbance of ongoing autonomic regulatory rhythms, particularly heart rate and respiration, together with a burst of diffuse motor discharge" (295). When the switch occurs, there is often a shift in expressed emotion (e.g., from depressed to euphoric or angry) sometimes a change in voice or speech frequency, rate, or volume, and occasionally a rearrangement of facial muscles in a stepwise fashion through a series of grimaces. There may be postural shifts after the initial switch as the new personality seems to get comfortable and exercise the body (Putnam 1994, 295).

The switch process is reminiscent of the shtick that impressionist comedians do when they change into a character they are impersonating—looking away, shrugging their shoulders, and then turning around with a new expression. And, indeed, some commentators have understandably wondered whether patients are voluntarily pretending. Joanne Woodward looked very convincingly different as the characters Eve White and Eve Black in *The Three Faces of Eve*, yet she was an actress, not a multiple. It makes sense that people might be acting their multiple personalities. Perhaps, like those who develop spirit possession in order to express forbidden impulses, people become susceptible to multiple personality for instrumental reasons. Perhaps, also as in possession, people develop multiple personality through a self-induction process that begins with pretending and proceeds into uncontrollable changes.

The strange transition of DID from a once rare disorder to the "flavor of the month" of psychological problems has raised concerns that the disorder is indeed a matter of faking or fashion (Spanos 1994). The most common suggestion is that DID is caused by psychotherapists who, though often well-meaning, have searched so hard for evidence in patients who are vulnerable to their suggestive procedures that they have ended up creating the disease. Accounts of how therapists treat DID show indications of cajoling, suggesting, coaxing, and even bullying clients into reporting evidence of alter personalities, and many of the names for alters indeed are created by therapists (Acocella 1999). Dissociative disorders may have been created, rather than treated, through seriously flawed therapeutic and self-help procedures like those that try to recover "repressed memories" (e.g., Bass and Davis 1988) and instead insert false memories into the minds of clients (Ofshe and Waters 1994). There is evidence that new multiple personality cases tend to arise in communities primarily when therapists who believe in this disorder come to town. Acocella (1999) recounts a number of such instances and also points out numerous cases in which people once diagnosed with DID have become "retractors" and have successfully sued their therapists for causing their disorder. She concludes that the study of multiple personality disorder is "not a science but a belief system" (Acocella 1999, 81).

In this sense, the current wave of DID diagnoses may be understood as arising from belief processes much like those that underlie the creation of possession in religious groups or of spirit channeling in new-age believers. Multiple personality may be less a fundamental psychological disorder than a manifestation of the human ability to assume multiple virtual agents in response to strong social pressures and deeply held beliefs. The stories of Eve and Sybil may have given many people cultural recipes for the self-induction of new virtual agents and simultaneously instructed unwitting therapists in how to help them along.[14]

What evidence is there for the reality of multiple personalities? Perhaps the most basic fact is the sense of involuntariness that patients feel for the behavior they perform while in other personalities. The change process, too, is not usually reported to feel voluntary. Although switches can often be made on demand, when the therapist asks a patient to change, the changes may occur without the patient's knowledge or feeling of will (Spiegel and Cardeña 1991). This means that patients can have difficulties maintaining effectiveness in work, relationships, and life in general. One personality may take a prescription medicine in the morning, for instance, and others may take their own doses as they emerge during the day, leading to an overdose by evening. Or one personality may make an appointment, but the personality in control at the time of the appointment is amnesic for the information and misses it. Given that the personalities can be at odds with each other, these inconveniences may be complicated further by serious internal struggles, in some cases culminating in extreme self-injurious behavior. Although DID may evolve from

14. There are a number of other examples of ideas popping up in fiction that quickly become major cultural myths and that then seem to come back as "real events" through reports by people who have come to accept imagined experiences of these events as real. People began talking about "satanic cults" and "satanic ritual abuse" in the 1980s, for example, and fears of such goings-on rapidly wound up fueling dramatic accounts of atrocities despite the fact that there is almost no verifiable evidence of such activity anywhere in North America (Ofshe and Watters 1994; Victor 1993). We also now have an astonishing number of people who report having been abducted by aliens, usually to have their genitals examined and anus probed (Newman and Baumeister 1996). No one has yet explained why the aliens are so darned interested in these things, but the image of this occurrence seems interesting enough to people that it flickers into "reality" with remarkable frequency. Susan Blackmore (1999) describes the imagined experiences as "memeplexes," sets of ideas that live and die by evolutionary principles in the environment of human thought and communication. Her account is the best I've seen.

self-induction processes, it develops into a problem that is not then susceptible to immediate conscious control (Gleaves 1996).

There are some other potential indications of the reality of DID: Different personalities or alters may have different bodily states. Some of the most convincing evidence suggests through eye exams that different alters may have different levels of visual acuity (Miller 1989; Miller, Blackburn et al. 1991). One may be myopic and another may have perfect vision. There is also some evidence that handedness and manual dexterity can vary among alters (Henninger 1992; Schenk and Bear 1981). But repeated investigations looking for differences in EEG patterns between personalities have yielded no consistent results (Brown 1994). Instead, there is some evidence that patients merely relax and so show EEG alpha patterns as they switch between personalities (Cocores, Bender, and McBride 1984). Studies examining cerebral evoked potential responses have shown some changes between personalities, as have some studies looking at respiratory and heart rates, but the evidence for these psychophysiological disparities between personalities must be viewed as mixed (Brown 1994). It is not clear that someone merely pretending to have another personality could not show the same kinds of changes.

Evidence on amnesia is also unclear. Studies of memory sharing among personalities indicate that the conscious recall of items encountered by one alter is often seriously impaired in other alters. This could be explained as a matter of conscious faking. In studies of *implicit memory*, however, researchers have examined influences of information on behavior and performance that occur without the person's awareness that memory is being tested. In one study, for instance, one personality was shown a list of words and was asked to rate the pleasantness of each word (Nissen et al. 1988). Later, another personality was given a list of three-letter word stems, many of which could form words from the original list, and was asked to complete each one with the first word that came to mind. Although most people tend to complete the stems with many words from the original list, the second personality responded with only very few such completions. When the first personality was tested later, she used many words from the pleasantness rating list. Subsequent studies of implicit memory have found that such compartmentalization occurs on some implicit tasks but not others, suggesting that the memory dissociation between personalities is real but far from complete (Eich et al. 1997).

Another hard-to-interpret set of findings concerns how people develop multiple personalities in the first place. The main researchers in the field hold that the development of dissociative identities is linked with the occurrence of early psychological trauma. In patients diagnosed with DID, the prevalence of early trauma (such as physical or sexual abuse, extreme neglect, chronic pain, incest, or witnessing violent death) is reported to be more than 80 percent (Coons and Milstein 1986; Kluft 1987; Putnam et al. 1986). These studies have not independently verified the traumas, however, relying instead on therapist reports. Some investigators nonetheless claim that the relation is so strong that the occurrence of early trauma should be understood as a defining feature of the syndrome (Ross 1989). Others note, though, that both DID and traumatic early abuse are dramatic and salient phenomena that may appear to be linked merely because their co-occurrences are even more dramatic and distinctive (Tillman, Nash, and Lerner 1994). It is particularly curious, for example, that while early abuse and trauma are especially prevalent in low-income households, cases of multiple personality occur almost exclusively among people of middle income (Acocella 1999).

In the same way that Freud came to question the validity of reports of early sexual abuse in his psychoanalytic cases (his abandonment of the "seduction theory"; Masson 1984), we can wonder whether the reports of such abuse in DID are true. Prince (1906) mentions trauma only in passing in his comments on Miss Beauchamp, and the major early review of multiple personality by Taylor and Martin (1944) did not note any special role of trauma. Suggestions of traumatic origins have coincided with the widespread media coverage of multiple personalities through reports of Eve and Sybil, and it may be that these stories have promoted a cultural theory that has grasped the imagination of therapists and their clients alike (Acocella 1999). People susceptible to the development of multiple personalities may be particularly prone to confabulate such reports, and research is only now beginning to examine the degree to which early traumas can be verified independently.

It does make some theoretical sense, however, to view traumatic experience as a potentially powerful motivator behind the profound rearrangement of mind that seems to occur in DID. Perhaps when people are in the process of developing their sense of will and perception of themselves as agents, there is still some fluidity or instability in the system whereby the self is constructed. If extreme traumas are visited upon the individual, as viewed through the lens of this early virtual agent, an effective way of blunting or avoiding thoughts of the traumas might be the construction of an alternative virtual agent, one that is "not there" during the trauma. Some victims of trauma report being "away" or "floating above" the scene, and this could be the first step in the development of an alternative sense of virtual agency. Once the trick is learned, then, the production of yet other personalities could become a standard way to respond to new or difficult situations.

What should we conclude? The occurrence of multiple personalities among troubled people seems to be a real phenomenon in one important sense. Like people who report unconscious spirit possession and trance channeling, a person with multiple personalities offers reports of amnesia and involuntary control by other personalities. These reports are accompanied by behaviors suggesting that these experiences are very real for the person (Gleaves 1996). Questions of how the person reached this pass—through a natural response to trauma or by responding to the earnest suggestions of therapists looking for the disorder—are important for understanding how it might be treated or prevented. However, these questions need not be answered at this time in order to appreciate the implications of multiple personality for the topic of conscious will.

The phenomena of dissociative identity disorder remind us that our familiar subjective sense of being and doing are open to remarkable transformations. The self is not locked into place somewhere an inch or so behind our eyes, a fixture in the mind. Rather, the agent self is a fabrication put in place by the mechanisms of thought, a virtual agent that has experiences and feels as though it is doing things but that could conceivably be replaced by some other virtual agent that is implemented in the same mind. The experience of consciously willing an action is something that happens in a virtual agent, not in a brain or mind. The sense of *being an agent* creates our sense of subjective self and identity.

Personal Identity

How do you know you're the same person this morning who went to bed in your pajamas last night? For that matter, what makes you the same person as that kid whose mouth is smeared with cake in those early birth-day snapshots? If you're convinced that in both of these cases there's really no difficulty in fashioning an answer, here's another question: Imagine a small part of your brain is removed and replaced with a part made in a secret brain replication facility, which copied the old part and made the new part perfectly. Would the person remaining in your body still be you? What if it were the whole brain, replaced exactly? Would that be you?[15] If not, at what point would you disappear and someone else appear? One more possibility: On *Star Trek,* you are "beamed up" by Scotty, but there is a technical hiccup in the transporter. Because of a malfunction, you are produced twice, one right next to the other. Would one copy be you and the other not you, or would both somehow have your identity? Which one would have your experiences now? The sense of personal identity and continuity that we each understand intuitively as part of sub-jective self turns out to be a slippery concept when examined up close.[16] These stories of brains and beamings remind us that we need to consider more carefully how personal identity is influenced by changes in virtual agency.

The essence of personal identity is memory. This was John Locke's (1690) view and has since formed the basis of several further develop-ments of the memory theory of identity (Grice 1941; Perry 1975).[17] If you recall or recognize at this time some experience that occurred to you at a prior time, there is a thread of personal identity linking now and then. The experience contains not only the events or episode you remem-ber but also "you," the rememberer. Personal identity can be understood

15. This is the same identity argument as Aristotle's question of whether a ship that was rebuilt timber by timber would in the end be the same ship.

16. There are excellent and entertaining discussions of personal identity that help to illustrate the issues in Hofstadter and Dennett (1981). Ethical and practical problems arising in this area are examined in depth by Radden (1996) and Wilkes (1988).

17. Identity can be understood as having two aspects: unity and continuity. The unity of a person's identity involves the coherence of aspects of identity at one time, whereas the continuity of identity involves linking aspects of self over time. The memory analysis examined here is primarily relevant to continuity. Questions of the unity of a person at one time are addressed in analyses of the "binding" of experience in the brain (e.g., Crick and Koch 1990) and of the psy-chological interrelations of brain, body, and experience (e.g., Greenwald 1982).

as a chain of such links, a connection linking the "you"s over time. Not all such selves need to be linked directly to your current self for you to claim continuity of identity. If you remember yourself last weekend (e.g., shopping for peat moss) and the self who was shopping for peat moss had, at that time, remembered a self from a prior weekend singing in the shower one morning and making the dog howl, then you currently could claim to be identical not just to the peat moss self but to the shower-singing self as well, even if right now you might not recall the singing incident at all. In this way of thinking, the continuity of personal identity over time might be symbolized through a host of these various links, some massively paralleling one another in some events, others connecting the selves over time with just a few links, and yet others showing single threads linking otherwise discontinuous temporal islands of identity. As long as there is any one link between such islands of self, it can be said that the thread of personal identity is maintained.

A break in this thread of personal identity occurs when the self has no memory of being a past self. If such a break occurs, there might be a current self that is not the same as the past self. This, then, is all that is really needed for the occurrence of a transition from one virtual agent to another. If the person experiences a self that doesn't remember being the person's prior self, then a new virtual agent has been created. The transition from one multiple personality to another, or from person to spirit, or from channel to channeled entity, involves the development of an agent self that simply doesn't remember the prior agent self. The poorer the memory of past episodes that a virtual agent has, the more likely it will feel as though it has no prior identity. This lack of memory is equally important when the person moves back to the original agent self. The DID person returning to the main personality, or the channel or medium returning to the self, will experience a return to the old virtual agent that is particularly impressive when the interloper agent is not well remembered.

The memories that are related to identity are different from other kinds of memory. Identity-relevant memories involve the agent, a perspective from which the memory item was experienced. Endel Tulving (1972) distinguished such *episodic* memories from the more general class of *semantic* memories. Recalling that you ate fish for dinner last night would be an episodic memory, for example, whereas remembering that fish swim in water would be a semantic memory. Knowledge stored in semantic memory is source-free, without a conscious agent that experienced and recorded it, and such memory could easily be something that animals or babies have available in various degrees. Tulving (1985; 1999) suspects that episodic memory, however, is uniquely a characteristic of conscious human adults because of its special identity-relevance. Having memories with *who, where,* and *when* attached to them allows us to remember not only *what*. Memory for episodes brings along the self, kind of piggyback, and so allows us to make distinctions between selves we remember being and selves we do not.

Such identity changes are often viewed as all-or-none, radical transitions between virtual agents. Miss Beauchamp changes to Sally, or Jane Roberts changes to Seth. But this impression is an oversimplification, just like our tendency to think that we are either happy or sad rather than to appreciate all the variations and blends of these feelings we truly experience. People may change virtual agents gradually, in a piecemeal fashion, because both consciousness and memory can vary in graduated segments. One can spend more or less time consciously in an agent, or ascribe more or less of the body's actions to an agent. One can remember some actions and experiences of an agent at some times, and lose track of these things at others. Instead of a starkly qualitative property, then, identity becomes something we can slide into and out of moment by moment. Identity is a variable quantity that allows more than one virtual agent to share the resources of body and mind.

Consider how it is that we perceive the continuity of any object over time. To examine this, the Belgian psychologist Michotte (1962; see also Bower 1974) showed people items that changed over time in various ways. When, for example, a blue triangle was covered up, and the cover was then removed to show a blue circle, most people watching the demonstration felt that the same object was present. It had merely changed shape from triangle to circle. If, however, a blue triangle was covered up and a red circle appeared when the cover was removed, most viewers thought the object itself had changed identity. As long as some proportion of the features of the object remain the same, it is possible to maintain the perception that it is the same thing. When features change beyond that proportion, there comes a point when it suddenly is something new. If we view personal identity in this way, we can see that a variety of small changes in perceived authorship could add up to a sudden sense that a whole new virtual agent is in place. Transitions as radical as multiple personality switches or spirit possessions may happen little by little at first, in moments of failing to remember what identity we currently possess. With more instances of action that are attributed to the new virtual agent, these small changes can develop over time into noteworthy transformations.

In the overall ebb and flow of events and memories, it is a major achievement for our memory systems to keep track of who we are as well as they do. How, then, does memory for identity keep us in one virtual agent at a time? The process of remembering thoughts and actions must carry on by allocating the body's acts to particular agents, in line with the perception of the source of thoughts. This process will seek a virtual agent to account for each thought-action unit, and will accumulate as an identity those thought-action units ascribed to the same source. One key function of this system, then, is to create a "home agent," a virtual agent that is perceived as the source of present thoughts and actions. This is the place thoughts and actions are perceived to be coming from—the subjective self, the agent one inhabits. The feeling of conscious will for actions occurs to this agent, and perception of this agent's thoughts is used to predict the body's current actions. Actions that don't follow from those thoughts will be collected as inconsistent and may eventually lead to the postulation of another agent to whom they can be ascribed.

How does one move from one agent to another? As long as one's actions are consistent with one's prior thoughts, the actions continue to feel consciously willed and the home agent remains in operation. However, acts may begin to appear that are inconsistent with the home agent's thoughts (or memories of prior thoughts). One way to deal with such thoughts is to rationalize them somehow, making them consistent with the home agent's point of view. This brings them back into the fold, in a sense, and allows one to continue inhabiting the home agent. The auditory hallucinations or voices heard by people with schizophrenia, for example, are understood by the person to be voices of other agents, not the self. This rationale makes sense of the voices, even though they are being created by one's own mind, and also makes it understandable why no feeling of will is experienced for what those voices say.

Thoughts that are inconsistent with the home agent's thoughts can also create a new agent. There is a breakdown in experience of will for the home agent and the creation of an experience of will for a new agent—what might be called an "away agent." As more such experiences of will accrue for the away agent, a sense of subjective self and identity begins to form for that agent. The mechanisms of mind that give rise to behavior are now seen in a new light, from the perspective of a new self. All the activities that transport the person to this point—the rituals leading to spirit possession, the earnest attempts at pretending to channel, the events that precipitate multiple personality—pale in comparison to the intriguing event they produce: the home agent is lost and an away agent takes over. The change in virtual agency produces an experience of consciously willing actions from the perspective of a different self.

The Self as Operating System

It is probably time now to trot out the inevitable computer metaphor. Virtual agents seem a lot like software shells or operating systems on computers—different versions of Windows or Linux or Mac OS. On their face, virtual agents bear an important likeness to the interface of the operating system, the *look and feel* of the computer. An operating system or shell creates a virtual world, an array of what is possible with the machine and what is easily remembered that sits there on the screen and creates the way in which the world is experienced. The virtual agent we experience at any given time similarly produces our experience of the world for us.

Brains and nonconcious mental structures and processes, in turn, might be compared to the hardware of the computer. The operating system typically covers up this stuff, leaving all the wiring and machine languages under the surface. When we want to access a disk drive, we click on a nice little icon on the screen—we don't have to worry about making the motor turn, finding the proper tracks on the drive, or running the underlying machinery of our search. The operating system can vary from one computer to another, of course, and can also be changed in one computer from day to day. Some machines can boot up in Windows and also boot up in Linux, for example. What seems to happen in people who experience possession, channeling, and DID is highly reminiscent of rebooting the machine and bringing up a changed operating system after the boot. All the different operating systems work the "body"—they each give access to disk drives and printer ports and the like—but they each provide different "front ends" for the machine.

This way of viewing virtual agency is a nice metaphor without much scientific implication. It is not clear how we would go about testing this metaphor, for example, or what it predicts beyond some of the basic resemblances between people and computers. The operating system/self link does highlight, however, how the subjective self might be a construction—a replaceable set of ways in which things seem to the person—rather than an etched-in-stone feature of the structure of the mind. The point of this chapter has been establishing whether and under what conditions people might change the sense of self they experience as they act. We've seen any number of such transformations and have reached the point now of being able to step back and view the system as a whole. And, yes, it does look remarkably like a computer with interchangeable operating systems.

The conclusion we reach is that virtual agents can vary within each person, and perhaps more broadly, that *there is generally a virtual agent for each person*. The sense of having a conscious mind that experiences and chooses and acts is a basic feature of being human. But the fact that this perspective can change with vagaries of memory and experience suggests that this is a basic component that must be added onto the hardware of our brains and mental mechanisms for us to exist in anything like the way we now know ourselves. The development of an agent self in human beings is a process that overlays the experience of being human on an undercarriage of brain and nerve connections. We achieve the fact of having a perspective and being a conscious agent by appreciating the general idea of agents overall and then by constructing a virtual agent in which we can reside (see Attneave 1959).

The human being without a virtual agent is, by this logic, something of a zombie. Someone who is in this no-agent position might be like a person who is moving between multiple personality alters, for example, or like someone who is no longer feeling like himself or herself but has not yet achieved the state of spirit possession. Perhaps sleepwalkers or people in fugue states with subsequent amnesia could be envisioned this way. The inner state of such a person is mysterious. It is not clear what it is like to be without a virtual agent, as we have no reports of this state to go on. No one who can talk about these things intelligently quite knows what it is like to fail to be someone. Perhaps this state is like a dream in which we have no sense of will, or perhaps it is like nothing at all. We are conscious only from the perspective of a virtual agent, and so, with no such agent available, we may simply be not conscious. To be sure, it is only through the construction of a first virtual agent—the self—that a person becomes capable of experiencing conscious will at all.

8

Hypnosis and Will

In hypnosis the person experiences a loss of conscious will. This loss accompanies an apparent transfer of control to someone else, along with the creation of some exceptional forms of control over the self.

The principal condition for the induction of the hypnotic state is a vivid idea of a passive surrender of the will to that of some other person, who is able to influence his subject by words, acts, or gestures.

Wilhelm Wundt, *Lectures on Human and Animal Psychology* (1912)

You're at someone's house for dinner, and you have absolutely stuffed yourself. You lean back, basking in the glow of serious overfeeding. But the host is not quite done with you and offers you a bit more stuffing. This you decline with a smile and wave of the hand. I've had quite sufficient, you think to yourself. But the host says "Are you sure? Not just a little more? Otherwise it will go to waste." You wag your head no and look searchingly in another direction, but the host goes on, "Really, just one tiny spoonful more—you already ate yours up so fast! You must like it. Have a little more, just for me. C'mon, just a little." Feeling now that you're on the verge of making a scene, you relent, accept the stuffing, and the incident is over. You've succumbed to social influence.

If you're like me, you leave this event feeling coerced. You didn't want the stuffing and then you got it anyway. Some proportion of social influence creates this feeling of defeat, occasioning an inner monologue on what you wanted, what the other person wanted, and on how they got what they wanted and you didn't get what you wanted. Hypnosis is a form of social influence that occasions a much reduced level of this kind of reflective grumbling. Instead, feelings of cooperation and of involuntariness prevail—a giving over of control to the hypnotist. When this happens, people can end up performing actions they might not have predicted in advance that they would do, or actions that spectators may find unusual and embarrassing. Instead of taking a bite of stuffing, the hypnotized person barks like a dog or acts as though she can't get up from a chair.

A common trick of the stage hypnotist (e.g., McGill 1947), for example, might be to tell someone who is hypnotized that "until I tell you otherwise, you will be stuck to your chair, unable to get up from your seat. . . . In all other respects, you will feel fine and perfectly normal, except it will be as though you are glued to your chair . . . and the harder you try, the more you will be stuck to the seat. . . . No matter how hard you try, you will not be able to get up out of your chair." Now, if someone said this to you at a party, you would probably get up smartly from your chair, deliver a defiant hip swivel, and then sit back down. Yet people who are hypnotized have no such reaction and instead wriggle uselessly and look nonplussed as they find themselves indeed stuck in their chairs until the hypnotist suggests otherwise. This is not a trick in the sense that the stage hypnotist has paid people off to help in the performance; it is one of the genuine phenomena of hypnosis.

Clearly, hypnosis involves a significant departure from the everyday experience and exercise of conscious will. The hypnotized person experiences the causation of his actions in an unusual way, as being generated less by the self and more by the hypnotist. This is not only a feeling but involves a kind of actual transfer of control from person to hypnotist. What is equally odd, though, is that the range of what can be controlled changes during hypnosis. People find that they are able to control the experience of pain or the recall of memory, for example, in ways that are not readily available to them when they are not hypnotized. In this sense, while hypnosis may undermine the experience of will, it seems paradoxically to expand and alter the force of will. This is why hypnosis has been implicated in many of the curiosities of will we have discussed, including possession, multiple personality, and automatisms. One way to explain what is happening when people experience departures from normal conscious will is to say that they've been subjected to some special process or state. Perhaps they are hypnotized.

But what, then, is hypnosis? This chapter examines what is known about hypnosis in current scientific psychology. The first focus is on induction—how people get to be hypnotized and who is most susceptible.

Second, we take up the major phenomena of hypnosis, the features that distinguish the psychology of the hypnotized person from that of the person in a standard waking state. The third concern is figuring out what causes hypnosis. The chapter reviews the major theories and examines how some of the effects of hypnosis might be explained in terms of the theory of apparent mental causation. It concludes that hypnosis really only makes sense when we recognize that the experience of conscious will can be influenced by factors that are independent of the factors that cause human action.

Hypnotic Induction

The induction of hypnosis is no different, in principle, from any attempt at direct social influence. Like the host who repeatedly pleads with you to have that spoonful of stuffing, the modern induction of hypnosis involves repeatedly asking a person to comply with requests. There is a sense, though, in which direct influence is about one thing—a single target behavior that is requested (the stuffing)—whereas hypnosis involves a series of requests, building from very minor suggestions to more major ones. Hypnotic induction is a *process of social interaction* in which one person comes to have influence over another without the other's feeling deeply coerced. The basic process follows from the simple fact that people can follow instructions given to them by another.

The Essence of Induction

A demonstration of something like hypnotic induction was provided by Frank (1944b). He asked people to eat unsalted soda crackers, one after another, until they would have no more. Then, like the pushy host, he asked them to please eat another. Some people did, others demurred, and eventually he got to the point with everyone where they would have no more at all. Then he changed tactics. He asked if they would be willing to take a cracker in their hand. People did this. Then, would they touch it to their lips? They did. Would they put the cracker between their lips? They did this. Between their teeth? This, too. Then, he asked them to go ahead and take a bite, and several went ahead and did it. Then when he asked them to finish it, they did that, too. Despite their fullness and all the protesting, they were led to perform this behavior seemingly against their will.

Was this hypnosis? It probably was not, in the sense that Frank did not produce in these people a general tendency to follow his suggestions in other areas. But this induction of cracker eating shares with hypnotic induction a key feature that seems to arise in many other cases of social influence: a process of *sequential agreement*. The person being influenced goes along with some one or a few minor explicit requests or implicit gestures of request by the influencer. She becomes inveigled, drawn into the interaction by assenting in a minor way to some seemingly inconsequential first influence attempts. This inveiglement may then involve a lengthy series of influences, all seemingly baby steps, but the "baby" keeps toddling along and eventually ends up performing target actions that she would have been highly unlikely to do had they been requested at the outset.

Sequential processes of agreement are well known among social influence researchers. One such process, for instance, is known as the "foot in the door" procedure. It is often impossible to get people to comply with a large request that they encounter cold, whereas they may be inclined to comply if they have previously complied with a smaller request. Freedman and Fraser (1966) tested this idea by going door-to-door asking people to place a large "Drive Carefully" sign on their lawns. Normally, most people would not do this. Some were asked by an experimenter before this happened, however, to display a small "Be a Safe Driver" sign in their window, which most of them did. The people induced to make this small gesture became far more likely to go along with the subsequent request and allow the big sign to be installed. Hypnotic induction is similarly a process of getting someone progressively involved with the plans and instructions of the hypnotist until following even the big instructions eventually seems like the thing to do.

This sequential process seems to be one of several ways of creating a key ingredient of hypnotic induction—the person's *assent to be influenced*. Now, there are many times, I'm sure, in which you've agreed to be influenced. When someone says, "Would you do me a favor?" without telling you what will be requested, for example, you may say "Sure. What do you want?" In so doing, you have given prior consent to be influenced.

You've given away the right to protest or say no to any action you are then asked to do—within the bounds of reason and the nature of the relationship, of course. He can ask you to run down to the store for a six-pack or to give him a back rub, and you're pretty much stuck because you've already agreed. This kind of *meta-influence* (influencing the person to be influenced) is the initial step in most hypnotic induction as well as in many forms of direct social influence. Frank (1994a, 23) commented on his soda-cracker studies in precisely these terms: "Resistance to an activity is strongly inhibited if [the activity] appears to be implied by a previous agreement."

The agreement to be influenced is sometimes used unfairly by salespeople, in what has come to be called the lowball technique for inducing compliance. The usual ploy occurs most often in automobile salesrooms, when the salesperson arranges all the details of your deal for the car you want, gets the whole thing on paper, and then goes to check with the boss to see whether they can accept your "offer." It then turns out that the boss can't let the car go for this amount because of X (fill in an appropriate costly excuse here), and you find that you will have to pay $500 more. Having now come this far, however, you're no longer willing to give it all up, so you go ahead and cough up the extra. You've been low-balled. Don't conclude that you're a dupe here, though, because this happens to many people. Cialdini and colleagues (1978), for example, invited people to participate in a psychology experiment that was scheduled for 7 A.M., and very few agreed to do this. However, if they were first asked whether they would be in an experiment and agreed to do it, and *then* were informed that the only time available was 7 A.M., they were far more likely to comply—and they even showed up. The initial commitment to be in an experiment amounted to a case of agreeing to be influenced.

The usual hypnotic induction starts, then, with getting people to agree to be influenced. People are told, for example, that hypnosis is not dangerous, that they won't be inclined in hypnosis to do anything they find morally wrong, that they may be endowed with a rare ability to follow hypnotic suggestions, and so on. These initial reassurances help people to make that initial decision to do it. They develop enough trust in the hypnotist at this point to sign a blank check, as it were, allowing further influence to take place unimpeded. Once this part of the procedure is over, the hypnotic induction becomes a cooperative action, something both people are trying to achieve. With a plan in place to do hypnosis, the sequential agreement process can proceed.

The hypnotist's first few requests often prompt subjects to do something they are already doing or something they can't discern that they're *not* doing. The hypnotist might say, "Please sit back comfortably in your chair," as though otherwise people might be perched in some awkward position ready to fall off and bump their heads. The hypnotist might say, "Relax your neck by tightening it and releasing it, and now your arms, now your legs, now your back." This seems innocuous enough, so people go along and do these things. They might already be relaxed and so have nothing to do, but this is a fine point they don't notice.[1] The hypnotist might then ask the person to fixate on something: "Find a spot on your hand now and fix your gaze on it. Look at it very constantly." This might be the first significant request the person could fail to follow, but by now most people go along with this, too. Then the induction proceeds, often by asking people to relax more, although most hypnotists have the sense to avoid the cliché "You're getting sleepy, very sleeeepy." The amount of repetition in the induction is quite notable to anyone who has not heard this before—clearly much more even than all that begging from the stuffing host.

The next steps of induction involve tests and demonstrations of involuntariness. The hypnotist might comment, "Your eyes are now getting a bit dry, somewhat heavy. They're feeling like they have been open for a long time. It might feel good to close them, to let them fall down shut. They are falling just a little now, just a little more, and all the while they are feeling heavier. They are so dry, so tired of being open. They are closing now, closing, closing. The lids are heavier and heavier, falling down, falling down shut." The hypnotist might repeat this several times in various ways, and like the dutiful stuffing-eater, many people will go ahead and placate the hypnotist by closing their eyes. You may be feeling an

1. The actual occurrence of relaxation is not an essential part of the induction. In one study, for example, people given an induction while riding an exercycle nonetheless exhibited comparable levels of hypnotic behavior (Banyai and Hilgard 1976). Relaxation techniques borrow much from hypnotic induction, however, and it is often easier to induce hypnosis with an accompanying relaxation script, perhaps because it gives the subject something to do (Edmonston 1981).

impulse to do this yourself, but then you would have to stop reading and miss the rest of the chapter. Perk back up, please.

Later tests and demonstrations then become more challenging. For instance, the hypnotist might ask people to hold their hands in front of them, palms together, fingers apart, and then to bring them together, clasp them, and let them drop lightly in their laps. The hypnotist asks them to clasp their hands together very tightly, repeating this request several times, and then asks them to notice how their hands seem to be so tightly clasped that they are not easy to pull apart. This odd suggestion—please clasp your hands but notice that when you try, they are difficult to pull apart—leads the person to experience a bit of involuntariness, the sense that the hands are not in voluntary control. They actually do feel sort of stuck; it seems quite possible for an instant to ignore the fact that you're clasping them together all the while. The attempt to pull them apart is not a success, perhaps, or it goes slowly, and this serves as a further demonstration of the hypnotist's control and your lack of influence over your own body. The induction might take the person through a series of such tests—involuntary arm heaviness (when you hold your arm out in front of you, it feels heavy and is falling down), head nodding (your head is falling forward), or the like.

During these tests, the hypnotist often says things to support the person's belief that hypnosis is actually occurring. For example, "As your hand gets heavier and heavier, your arm feels like it is being pulled down by a heavy weight. And as it falls, falling, falling down, you find you are falling deeper and deeper into hypnosis." Induction procedures differ widely, of course, and some are more successful than others. Nobody knows exactly the right way to proceed, and the history of hypnotic induction reveals a menagerie of techniques.[2] Eventually, however, it works, at least for some of the people some of the time. Then people usually need to be talked out of hypnosis just as they were talked into it. A suggestion for waking is given: "When I count to three and say 'Wide awake,'

2. Many hypnotists make their induction speech sing-songy and repetitive, with a kind of rhythm that gets monotonous. It is not clear if this has any actual influence, as might follow from the rhythmic driving hypothesis of spirit possession, or whether it just happens to be the fashion. Brown (1991) writes about the rhythms of hypnosis.

you will awake relaxed and refreshed. You will open your eyes and stretch your arms and you will feel good. Okay, here we go ... 1 ... 2 ... 3 ... Wide awake!"

Strange Inductions

Hypnosis did not come into being suddenly, with a handy name and the induction techniques all spelled out. It was discovered over time. People have experimented in countless sessions with almost as many techniques of hypnotic induction as there are hypnotists. Historical tradition points to the discovery of "animal magnetism" by Franz Anton Mesmer, however, as the first widespread use of hypnotic procedure (Ellenberger 1970; Gauld 1992). This technique, later named hypnotism by James Braid (1843), started out as a kind of healing ritual.

Mesmer was a Viennese physician who developed a reputation for healing patients in France at the turn of the eighteenth century through the use of what he believed was a magnetic force influencing human beings. He performed activities with his patients that we now classify as hypnotic induction procedures but that he claimed were techniques for focusing and directing "animal magnetism." The induction of what was later called mesmerism is described by Laurence and Perry (1988) as follows:

Upon arrival at Mesmer's clinic, patients were taken to a dimly lit room which was adorned with heavy drapes and zodiacal and masonic signs painted on the walls. The patients were asked to sit around a table that was the cover of a circular oak box, 18 inches high and 6 feet in diameter. This *baquet* ... contained water, broken glass, and iron filings ... covered by a wooden panel which had a number of holes, through which either glass or iron rods protruded. Each rod was bent at an angle that allowed one extremity to be in water while the other could be applied to the patient's body. (58)

Mesmer often roped all the participants loosely together, with one end of the rope in the tub and the other tied to himself. He then made *passes*, moving his hands or an iron or glass rod near each person repeatedly without actually touching the person.[3] The person might watch, or perhaps would have eyes closed and experience the passes just by

3. The use of passes in hypnosis was particularly popular later in its history and still enjoys a certain popularity in an alternative health care technique called "healing hands" or "therapeutic touch" (e.g., Macrae 1987). Practitioners, most

Figure 8.1
Group assembled for a mesmeric session. Participants seated at the *baquet* already have iron rods in hand, whereas standing spectators are talking about how much the fellow at the far left looks like George Washington. From Hull (1933).

hearing Mesmer's movements (fig. 8.1). This would go on at length, yielding responses that varied among people as a function of their previous experiences:

The neophytes usually did not feel anything unless Mesmer himself came to magnetize them. For the more experienced patients, there were different types of reaction. Some would laugh, sweat, yawn, shiver; most of them had bowel movements, a sure sign of the effect of the magnetism, though this appears to have been the result of ingesting cream of tartar, a light laxative. . . . In a small proportion of patients, the effects were more intense. They shouted, cried, fell asleep, or lost consciousness. They sweated profusely; laughter and shivers became convulsive. In all this, Mesmer appeared like the conductor of an orchestra. With his glass or iron rod, he directed the ensemble. (Laurence and Perry 1988, 59)

Mesmer's magnetism became a popular sensation and spread rapidly through France and Europe, developing a large following of practitioners

---

often nurses or other health care workers, have developed a detailed ideology surrounding the practice that unfortunately includes occult themes of which it is easy to be skeptical.

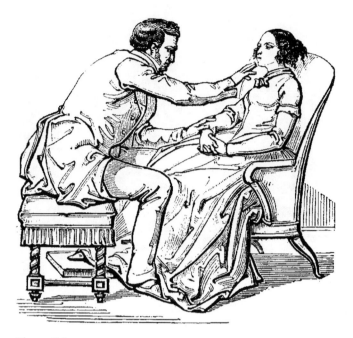

Figure 8.2
Mesmeric passes. From Dupotet (1862).

(fig. 8.2). The idea became a well-developed cultural knowledge system in short order, just like the current widespread "sleeeeeepy" understanding of hypnosis. This no doubt helped in the implementation of the key procedures of induction—the sequential agreement process and the agreement to be influenced. The sequential agreement process was subtle in Mesmer's approach, but we know that patients came to him with hopes of being healed of a variety of complaints, that they had heard of his successes, and that they paid him in advance for his services (Winter 1998). Sitting by the plumber's nightmare *baquet* and allowing the mesmerist to make passes are initial steps to which people assented on the way to their bizarre behavior. No doubt, the presence of a company of people being magnetized helped to secure the success of the process as well, as more experienced patients served as models for the less experienced and all served as expectant audiences for one another.

Mesmer's success was not dependent on his ability to make people convulse, of course, but on the cures he produced through his methods. Beyond all the strange behavior of his subjects was an underlying tendency to follow suggestions for the relief of symptoms—pain such as headache or backache, some cases of paralysis, blindness, lameness, and other complaints. His flourishes had the effect of influencing the expression of symptoms that are traditionally viewed as *hysterical* in origin—physical complaints without clear physical cause. Later, the psychiatrist Jean Charcot employed hypnotic techniques more like modern ones to much the same end and became famous for his treatment of hysterical symptoms (Ellenberger 1970). Pierre Janet and Sigmund Freud, in turn, each used varieties of hypnosis among the same sorts of patients, creating cures or rearrangements of symptoms by the use of suggestion (Showalter 1997).

Many of the most unusual hypnotic induction techniques depend on just the sorts of preparatory experiences evident in mesmerism. Hypnotic induction that seems instantaneous is commonly seen among faith healers, for example, when a belief system and a worship service provide the context of sequential agreement in which a single touch is enough to produce hypnotic effects. You may have come across the faith healer Benny Hinn on late-night TV, for example, putting people into trances by merely pushing them down by the forehead. Abell (1982) describes this particular move in the case of a Pentecostal church meeting:

Whether it is at the prayer line for persons seeking physical healing, or at the altar where a person is seeking the Holy Ghost, a significant stimulus . . . is "the push." . . . As a potential convert is facing the minister, the minister will grip the convert's forehead . . . [and] slightly (but very significantly) push the convert backwards. It is usually enough of a push that the potential convert will fall over backwards if he does not quickly attempt to regain his balance. . . . So the potential convert is forced both to take a step backwards as quickly as possible and to jerk his head and trunk forward. . . . It is precisely at the moment of the jerk that potential converts often go into a trance—dancing and quivering rapidly and violently, often accidentally hitting people and even falling down. (132–133)

The speedy induction through "the push" bears some resemblance to the fast inductions that occur among people who have had prior hypnosis. A hypnotist may specifically suggest this, saying, "You will wake up now, but later when I give you a special signal, when I say, 'Relax,' you will very quickly relax back into your deepest hypnotic trance." This expedient makes the next hypnotic session take less time to initiate. Such rapid reinduction is one form of posthypnotic suggestion, the technique whereby people are given suggestions during hypnosis that they then perform later (sometimes unconsciously) when they return to a waking state. A rapid reinduction strategy is also used in stage hypnosis, as people who have been hypnotized earlier may be approached again during the show for what appears to be their first induction and be instantaneously hypnotized for the audience with one prearranged gesture or word (McGill 1947). The hypnotist says, "*Be* the dog," and suddenly the audience member is down on all fours yipping.

Hypnotic induction procedures can differ widely because of the strong influence of expectation on the entire hypnotic process (Kirsch 1999). It may matter far less what the hypnotist does than just that the hypnotist is doing *something* that is expected to have some effect. Hypnosis may be another version of the placebo effect, a way in which people behave when they think something is going to have an influence on them. The various hypnosis gadgets available in the media back pages may be quite effective in their own way for this reason—merely because people suspect that they might work (fig. 8.3). Perhaps if people generally believed that clog

Figure 8.3
One of many versions of the hypno-coin. These can be dangerous if swallowed. Courtesy of Terry O'Brien.

dancing would effect hypnotic induction, people could be clogged into a trance.

Hypnotic Susceptibility

The tendency to follow hypnotic suggestions as well as to experience a reduction in the sense of conscious will in hypnosis varies widely in the general population. There are virtuosos, and there are those who can't or won't carry the tune. Most of us are between these extremes; most people are susceptible enough so that some kinds of hypnotic effects can be produced in over half of the population. Only about 10 percent, however, fall into what might be called the highly susceptible range on tests such as the Harvard Group Scale of Hypnotic Susceptibility (Shor and Orne 1962) and the Stanford Hypnotic Susceptibility Scale (Hilgard 1965; Weitzenhoffer and Hilgard 1962). These scales are not questionnaires but instead are standard hypnotic inductions made up of a series of tests of behavioral responsiveness to induction and experienced involuntariness. These scales are correlated with each other and with other indications of the success of induction but are only moderately associated with other personality dimensions that would seem as though they ought to be indicative of hypnotizability.

To nobody's surprise, for instance, hypnotic susceptibility is moderately correlated with the tendency to say yes in response to questionnaire items (what is called the acquiescence response set; Hilgard 1965). Susceptibility is also somewhat related to imagination (the ability to experience vivid visual imagery; Sheehan 1979) and to absorption (the tendency to become deeply absorbed in experience; Tellegen and Atkinson 1974). Susceptibility is also correlated with the self-prediction of hypnotizability—people who think they can be hypnotized often indeed can be hypnotized (Hilgard 1965). This finding is in line with the aforementioned principle that expecting to be hypnotized may be a key cause of becoming hypnotized (Council, Kirsch, and Grant 1996; Kirsch 1999).

That's about it, however, for personality correlates of hypnotizability. There does not seem to be a strong relation between hypnotizability and any of the major dimensions of personality identified by standard personality inventories, or between hypnotizability and dimensions of psychopathology assessed by usual measures such as the MMPI (Hilgard 1965; Kihlstrom 1985). So, for example, hypnotizable people are no more likely than others to be emotional or neurotic. It turns out, too, that there is no clear gender difference in hypnotic susceptibility (Hilgard 1965) despite the greater representation of females in several of the dissociative disorders and practices. Although hypnotizability is very stable over time, showing very similar levels even over the course of twenty five years (Piccione, Hilgard, and Zimbardo 1989), the hypnotizable person is not an easily characterized individual.

These findings are disappointing for those who have tried to explain the phenomena of dissociation, such as spirit mediumship or multiple personality, by connection to hypnotizability. It is tempting to suspect that there is one kind of person who is responsible for all this spooky stuff. But, as it turns out, there is no appreciable relation between measures of dissociation (such as the Dissociative Experiences Scale; Bernstein and Putnam 1986) and hypnotic susceptibility (e.g., Faith and Ray 1994). This may be due to the lack of a unified "dissociative personality," and the tendency instead for different dissociative experiences to happen to different people. The general absence of a relation between hypnotic susceptibility and most tests of psychopathology, in turn, is problematic for theorists who perceived a connection between the phenomena of hysteria and the occurrence of hypnotizability (Ellenberger 1970; Gauld 1992; Kihlstrom 1994; Showalter 1997). After all, the similarity of hysterical conversion reactions (blindness, paralysis, convulsions, anomalous pain) to the results of hypnosis led many clinical theorists over the years, such as Charcot, Janet, and Freud, to the conclusion that hysterics were hypnotizable and hypnotizables were hysterics. This does not seem to be the case.

Instead, it seems that the unusual pliability of the hypnotized subject allows such subjects to mimic various psychopathologies. As mentioned earlier in the discussion of dissociative identity disorder (chapter 7), many cases of multiple personality seem to have arisen through the use of hypnosis in therapy (Acocella 1999). It is not particularly difficult, in fact, to get hypnotically susceptible people to produce vivid symptoms of DID in one or a few hypnosis sessions. In one study, subjects under suggestion produced automatic writing that they could not decipher but that on further suggestion they could understand and translate in full (Harriman 1942). About 7 percent of subjects in another study were able to respond to suggestions to create a secondary personality, a personality for which the main personality was then amnesic (Kampman 1976). The remarkable flexibility of the hypnotized individual has created a serious confusion between psychopathology and what might be no more than the chronic result of *suggestions* of psychopathology.

To summarize, the induction of hypnosis requires two things: the right situation and the right person. The situation is the actual induction process, and as we have seen, this can vary quite widely from the standard induction we reviewed in detail. The induction can occur, moreover, quite without anyone's awareness that a process of hypnosis is underway. The response of the faith healer's subjects to "the push" is undoubtedly of the hypnotic variety, but both the healer and the faithful would likely balk at any description of their interaction as hypnotic induction. The induction of hypnosis also requires a special sort of person. Although most people can experience some of the effects of hypnosis, only a few will show evidence of strong influence along with extreme reductions in the sense of voluntariness across a range of hypnotic tests.

The findings regarding hypnotic susceptibility suggest a cautionary note for our study of the will. In essence, we can't be sure that what we learn about the nature of conscious will through the study of hypnosis is true of all people. Any anomalies in the experience of will that we observe happening during hypnosis are, in fact, limited to that portion of the population that is hypnotically susceptible. In the words of the early hypnosis researcher Albert Moll, "Though hypnosis is not a pathological state it is an exceptional one, from which we must not draw general conclusions. Few who have made such experiments often can fail to feel occasional subjective doubts of freedom of will, but from these doubts to scientific proof is an immense step. Further, it should not be forgotten that we do not by any means find these deep hypnoses and subjective delusions of the judgment in all subjects" (1889, 155).

Hypnotic Phenomena

What does hypnosis do? The main questions about the influence of hypnosis seem to come down to three: What does it feel like? Can people be hypnotized to do things they would otherwise not do? and Can people be hypnotized to do things that they would otherwise not be *able* to do? The first question is really about what consciousness is like in hypnosis and whether the experience of conscious will is preserved. The second is about whether the will of the hypnotist is truly imposed on the subject. And the third is a question about special talents—whether there are human abilities that are available to us only through hypnosis.

The Experience

For some reason, hypnosis researchers have devoted a tremendous amount of effort to discerning whether people who are hypnotized are in a "trance." The same hand-wringing we found around this word in the case of spirit possession shows up here (Chaves 1997). One camp wants to use this word (e.g., Hilgard 1986) and another finds it objectionable (e.g., Spanos 1986). The main objection is that "trance" or "altered state of consciousness" might be interpreted as a causal explanation rather than as a description of a feeling. The hypnotized person often describes the experience as one in which consciousness is not quite the same as usual—an altered state, maybe with some grogginess or a feeling of blankness. If we stop at this point and appreciate that this might be called a trance, then the term is usefully descriptive. Indeed, being hypnotized can seem like a dream or sleep state (Edmonston 1981); there was an early period of hypnosis research in which the state was even called *somnambulism*, the term now applied to sleepwalking.[4] In hypnosis, at any rate, people do report that something is different—they say they are hypnotized (e.g., Spanos and Katsanis 1989).

The experience of being hypnotized is usually accompanied by a sense of involuntariness regarding the suggested behavior, a feeling that one's action is happening rather than that one is doing it. In a study by Bowers, Laurence, and Hart (1988), people were asked to perform a series of twelve hypnotic tests. In one test, for instance, people were asked to hold their arms straight out ahead, palms a few inches apart, and it was

---

4. The historical confusion between hypnosis and sleepwalking is why one often sees cartoon depictions of hypnotized people walking with their arms out-stretched. People who are sleepwalking are usually shown with eyes closed and arms outstretched, although this isn't typically what happens in fact. (Shakespeare said of the sleepwalking Lady Macbeth: "You see, her eyes are open, but their sense is shut!")

suggested to them that their hands were coming together. In this sample of respondents doing the twelve tests, 63 percent of the suggested behaviors were experienced (e.g., people said they found their hands coming together). Considering now only those people who experienced actually following the suggestion, some 32 percent of these experienced complete involuntariness ("I found my hands moving together without my helping them"), 26 percent experienced the development of involuntariness ("I found I directed the movement of my hands and then later they continued to move together with no effort on my part"), 22 percent experienced partial involuntariness ("The feelings of purposefully moving my hands were completely mixed with feelings that they were moving on their own"), and only 12 percent experienced complete voluntariness ("I purposefully directed the movement of my hands most of the time").

The instructions in most hypnotic inductions stress involuntariness. Perhaps hypnosis creates the experience of involuntariness merely by saying that this is the way things will be. Just as someone saying again and again how sick you must be can make you sick, or someone saying how guilty you must feel can make you feel guilty, perhaps someone saying you have no conscious will makes you lose the feeling of doing. When hypnotic test instructions are put into words that imply involuntariness ("Your hands are coming together"), in fact, people report stronger feelings of involuntariness than when the instructions are put into words that emphasize volition ("Please bring your hands together"; Gorassini and Perlini 1988; Spanos and Gorassini 1984). This suggests that the experience of involuntariness is the result of an interpretive exercise, a self-observation in which one's behavior performed in this context comes to be understood as involuntary because of the way it is described (Sarbin and Coe 1972; Spanos 1986). It makes sense in this light that people given "permissive" hypnotic suggestions ("Let your hand become heavy") report feeling more voluntary than those given "authoritative" suggestions ("Your hand will become heavy"). When the tone and language suggest that you're being pushed around, you feel pushed around (Lynn et al. 1988). Finally, experiencing one's behavior as unwilled should not happen if one doesn't actually perform the suggested action, and indeed involuntariness is experienced to the degree that the suggested action is actually carried out (Barber 1969; Bowers 1981; Gorassini 1999).

Hypnotic Influence

It is easy to code the interaction between hypnotist and subject as a battle of wills. The hypnotist influences the subject to do something he or she wouldn't normally do, and the subject's feeling of will dissipates in direct relation to the loss of willful control. As it turns out, the full story on the nature of hypnotic influence is more complex than this (have you ever heard of the full story being simpler?). The actual control of the subject's behavior must be distinguished from the perceived control. The idea we've been pursuing throughout this book is that the experience of conscious will is not a direct indicator of a causal relation between thought and behavior. In the case of hypnosis, this means that the subject's perception of involuntariness is not a direct indicator of the role of the subject's thought in causing the subject's behavior. Although the subject may perceive a draining away of conscious will during hypnosis, and the hypnotist may in turn experience some sort of surge in perceived control over the subject (we don't actually know this because no one has studied hypnotists), these perceptions and experiences are not the final word on hypnotic influence. We need to establish what actual transfer of control is occurring, not only how it seems.

Let's look into such hypnotic influence with some examples. Take, for instance, voodoo death. In 1942 the psychophysiologist Walter B. Cannon published a paper on this topic that summarized the anthropological and medical evidence available at the time. He described multiple cases of this phenomenon so extraordinary and so foreign that it seems incredible. One case, taken from Basedow (1925), illustrates the effect of the belief among Australian Aboriginal peoples that having someone point a bone at you is fatal:

The man who discovers he is being boned by an enemy is, indeed, a pitiable sight. He stands aghast, with his eyes staring at the treacherous pointer, and with his hands lifted as though to ward off the lethal medium, which he imagines is pouring into his body. . . . He attempts to shriek but usually the sound chokes in his throat . . . his body begins to tremble and the muscles twist involuntarily. He sways backwards and falls to the ground, and . . . appears to be in a swoon. After a short time he becomes very composed and crawls to his wurley. From this time onwards he sickens and frets, refusing to eat and keeping aloof from the daily affairs of the tribe. Unless help is forthcoming in the shape of a counter-charm administered by the . . . medicine man, his death is only a matter of a comparatively short time. (178–179)

Of course, events of this kind cannot be produced in the laboratory, and so it is difficult to offer a confident judgment of whether they even exist—let alone what caused them. However, Cannon (1942) observed a variety of similar effects in laboratory animals and in people subjected in life to intense physical traumas, leading him to propose that death might be caused psychologically through "lasting and intense action of the sympathetico-adrenal system" (187). The same reaction, known medically as *shock,* might be responsible for fatal responses to psychological threats. Although Cannon did not implicate hypnosis directly in his analysis, he pointed to the crucial importance of the individual's belief in the threat for the occurrence of the effect: "This belief is so firmly held by all members of the tribe that the individual not only has the conviction himself but is obsessed by the knowledge that all his fellows likewise hold it. . . . Amid this mysterious murk of grim and ominous fatality, . . . an immediate threat of death fills the terrified victim with powerless misery" (186).

So at the extreme something like hypnosis seems to be capable of the ultimate social influence—death. But this example is pretty much out on the fringe, requiring the operation of a full-blown belief system shored up by thoroughly convincing cultural support. Are there any demonstrations of one lone hypnotist's having anything like this kind of influence? As it happens, there is at least one reported case of apparent death by hypnosis (Schrenk-Notzing 1902). In 1894 the stage hypnotist Franz Neukomm was working with a highly susceptible subject, one Ella Salamon, who had experience being hypnotized many times in his show. In their routine, Neukomm would invite an ailing volunteer from the audience up on stage, hypnotize Ella, and give her a suggestion to place herself in the mind of the patient and provide information about his or her health. One night he changed his hypnotic instructions slightly and told Ella, "Your soul will leave your body in order to enter that of the patient." Ella was unusually resistant to the suggestion and said she would not do this. Neukomm firmly repeated the "leave your body" command, deepened the trance, and repeated the command again. Ella died, apparently of heart failure. Although there is no way scientifically to establish whether hypnosis caused her death—it may well have been coincidence—Neukomm was charged with manslaughter and found guilty.

Figure 8.4
The lovely Trilby is hypnotized by Svengali into being able to sing. Illustration by
du Maurier for a serialized version of *Trilby.*

The power of hypnosis was a particularly active cultural theme in
the late nineteenth century, and this story fits right in. This was the age in
which du Maurier (1894) published his novel *Trilby,* for example,
recounting the travails of a young female subject at the hands of the
evil hypnotist Svengali (fig. 8.4). She was hypnotized against her will and
made his slave, and the possibility of such perils created a widespread
public distrust of hypnosis. The question of whether people can be induced to perform immoral or criminal acts by hypnosis gained the popular eye and since then has recurred perennially whenever anyone speaks
of hypnosis. What's the answer? Is it really so powerful?

There have been several studies in which people were asked in hypnosis to perform dangerous or criminal actions. In some cases, hypnotized
subjects have been asked to pick up a dangerous snake or to throw acid
at the experimenter (Rowland 1939; Young 1948), with safeguards in

place to make sure that nobody would get hurt (unbeknownst to the subject, a plate of glass was between the subject and the snake and experimenter). The great majority of subjects in these studies did the awful acts—they reached out to the snake, or they threw the acid. Such findings suggest that hypnosis is truly powerful. They also suggest that the initial disclaimer of some hypnotists that hypnosis is not dangerous, and you can't be forced to do something you don't want to do, is not truthful advertising. However, there is a catch. A remarkable experiment performed by Orne and Evans (1965) followed up the snake and acid studies and discovered an important caveat.

In this research, six participants selected for their high hypnotizability were placed in a deep trance and were then given very emphatic suggestions to carry out the acts: Reach out a hand to a dangerous snake, and throw a flask of acid in the experimenter's face. Just as in the earlier studies by Rowland and Young, five of the six did as they were told, reaching for the reptile and throwing the acid at the experimenter. In another condition of the experiment, however, six people who were low in hypnotizability were asked to *simulate* being hypnotized. They were simply asked to try to fool the experimenter into thinking that they also were in trances. When these people were pretending to be hypnotized, and were given emphatic instructions to do the dangerous acts, all six reached for the reptile and threw the acid! Apparently, hypnosis had no special impact on the effectiveness of the experimenter's demands that people perform these nasty acts.

To top it off, an additional group of people who were not hypnotized and were not even simulating hypnosis were given the dangerous instructions–again, forcefully, as in the other conditions of the study. Of these, three of six reached for the snake and five of six threw the acid at the experimenter. Apparently, a deep trance was not necessary to get people to create mayhem. All that was needed was a very pushy experimenter. Participants afterwards had all sorts of justifications, of course. They claimed that they knew at some level that the whole thing was an experiment and that no one in such a setting would actually force them to do something so horrible. The experimenter, they said, was the responsible party and wouldn't make them do something without its being safe. Still, there was no guarantee of this in the study, and these people mostly just stepped right up and did bad things.

This demonstration is reminiscent of a number of studies in which people have been led to do their worst without any hypnosis at all. The well-known obedience experiments by Stanley Milgram (1974), for instance, showed that people can be influenced in the course of a laboratory study to perform an action that most observers judge to be so harmful it would only be done by a psychopath. Still, some 60 percent of people in Milgram's basic studies followed the instructions of an experimenter apparently to administer strong electric shocks to a person in an adjoining room up to and beyond the point at which the person exclaimed, "My heart, my heart!" and stopped responding. The fact is, people can be influenced to do harm to others and to themselves without the benefit of any hypnosis at all. The sequential agreement process that works in hypnosis works just as well in everyday life; we often find ourselves entangled in situations from which one of the few escapes involves doing something evil (Baumeister 1997). And we may do it, hypnotized or not.

One of the reasons hypnosis seems so influential may be that it releases the hypnotist to demand exaggerated levels of influence. Perhaps the occasion of performing hypnosis makes a person more brazen and persistent, more likely to ask someone to do odd or unexpected things, and judge that influence has taken place. In the normal give-and-take of polite social exchange, people may not be inclined to give each other major body blocks or loopy requests. They don't ask others to "watch as your arm rises up," "forget everything I've told you," or "hop around like a bunny." But in the hypnotic encounter, there is license to ask for much, and so, much is given. The social interaction that we call hypnotism may have evolved into a special situation in which it is okay to ask people to do weird things and then to notice that they've done exactly what was asked.

The hypnotist's control over a subject does not seem to surpass the control available in everyday social influence. This is basically true because everyday social influence is itself so astonishingly potent. One study in which suggestions were given to fall forward, for instance, produced the conclusion that "suggestion was not at all necessary in order to procure the desired effects; a simple order ("Imagine that you are falling forward") had precisely the same effect" (Eysenck and Furneaux 1945, 500).

When we focus on standard human actions, it seems that hypnosis may be normal social interaction masquerading under another name (Barber 1969). We must look beyond everyday behaviors, and even beyond the extremes of human social influence, to find special effects of hypnosis. But there do seem to be some special effects here—in the realm of unique abilities possessed by those who are hypnotized.

Hypnotic Control Abilities

It has long been suspected that hypnotized people might have super-human abilities. Fictional (or just gullible) accounts give us hypnotized individuals who can foretell the future, walk through fire, levitate, or regress in age until they reach past lives.[5] These special abilities are not substantiated by research. Studies do identify, however, a few special things that hypnotized people are able to do that appear to exceed standard human abilities:

Pain Control   Hypnosis provides some people with an unusual ability to reduce their experience of pain. For example, in a study of pain induced in the laboratory (ischemic pain, produced by a tourniquet reducing blood flow to the forearm, and cold-pressor pain, produced by immersion of the hand in ice water), hypnosis was found to be more effective in reducing reported pain than morphine, diazepam (Valium), aspirin, acupuncture, or placebos (Stern et al. 1977). Reviews of a large number of studies on hypnotic pain control in laboratory and clinical settings indicate that this is indeed a remarkably useful technique (Hilgard and Hilgard 1983; Kihlstrom 1985; 1994; Wadden and Anderton 1982). Hypnosis with highly hypnotizable patients has been found to control pain even in lengthy surgeries and dental procedures, in some cases more effectively and safely than any form of anesthesia (fig. 8.5).

Mental Control   Hypnosis can yield higher levels of mental control than are attainable otherwise. For example, Bowers and Woody (1996) found that highly hypnotizable subjects who were administered suggestions to stop thinking about their favorite kind of automobile were in fact able to

5. A Web site by Terry O'Brien (2001) collects accounts of hypnosis from the media, and pokes fun at the more fantastic imaginings.

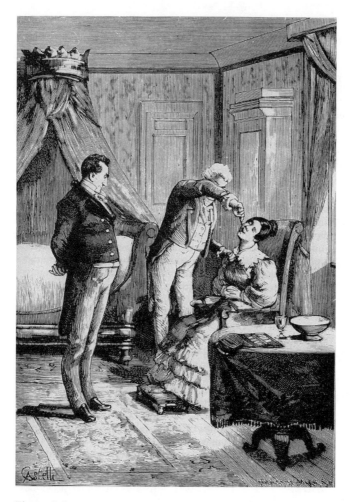

Figure 8.5
Dr. Oudet performs a tooth extraction with the assistance of Hamad the magnetizer in 1836. From Figuier's *Mystères de la Science* (1892).

do so. They reported by means of button presses that the thought occurred less than once in two minutes, and some 50 percent of these subjects couldn't even remember what car it was. Nonhypnotizable subjects who are not hypnotized, in contrast, reported experiencing the unwanted thought over three times per minute. This latter group exhibited the usual poor mental control ability shown by normal individuals asked to suppress thoughts in the laboratory (Wegner 1989; 1992; 1994; Wenzlaff and Wegner 2000). In another mental control study, Ruehle and Zamansky (1997) gave hypnotized and simulating subjects the suggestion to forget the number 11 and replace it with 12 while they did addition problems. Hypnotized subjects were faster than simulators at doing the math with this transposition. Miller and Bowers (1993) found a related effect in hypnotic pain control. Although waking attempts at the control of pain interfered with subjects' abilities to perform a demanding, secondary task, hypnotic pain control did not show such interference, suggesting that it reduced pain without effortful mental control.

Retrieval Control   Hypnosis enhances the individual's ability to control memory retrieval, particularly in the direction of *reduced* retrieval. Studies of hypnotically induced amnesia suggest that people can forget material through hypnosis; they either fail to retrieve items or develop disorganized ways of thinking about the items that undermine their retrieval attempts (Kihlstrom and Evans 1979; Kihlstrom and Wilson 1984). Hypnosis seems to be a good way to forget. The remarkable thing is that people can recover these memories through hypnosis as well. Items that are apparently lost to retrieval at one point may be regained through hypnotic intervention. However, research does *not* find that people can remember through hypnosis items that were not originally lost through hypnosis. Instead, hypnotized individuals do try to report memories in line with the hypnotist's preferences. This inclination has often been mistaken for accuracy of memory report, but it is simply another indication of the malleability of the hypnotized subject's behavior at the hands of the hypnotist. In one study, for example, twenty-seven highly hypnotizable subjects were given suggestions during hypnosis that they had been awakened by some loud noises in the night a week before. After hypnosis, thirteen of them said that this event had indeed occurred (Laurence and Perry 1983). Scores of studies show that hypnosis does not enhance the accuracy of memory and instead merely increases the subject's confidence in false memory reports (Kihlstrom 1985; McConkey, Barnier, and Sheehan 1998; Pettinati 1988).

Wart Control   Yes, wart control. There are a number of studies indicating that people who have undergone hypnosis for wart removal have achieved noteworthy improvement. Noll (1994), for instance, treated seven patients who had not benefited from prior conventional therapies (e.g., cryotherapy, laser surgery). They suffered from warts that would respond to treatment and then return later at the same or another site. Hypnosis was presented to them as a method for learning to control the body's immune system, and they were given both hypnotherapy sessions and encouragement to practice visualization of healing on their own. In from two to nine sessions of treatment, six of seven patients were completely cured of all their warts and the seventh had 50 percent improvement. This sounds quite miraculous until you start to wonder: Compared to what? Would these people have improved without hypnosis or with some other kind of psychological or placebo intervention? Perhaps these were spontaneous remissions. However, studies comparing hypnosis to untreated control groups have found hypnosis successful as well (Surman et al. 1973; Spanos, Stenstrom, and Johnston 1988), so there's definitely something to this. Warts do also appear to respond to placebo treatments, though, suggesting that the effect of hypnosis may be part of a more general kind of psychological control over this problem.

Experience Control   Hypnotized individuals show a remarkable reduction in the tendency to report the experience of conscious will. This change in experience appears to be genuine and not feigned, as it even surfaces in reports given with lie detectors. Kinnunen, Zamansky, and Block (1994) questioned hypnotized and simulating people about their experiences of several hypnotic symptoms (e.g., during hand levitation, "When your hand was moving up did it really feel light?") and also about innocuous things ("Can you hear me okay?"). Their elevated skin conductance responses (a measure of anxiousness) suggested that the simulators were lying on the hypnotic symptoms as compared to the innocuous items but that the hypnotized subjects were not.

There are many claims for hypnotic abilities beyond these. Such claims often need to be viewed with skepticism. The idea that people in hypnosis can be age-regressed back to childlike modes of mental functioning, for example, is supported by a few case examples but little research. In one case, for instance, a Japanese-American student who had spoken Japanese as a child but who denied knowledge of the language in adulthood was age-regressed in hypnosis (Fromm 1970). She broke into fluent but childish Japanese. More generally, though, when people in hypnosis are asked to "go back in time," they appear to act in a manner characteristic of their own conception of children at an earlier age, not in a way consistent with actual earlier psychological functioning (Kihlstrom and Barnhardt 1993; Kihlstrom and Eich 1994; Nash 1987).

The five noteworthy hypnotic control abilities just discussed are ones that have been distilled from a large volume of research. Questions of unusual human abilities are, of course, matters of great scientific interest and considerable contention. Other claimed abilities that might be added to this list have been left out because insufficient evidence exists at present on which to base firm conclusions. Still, we have here a small but remarkable set of ways in which people who are under the control of others in hypnosis in fact exhibit greater control of themselves. Despite the absence of the feeling of will in hypnosis, there is in these several instances an advantage in the exercise of control. Curiously, the experience of will in this case fails entirely to track the force of will.

The Explanation of Hypnosis

The malleability of the hypnotized person is the central impediment to the development of theories of hypnosis. Imagine, for example, trying to make up a theory of "The Thing That Changes into What You Think It Is." For no particular reason you start thinking to yourself, "Gee, maybe it has wheels," and it turns out to have wheels. You think, "Perhaps it is large and green and soft," and a big green blob shows up in the yard. The wheels are still there, of course, but only as long as you think they are. You wonder if this Thing could be alive, and soon it starts throbbing and opens a big eye that is now staring at you. Be careful not to think it is coming this way. This kind of Thing is not just scary, it is the worst possible topic of scientific study. In fact, this is a step beyond even the shape-shifter aliens that the heroes of science fiction so often encounter. Something that can take on different identities or shapes for its own purposes at least can be fooled occasionally into taking on a shape that gives it away. The Thing we're talking about here will forever be camouflaged by our own guesses about what it is.

Nightmare Science

Theories of hypnosis are faced with exactly this bewildering problem. If any theory says that hypnotized people ought to behave in a particular way under certain conditions, the hypnotist who wants to test that theory can usually get hypnotized people to do exactly what the theory predicts. After all, the hallmark of hypnosis is the pliability of the subject. If the hypnotist is interested in finding out whether the subject enters a deep, sleepy trance, subjects are normally ready to say that this is what they are experiencing. If the hypnotist is interested in determining whether the subject is really quite conscious and is merely being deceptive during hypnosis, it is not hard to get evidence of this as well. Hypnosis, it turns out, is the Thing.

The history of the science of hypnosis is brimming with stories of what happens when one scientist's Thing meets another scientist's Thing (please try not to form a mental image of this). Consider, for example, an interesting idea introduced by Ernest Hilgard—the notion of the hidden observer. Hilgard investigated the possibility that the psyche of the hypnotized person might have two levels, one that seems hypnotized and another that is not. In studies of laboratory-induced pain (cold-pressor tasks in which subjects immersed hands in ice water), it was found that highly hypnotizable subjects in trance, to whom analgesia was suggested, were likely to report far less pain than comparison subjects (Hilgard, Morgan, and Macdonald 1975). However, these subjects could often be induced to report higher levels of pain by asking them about their feelings in a different way. The subject would be asked, for instance, if "a hidden part of you" is experiencing something other than what was just reported. Often, subjects concurred, and in many cases this "hidden observer" could then be coaxed into talking and commenting on what was happening. In pain studies, the hidden observer often reported experiencing much more pain than the subject did, suggesting to Hilgard that there might be a dissociated part of the individual's mind that continued to be conscious of pain even during hypnotic analgesia. The hidden observer seemed to be a pocket of conscious normality somewhere inside the hypnotized subject (Hilgard, 1986).

The spotlight on this discovery in hypnosis research was dimmed, however, by the counterdiscovery of Spanos and Hewitt (1980). These researchers thought the hidden observer might be a fabrication, just like other wild things highly hypnotized people do when asked. To test this, Spanos and Hewitt hypnotized highly hypnotizable subjects and suggested that they would feel no pain during a cold-pressor task. The subjects were asked to indicate how their "hidden part" rated cold-pressor pain using Hilgard's usual instructions, and—so far, so good—the hidden observer complained of more pain than did the hypnotized subjects. However, some subjects in the study were given a reversed version of the hidden observer instruction, in which they were led to believe that some hidden part of them might be feeling *even less* pain than they reported during hypnosis. And indeed, these subjects concocted hidden observers whose reports of the ice water pain were lower than those of the subjects themselves. In the words of the researchers, "'Hidden observer' reports are engendered, shaped, and maintained by the very procedures used for their investigation" (Spanos and Hewitt 1980, 1210). Apparently, people may be packed full of an unlimited supply of hidden observers, one for each "hidden part" of them that follows the expectations of a different hypnosis theorist.

Needless to say, there continues to be controversy over the status of the hidden observer, with a lot of rhetoric and evidence accumulating on each side and no clear consensus about what is going on. This controversy is entirely typical of the scientific study of hypnosis. Discoveries and counterdiscoveries abound in this field, making it impossible on reading the research literature not to get the feeling that every researcher in this area is studying something different. Some even insist that hypnosis is nothing at all (e.g., Coe 1992). Scientists studying hypnosis seem more eager to undermine each other's ideas than to establish an explanation for hypnosis. It is easy to develop the unflattering suspicion that researchers of hypnosis may be domineering and argumentative by nature. People who have gravitated to the study of hypnosis may be self-selected for an unusually strong desire to exert social influence, so perhaps all the squabbling arises because they can't all hypnotize each other and get their own way. This seems unlikely, however, now that I've started studying hypnosis myself.

The hypothesis we must come back to is that hypnosis is the Thing. The intransigence of this topic is due to the extraordinary flexibility of the hypnotized subject. The topic is slippery by its very nature. Although it is possible to get a general sense of how much influence hypnosis exerts, and to develop a smattering of fairly trustworthy conclusions about the abilities that it creates, the deep understanding of hypnosis is still a distant goal because of the chimeric properties of the topic of study. Hypnosis becomes what people think it is.

An Assortment of Theories

What, then, have people thought it is? We know Mesmer thought it was "animal magnetism," a colorful idea that inspires nice images of people being stuck to cattle but which has little else to recommend it. The more modern theories can be divided neatly into much the same two camps we observed in the study of spirit possession, the trance theories and the faking theories. Trance theorists have taken the hypnotized person's word for it and assumed that there is a unique state of mind in the hypnotic trance which may indicate a particular brain state and which causes hypnotic phenomena. Faking theorists have taken a more skeptical view, in which the hypnotic subject is appreciated as someone who is placed in a social situation with strong constraints on behavior and who behaves in accord with those constraints and perhaps feigns inner states in accord with them as well. Not all these theorists would agree with this crude partition, so we should review the specific theories in a bit more detail.

Hypnosis has always been considered a trancelike state of mind. It was initially named by Braid for its resemblance to sleep (Gauld 1992). The trance theories can be said really to have gotten off the ground with the *dissociation theory* of Janet (1889). This theory holds that the mind allows divided consciousness in that separate components of mind may regulate mental functioning without intercommunication. Perceptions of involuntariness in hypnosis are thus the result of dissociation between the mental subsystems that cause action and those that allow consciousness. Ideas and their associated actions can be dissociated or split off from normal consciousness such that they no longer allow consciousness of will. This notion was elaborated by Sidis (1906), who believed that hypnosis could be explained by the specific bifurcation of the individual psyche into two selves. He thought that in addition to the normal waking self, each of us has a subconscious self, "a presence within us of a secondary, reflex, subwaking consciousness—the highway of suggestion"

(179). Whereas the waking self is responsible for actions that occur with conscious will, the subconscious self produces those actions that occur through suggestion. Sidis believed the subconscious self to be a homunculus of the first order, with its own memory, intelligence, and personality.

A more contemporary version of this is the *neodissociation theory* of Hilgard (1986). Like Janet and Sidis, Hilgard proposed that dissociated subsystems of mind in hypnosis underlie subjects' reduced control over muscular movements, in comparison to the conscious, voluntary processes that cause waking actions. Actual control is thus reduced in hypnosis along with the experience of will. According to this viewpoint, the feeling of conscious will is associated specifically with an executive or controlling module of mind. Actions that occur without this feeling are processed through some other mental module and simply do not contact that part of the mind that feels it does things. The *dissociated control* theory of Woody and Bowers (1994) goes on to suggest that hypnotic action and thought might require less cognitive effort because of this dissociation.

Neodissociation theory is also related to the *ideomotor theory* of hypnosis elaborated by Arnold (1946; see also Hull 1933). Arnold proposed that the processes involved in ideomotor action produce automatisms, and that the production of such automatisms is the fundamental phenomenon of hypnosis. The hypnotized person's tendency to report involuntary action arises, in this view, because the action is indeed produced directly by the thought, not through any process of intention or will (fig. 8.6). She suggested that "in all these cases the supposedly 'central' process of thinking or imagining seems to initiate directly certain peripheral changes. Probably because of this direct connection, movements are experienced as different from ordinary 'willed' movements" (Arnold 1946, 115). Like the family of dissociation theories, this perspective suggests that behavior can be caused in two different ways: the hypnotized way and the normal, willful way.

Perhaps the most entrancing of the trance theories are those that point out the resemblance of hypnosis to brain states like those of sleep, sleepwalking, and relaxation (Edmonston 1981). The proponents of most of the trance theories would be happy to learn that recent studies of brain

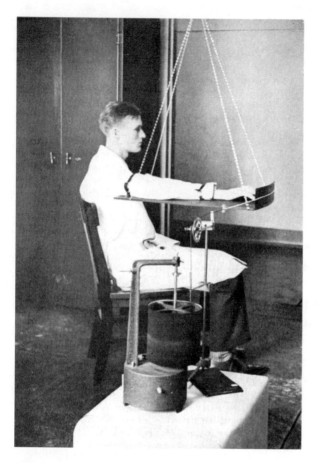

Figure 8.6
This arm suspension device allowed for precise measures of the degree of arm movement produced by ideomotor suggestions ("Think about your arm moving to the left"). Clark Hull, better known for his work on learning, applied scientific measurement in studying hypnosis as well. From Hull (1933). Courtesy Irvington Publishers.

processes in hypnosis have suggested some key differences between the brain state of the hypnotizable subject in trance and not in trance. Although brain activity in trance is not very much like brain activity in sleep, it does seem to differ from that of the waking state. Evidence from neuropsychological research using various brain scan methods and measures of brain electrical activity indicates that hypnosis prompts unique patterns (Crawford, Knebel, and Vendemia 1998; Maquet et al. 1999; Rainville et al. 1999).

A study of the influence of hypnosis on hallucinations provides a good example of the role of the brain in the hypnotic state (Szechtman et al. 1998). Highly hypnotizable subjects who were prescreened for their ability to hallucinate during hypnosis were tested while they lay in a PET (positron emission tomography) scanner. They first heard a recording of the line "The man did not speak often, but when he did, it was worth hearing what he had to say." Then, they followed instructions to imagine hearing this line again, or they listened while the hypnotist suggested that the tape was playing once more, although it was not. This suggestion was expected to produce an auditory hallucination of the line, and these subjects reported that indeed it did. The PET scan revealed that the right anterior cingulate cortex was just as active while the subjects were hallucinating as when they were actually hearing the line. However, that brain area was not active while the subjects merely imagined the line. Hypnosis had apparently stimulated that area of the brain to register the hallucinated voice as real. It is likely that with further developments in brain imaging technology, much more will be known very soon about the brain substrate of hypnosis. For now, we can at least begin to see the outline of a brain state theory of hypnosis in these preliminary findings.

There is, however, another whole camp of hypnosis theories for which news of brain states is a major catastrophe. These are the theorists committed to various versions of the faking theory. The initial development of this theory came as a skeptical response to all trance talk and can be traced to the *role theory* of Sarbin (1950; Sarbin and Coe 1972). This account explains hypnosis in the same way one might explain the behavior of someone trying to be, say, a bank teller or to fit into any other social role. In this analysis, hypnosis is a performance, and some people are better performers than others. The best performers give performances that are convincing not only to their audience but to themselves. This theory suggests that early efforts at being hypnotized might be conducted only with much secret-keeping and conscious deception, and perhaps later replaced by more well-learned role enactment and less need for conscious duplicity. A highly trained bank teller, for instance, need not work each day while rehearsing "I must try to act like a bank teller, I must try to act like a bank teller." With practice, this comes naturally along with the appropriate thoughts and even mental states. Hypnotic subjects learn their roles, and the faking becomes second nature.[6]

A version of role theory by Barber (1969) draws on the observation that hypnotic behavior is often no more extreme than behavior in response to strong social influence, as in the snake-touching and acid-throwing examples. This *task motivation* theory says that people will do the odd things they find themselves doing in hypnosis whenever they are sufficiently motivated by social influence to perform such actions. Like role theory, this explanation says people are performing the hypnotic behaviors voluntarily. A related theory, labeled *social psychological* (Spanos 1986), *sociocognitive* (Wagstaff 1991), or *social cognitive* theory (Kirsch and Lynn 1998), draws upon both the role theoretic and task motivation ideas to suggest that people do hypnotic behaviors and report experiencing hypnotic mental states because they have become involved in social situations in which these behaviors and reports are highly valued. The idea is that the abridgement of reported conscious will that occurs in hypnosis arises not because of a reduction in willed action but as a result of strong social influences that promote the alteration of the report. Some versions of this theory suggest that full-tilt faking is not needed because the social influences often help people to develop imagery consistent with the suggestion, and this then aids them in experiencing involuntariness (Lynn, Rhue, and Weekes 1990).

---

6. There is a natural tendency to assume that people remain conscious of the pretense when they fake. This idea that role adoption is conscious, or remains even partially conscious, however, is not usually defended by social cognitive theorists (e.g., Kirsch 1998). People are surely not conscious of faking, at least after the first little while, when they play the roles of everyday life. A lack of consciousness of the processes whereby one has achieved a mental state, however, suggests a kind of genuineness—a sense in which the state is an "altered state of consciousness"—and this is what many of the trance theorists would prefer to call hypnosis (e.g., Spiegel 1998). Much of the interchange between the "trance" and the "faking" theorists is nominally about other things yet actually hinges in a subtle way on this issue. There are hundreds of mental states we achieve every day in which, during the state, we are no longer conscious of having tried to or wanted to achieve that state (Wegner and Erber 1993). The argument between the "trance" and the "faking" theorists seems to result from different viewpoints: thinking about hypnosis with respect to *how it seems* (trance) or *how one got there* (faking).

So, where are we? At this point in the development of an explanation of hypnosis, none of these theories is winning. All seem to be losing ground. Trance theories have difficulty dealing with the social influence processes that give rise to hypnosis, and faking theories leave out the brain and body entirely, warts and all. The conflict between the trance theorists and the faking theorists has collapsed into mayhem, to the point that some are calling for a truce (Chaves 1997; Kirsch and Lynn 1995; Perry 1992; Spiegel 1998).

It should be clear from the evidence we have reviewed regarding hypnosis and other instances of the loss of conscious will that there is a vast middle ground now available for encampment. A theory that takes into account both the social forces impinging on the individual and the significant psychological changes that occur within the individual as a result of these forces must be the right way to go. Something along the lines of the self-induction theory of spirit possession, in which people's pretendings and imaginings turn into reality for them, seems fitting. As with possession, some people seem to be able to fake themselves into a trance. Such a theory of "believed-in imaginings" has in fact been proposed in several quarters of the hypnosis debates (Perry 1992; Sarbin and Coe 1972; Sutcliffe 1961), and further progress in the study of hypnosis may depend on the development of a more complete theory along these lines.

The theory of apparent mental causation is not a complete theory of hypnosis, so we don't need to worry about joining the fray. The idea that the experience of will is not an authentic indication of the force of will, however, can help to clear up some of the difficulties in the study of hypnotic involuntariness. Our analysis of the experience of conscious will suggests that we could make some headway toward understanding hypnosis by examining how people perceive the causation of behaviors they are asked, instructed, or pressured to perform.

Partitioning Apparent Mental Causation

Hypnosis presents an action authorship problem to the hypnotic subject. This occurs because the actual causal situation in any case of social influence is more complicated than the causal situation in basic individual action. In the usual waking state, things are relatively simple. A person's perception of apparent mental causation often tracks the actual relation

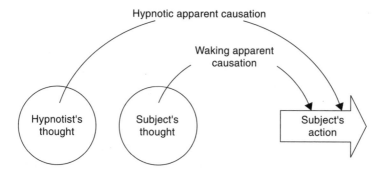

Figure 8.7
Experience of will during waking state and hypnotic state. In waking, the subject perceives an apparent influence of own thought on own action that may reflect the actual influence. In hypnosis, the subject perceives an apparent influence of the hypnotist's thought on own action, bypassing the influence of own thought and so reducing the experience of will.

between conscious thought and behavior (fig. 8.7). Conscious thoughts come to mind before the behavior and play a role in the mechanisms that produce the behavior. But, at the same time, the apparent causal relation between thought and behavior is perceived and gives rise to an experience of will. When everything is well-oiled and working normally, the person experiences will in a way that maps at least approximately onto the actual causal relation between conscious thought and behavior, and the person thus experiences a sense of voluntariness. The experience of will tracks the force of will.

In the case of hypnosis, the perception of apparent causation must now take into account two actual causal links: the hypnotist's thought influencing the subject's thought, and the subject's thought influencing his or her own action. This is where the perception process takes a shortcut. Perhaps not immediately, but at some point in the process of hypnosis, the subject's awareness of the role of his or her own thought in this sequence drops out. The hypnotist's thought is perceived as having a direct causal influence on the subject's action, and the experience of will thus declines. Feelings of involuntariness occur even though there remains an actual link between the subject's thought and action. The subject's thought may actually become more subtle at this time, perhaps even dropping from consciousness. But there must be mental processes involved in taking in the information from the hypnotist and transforming it into action. They may not have a prominent role in the subject's consciousness, however, and so do not contribute to sensed will.

People in hypnosis may come to interpret their thoughts, even if they are conscious, as only part of a causal chain rather than as the immediate cause of their action. There is evidence of a general tendency to attribute greater causality to earlier rather than later events in a causal chain—a causal primacy effect (Johnson et al. 1989; Vinokur and Ajzen 1982). So, for instance, on judging the relative causal importance of the man who angered the dog who bit the child, we might tend under some conditions to hold the man more responsible than the dog. This should be particularly true if the man's contribution itself increased the probability of the bite more than did the dog's contribution (Spellman 1997). Moreover, this effect may gain influence with repetition of the sequence (Young 1995). The development of involuntariness in hypnosis may occur, then, through the learning of a causal interpretation for one's action that leaves out any role for one's own thoughts, conscious or not. Over time and repetition, the hypnotist's suggestions are seen as the direct causes of one's actions.

How might people stop noticing the causal role of their own thoughts? One possibility is suggested by Miller, Galanter, and Pribram (1960) in *Plans and the Structure of Behavior:*

> Most of our planned activity is represented subjectively as listening to ourselves talk. The hypnotized person is not really doing anything different, with this exception: the voice he listens to for his Plan is not his own, but the hypnotist's. The subject gives up his inner speech to the hypnotist. . . . It is not sufficient to say merely that a hypnotized subject is listening to plans formulated for him by the hypnotist. Any person . . . listening to the same plans . . . would not feel the same compulsion to carry them out. . . . [The] waking person hears the suggested plans and then either incorporates them or rejects them in the planning he is doing for himself. But a hypnotized subject has stopped making plans for himself, and therefore there can be no question of coordination, no possible translation from the hypnotist's version to his own. The hypnotist's version of the plan is the only one he has, so he executes it. . . . How does a person stop making plans for himself? This is something each of us accomplishes every night of our lives when we fall asleep. (104–105)

These theorists suggest that the standard procedure for sleep induction, like that for hypnosis, involves turning down the lights, avoiding excessive stimulation, getting relaxed, and either closing the eyes or focusing on something boring. They propose that unless insomnia sets in, this shuts down the person's plan generator. One stops talking to oneself, and action is generally halted. In hypnosis, the person doesn't fall asleep because another person's voice takes over the plan generation function and keeps the body moving.

This approach suggests that people may interpret their thoughts about their behavior as causal or not. They may see some thoughts about upcoming actions as intents or plans, whereas they see other thoughts about those actions as noncausal—premonitions, perhaps, or imaginings, or even echoes of what has come before or of what they are hearing. When the thoughts occurring before action are no longer viewed as candidates for causal status, the experience of will is likely to recede. In the case of hypnosis, then, the exclusivity principle may be operating to yield reduced feelings of will. The presence of the hypnotist as a plausible cause of one's behavior reduces the degree to which one's own thoughts are interpreted as candidate causes, and so reduces the sense of conscious will.

Thoughts that are consistent with an action in hypnosis might not be appreciated as causal if they happen to be attributed to the hypnotist. A lack of exclusivity could preempt this inference, as might often happen whenever a person is given an instruction and follows it. Someone says, "Please wipe your feet at the door," and you do so. Although there could be a sense that the act is voluntary, there might also be the immediate realization that the thought of the act was caused by your asker's prior thoughts. In essence, both the self's thought and the other's thought are consistent with the self's action in this case, and the inference of which thought is causal then is determined by other variables. There may be a general inclination to think that self is causal, or an inclination to think that other is causal, as determined by any number of clues from the context of the interaction.

The ambiguities of causation inherent in instructed or suggested actions open the judgment of apparent mental causation to general expectations. A sense of involuntariness may often emerge as the result of a prior expectation that one ought not to be willful in hypnosis. In research by Gorassini (1999), for example, people were asked what they were planning to do in response to hypnotically suggested behaviors. Their plans fell into four groups we might name as follows: *wait and see* (planned to wait for the suggested behavior to occur on its own), *wait and imagine* (planned to wait for the suggested behavior and imagine it happening), *intend to act and feel* (planned to go ahead and do the act and try to generate a feeling of involuntariness), and *cold acting* (planned to go ahead and do the act but not try to experience involuntariness). Gorassini described the third group here, those who intended to do the act and try to get the feeling, as the "self-deception plan" group. These people planned to fake the behavior and also try to fake the feeling.

The relation between these plans and actual hypnotic behavior was assessed in a variety of studies, and it was generally found that plans to wait didn't produce much. *Wait and see* yielded few hypnotic responses, and *wait and imagine* was a bit better but still did little. *Cold acting* produced hypnotic responses but little experience of involuntariness. The people who were self-deceptive, in that their plan was *intend to act and feel*, produced both the most frequent suggested behavior and the strongest reports of involuntariness. Apparently, those people who followed the suggestions and actively tried to experience the feeling of involuntariness were the ones who succeeded in producing a full-blown hypnotic experience.

Now, in normal waking action, the thought, act, and feeling arise in sequence. We think of what we will do, we do it, and the feeling of conscious will arises during the action. Gorassini's findings suggest that in hypnosis, the feeling of involuntariness may be substituted in advance as a counterfeit for the usual feeling of voluntariness. A distinct lack of will is something we're looking for and trying to find even as we are aware of our thoughts and our behaviors. Such readiness to perceive involuntariness may thus short-circuit our usual interpretive processes. We no longer notice the fact that our thoughts do appear prior to the action and are consistent with the action because the overall set to experience the action as unwilled—because of the clear absence of exclusivity (the hypnotist, after all, is an outside cause)—overwhelms the interpretive weight we might usually assign to these factors. Instead, the behavior is perceived as emanating from the hypnotist's suggestions and, for our part, as happening involuntarily.

Control through Involuntariness

The analysis of apparent mental causation can account for the experience of involuntariness. But how do we account for hypnotic behavior? The theory of apparent mental causation is not clear in its implications in this regard, which is why it is not a complete theory of hypnosis. It is not really necessary to have a special theory to explain the high degree of social influence that occurs in hypnosis. As we've seen, this may be due entirely to factors having little to do with hypnosis per se and more to do with the power of social influence itself. However, the unusual abilities of hypnotized people do need a theory. They do not appear, however, to arise from variations in experienced voluntariness, and thus far these variations are all we've been able to begin to explain. How would involuntariness prompt the enhanced levels of control we have observed over pain, thought, memory, and the like?

Perhaps the experience of involuntariness helps to shut down a mental process that normally gets in the way of control. And, oddly, this mental process may be the actual exercise of will. It may be that the feeling of involuntariness reduces the degree to which thoughts and plans about behavior come to mind. If behavior is experienced as involuntary, there may be a reduced level of attention directed toward discerning the next thing to do or, for that matter, toward rehearsing the idea of what one is currently doing. A lack of experienced will might thus influence the force of will in this way, reducing the degree to which attention is directed to the thoughts normally preparatory to action. And this could be good.

The ironic processes of mental control (Wegner 1994) suggest that there are times when it might be good to stop planning and striving. It is often possible to try too hard. The initiation of plans for action and for thought is normally a useful enterprise, of course, as it typically leads to the exercise of successful operations of mental control. We plan to stand up and we do so, we intend to concentrate and we do so, we intend to relax, to sleep, to eat, to go outside, or to write a letter, and we do so. However, sometimes the formation of a conscious plan leads to a paradoxical effect—the implementation of the plan creates the opposite of what was planned. The example mentioned at several points in this book is the case of thought suppression; when we try not to think of something, we seem to create an automatic and ironic tendency to think of that very thing. The usual usefulness of our planning and intention procedures makes us go ahead and try to do many things, even those that have inherent ironies.

This ironic effect can undermine effective action and thought in a variety of domains, particularly when people try to perform the planned actions under mental load or stress. The conscious desire to sleep, for example, can cause wakefulness under stress (Ansfield, Wegner, and Bowser 1996); the conscious desire to forget can cause remembering, particularly under mental load (Macrae et al. 1997); the conscious desire to relax can cause anxiety during stress (Wegner, Broome, and Blumberg 1997); the conscious desire to be fair can cause stereotyping and prejudiced behavior under mental load (Macrae et al. 1994). Many of our favorite goals, when pursued consciously, can be undermined by distractions and stressors to yield not just the failure of goal attainment but the ironic opposite of that attainment. We achieve exactly what we most desired not to do.

Think of this now in the case of hypnosis. It may be that some of the special abilities accruing from hypnosis arise because the hypnotic state bypasses the ironies of mental control (King and Council 1998; Bowers and Woody 1996). In essence, hypnosis may save us from the foibles of the normal conscious willing process. When goals are not consciously salient, people may be able to achieve those goals more readily. The mechanistic processes of mind come forward to cause the desired behavior without the ironic monitoring processes that normally yield the counterintentional lapses that are inherent in conscious control. The desire to distract oneself from pain, for example, normally initiates a monitoring process that sensitizes one to the very pain one is hoping to ignore (Cioffi 1993; Cioffi and Holloway 1993; Wegner 1994). If this conscious desiring process can somehow be dismantled, then the ironic return of pain to mind might be sidestepped as well. A similar analysis can be made for the unusual mental control of memory that occurs in hypnosis. The conscious desire not to remember will normally highlight any to-be-forgotten items, making them all the more memorable. In hypnosis, perhaps the processes of conscious desiring are undermined, yielding an enhanced ability to forget (Wenzlaff and Wegner 2000).

The hypnotized person has the unique ability to achieve certain sorts of control over the mind and body that are not within the capability of the waking individual. It is as though in hypnosis a normal layer of conscious controlling apparatus is cleared away to yield a more subtle and effective set of techniques. A variety of self-control techniques that work without the exertion of conscious will—such as the response to placebos and expectations (Kirsch 1999)—may be models for the sorts of control that become available in hypnosis. People seem to experience strong influences of ideas, as has been found in studies of unconscious priming among people in waking states (e.g., Bargh and Chartrand 1999). These effects may be amplified, or at least uncovered, in hypnosis because of a general relaxation of attention to conscious thoughts about action. By this analysis, hypnosis may leave people conscious in the general sense but not conscious of their thoughts about action. As a result, their tendency to check or inhibit their unconsciously primed behaviors, and their tendency to undermine their own conscious purposes through ironic processes, may be set aside during the hypnotic state (Kirsch and Lynn 1999; Lynn 1997). It may be that in this special sense the behavior of the hypnotized person may not only be an automatism (occurring without the experience of conscious will) but also be automatic (occurring without prior conscious thought).

Hypnotized behavior may be special for the fact that it goes *unmonitored*. Most of what we consciously set out to do, as when we decide to walk across a room with a full cup of coffee, is something we watch for success or failure. We are checking all the while as we walk to see if that coffee is remaining unspilled. And in a perverse sense it is the very consciousness of this goal not to spill that creates the precariousness of the action, adding just a bit of the jitters that seem to make us ready to tilt it onto the floor. There are times when we are thinking of other things or are not conscious of spilling, however; at these times we may be remarkably adept with a cup that is otherwise just as spillable as the first. In hypnosis, it could be that the lack of an experience of will renders our conscious willing process less active, reducing the ironies of conscious willing and so enhancing certain aspects of mental control.

Just how the reduction in an experience of will might influence the force of will is an open matter at this point. A variety of theories and research findings suggest that lapses in the perception of control can induce reductions in the exertion of control (Bandura 1997a; Langer 1983; Seligman 1975), and this might be how such things happen. As a rule, such theories have taken a motivational stance, suggesting that the lack of a feeling of conscious will reduces the person's empirical will by undermining the desire for control. It may be, though, that the lack of a feeling of conscious will reduces the degree to which thoughts about action occur in consciousness at all, or the degree to which they are given conscious attention even if they are generally accessible. Feelings of involuntariness may reduce the person's attention to those thoughts that normally would form the basis for exertions of the force of will.

The Circle of Influence

Hypnosis is a social interaction. This observation is a fitting point of closure for a chapter that has emphasized the social influences on individual mind and action. Social influences are very seldom unidirectional because they happen not just in a one-shot event but in a repeated sequence of events that create pathways for feedback and transformation. When you yell at your friend, for example, there is a one-shot version of the story in which you do the yelling and he does the hearing (and suffering or shrugging or wincing). But in episode two of this story, the friend has a reaction, which in turn influences you. If your friend breaks down weeping, you feel guilty and yell less next time. If your friend yells back, you might yell back immediately, and so on. The circle of influence means that one influence sets off a chain of events that influences everyone.

Circular influence happens regularly in hypnosis, and this process has had a lot to do with shaping the modern format of hypnosis—what we think it is and does. A fine example of this was the development of the strange set of behaviors observed by Jean Charcot in his early clinical uses of hypnosis. In 1862, Charcot became physician to the Salpêtrière, the Paris asylum for women, and inherited the supervision of a ward that housed epileptics and hysterics (Gauld 1992). The hysterics, because of their fine imitative tendencies and, in this case, their exposure to people with epilepsy, also tended to have seizures. Charcot eventually took up hypnosis as a treatment for both groups, finding seizures and "crises" in most of his patients, and developed an extraordinarily detailed theory of the effects of hypnosis. Apparently, people responded to hypnotism in a series of stages, progressing from catalepsy (pliable immobility) to lethargy to somnambulism (suggestibility). Charcot gave regular demonstrations of his findings and had a number of "star" patients who performed almost as if on stage. Catalepsy was particularly entertaining because patients could be arranged into positions they would hold indefinitely, thus replacing certain items of furniture.

The Thing strikes again. In an attack on Charcot's work, Delboeuf (1886) suggested that the entire display of symptoms was contrived. He proposed that all this occurred because the effect of suggestion passes not only from hypnotist to subject but from subject to hypnotist. One patient with certain remarkable symptoms can create beliefs in the hypnotist about the forms that hypnotic manifestations will take. These can then be transmitted unwittingly as suggestions to other patients, who then act so as to confirm the hypnotist's expectations. An epidemic of standard responses to hypnosis results. The circle of influence can also promote a kind of social memory. Previous performances by the subject are recalled by the hypnotist and suggested again, then to be performed again by the subject. Thus, the hypnotist develops the conviction that there is a pattern in the subject's behavior when none would have arisen otherwise. It is easy to see how the hypnotist's theory of the Thing changes the Thing, which then changes the hypnotist's theory—a cycle that can move along to produce an evolving picture of hypnosis. Because of this process, hypnosis doesn't seem to hold still.

The circle of influence is also evident in everyday social interaction. The way in which groups and cultures move along, changing their expectations of each other and themselves, produces an odd situation we might call the "suggested society." People become what they think they are, or what they find that others think they are, in a process of negotiation that snowballs constantly. In some of this influence, the computation of will is correct in that people come to experience will that maps accurately onto the influence of their own thoughts on their behavior. In other cases of such influence, perhaps the larger portion, the experience of will does not signal very accurately the actual causal relations linking people together. The circle of influence that occurs in reality is accompanied by a vaguely similar set of causal relations that are consciously apprehended by the individuals involved. The causal influences people have on themselves and each other, as they are understood, capture only a small part of the actual causal flux of social relations (Wegner and Bargh 1998).

In *Unconscious Influence,* Horace Bushnell spoke of this phenomenon wisely: "Men are ever touching unconsciously the springs of motion in each other; one man, without thought or intention or even consciousness of the fact, is ever leading some others after him. . . . There are two sorts of influence belonging to Man: that which is active and voluntary, and that which is unconscious; that which we exert purposely, or in the endeavor to sway another, as by teaching, by argument, by persuasion, by threats, by offers and promises, and that which flows out from us, unawares to ourselves" (quoted in Carpenter 1888, 541).

In hypnosis, conscious and unconscious processes of influence live parallel lives. The hypnotist and subject view the event at the conscious level, appreciating it as "the subject obeys the conscious will of the hypnotist." This much of hypnosis can be understood as a transformation in the way that the subject's apparent mental causation is viewed by both participants. The subject experiences less will and more compulsion, and the hypnotist may feel empowered and more willful in directing the subject's actions. These conscious experiences of will are layered over a set of actual causal changes, however, that are poorly understood by both participants and only beginning to be understood by scientists. At this level, we know now that in certain subjects who seem to have this ability, a subtle sequence of events in social interaction brings about changes in the subject's mind, brain, and capacity for control.

9

The Mind's Compass

Although the experience of conscious will is not evidence of mental causation, it does signal personal authorship of action to the individual and so influences both the sense of achievement and the acceptance of moral responsibility.

Volition . . . is an emotion *indicative* of physical changes, not a *cause* of such changes. . . . The soul stands to the body as the bell of a clock to the works, and consciousness answers to the sound which the bell gives out when struck. . . . We are conscious automata.

T. H. Huxley, *Methods and Results* (1910)

Does the compass steer the ship? In some sense, you could say that it does, because the pilot makes reference to the compass in determining whether adjustments should be made to the ship's course. If it looks as though the ship is headed west into the rocky shore, a calamity can be avoided with a turn north into the harbor. But, of course, the compass does not steer the ship in any physical sense. The needle is just gliding around in the compass housing, doing no actual steering at all. It is thus tempting to relegate the little magnetic pointer to the class of epiphenomena—things that don't really matter in determining where the ship will go.

Conscious will is the mind's compass. As we have seen, the experience of consciously willing action occurs as the result of an interpretive system, a course-sensing mechanism that examines the relations between our thoughts and actions and responds with "I willed this" when the two correspond appropriately. This experience thus serves as a kind of compass, alerting the conscious mind when actions occur that are likely to be the result of one's own agency. The experience of will is therefore an indicator, one of those gauges on the control panel to which we refer as we steer. Like a compass reading, the feeling of doing tells us something about the operation of the ship. But also like a compass reading, this information must be understood as a conscious experience, a candidate for the dreaded "epiphenomenon" label. Just as compass readings do not steer the boat, conscious experiences of will do not cause human actions.

This chapter examines why the conscious experience of will might exist at all. Why, if this experience of will is not the cause of action, would we even go to the trouble of having it? What good is an epiphenomenon? The answer becomes apparent when we appreciate conscious will as a feeling that organizes and informs our understanding of our own agency. Conscious will is a signal with many of the qualities of an emotion, one that reverberates through the mind and body to indicate when we sense having authored an action. The idea that conscious will is an *emotion of authorship* moves beyond the standard way in which people have been thinking about free will and determinism, and presses toward a useful new perspective. This chapter explores how the emotion of authorship serves key functions in the domains of achievement and morality. It seems that the feeling that we are doing things serves as a basis for what we attempt to accomplish and how we judge ourselves to be morally right or wrong.

Free Will and Determinism

A book called *The Illusion of Conscious Will* certainly gives the impression of being a poke in the eye for readers who believe in free will. It is perfectly reasonable to look at the title and think the book is all about determinism and that it will not give the idea of free will a fair hearing. Of course, the line of thought here does take a decidedly deterministic approach. For all this, though, our discussion has actually been *about* the experience of free will, examining at length when people feel it and when they don't. The special idea we have been exploring is to explain the experience of free will in terms of deterministic or mechanistic processes.

On the surface, this idea seems not to offer much in the way of a solution to the classic dichotomy between free will and determinism. How does explaining the feeling of will in terms of deterministic principles help us to decide which one is true? Most philosophers and people on the street see this as a conflict between two big ideas, and they call for a decision on which one is the winner. As it turns out, however, a decision is not really called for. The usual choice we are offered between these extremes is a false dichotomy. It is like asking, Shall we dance, or shall we move about the room in time to the music? The dichotomy melts when we explain one pole of the dimension in terms of the other. Still, this doesn't sit well with anyone who is wedded to the standard view, so we need to examine just how the usual choice leads us astray.

The Usual Choice

Most of us think we understand the basic issue of free will and determinism. The question seems to be whether all our actions are determined by mechanisms beyond our control or whether at least some of them are determined by our free choice. When the alternatives are described this way, many people are happy to side with one or the other. Those who side with free will view members of the opposition as nothing but *robogeeks*, creatures who are somehow disposed to cast away the very essence of their humanity and embrace a personal identity as automatons (fig. 9.1). Those who opt for the deterministic stance view the opposition as little more than *bad scientists,* a cabal of confused mystics with no ability to understand how humanity fits into the grand scheme of things in the universe (fig. 9.2). In each other's eyes, everyone comes out a loser.

The argument between these two points of view usually takes a simple form. The robogeeks point to the array of evidence that human behavior follows mechanistic principles and take great pride in whatever data or experiences accumulate to indicate that human beings are predictable by the rules of science. Meanwhile, the bad scientists ignore all this and simply explain that their own personal experience carries the day: They know they have conscious will.[1] My favorite illustration of the impasse between these combatants is a dialogue that Mark Twain (1906, 7–8) imagined between an old man and a young man in *What Is Man?*

Young Man: You have arrived at man, now?
Old Man: Yes. Man the machine—man the impersonal engine. Whatsoever a man is, is due to his *make,* and to the *influences* brought to bear

---

1. At a session on conscious will at the Tucson 2000 Consciousness conference, for instance, the philosopher John Searle raised his hand (in response to his desire to do so) no less than four times in a fifteen-minute period to show that he indeed had conscious will. As noted by Datson (1982), "Defenders of the traditional theory of volition ultimately base their case on introspective empiricism."

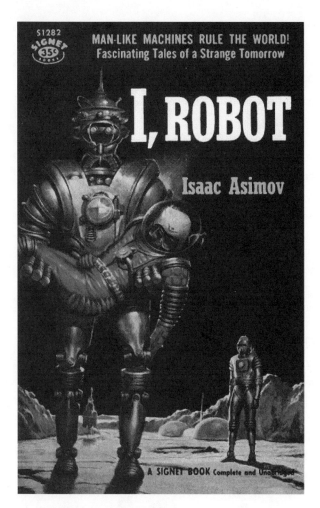

Figure 9.1
Admission of guilt by robogeeks.

upon it by his heredities, his habitat, his associations. He is moved, directed, *commanded,* by *exterior* influences—*solely.* He *originates* nothing, not even a thought.

Y. M.:   Oh, come! Where did I get my opinion that this which you are talking is all foolishness?

O. M.:   It is a quite natural opinion—indeed an inevitable opinion—but *you* did not create the materials out of which it is formed. They are odds and ends of thoughts, impressions, feelings, gathered unconsciously from

Figure 9.2
Good scientist being bad. Courtesy Corbis Picture Library.

a thousand books, a thousand conversations, and from streams of thought and feeling which have flowed down into your heart and brain out of the hearts and brains of centuries of ancestors. *Personally* you did not create even the smallest microscopic fragment of the materials out of which your opinion is made; and personally you cannot claim even the slender merit of *putting the borrowed materials together.* That was done *automatically*—by your mental machinery, in strict accordance with the law of that machinery's construction. And you not only did not make that machinery yourself, but you have *not even any command over it.*

Y. M.: This is too much. You think I could have formed no opinion but that one?

O. M.: Spontaneously? No. And *you did not form that one;* your machinery did it for you—automatically and instantly, without reflection or the need of it.

Y. M.: But don't I tell it what to say?

O. M.:   There are certainly occasions when you haven't time. The words leap out before you know what is coming.

Y. M.:   For instance?

O. M.:   Well, take a "flash of wit"—repartee. Flash is the right word. It is out instantly. There is no time to arrange the words. There is no thinking, no reflecting. Where there is a wit-mechanism it is automatic in its action, and needs no help. Where the wit-mechanism is lacking, no amount of study and reflection can manufacture the product.

Y. M.:   You really think a man originates nothing, creates nothing.

O. M.:   I do. Men perceive, and their brain-machines automatically combine the things perceived. That is all.

The protagonists here are arguing on different premises and so are getting nowhere. The young man (playing bad scientist) assumes as given the feeling of free will and thus marvels, apparently mouth agog, that someone could even begin to claim it is not causal. The old man (playing robogeek) points out examples that belie the feeling. And no one wins the argument. The usual clash fails on both sides because free will is a feeling, whereas determinism is a process. They are incommensurable.

The illogic of treating free will and determinism as equal opposites becomes particularly trenchant when we try to make free will do determinism's causal job. What if, for example, we assume that free will is just like determinism, in that it is also a process whereby human behavior can be explained? Rather than all the various mechanistic engines that psychologists have invented or surmised in human beings that might cause their behavior, imagine instead a person in which there is installed a small unit called the Free Willer. This is not the usual psychological motor, the bundle of thoughts or motives or emotions or neurons or genes—instead, it is a black box that just *does things*. Many kinds of human abilities and tendencies can be modeled in artificially intelligent systems, after all, and it seems on principle that we should be able to design at least the rudiments of a psychological process that has the property of freely willing actions.

But what exactly do we install? If we put in a module that creates actions out of any sort of past experiences or memories, that fashions choices from habits or attitudes or inherited tendencies, we don't get freedom—we get determinism. The Free Willer must be a mechanism that is *unresponsive to any past influence*. In *Elbow Room: The Varieties of Free Will Worth Wanting*, Daniel Dennett (1984) illustrates how hollow and unsatisfying free will of this kind might be. In essence, any such system makes sense only if it inserts some fickle indeterminacy into the person's actions. Dennett points out that it is not particularly interesting or fun to have a coin flipper added to the works somewhere between "sensory input" and "behavior output." Who would want free will if it is nothing more than an internal coin flip? This is not what we mean when we talk about our own conscious will. Trying to understand free will as though it were a kind of psychological causal process leads only to a mechanism that has no relation at all to the experience of free will that we each have every day.

People appreciate free will as a kind of personal power, an ability to do what they want to do. Voltaire (1694–1778) expressed this intuition in saying, "Liberty then is only and can be only the power to do what one will" (1752, 145). He argued that this feeling of freedom is not served at all by the imposition of randomness, asking, "Would you have everything at the pleasure of a million blind caprices?" (144). The experience of will comes from having our actions follow our wishes, not from being able to do things that do not follow from anything. And, of course, we do not cause our wishes. The things we want to do come into our heads. Again quoting Voltaire, "Now you receive all your ideas; therefore you receive your wish, you wish therefore necessarily. . . . The will, therefore, is not a faculty that one can call free. The free will is an expression absolutely devoid of sense, and what the scholastics have called will of indifference, that is to say willing without cause, is a chimera unworthy of being combated" (143). A Free Willer, in short, would not generate the experience of conscious will.

Our personal Free Willer also wouldn't satisfy our desire to establish causality in the person. This classic problem with the theory of free will was described nicely by William James in his essay on *Pragmatism:* "If a 'free' act be a sheer novelty, that comes not *from* me, the previous me, but *ex nihilo*, and simply tacks itself on to me, how can *I*, the previous *I*, be responsible? How can I have any permanent *character* that will stand still long enough for praise or blame to be awarded? The chaplet of my days tumbles into a case of disconnected beads as soon as the thread of inner necessity is drawn out by the preposterous indeterminist doctrine" (1910, 53). It seems quite arbitrary to single out the person for praise or blame when nothing about the person other than this random causation module can be assigned causality or responsibility. Responsibility would seem to be something we would want to attach to some lasting quality of the person. The Free Willer leaves the person responsible merely for having such a device (Miller, Gordon, and Buddie 1999).

So a Free Willer doesn't serve the purposes we would wish it to serve. It doesn't cause action in a way that leaves the person responsible, and it doesn't create an experience of free will either. For these reasons, free will is regularly left out of psychological theory.[2] The major deterministic theory of the past century, the behaviorism of B. F. Skinner, not only left out free will but explicitly belittled the idea (e.g., Skinner 1971). In his words, "We do not hold people responsible for their reflexes—for example, for coughing in church. We hold them responsible for their operant behavior—for example, for whispering in church or remaining in church while coughing. But there are variables which are responsible for whispering was well as coughing and these may be just as inexorable. When we recognize this, we are likely to drop the notion of responsibility altogether and with it the doctrine of free will as an inner causal agent" (1953, 115–116).

This approach argued that the mind does not cause action, and behaviorists developed extensive evidence that behavior can be effectively predicted by conditions that precede and follow it, without any reference to the mind. It turns out, of course, that knowing what is on the mind is indeed useful for predicting behavior. With the cognitive revolution that recognized this, psychology has included thought mechanisms in its theorizing, but along with Skinner, it still has left the experience of conscious will quite out in the cold. Psychologists continuing the emphasis on determinism by studying automatic thought and behavior (e.g., Bargh and Ferguson 2000) have presented convincing blueprints for the human mechanism that leave out a Free Willer of any kind. Free will is not an effective theory of psychology and has fallen out of use for the reason that it is *not the same kind of thing* as a psychological mechanism.

2. Sappington (1990) reports on a number of psychological theories that purport to include some kind of nondeterminism in their formulations. He also argues that theories including free will can be compatible with the scientific tasks of prediction and control. I remain to be convinced. I believe that most of these Free Willer theories have confused having free will with experiencing free will, and the two are vastly different. Having it doesn't happen, whereas experiencing it goes on pretty much constantly.

We are left, then, with a major void. In leaving out a mechanism that might act like free will, theories have also largely ignored the experience of free will. The feeling of doing is a profoundly regular and important human experience, however, one that each of us gets enough times in a day to convince us that we are doing things (nonrandomly) much of the time. This deep intuitive feeling of conscious will is something that no amount of philosophical argument or research about psychological mechanisms can possibly dispel. Even though this experience is not an adequate theory of behavior causation, it needs to be acknowledged as an important characteristic of what it is like to be human.[3] People feel will, and scientific psychology needs to know why. Clearly, people don't feel will because they are somehow immediately knowing their own causal influence as it occurs. The experience is the endpoint of the very elaborate inference system underlying apparent mental causation, and the question becomes, Why do we have this feeling?

Authorship Emotion

Perhaps we have conscious will because it helps us to appreciate and re-member what we are doing. The experience of will marks our actions for us. It helps us to know the difference between a light we have turned on at the switch and a light that has flickered alive without our influence. To label events as our personal actions, conscious will must be an experience that is similar to an emotion. It is a feeling of doing. Unlike a cold thought or rational calculation of the mind alone, will somehow happens both in body and in mind. This embodied quality gives the will a kind of weight or bottom that does not come with thoughts in general. In the same sense that laughter reminds us that our bodies are having fun, or that trembling alerts us that our bodies are afraid, the experience of will reminds us that we're doing something. Will, then, makes the action our own far more intensely than could a thought alone. Unlike simply saying, "This act is mine," the occurrence of conscious will brands the act deeply, associating the act with self through feeling, and so renders the act one's own in a personal and memorable way. Will is a kind of authorship emotion.

3. Dan Gilbert and I got all frothed up about the importance of experience in psychology and spent several days ruminating on the excessive interest most psy-chologists have shown in nonexperiential things such as behavior. See Wegner and Gilbert (2000) for the result.

The idea that volition is an emotion is not new. In fact, the quote from T. H. Huxley at the beginning of this chapter makes the equation explicit. Will is a feeling, not unlike happiness or sadness or anger or anxiety or disgust. Admittedly, conscious will doesn't have a standard facial expression associated with it, as do most other basic emotions (Ekman 1992). The look of determination or a set brow that is sometimes used to caricature willfulness is probably not identifiable enough to qualify as a truly communicative gesture. Still, will has other characteristics of emotion, including an experiential component (how it feels), a cognitive component (what it means and the thoughts it brings to mind), and a physiological component (how the body responds). Although conscious will is not a classic emotion that people would immediately nominate when asked to think of an emotion, it has much in common with the emotions.

Conscious will might be classed as one of the *cognitive feelings* described by Gerald Clore (1992). He points out that there are a set of experiences, such as the feeling of knowing, the feeling of familiarity, or even the feeling of confusion, that serve as indicators of mental processes or states and that thus inform us about the status of our own mental systems. The experience of willing an action is likewise an informative feeling, a perception of a state of the mind and body that has a unique character. Although the proper experiments have not yet been done to test this, it seems likely that people could discriminate the feeling of doing from other feelings, knowing by the sheer quality of the experience just what has happened. The experience of willing is more than a perception of something outside oneself; it is an experience of one's own mind and body in action.

Now, the body serves as an anchor to thinking in many ways. Antonio Damasio (1994) has described the general function of emotions as "somatic markers," deep and unavoidable reminders of the body's interests in what we do and what we experience. It is rare that conscious thought or rational argument can lead a person of sound mind to jump off a bridge, for instance, or to challenge a bear for a fish, reject a loving gesture, or walk away from a large cash windfall. The emotions that these incidents provoke tend to clear away irrelevant or conflicting thoughts and draw the person's attention strongly toward the emotional point of the situation. We attack things that make us angry, run from things that make us afraid, approach things that make us happy, avoid things that make us sad, and otherwise behave in quite simple self-preserving ways in the presence of these bodily signals of our best interests.

Emotions have evolved as automatic signals for this reason (Plutchik 1980; Wegner and Bargh 1998). Damasio finds that people who behave on the basis of seemingly rational and intelligent thought, but whose damaged frontal lobes reduce their emotional reactions to situations, often act in ways that come to undermine their own pursuit of well-being. When patients with frontal damage are shown emotionally disturbing pictures that stimulated surges in skin conductance level (sweating of the fingers) among normal individuals, they exhibit remarkably little response (Damasio, Tranel, and Damasio 1991). It makes sense, then, that such frontal patients in a gambling experiment picked a strategy that earned them slightly higher payoffs on most trials while not noticing that the same strategy often yielded major losses (Bechara et al. 1994). The usual bodily signals that indicate dangerous behavior are not present in these cases and deprive people of the somatic markers that normally guide them away from serious risk.

Conscious will is the somatic marker of personal authorship, an emotion that authenticates the action's owner as the self. With the feeling of doing an act, we get a conscious sensation of will attached to the action. Often, this marker is quite correct. In many cases, we have intentions that preview our action, and we draw causal inferences linking our thoughts and actions in ways that track quite well our own psychological processes. Our experiences of will, in other words, often do correspond correctly with the empirical will—the actual causal connection between our thought and action. The experience of will then serves to mark in the moment and in memory the actions that have been singled out in this way. We know them as ours, as authored by us, because we have felt ourselves doing them. This helps us to tell the difference between things we're doing and all the other things that are happening in and around us. In the melee of actions that occur in daily life, and in the social interaction of self with others, this body-based signature is a highly useful tool. We *resonate* with what we do, whereas we only *notice* what otherwise happens or what others have done. Thus, we can keep track of our own contributions without pencils or tally sheets.

Conscious will can be understood as part of an accounting system. Its regular appearance in actions of all kinds serves as an aid to remembering what we are doing and what we have done. This, in turn, allows us to deserve things. One of the key reasons for describing actions and ascribing them to persons is as a way of determining who deserves what (Feinberg 1970). Action descriptions mark up the flow of human events into convenient packages ("He repaired my motorbike," "She shot the winning basket at the final buzzer," "They sang a musical program at the retirement home"). But each such description of action comes with an ascription, a notation of who is author. Although it could be useful to all of us to remember all the various ascriptions, it is most pressing that we remember our own. We must remember what we have done if we are going to want to claim that our actions have earned us anything (or have prevented us from deserving something nasty). Although the whole team might secretly want to lay claim to that final basket that won the game, for instance, the player who made the shot would be particularly remiss if she didn't know, or later forgot, that she did it. It is good that when she did it, she had an emotion, an experience of conscious will, that certified it as her own.

Conscious will is particularly useful, then, as a guide to ourselves. It tells us what events around us seem to be attributable to our authorship. This allows us to develop a sense of who we are and are not. It also allows us to set aside our achievements from the things that we cannot do. And perhaps most important for the sake of the operation of society, the sense of conscious will also allows us to maintain the sense of responsibility for our actions that serves as a basis for morality. In the remainder of the chapter, we explore these benefits of the authorship emotion.

Achievement and Confidence

In the causal puzzle that is the world, we are overwhelmed with a large number of events and a large number of causal candidates. So much stuff is going on, and some of the things that are going on are causing other things to go on. Making sense of all this is daunting, and so it is indeed fortunate that we have a handy bonus hint whenever an event seems to be caused by ourselves: the feeling of will. It is as though we were putting together a jigsaw puzzle of male rock stars, for instance, with thousands of little pieces of Dylan and Hendrix and Springsteen and Bowie and Prince and Beck, with the convenient feature that whenever we happen to touch a piece of the Boss, we distinctly hear the tune of *Born to Run*.

We would soon finish the Springsteen part of the puzzle, leaving the rest in pieces. Similarly, the experience of conscious will acts as a unifying clue in our causal analysis, leading us to do a better job of appreciating our own potential causality than the causality of anyone or anything else. Conscious will puts the agent self together in the puzzle of life.

The authorship emotion is one of the things people intuitively believe that they would miss if it were gone. It would not be particularly satisfying to go through life causing things—say, making scientific discoveries, winning sports victories, creating social harmony, helping people, or even digging nice big holes in the yard—if we had no personal recognition of these achievements. If such fine and commendable acts were jumbled into an indistinguishable rubble with all the acts ever done by anyone else we'd ever known and with all the occurrences caused by events outside any human agent, we'd be unable to piece together much of a picture of our abilities. Such a featureless landscape, in which self is indistinguishable among all the other causal forces at work in the world, would be deeply depressing. And, indeed, it is this profound lack of an achieving, causal self that people most regret when they envision life as a robogeek. With the loss of a sense of conscious will comes a loss of the organizing theme that helps us to find the thread of our own abilities and achievements in the context of everything else we perceive and remember.

This key feature of conscious will has been celebrated in the findings of a number of researchers. The term *perceived control* is usually used to refer to the experience of conscious will in the achievement domain, and there are many studies indicating that feelings of perceived control are essential for psychological health.[4] We know that people who believe they are the cause of events in their lives tend to be more active in controlling those events. A classic example of this can be found in a study of

4. Haidt and Rodin (1999) and Skinner (1995) have provided reviews of this voluminous literature. Researchers have studied the effects of perceived control under many names: perceived control (Glass and Singer 1972), locus of control (Rotter 1966; Weiner 1974), psychological reactance (Brehm 1966), personal causation (DeCharms 1968), intrinsic motivation (Deci 1975), illusion of control (Langer 1975), self-efficacy (Bandura 1977; 1997a), personal control (Folkman 1984), optimism (Scheier and Carver 1985), personal agency (Vallacher and Wegner 1989), positive illusions (Taylor and Brown 1988), attributional style (Peterson, Maier, and Seligman 1993), and control motivation (Weary, Gleicher, and Marsh 1993).

people's responses to uncontrollable and unfortunate events. Bulman and Wortman (1977) investigated the attributions made by the victims of paralyzing accidents, classifying the explanations people gave for the events as either internal ("I was responsible") or external ("Someone else did it," "It was random"). The noteworthy finding was that people who believed that their victimization was their own responsibility were more inclined to cope well afterwards. Although you might think that these people would be most disappointed in themselves for causing their calamities, the habit of taking responsibility seemed to carry over from the accident into the pursuit of adjustment in the aftermath.

Perceived control is usually understood as a global feeling of competence or confidence. Thus, it is reasonable for a person who perceives control in one area to suspect the possibility of such control in another. In fact, the early study of perceived control (initiated by Julian Rotter in 1966) focused specifically on the idea that the tendency to attribute control to self is a personality trait. Some people have more of it than others, and this generalized expectancy for control influences a person's actions and choices across a wide range of circumstances. Perceiving control is a lot like optimism in that it portends confidence and exuberance in many domains of life; little perceived control, in turn, is like pessimism in that it leads to a general underestimation of what can be done. People who don't perceive that they are controlling things in their lives often attribute events to chance, fate, or powerful others.

The benefits of new perceived control can be particularly positive for people who believe they have little control. This was discovered through the use of control interventions, the addition of control opportunities or demonstrations in a person's life. Among elderly people, for instance, there is a progressive natural decline in actual ability to control aspects of life. With reduced mobility, retirement from work, and increasing health problems, people seem to experience an overall loss of actual control, often accompanied by reductions in perceived control. When elderly people are given new control opportunities, even minor ones such as being asked to take care of themselves and to water a plant (rather than being told they will be cared for and their plant will be watered by others), they show renewed resilience in psychological and physical well-being (Langer and Rodin 1976; Rodin and Langer 1977; Schulz 1976). Perceived control seems to lessen the negative effects of actual reductions in control in many areas, making people feel and perform better in stressful environments (Glass and Singer 1972), for example, and improving their adjustment to health problems (Gatchel and Baum 1983; Taylor and Aspinwall 1993).

In addition to this global "I can do anything" kind of perceived control, there is a more specific "I can do this" variety. This action-specific form of perceived control is really quite like the experience of conscious will. And, as one might expect, having such specific self-confidence is an important element in the likelihood that a person will even try to undertake a specific action. Albert Bandura (1977; 1997a) has studied such perceived control under the rubric of self-efficacy, focusing attention on what happens when this is absent—the cases of actions for which people express zero self-confidence. Self-efficacy seems to be conspicuously missing for actions associated with fears and phobias.

A person who has a phobic reaction to spiders, for instance, finds that fear of spiders is only a part of the problem. The more weighty concern is the person's lack of a feeling that he or she could even *approach* a spider without collapsing into a quivering heap on the floor. The absence of any memory of consciously willing an effective act in this circumstance robs the person of all inclination to approach spiders and replaces it instead with the desire to run away. Without any history of self-efficacy, then, the person is acutely incapacitated in any situation in which this action is potentially required. This unpleasant state of affairs is something each of us has experienced at one time or another. If we don't worry about spiders, we may have fears of flying or falling or crowds or loneliness or public speaking or test taking or financial ruin. Whichever of these circumstances happens to be our personal crippler, the essential ingredient in each case is that, in this particular situation, we simply don't know what to do and have no memory of doing anything right in the past.

What to do? Bandura and others (e.g., Bandura, Reese, and Adams 1982) have championed therapies in which people are encouraged to do very small things in the direction of acting. People who fear spiders, for instance, might be encouraged at the outset to watch someone else draw a picture of a spider. This seems innocuous enough and may be tolerated. But then the therapy escalates, and phobics are asked, perhaps, to draw their own picture of the beast, to watch someone touching a photo of one, to touch the photo themselves, to watch a person touch a real spider, and so on. The phobia sufferer is encouraged to relax along the way and in this process gets a sense of being able to will each of a series of actions all the way up to the target act. Finally, the person may be able at least to enter a room with a spider and may even assemble the nerve to contact a spider in the way most people do, by flattening it with a rolled-up newspaper. The incremental approach of such systematic desensitization works its magic by building up an experience of conscious will for acts that progressively approximate the act the person has not been able to do.

In all these examples of perceived control, the perception of control is not the same thing as actual control. The point we have rehearsed to exhaustion throughout this book—that the feeling of will is not the same as the force of will—arises again here. Perceived control can depart from actual control significantly and repeatedly in life, and the consequences of this variation are not trivial.[5] Consider, for instance, what happens when people have too little perceived control—less than is warranted by the actual causal connection between their thoughts and their actions. In this circumstance they are likely to attempt little or nothing (like the spider phobics) and so may seldom if ever learn that they should perceive more control. This is the classic dilemma of the underachiever. Having tried nothing, the person expects that exertions of conscious will are likely to be futile and so continues to try nothing. This can be a road to depression and despair.

All in all, then, it might be better to err on the side of too much perceived control. And, indeed, this seems to be what most people do. Shelley Taylor (1983; Taylor and Brown 1988; Taylor, Wayment, and Collins 1993) has explored the role of such a *positive illusion* in psychological and mental health, and has catalogued many instances in which it seems to be better to think you have control than not. This sometimes seems to be true even if no real control exists at all. The belief that one has control can be beneficial even in the case of dire circumstances—among people who have terminal illnesses that make their future uncontrollable, for example, or who have suffered serious traumas and so are left with memories of uncontrollable events in the past. It could be unpleasant and potentially disheartening to be brought down from this cloud of fantasy to

5. Not everyone remembers this point all the time, as it is easy to blur the distinction between real and perceived control when speaking generically of "human agency"; see, for example, Bandura (1997b).

the reality of a lack of actual control, but an inflated perception of control seems generally to be better even than an accurate view of control.

But there might be benefits, too, to losing one's illusions. Albert Einstein, the epitome of the *good* scientist, remarked on the mental peace that can come from relaxing the striving for control and accepting a philosophy of resignation to determinism: "The conviction that a law of necessity governs human activities introduces into our conception of man and life a mildness, a reverence and an excellence, such as would be unattainable without this conviction" (quoted in Home and Robinson 1995, 172). Religious traditions such as Zen Buddhism teach a philosophy of relinquishing the pretense of control and view a break with the illusion of conscious will as the ultimate form of enlightenment (Breer 1989). One wonders, however, whether it is possible purposefully to renounce the illusion of purpose or whether one must only sit back and wait for the loss of the illusion to happen.

Whether we embrace the illusion of control or reject it, the presence and absence of the illusion remain useful as clues to what is real. Just as the experience of will allows us to know what we can control, the lack of this feeling alerts us to what we *can't* control, what surely exists beyond our own minds. As Marcia Johnson (1988) has observed, the uncontrollableness of any given percept or memory gives us a hint that we're dealing with reality rather than with imagination. Perceptions with no sense of will attached to them are likely to be indications of reality rather than figments of our minds. The experience of conscious will is thus a friendly sign, a marker of things that have some "give" in that we have felt we could influence them by virtue of our thoughts. The experience of will marks the indulgent areas, the places where we remember having known what we were doing and then doing it. This is good. Even if conscious will isn't an infallible sign of our own causation, it is a fairly good sign and so gives us a rough-and-ready guide to what part of experience is conjured by us and what part is bedrock reality.

The role of conscious will in psychological well-being, in this light, may be a very useful one. Even though conscious will does not signal the actual occurrence of mental causation, it serves as a hint that such causation is happening. Each surge of will we feel accrues very quickly into our overall experience of effectiveness and achievement. Admittedly, this experience of will can be mistaken. A person who fails to sense the willfulness of an automatism, for example, has failed to keep score correctly and may attribute to outside agents the actions actually caused by the self's thoughts. And people can also experience will for actions they did not perform, as in the *I Spy* study (Wegner and Wheatley 1999), which led people to feel they had chosen to do things they had actually been forced to do. But for a significant range of everyday experiences, the feeling of will does measure and accumulate a record of the force of will. This function turns out to be vastly useful, and that might be why people feel will as they do.

Responsibility and Morality

Conscious will is strongly linked to responsibility and morality. As the logic goes, a person is morally responsible only for actions that are consciously willed. Thus, the idea that conscious will might be no more than an illusion stirs up a torrent of moral worries: If conscious will is illusory, how can we continue to hold people responsible for what they do? If behavior is determined and people are merely automatons, how can a person be any more moral or immoral than a machine—a toaster, say, or a Buick? How can we blame people for despicable acts if they didn't will them? How can we reward people for good acts if there is no doing things on purpose? And what about heaven and hell? How will we know what we deserve in the eyes of God? And who shall we blame for all these darned questions?

There is a foundation for many of these worries. There are indeed some contradictions between the standard ways in which people think of moral responsibility and the new ways suggested by the theory of apparent mental causation. However, the contradictions are not nearly as devastating as these questions suggest. Unlike the major moral paradigm changes suggested by some forms of deterministic psychology—behaviorism, for example (Skinner 1971), or theories of automatic behavior (Bargh and Ferguson 2000)—the changes suggested by the present theory are relatively small. After all, the apparent mental causation approach does not throw out conscious will entirely; it instead explains how the experience comes to be. To understand exactly where the real conflicts arise, and which conflicts are merely misunderstandings, it is useful to explore the basic theory of free will that underlies most commonsense moral thinking.

The Free Will Theory

Moral judgments are based not just on what people do but on what they consciously will. In the case of the law, this means that we are concerned not just with what damage might have been caused by an action but with what the person meant to do by so acting. Hart (1968) describes the practice this way: "All civilized penal systems make liability to punishment . . . dependent not merely on the fact that the person to be punished has done the outward act of a crime, but on his having done it in a certain frame of mind or will. These mental and intellectual elements are many and various and are collected together in the terminology of English jurists under the simple sounding description of *mens rea,* a guilty mind. But in many ways the most prominent is a man's intention . . ." (114). So what people intend and consciously will is a basis for how the moral rightness or wrongness of the act is judged.[6]

Religion often emphasizes conscious will even more forcefully than does the law. What people consciously will becomes the arbiter of what they deserve on earth and of their fate in the hereafter. The idea that conscious will might be an illusion is radically disturbing to those who believe that our conscious choices determine our eternal futures. Winter (1998) noted, for example, how doubts about the will that were aroused by the popular discovery of automatism during the spiritualist era came to prompt religious concerns: "The struggle over the natural or supernatural character of mesmerism, table-turning, and early spiritualism developed into a pamphlet war during the early 1850s. . . . The concept of a voluntary or willed action being carried out *unconsciously* was not only objectionable to many Evangelicals but even unimaginable. To make what were in effect unconscious choices would make it impossible to be on one's guard against satanic influence" (264–267). The role of a person's conscious will in choosing what is right and rejecting what is wrong

---

6. The issue of conscious will is taken up in detail in the American Law Institute's, (1995) *Model Penal Code* (Article 2, "General Principles of Liability"), where the requirements for calling an act "voluntary" are said to involve "inquiry into the mental state of the actor" (216). In a major text on criminal law, for instance, criminal responsibility is said to be precluded in situations involving "disturbances of consciousness in persons who retain the capacity to engage in goal-directed conduct based on prior learned responses" (Bonnie et al. 1997, 107). The problem of defining consciousness and mental states is nevertheless one of continual debate and contention in the law (e.g., Keasey and Sales 1977).

makes it a theological issue, and much of the concern about mechanistic explanations of human behavior may be traced to an origin in Western culture and its religious ideologies (Lillard 1998).

Both the legal and the religious free will theories assume that the person's experience of conscious will is a direct sensation of the actual causal relation between the person's thought and action. This is the point at which the theory of apparent mental causation diverges from these theories. Apparent mental causation suggests that the experience of consciously willing an act is merely a humble estimate of the causal efficacy of the person's thoughts in producing the action. Conscious will is the mind's way of signaling that it might have been involved in causing the action. The person's experience of doing the act is only one source of evidence regarding the actual force of the person's will in causing the action, however, and it may not even be the best source.

The gold standard of evidence here would be a scientific experiment in which we set up replicable conditions: The person would be led to think of the act in the exact circumstances in which it was performed, and we would observe repeatedly in these circumstances whether or not the act was done. These conditions are largely impractical, however, and often impossible to produce—we'd have great difficulty wiping the person's mind clean of memory for all the experiments each time we wanted to check again whether the thought caused the action. So we fall back to the tin standard: We gather evidence from multiple sources about the causation of the person's act. The person's experience of conscious will is only one of these sources, not the definitive one.

In the law and in religion, this wishy-washy approach to reports of will makes everyone deeply uncomfortable. It would be nice, after all, to have an infallible source of information about whether the person caused the action. When life or death, or life after death, are at stake, people aspire to this ideal and rely very heavily on the person's reports of the feeling of conscious will, sometimes ignoring in the process better evidence of the role of the force of will in the action. We look to confessions, to expressions of intent, and to other hints of conscious will as indications that a person's mind indeed caused the action.

The reports people make of what they were thinking and experiencing when they committed crimes (or sins) are notoriously unreliable, however. Culprits often deny entirely having conscious thoughts about a crime in advance or deny having an experience of conscious will while performing the crime. The former U. S. Housing Secretary Henry Cisneros, for example, explained why he lied to the FBI about payments to his mistress by saying, "I've attributed it to the pressure and confused sort of fog of the moment where I gave an incorrect number" (*Newsweek,* September 20, 1999, 21).

The same *fog of the moment* is apparent in the statement of Lonnie Weeks, convicted killer of a state trooper who had pulled him over for speeding: "As I stepped out of the car, it was just like something just took over me that I couldn't understand. . . . I felt like it was evil, evil spirit or something. That's how I feel. That's the way I describe it" (Associated Press, September 2, 1999). Another twisted sense of authorship of a crime was conveyed by Mitchell Johnson, one of two boys in jail for the Jonesboro, Arkansas, school shootings in which five people were killed in March 1998: "I honestly didn't want anyone to get hurt. You may not think of it like this, but I have the same pain y'all have. I lost friends like you did. The only difference is, I was the one doing the killing" (Cuza 1999, 33). And perhaps the densest fog is reported by an anonymous respondent in the Feeney (1986) survey of robbers: "I have no idea why I did this" (57).

One view of foggy accounts of crimes is that criminals are ashamed of their actions after the fact and won't admit conscious will. Maybe they try to divorce themselves from the acts by lying about the mental states they had during the action. This makes particular sense if there is something to be gained by the lying, and often there may be some such benefit. The matter-of-fact, concrete accounts of their acts of murder given by German police and soldiers following the Holocaust of World War II, for instance, reflect little experience of conscious will and more of the "I was only following orders" logic we have come to expect of people who are obeying commands (e.g., Browning 1992). Underplaying the sense of conscious will makes good sense if one is hoping to avoid moral condemnation for the sin or retribution for the crime. However, even among people who are unrepentant or have little to gain by disavowing their complicity, there is a widespread tendency to describe crimes and morally reprehensible actions in benign, mindless terms (Katz 1988; Schopp 1991; Wegner and Vallacher 1986).

The causes of evil acts are often only poorly represented in a person's conscious mind. Studies of how criminals choose what crime opportunities to pursue, for example, suggest that they regularly lack insight into the variables that ultimately influence their judgment (e.g., Cornish and Clarke 1986). A criminal may report having robbed a store, for example, because there were no TV surveillance cameras and he hadn't seen police nearby—when research has demonstrated that the strongest consideration influencing most robbers' choice of crime opportunities is the size of the likely haul (Carroll 1978). Such lack of insight can even extend to whether a crime was committed, particularly when the offender is drunk, drugged, sleepwalking, insane, or otherwise incapacitated. People may claim they did nothing at all. In this light, although it makes sense to *ask* people whether they willed their actions, their answers would not seem to be the sole basis for a sound moral judgment of the role of their thoughts in causing their actions. Personal responsibility can't be founded only on self-reports of will. The experience of conscious will is just not a very clear or compelling indication that actions were accomplished by force of will.

This realization has influenced the legal community, particularly among those concerned with the fairness of the insanity defense. John Monahan (1973) examined the way in which psychological science impinges on this legal issue and concluded that the "free will theory" is often challenged these days by the "behavioral position," in which the trial court considers solely whether the defendant committed the physical act with which he or she was charged. After conviction, *mens rea* and any other information available regarding the defendant might then be considered by a group of experts in deciding on the disposition of the case. In this way, people who did not know what they were doing when they committed crimes would be treated just like those who did, at least during the trial. Whether they ended up being sentenced to prison or given psychological or other treatment would be a matter to be determined later. Monahan indicates that "the advocates of this position see it as more scientific, rational, humane, and forward-looking than the punishment-oriented free will system" (733). Monahan was not convinced of the correctness of this position, however, and went on to note the usefulness of considering the criminal's mental state at several points in the legal judgment process.

Robot Morality

One useful way to consider the role of conscious will in moral judgment is to examine the extreme case. Imagine for a moment that we simply throw out the person's statements about conscious will in every case. This extreme version of the "behavioral position" is reminiscent of a kind of moral system one might construct for robots. In a series of science fiction stories set forth in the book *I, Robot* (1970), Isaac Asimov recommended rules for the operating systems of an imaginary fleet of intelligent robots. His Three Laws of Robotics are as follows:

1. A robot may not harm a human being, or through inaction, allow a human being to come to harm.
2. A robot must follow the orders given it by a human being except where such orders would conflict with the First Law.
3. A robot must protect its own existence so long as such protection does not conflict with the First or Second Laws.

The plots of Asimov's stories in this book investigate the potential conflicts among these laws and prompt some clever robot morality plays. The odd feature of these laws is that they make no mention of what the robot might think in advance of action, or what it might feel it is doing. There is no room for this kind of talk because we assume robots are not conscious.

A morality based on such laws might be crudely workable, like the "behavioral position" described by Monahan. If we applied only these basic robot rules to humans, we would judge all action according to its objective consequences. We could merely say that if someone killed a person, the culprit was essentially a faulty robot and could be dropped in the bad robot bin for reprocessing into spark plugs and radios. Intentional murder would be equivalent, in this way of judging morality, to clumsiness that happens to take a life. "Die, you scum!" would be equal to "Whoops, I'm really sorry." This approach is something we may be tempted to take when a person performs a morally reprehensible action that the person claims not to have willed. Without a sense of conscious will, people do not claim to be conscious agents, and it is tempting to judge their behavior by its consequences alone.

On closer analysis, however, Asimov's laws can be understood to imply something much like a concept of conscious will. We seem to need intention and will to keep robots out of the bin. Suppose, for example, that we built a robot that had no action previewing system. It would behave without any prior readout or announcement of its likely behavior, most of the time performing very effectively—but once in a while making the inevitable error. Without some internal mechanism for predicting its own action, and then warning others about it if the action might be harmful, the robot might break Asimov's laws every day by noon. This could quickly doom it to reprocessing.

We would also want the robot to be able to keep track of what it was doing, to distinguish its own behavior from events caused by other things. A robot thus should have an automatic authorship detection system installed at the factory. A good system for detecting authorship would be one in which the robot's previews of its actions were compared with the behaviors it observed itself doing. Matches between previews and actions would suggest that the action was authored by the robot, whereas mismatches would suggest that the action was caused by other forces. The robot would need to keep track of these things, after all, to be able to assess its behavior with respect to the laws. If it happened to be involved in the death of a human because the human ran full speed into it from the rear, the robot could report this and keep itself from being binned while innocent. A record of authorship would also be useful for the robot to record its own past problems and avoid future situations in which it might break laws. None of these functions of the robot would need to be conscious, but all should be in place to allow it to function successfully in Asimov's robot world.

This way of viewing robot morality helps us make sense of the moral role of intention and will in human beings. The intentions and conscious thoughts we have about our actions are cues to ourselves and to others about the meaning and likely occurrence of our behavior. These thoughts about action need not be causes of the action in order to serve moral functions. In his analysis of the insanity defense, Monahan (1973) critiques the "behavioral position" on just this basis. He observes that information about a person's state of mind is important for determining what the crime is, how the person should be treated after the crime, how the person's tendency to commit further crime should be predicted, and whether the person's tendency to perform the crime might be modified in the future. Just because the person may not have infallible knowledge of whether he willed the action is no reason to throw the rest of this crucial information away.

Illusory or not, conscious will is the person's guide to his or her own moral responsibility for action. If you think you willed an act, your ownership of the act is established in your own mind. You will feel guilty if the act is bad, and worthy if the act is good. The function of conscious will is not to be absolutely correct but to be a compass. It tells us where we are and prompts us to feel the emotions appropriate to the morality of the actions we find ourselves doing. Guilt (Baumeister, Stillwell, and Heatherton 1994), pride, and the other moral emotions (Haidt 2001) would not grip us at all if we didn't feel we had willed our actions. Our views of ourselves would be impervious to what we had done, whether good or bad, and memory for the emotional consequences of our actions would not guide us in making moral choices in the future.

We can feel moral emotions inappropriately, of course, because our experience of conscious will in any given case may be wrong. The guilt we feel for mother's broken back may arise from the nonsensical theory that we caused her injury by stepping on a crack. More realistically, we can develop guilty feelings about all sorts of harms we merely imagine before they occur, simply because our apparent mental causation detector can be fooled by our wishes and guesses into concluding that we consciously willed events that only through serendipity have followed our thoughts about them. By the same token, the pride we feel in helping the poor may come from the notion that we had a compassionate thought about them before making our food donation, whereas we actually were just trying to clear out the old cans in the cupboard. But however we do calculate our complicity in moral actions, we then experience the emotional consequences and build up views of ourselves as certain kinds of moral individuals as a result. We come to think we are good or bad on the basis of our authorship emotion. Ultimately, our experience of conscious will may have more influence on our moral lives than does the actual truth of our behavior causation.

How Things Seem

Sometimes how things seem is more important than what they are. This is true in theater, in art, in used car sales, in economics, and—it now turns out—in the scientific analysis of conscious will. The fact is, it seems to each of us that we have conscious will. It seems we have selves. It seems we have minds. It seems we are agents. It seems we cause what we do. Although it is sobering and ultimately accurate to call all this an illusion, it is a mistake to conclude that the illusory is trivial. On the contrary, the illusions piled atop apparent mental causation are the building blocks of human psychology and social life. It is only with the feeling of conscious will that we can begin to solve the problems of knowing who we are as individuals, of discerning what we can and cannot do, and of judging ourselves morally right or wrong for what we have done.

The illusion is sometimes fragile. There are days when we wonder whether we're willing anything at all. In *The Reader* (1995), Bernard Schlink captures this feeling: "Often enough in my life I have done things I had not decided to do. Something—whatever that may be—goes into action; 'it' goes to the woman I don't want to see anymore; 'it' makes the remark to the boss that costs me my head; 'it' keeps on smoking although I have decided to quit, and then quits smoking just when I've accepted the fact that I'm a smoker and always will be. I don't mean to say that the thinking and reaching decisions have no influence on behavior. But behavior does not merely enact whatever has already been thought through and decided. It has its own sources . . ." (20).

But usually we assume that how things seem is how they are. We experience willing a walk in the park, winding a clock, or smiling at someone, and the feeling keeps our notion of ourselves as persons intact. Our sense of being a conscious agent who does things comes at a cost of being technically wrong all the time. The feeling of doing is how it seems, not what it is—but that is as it should be. All is well because the illusion makes us human. Albert Einstein (quoted in Home and Robinson 1995, 172) had a few words on this that make a good conclusion:

If the moon, in the act of completing its eternal way around the earth, were gifted with self-consciousness, it would feel thoroughly convinced that it was traveling its way of its own accord. . . . So would a Being, endowed with higher insight and more perfect intelligence, watching man and his doings, smile about man's illusion that he was acting according to his own free will.

References

Abbey, A., and C. Melby. 1986. The effects of nonverbal cues on gender differences in perceptions of sexual intent. *Sex Roles* 15: 283–298.

Abbott, K., and J. H. Flavell. 1996. Young children's understanding of intention. Unpublished manuscript.

Abell, T. D. 1982. *Better felt than said: The holiness-pentecostal experience in Southern Appalachia.* Waco, TX: Markham Press.

Acocella, J. 1999. *Creating hysteria: Women and multiple personality disorder.* San Francisco: Jossey-Bass.

Ajzen, I. 1985. From intentions to actions: A theory of planned behavior. In *Action control: From cognition to behavior,* eds. J. Kuhl and J. Beckmann, 11–39. New York: Springer-Verlag.

———. 1991. The theory of planned behavior. *Organizational Behavior and Human Decision Processes* 50: 179–211.

Aldridge-Morris, R. 1989. *Multiple personality: An exercise in deception.* Hillsdale, NJ: Erlbaum.

Alexander, M. P., D. T. Stuss, and D. F. Benson. 1979. Capgras' syndrome: A reduplicative phenomenon. *Neurology* 29: 334–339.

Alloy, L. B., and L. Y. Abramson. 1979. Judgment of contingency in depressed and nondepressed students: Sadder but wiser? *Journal of Experimental Psychology: General* 108: 441–485.

Alloy, L. B., and N. Tabachnik. 1984. Assessment of covariation by humans and animals: The joint influence of prior expectations and current situation information. *Psychological Review* 91: 112–149.

American Law Institute. 1985. General provisions. In *Model penal code and commentaries,* 212–268. Philadelphia: American Law Institute.

Angel, L. 1989. *How to build a conscious machine.* Boulder, CO: Westview Press.

Anscombe, G. E. M. 1957. *Intention.* London: Blackwell.

Ansfield, M. E., and D. M. Wegner. 1996. The feeling of doing. In *The psychology of action: Linking cognition and motivation to behavior,* eds. P. M. Gollwitzer and J. A. Bargh, 482–506. New York: Guilford.

Ansfield, M. E., D. M. Wegner, and R. Bowser. 1996. Ironic effect of sleep urgency. *Behaviour Research and Therapy* 34(7): 523–531.

Arnold, M. 1946. On the mechanism of suggestion and hypnosis. *Journal of Abnormal and Social Psychology* 41: 107–128.

Aronson, E., C. Fried, and J. Stone. 1991. Overcoming denial and increasing the intention to use condoms through the induction of hypocrisy. *American Journal of Public Health* 81: 1636–1638.

Asimov, I. 1970. *I, robot.* New York: Fawcett Crest.

Astington, J. W. 1991. Intention in the child's theory of mind. In *Children's theories of mind: Mental states and social understanding,* eds. D. Frye and C. Moore, 157–172. Hillsdale, NJ: Erlbaum.

———. 1993. *The child's discovery of mind.* Cambridge, MA: Harvard University Press.

Astington, J. W., P. L. Harris, and D. R. Olson. 1988. *Developing theories of mind.* New York: Cambridge University Press.

Attneave, F. 1959. Comments: In defense of homunculi. In *Sensory communication: Contributions to the symposium on principles of sensory communication, July 19–August 1,* ed. W. A. Rosenblith, 777–781. Cambridge, MA: MIT Press.

Baars, B. J. 1988. *A cognitive theory of consciousness.* New York: Cambridge University Press.

Baddeley, A. C. 1986. *Working memory.* New York: Oxford University Press.

Bair, J. H. 1901. Development of voluntary control. *Psychological Review* 8: 474–510.

Baldwin, J. M., ed. 1902. Muscle reading. In *Dictionary of philosophy and psychology.* Vol. 2, 120–121. New York: Macmillan.

Bandura, A. 1977. Self-efficacy: Toward a unifying theory of behavioral change. *Psychological Review* 84: 191–215.

———. 1988. Human agency in social cognitive theory. Paper, 24th International Congress of Psychology, Sydney, Australia, August.

———. 1997a. *Self-efficacy: The exercise of control.* San Francisco: Freeman.

———. 1997b. Human agency: The emperor does have new clothes. Paper, CPA Conference, Toronto, 1–18.

Bandura, A., L. Reese, and N. E. Adams. 1982. Microanalysis of action and fear arousal as a function of differential levels of perceived self-efficacy. *Journal of Personality and Social Psychology* 43: 5–21.

Banks, G., P. Short, A. J. Martinez, R. Latchaw, G. Ratcliff, and F. Boller. 1989. The alien hand syndrome: Clinical and postmortem findings. *Archives of Neurology* 46: 456–459.

Banyai, E. I., and E. R. Hilgard. 1976. A comparison of active-alert hypnotic induction with traditional relaxation induction. *Journal of Abnormal Psychology* 85: 218–224.

Barber, T. X. 1969. *Hypnosis*. New York: Van Nostrand Reinhold.

Bargh, J. A. 1984. Automatic and conscious processing of social information. In *Handbook of social cognition*, eds. R. S. Wyer, Jr., and T. K. Srull. Vol. 3, 1–43. Hillsdale, NJ: Erlbaum.

———. 1994. The four horsemen of automaticity: Awareness, intention, efficiency, and control in social cognition. In *Handbook of social cognition*, 2d ed., eds. R. S. Wyer, Jr., and T. K. Srull, 1–40. Hillsdale, NJ: Erlbaum.

———. 1997. The automaticity of everyday life. In *Advances in social cognition*, ed. R. S. Wyer, Jr. Vol. 10, 1–62. Hillsdale, NJ: Erlbaum.

Bargh, J. A., S. Chaiken, P. Raymond, and C. Hymes. 1996. The automatic evaluation effect: Unconditionally automatic attitude activation with a pronunciation task. *Journal of Experimental Social Psychology* 32: 185–210.

Bargh, J. A., and T. L. Chartrand. 1999. The unbearable automaticity of being. *American Psychologist* 54: 462–479.

———. 2000. Studying the mind in the middle: A practical guide to priming and automaticity research. In *Handbook of research methods in social psychology*, eds. H. Reis and C. Judd, 253–285. New York: Cambridge University Press.

Bargh, J. A., M. Chen, and L. Burrows. 1996. Automaticity of social behavior: Direct effects of trait construct and stereotype activation on action. *Journal of Personality and Social Psychology* 71: 230–244.

Bargh, J. A., and M. J. Ferguson. 2000. Beyond behaviorism: On the automaticity of higher mental processes. *Psychological Bulletin* 126: 925–945.

Bargh, J. A., and F. Pratto. 1986. Individual construct accessibility and perceptual selection. *Journal of Experimental Social Psychology* 22: 293–311.

Baron-Cohen, S. 1995. *Mindblindness*. Cambridge, MA: MIT Press.

Barresi, J., and C. Moore. 1996. Intentional relations and social understanding. *Behavioral and Brain Sciences* 19: 107–154.

Barrett, D. L. 1994. Dreaming as a normal model for multiple personality disorder. In *Dissociation: Clinical and theoretical perspectives*, eds. S. J. Lynn and J. W. Rhue, 123–135. New York: Guilford.

Barrett, J. L., and F. C. Keil. 1996. Conceptualizing a nonnatural entity: Anthropomorphism in God concepts. *Cognitive Psychology* 31: 219–247.

Barrett, W., and T. Besterman. 1926. *The divining rod: An experimental and psychological investigation*. London: Methuen.

Basedow, H. 1925. *The Australian Aboriginal*. Adelaide, Australia: Preece.

Baskin, A. 1994. The spirit of Barbie. *Omni* 76 (March).

Bass, E., and L. Davis. 1988. *The courage to heal: A guide for women survivors of child sexual abuse*. New York: Perennial Library.

Bateson, G., and D. D. Jackson. 1964. Some varieties of pathogenic organization. In *Disorders of communication*, ed. D. M. Rioch. Vol. 42, 270–283. New York: Association for Research in Nervous and Mental Disease.

Baumeister, R. F. 1997. *Evil: Inside human violence and cruelty.* San Francisco: Freeman.

———. 1998. The self. In *Handbook of social psychology,* 4th ed., eds. D. T. Gilbert, S. T. Fiske, and G. Lindzey. Vol. 1, 680–740. Boston: McGraw-Hill.

Baumeister, R. F., T. F. Heatherton, and D. M. Tice. 1995. *Losing control.* San Diego, CA: Academic Press.

Baumeister, R. F., A. M. Stillwell, and T. F. Heatherton. 1994. Guilt: An interpersonal approach. *Psychological Bulletin* 115: 243–267.

Beard, G. M. 1877. Physiology of mind reading. *Popular Science Monthly* 10: 459–473.

———. 1882. *The study of trance, muscle-reading, and allied nervous phenomena.* New York.

Bechara, A., A. R. Damasio, H. Damasio, and S. Anderson. 1994. Insensitivity to future consequences following damage to human prefrontal cortex. *Cognition* 50: 7–12.

Begg, I. M., R. K. Robertson, V. Gruppuso, A. Anas, and D. R. Needham. 1996. The illusory-knowledge effect. *Journal of Memory and Language* 35: 410–433.

Bem, D. J. 1967. Self-perception: An alternative interpretation of cognitive dissonance phenomena. *Psychological Review* 74: 183–200.

———. 1972. Self-perception theory. In *Advances in experimental social psychology,* ed. L. Berkowitz. Vol. 6, 1–62. New York: Academic Press.

Bem, D. J., and H. K. McConnell. 1970. Testing the self-perception explanation of dissonance phenomena: On the salience of premanipulation attitudes. *Journal of Personality and Social Psychology* 14: 23–31.

Bentley, M. 1944. The theater of living in animal psychology. *American Journal of Psychology* 67: 1–48.

Bergen, C. 1984. *Knock wood.* New York: Simon and Schuster.

Bernheim, H. 1889. *Suggestive therapeutics: A treatise on the nature and uses of hypnotism.* New York: Putnam.

Bernstein, E. M., and F. W. Putnam. 1986. Development, reliability, and validity of a dissociation scale. *Journal of Nervous and Mental Disease* 174: 727–735.

Bernstein, M. 1965. *The search for Bridey Murphy.* New York: Doubleday.

Berson, R. J. 1983. Capgras' syndrome. *American Journal of Psychiatry* 140: 969–978.

Besnier, N. 1996. Heteroglossic discourses on nukulaelae spirits. In *Spirits in culture, history, and mind,* eds. J. M. Mageo and A. Howard, 75–98. New York, Routledge.

Biklen, D., M. W. Morton, D. Gold, C. Berrigan, and S. Swaminathan. 1992. Facilitated communication: Implications for individuals with autism. *Topics in Language Disorders* 12: 1–28.

Biklen, D., M. W. Morton, S. Saha, J. Duncan, D. Gold, M. Hardardottir, E. Karna, S. O'Connor, and S. Rao. 1991. "I AM NOT A UTISTIC OH THJE TYP" (I am not autistic on the typewriter). *Disability, Handicap, and Society* 6: 161–180.

Biklen, D., and D. N. Cardinal, eds. 1997. *Contested words, contested science: Unraveling the facilitated communication controversy.* New York: Teachers College Press.

Binet, A. 1896. *On double consciousness.* Chicago: Open Court.

Blackmore, S. 1999. *The meme machine.* New York: Oxford University Press.

Bloch, S., P. Orthous, and G. Santibañez-H. 1995. Effector patterns of basic emotions: A psychophysiological method for training actors. In *Acting (re)considered: Theories and practices,* ed. P. Zarrilli, 197–218. New York: Routledge.

Boddy, J. 1994. Spirit possession revisited: Beyond instrumentality. *Annual Review of Anthropology* 23: 407–434.

Bonnet, C. 1755. *Essai de psychologie.* New York: George Olms, 1978.

Bonnie, R. J., A. M. Coughlin, J. C. Jeffries, Jr., and P. W. Low. 1997. *Criminal law.* Westbury, NY: Foundation Press.

Boswell, J. 1791. *Life of Johnson.* London: Oxford University Press, 1970 (3d ed.).

Botvinick, M., and J. Cohen. 1998. Rubber hands "feel" touch that eyes see. *Nature* 391: 756.

Bourguignon, E. 1973. Introduction: A framework for the comparative study of altered states of consciousness. In *Religion, altered states of consciousness, and social change,* ed. E. Bourguignon, 3–35. Columbus: Ohio State University Press.

———. 1976. *Possession.* San Francisco: Chandler and Sharp.

Bower, G. H. 1994. Temporary emotional states act like multiple personalities. In *Psychological concepts and dissociative disorders,* eds. R. M. Klein and B. K. Doane, 207–234. Hillsdale, NJ: Erlbaum.

Bower, T. G. R. 1974. *Development in infancy.* 2d ed. San Francisco: Freeman.

Bower, T. G. R., J. M. Broughton, and M. K. Moore. 1970. Demonstration of intention in the reaching behavior of neonate humans. *Nature* 228: 679–680.

Bowers, K. S. 1981. Do the Stanford scales tap the "classic suggestion effect?" *International Journal of Clinical and Experimental Hypnosis* 29: 42–53.

Bowers, K. S., and E. Z. Woody. 1996. Hypnotic amnesia and the paradox of intentional forgetting. *Journal of Abnormal Psychology* 105(3): 381–390.

Bowers, P., J. R. Laurence, and D. Hart. 1988. The experience of hypnotic suggestions. *International Journal of Clinical and Experimental Hypnosis* 36: 336–349.

Braid, J. 1843. *Neurhypnology, or the rationale of nervous sleep considered in relation with animal magnetism.* London: J. Churchill.

Brandimonte, M. A., G. O. Einstein, and M. A. McDaniel. 1996. *Prospective memory: Theory and applications.* Hillsdale, NJ: Erlbaum.

Brandon, R. 1983. *The spiritualists: The passion for the occult in the nineteenth and twentieth centuries*. New York: Knopf.

Brasil-Neto, J. P., A. Pascual-Leone, J. Valls-Solé, L. G. Cohen, and M. Hallett. 1992. Focal transcranial magnetic stimulation and response bias in a forced choice task. *Journal of Neurology, Neurosurgery, and Psychiatry* 55: 964–966.

Bratman, M. E. 1984. Two faces of intention. *Philosophical Review* 93: 375–405.

———. 1987. *Intentions, plans, and practical reason*. Cambridge, MA: Harvard University Press.

Breen, N. 1999. Misinterpreting the mirrored self. Paper, Third Annual Meeting of the Association for the Scientific Study of Consciousness, London, Ontario, Canada, June.

Breer, P. 1989. *The spontaneous self: Viable alternatives to free will*. Cambridge, MA: Institute for Naturalistic Philosophy.

Brehm, J. W. 1966. *A theory of psychological reactance*. New York: Academic Press.

Brickman, P. 1978. Is it real? In *New directions in attribution research,* eds. J. H. Harvey, W. Ickes, and R. F. Kidd. Vol. 2, 5–34. Hillsdale, NJ: Erlbaum.

Brown, D. D. 1986. Umbanda ritual. In *Umbanda religion and politics in urban Brazil,* ed. D. D. Brown, 79–92. Ann Arbor, MI: UMI Research Press.

Brown, J. W. 1989. The nature of voluntary action. *Brain and Cognition* 10: 105–120.

———. 1996. *Time, will, and mental process*. New York: Plenum.

Brown, J. W., ed. 1988. *Agnosia and apraxia: Selected papers of Liepman, Lange, and Pötzl*. Hillsdale, NJ: Erlbaum.

Brown, M. F. 1997. *The channeling zone*. Cambridge, MA: Harvard University Press.

Brown, P. 1991. *The hypnotic brain: Hypnotherapy and social communication*. New Haven, CT: Yale University Press.

———. 1994. Toward a psychobiological model of dissociation and post-traumatic stress disorder. In *Dissociation: Clinical and theoretical perspectives,* eds. S. J. Lynn and J. W. Rhue, 94–122. New York: Guilford.

Brown, R. 1973. *A first language: The early stages*. Cambridge, MA: Harvard University Press.

Browning, C. R. 1992. *Ordinary men: Reserve police battalion 101 and the final solution in Poland*. New York: Harper Perennial.

Bruner, J. S. 1957. On perceptual readiness. *Psychological Review* 64: 123–152.

———. 1964. The course of cognitive growth. *American Psychologist* 19: 1–15.

Brunia, C. H. M. 1987. Brain potentials related to preparation and action. In *Perspectives on perception and action,* eds. H. Heuer and A. F. Sanders, 105–130. Hillsdale, NJ: Erlbaum.

Bryan, W. L., and L. Harter. 1899. Studies on the telegraphic language: The acquisition of a hierarchy of habits. *Psychological Review* 6: 345–378.

Buchanan, J. 1812. *The philosophy of human nature.* Richmond, KY: Grimes.

Bulman, J. R., and C. B. Wortman. 1977. Attributions of blame and coping in the "real world": Severe accident victims react to their lot. *Journal of Personality and Social Psychology* 35: 351–363.

Burgess, C. A., I. Kirsch, H. Shane, K. L. Niederauer, S. M. Graham, and A. Bacon 1998. Facilitated communication as an ideomotor response. *Psychological Science* 9: 71–74.

Burgess, P. W. 1997. Theory and methodology in executive function research. In *Methodology of frontal and executive function,* ed. P. Rabbitt, 81–116. Hove, East Sussex, UK: Psychology Press.

Cabay, M. 1994. A controlled evaluation of facilitated communication using open-ended and fill-in questions. *Journal of Autism and Developmental Disorders* 24: 517–527.

Campbell, D. T. 1958. Common fate, similarity, and other indices of the status of aggregates of persons as social entities. *Behavioral Science* 3: 14–25.

Cannon, W. B. 1942. "Voodoo" Death. *American Anthropologist* 44: 182–190.

Carey, S. 1996. Cognitive domains as modes of thought. In *Modes of thought: Explorations in culture and cognition,* eds. D. R. Olson, and N. Torrance, 187–215. New York: Cambridge University Press.

Carlson, E. B., and F. W. Putnam. 1993. An update on the dissociative experiences scale. *Dissociation* 6: 16–27.

Carpenter, W. B. 1888. *Principles of mental physiology, with their applications to the training and discipline of the mind and the study of its morbid conditions.* New York: Appleton.

Carroll, J. S. 1978. A psychological approach to deterrence: The evaluation of crime opportunities. *Journal of Personality and Social Psychology* 36: 1512–1520.

Carroll, L. 1882. *Alice's adventures in wonderland.* New York: Armont, 1965.

Carver, C. S., and M. F. Scheier. 1998. *On the self regulation of behavior.* Cambridge: Cambridge University Press.

Castiello, U., Y. Paulignan, and M. Jeannerod. 1991. Temporal dissociation of motor responses and subjective awareness: A study in normal subjects. *Brain* 114: 2639–2655.

Chadwick, P., and M. J. Birchwood. 1994. The omnipotence of voices: A cognitive approach to auditory hallucinations. *British Journal of Psychiatry* 164: 190–201.

Chalmers, D. J. 1996. *The conscious mind.* New York: Oxford University Press.

Chapman, J. P. 1966. The early symptoms of schizophrenia. *British Journal of Psychiatry* 12: 221–251.

Chapman, L. J., and J. P. Chapman. 1988. The genesis of delusions. In *Delusional beliefs*, eds. T. F. Oltmanns and B. A. Maher, 167–184. New York: Wiley.

Charleton, W. 1988. *Weakness of will: A philosophical introduction*. New York: Blackwell.

Chaves, J. F. 1997. The state of the "state" debate in hypnosis: A view from the cognitive-behavioral perspective. *International Journal of Clinical and Experimental Hypnosis* 45: 251–265.

Chevreul, M. E. 1833. Lettre à M. Ampère sur une classe particulaire. *Review des Deux Mondes* 2: 258–266.

Cialdini, R. B., J. T. Cacioppo, R. Bassett, and J. A. Miller. 1978. Low-ball procedure for producing compliance: Commitment then cost. *Journal of Personality and Social Psychology* 36: 463–476.

Cioffi, D. 1993. Sensate body, directive mind: Physical sensations and mental control. In *Handbook of mental control*, eds. D. M. Wegner and J. W. Pennebaker, 410–442. Englewood Cliffs, NJ: Prentice Hall.

Cioffi, D., and J. Holloway. 1993. Delayed costs of suppressed pain. *Journal of Personality and Social Psychology* 64: 274–282.

Clarke, A. C. 1973. *Profiles of the future: An inquiry into the limits of the possible*. Rev. ed. New York: Harper and Row.

Claxton, G. 1999. Whodunnit? Unpicking the "seems" of free will. *Journal of Consciousness Studies* 6: 99–113.

Clore, G. 1992. Cognitive phenomenology: Feelings and the construction of judgment. In *The construction of social judgments*, ed. L. L. Martin, 133–163. Hillsdale, NJ: Erlbaum.

Cocores, J. A., A. L. Bender, and E. McBride. 1984. Multiple personality, seizure disorder, and electroencephalogram. *Journal of Nervous and Mental Diseases* 172: 436–438.

Coe, W. E. 1992. Hypnosis: Wherefore art thou? *International Journal of Clinical and Experimental Hypnosis* 40: 219–237.

Cohen, A. R. 1962. An experiment on small rewards for discrepant compliance and attitude change. In *Explorations in cognitive dissonance*, eds. J. W. Brehm and A. R. Cohen, 73–78. New York: Wiley.

Cohen, B. H. 1986. The motor theory of voluntary thinking. In *Consciousness and self-regulation*, eds. R. J. Davidson, G. E. Schwartz, and D. Shapiro. Vol. 4, 19–54. New York: Plenum.

Cole, H., and D. Ross. 1977. *The Arts of Ghana*. Santa Barbara, CA: Regents of the University of California.

Cole, J. 1986. Observations on the sense of effort in a man without large myelinated cutaneous and proprioceptive sensory fibers below the neck. *Journal of Physiology* 382: 80.

———. 1995. *Pride and a daily marathon*. Cambridge, MA: MIT Press.

Cole, J., and J. Paillard. 1995. Living without touch and peripheral information about body position and movement: Studies with deafferented subjects. In *The body and the self*, eds. J. L. Bermudez, A. Marcel and N. Eilan, 245–266. Cambridge, MA: MIT Press.

Cooley, C. H. 1902. *Human nature and the social order.* New York: Scribners.

Coons, P. M., and V. Milstein. 1986. Psychosexual disturbances in multiple personality: Characteristics, etiology, and treatment. *Journal of Clincial Psychiatry* 47: 106–110.

Cooper, J., and R. H. Fazio. 1984. A new look at dissonance theory. In *Advances in experimental social psychology*, ed. L. Berkowitz. Vol. 17, 229–266. San Diego, CA: Academic Press.

Cornish, D. B., and R. V. Clarke, eds. 1986. *The reasoning criminal: Rational choice perspectives on offending.* New York: Springer-Verlag.

Council, J. R., I. Kirsch, and D. L. Grant. 1996. Imagination, expectancy, and hypnotic responding. In *Hypnosis and imagination*, eds. R. G. Kunzendorf, N. P. Spanos, and B. Wallace, 41–65. Amityville, NY: Baywood.

Crawford, H. J., T. Knebel, and J. M. C. Vendemia. 1998. The nature of hypnotic analgesia: Neurophysiological foundation and evidence. *Contemporary Hypnosis* 15: 22–33.

Crewes, W. D., et al. 1995. An evaluation of facilitated communication in a group of nonverbal individuals with mental retardation. *Journal of Autism and Developmental Disorders* 25: 205–213.

Crick, F., and C. Koch. 1990. Towards a neurobiological theory of consciousness. *Seminars in the Neurosciences* 2: 263–275.

Crossley, R. 1992. Lending a hand—a personal account of facilitated communication training. *American Journal of Speech-Language Pathology* 2: 18–21.

Crossley, R., and A. McDonald. 1980. *Annie's coming out.* Melbourne, Australia: Penguin.

Crossley, R., and J. Remington-Gurney. 1992. Getting the words out: Facilitated communication training. *Topics in Language Disorders* 12: 29–45.

Cuza, B. 1999. Detained and confused. *Time*, August 16, 32–33.

Damasio, A. R. 1994. *Descartes' error: Emotion, reason, and the human brain.* New York: Avon.

Damasio, A. R., D. Tranel, and H. Damasio. 1991. Somatic markers and the guidance of behavior: Theory and preliminary testing. In *Frontal lobe function and dysfunction*, eds. H. S. Levin, H. M. Eisenberg, and A. L. Benson, 217–229. New York: Oxford University Press.

Danto, A. 1963. What we can do. *Journal of Philosophy* 40: 435–445.

Daprati, E., N. Franck, N. Georgieff, J. Proust, E. Pacherie, J. Dalery, and M. Jeannerod. 1997. Looking for the agent: An investigation into consciousness of action and self-consciousness in schizophrenic patients. *Cognition* 65: 71–86.

Datson, L. J. 1982. The theory of will versus the science of mind. In *The problematic science: Psychology in nineteenth-century thought,* eds. W. R. Woodward and M. G. Ash, 88–115. New York: Praeger.

Davidson, D. 1963. Actions, reasons, and causes. *Journal of Philosophy* 60: 685–700.

De Pauw, K. W., T. K. Szulecka, and T. L. Poltock. 1987. Frégoli syndrome after cerebral infarction. *Journal of Nervous and Mental Diseases* 175: 433–438.

DeCharms, R. 1968. *Personal causation.* New York: Academic Press.

Deci, E. L. 1975. *Intrinsic motivation.* New York: Plenum.

Deecke, L., B. Grozinger, and H. H. Kornhuber. 1976. Voluntary finger movement in man: Cerebral potentials and theory. *Biological Cybernetics* 23: 99–119.

Deecke, L., P. Scheid, and H. H. Kornhuber. 1969. Distribution of readiness potential, pre-motion positivity, and motor potential of the human cerebral cortex preceding voluntary finger movements. *Experimental Brain Research* 7: 158–168.

Deese, J. 1978. Thought into speech. *American Scientist* 66: 314–321.

Delboeuf, J. 1886. De l'influence de l'imitation et de l'education dans le somnambulisme provoqué. *Revue philosophique* 22: 146–171.

Delgado, J. M. R. 1969. *Physical control of the mind: Toward a psychocivilized society.* New York: Harper and Row.

Dennett, D. C. 1984. *Elbow room: The varieties of free will worth wanting.* Cambridge, MA: MIT Press.

———. 1987. *The intentional stance.* Cambridge, MA: MIT Press.

———. 1991. *Consciousness explained.* New York: Basic Books.

———. 1992. The self as a center of narrative gravity. In *Self and consciousness: Multiple perspectives,* eds. F. Kessel, P. Cole, and D. Johnson. Hillsdale, NJ: Erlbaum.

———. 1996. *Kinds of minds.* New York: Basic Books.

———. 2000. In Darwin's wake, where am I? Presidential address, American Philosophical Association, December 29.

Dennett, D. C., and M. Kinsbourne. 1992. Time and the observer: The where and when of consciousness in the brain. *Behavioral and Brain Sciences* 15: 183–247.

Descartes, R. 1647. *Meditations on first philosophy,* trans. J. Veitch. New York: Prometheus Books, 1901.

Devor, M. 1997. Phantom limb phenomena and their neural mechanism. In *The mythomanias: The nature of deception and self-deception,* ed. M. S. Myslobodsky, 327–361. Mahwah, NJ: Erlbaum.

Diagnostic and statistical manual of mental disorders, IV. 1994. Washington, DC: American Psychiatric Association.

Diener, E. 1979. Deindividuation, self-awareness, and disinhibition. *Journal of Personality and Social Psychology* 37: 1160–1171.

Diener, E., S. C. Fraser, A. L. Beaman, and R. T. Kelem. 1976. Effects of deindividuating variables on stealing by Halloween trick-or-treaters. *Journal of Personality and Social Psychology* 33: 178–183.

Dijksterhuis, A., J. A. Bargh, and J. Miedema. 2001. Of men and mackerels: Attention and automatic social behavior. In *Subjective experience in social cognition and behavior,* eds. H. Bless and J. Forgas. Philadelphia: Psychology Press.

Dijksterhuis, A., and A. van Knippenberg. 1998. The relation between perception and behavior, or how to win a game of Trivial Pursuit. *Journal of Personality and Social Psychology* 74: 865–877.

———. 2000. Behavioral indecision: Effects of self-focus on automatic behavior. *Social Cognition* 18: 55–74.

Dijksterhuis, A., D. M. Wegner, and H. Aarts. 2001. Unconscious priming of conscious will. Unpublished manuscript.

Dillon, K. 1993. Facilitated communication, autism, and ouija. *Skeptical Inquirer* 17: 281–287.

Double, R. 1991. *The non-reality of free will.* New York: Oxford University Press.

Downey, J. D., and J. E. Anderson. 1915. Automatic writing. *American Journal of Psychology* 26: 161–195.

du Maurier, G. 1894. *Trilby.* New York: Oxford University Press, 1998.

Duchenne de Boulogne, G. B. 1862. *The mechanism of human facial expression,* trans. and ed. R. A. Cuthbertson. Cambridge: Cambridge University Press, 1990.

Dupotet de Sennevoy, C. 1862. *L'Art du Magnetiséur.* Paris: A. Réné.

Duval, S., and R. A. Wicklund. 1972. *A theory of objective self awareness.* New York: Academic Press.

———. 1973. Effects of objective self-awareness on attribution of causality. *Journal of Experimental Social Psychology* 9: 17–31.

Eagly, A. H., and S. Chaiken. 1993. *The psychology of attitudes.* Orlando, FL: Harcourt Brace Jovanovich.

Earman, J. 1986. *A primer on determinism.* Dordrecht, Netherlands: D. Reidel.

Easton, R. D., and R. E. Shor. 1975. Information processing analysis of the Chevreul pendulum illusion. *Journal of Experimental Psychology: Human Perception and Performance* 1: 231–236.

———. 1976. An experimental analysis of the Chevreul pendulum illusion. *Journal of General Psychology* 95: 111–125.

———. 1977. Augmented and delayed feedback in the Chevreul pendulum illusion. *Journal of General Psychology* 97: 167–177.

Eccles, J. C. 1976. Brain and free will. In *Consciousness and the brain,* eds. G. Globus, G. Maxwell, and I. Savodnik, 101–121. New York: Plenum.

———. 1982. How the self acts on the brain. *Psychoneuroendocrinology* 7: 271–283.

Edmonston, W. E., Jr. 1981. *Hypnosis and relaxation: Modern verification of an old equation.* New York: Wiley.

Edwards, G. 1963. The duration of post-hypnotic effect. *British Journal of Psychology* 109: 259–266.

———. 1965. Post-hypnotic amnesia and post-hypnotic effect. *British Journal of Psychiatry* 111: 316–325.

Eich, E., D. Macaulay, R. J. Loewenstein, and P. H. Dihle. 1997. Implicit memory, interpersonality amnesia, and dissociative identity disorder: Comparing patients and simulators. In *Recollections of trauma: Scientific research and clinical practice,* eds. J. D. Read and D. S. Lindsay, 469–474. New York: Plenum.

Einhorn, H. J., and R. M. Hogarth. 1986. Judging probable cause. *Psychological Bulletin* 99: 3–19.

Ekman, P. 1985. *Telling lies.* New York: W. W. Norton.

———. 1992. An argument for basic emotion. *Cognition and Emotion* 6: 169–200.

Ekman, P., R. J. Davidson, and W. V. Friesen. 1990. The Duchenne smile: Emotional and brain physiology II. *Journal of Personality and Social Psychology* 58: 342–353.

Ekman, P., and W. V. Friesen. 1975. *Unmasking the face.* Englewood Cliffs, NJ: Prentice Hall.

Ekman, P., W. V. Friesen, and R. C. Simons, 1985. Is the startle reaction an emotion? *Journal of Personality and Social Psychology* 49: 1416–1426.

Eliade, M. 1972. *Shamanism: Archaic techniques of ecstasy,* trans. W. R. Trask. Princeton, NJ: Princeton University Press.

Ellenberger, H. F. 1970. *The discovery of the unconscious.* New York: Basic Books.

Ellis, H. D., and A. W. Young. 1990. Accounting for delusional misidentifications. *British Journal of Psychiatry* 157: 239–248.

Erickson, M. H., and E. M. Erickson. 1941. Concerning the nature and character of posthypnotic behavior. *Journal of General Psychology* 24: 95–133.

Ericsson, K. A., and H. A. Simon. 1984. *Protocol analysis: Verbal reports as data.* Cambridge, MA: MIT Press.

Eysenck, H. J., and W. D. Furneaux. 1945. Primary and secondary suggestibility: An experimental and statistical study. *Journal of Experimental Psychology* 35: 485–503.

Faith, M., and W. J. Ray. 1994. Hypnotizability and dissociation in a college age population: Orthogonal individual differences. *Personality and Individual Differences* 17: 211–216.

Faraday, M. 1853. Experimental investigation of table turning. *Athenaeum,* July, 801–803.

Farmer, P. 1998. *Elvis Aaron Presley: His growth and development as a soul spirit within the universe.* New York: Prime.

Farrington, E. (pseud.). 1922. *Revelations of a Spirit Medium.* London: Kegan Paul, Trench, Trubner.

Fazio, R. H. 1987. Self-perception theory: A current perspective. In *Social influence: The Ontario symposium,* eds. M. P. Zanna, J. M. Olson, and C. P. Herman. Vol. 5, 129–150. Hillsdale, NJ: Erlbaum.

Fazio, R. H., M. P. Zanna, and J. Cooper. 1977. Dissonance and self-perception: An integrative view of each theory's proper domain of application. *Journal of Experimental Social Psychology* 13: 464–479.

Feeney, F. 1986. Robbers as decision-makers. In *The reasoning criminal: Rational choice perspectives on offending,* eds. D. B. Cornish and R. V. Clarke, 53–71. New York: Springer-Verlag.

Feinberg, I. 1978. Efference copy and corollary discharge: Implications for thinking and its disorders. *Schizophrenia Bulletin* 4: 636–640.

Feinberg, J. 1970. *Doing and deserving.* Princeton, NJ: Princeton University Press.

Feinberg, T. 2001. *Altered egos: How the brain creates the self.* New York: Oxford University Press.

Felce, D. 1994. Facilitated communication: Results from a number of recently published evaluations. *Mental Handicap* 22: 122–126.

Fernald, D. 1984. *The Hans legacy: A story of science.* Hillsdale, NJ: Erlbaum.

Festinger, L. 1957. *A theory of cognitive dissonance.* Palo Alto, CA: Stanford University Press.

Festinger, L., S. Schacter, and K. Back. 1950. *Social pressures in informal groups: A study of human factors in housing.* New York: Harper.

Fine, G. A. 1983. *Shared fantasy: Role playing games as social worlds.* Chicago: University of Chicago Press.

Flavell, J. H., P. Botkin, C. L. Fry, Jr., J. W. Wright, and P. E. Jarvis. 1968. *The development of role-taking and communication skills in children.* New York: Wiley.

Flavell, J. H., F. L. Green, and E. R. Flavell. 1995. The development of children's knowledge about attentional focus. *Developmental Psychology* 31: 706–712.

Folkman, S. 1984. Personal control and stress and coping processes: A theoretical analysis. *Journal of Personality and Social Psychology* 46: 839–852.

Foster, W. S. 1923. Experiments on rod-divining. *Journal of Applied Psychology* 7: 303–311.

Frank, J. D. 1944a. Experimental studies in personal pressure and resistance: I. Experimental production of resistance. *Journal of General Psychology* 30: 23–41.

———. 1944b. Experimental studies in personal pressure and resistance: II. Methods of overcoming resistance. *Journal of General Psychology* 30: 45–56.

Freedman, J. L., and S. C. Fraser. 1966. Compliance without pressure: The foot-in-the-door technique. *Journal of Personality and Social Psychology* 4: 195–203.

Freud, S. 1900. *The interpretation of dreams*. The Standard Edition of the Complete Psychological Works of Sigmund Freud, ed. and trans. J. Strachey. Vols. 4 and 5. London: Hogarth Press, 1953.

Frigerio, A. 1989. Levels of possession awareness in Afro-Brazilian religions. *Journal of the Association for the Anthropological Study of Consciousness* 5: 5–11.

Frith, C. D. 1987. The positive and negative symptoms of schizophrenia reflect impairments in the perception and initiation of action. *Psychological Medicine* 17: 631–648.

———. 1992. *The cognitive neuropsychology of schizophrenia*. Hillsdale, NJ: Erlbaum.

———. 1994. Theory of mind in schizophrenia. In *The neuropsychology of schizophrenia*, eds. A. S. David and J. Cutting, 147–161. Hillsdale, NJ: Erlbaum.

Frith, C. D., S. Blakemore, and D. M. Wolpert. 1999. Abnormalities in the perception and control of action. Unpublished study, Institute of Neurology, University College, London.

Frith, C. D., and D. J. Done. 1989. Experiences of alien control in schizophrenia reflect a disorder in the central monitoring of action. *Psychological Medicine* 19: 359–363.

Frith, C. D., and P. Fletcher. 1995. Voices from nowhere. *Critical Quarterly* 37: 71–83.

Fromm, E. 1970. Age regression with unexpected reappearance of a repressed childhood language. *International Journal of Clinical and Experimental Hypnosis* 18: 79–88.

Gandevia, S. C. 1982. The perception of motor commands or effort during muscular paralysis. *Brain* 105: 151–159.

———. 1987. Roles for perceived voluntary motor commands in motor control. *Trends in Neuroscience* 15: 81–85.

Gardner, M. 1957. *Fads and fallacies in the name of science*. New York: Dover.

Garrett, C. 1987. *Spirit possession and popular religion: From the Camisards to the Shakers*. Baltimore: Johns Hopkins University Press.

Gasquoine, P. G. 1993. Alien hand sign. *Journal of Clinical and Experimental Neuropsychology* 15: 653–667.

Gatchel, R. J., and A. Baum. 1983. *An introduction to health psychology*. Reading, MA: Addison-Wesley.

Gauld, A. 1992. *The history of hypnotism*. Cambridge: Cambridge University Press.

Gazzaniga, M. S. 1983. Right hemisphere language following brain bisection: A 20-year perspective. *American Psychologist* 38: 525–537.

————. 1988. Brain modularity: Towards a philosophy of conscious experience. In *Consciousness in contemporary science,* eds. A. J. Marcel and E. Bisiach, 218–238. Oxford: Clarendon Press.

————. 1995. Consciousness and the cerebral hemispheres. In *The cognitive neurosciences,* ed. M. S. Gazzaniga, 1391–1400. Cambridge, MA: MIT Press.

Gazzaniga, M. S., and J. E. LeDoux. 1978. *The integrated mind.* New York: Plenum.

Gelfano, M. 1998. B. B. King's blues: A journey into the soul of modern blues guitar. *Musician,* June, 28–42.

Gelman, R. 1990. First principles organize attention to and learning about relevant data: Number and the animate-inanimate distinction as examples. *Cognitive Science* 14: 79–106.

Gelman, R., F. Durgin, and L. Kaufman. 1995. Distinguishing between animates and inanimates: Not by motion alone. In *Causal cognition,* eds. D. Sperber, D. Premack, and A. J. Premack, 150–184. Oxford: Clarendon Press.

Geschwind, D. H., M. S. Iacoboni, D. W. Mega, W. Zaidel, T. Cloughesy, and E. Zaidel. 1995. Alien hand syndrome: Interhemispheric motor disconnection due to a lesion in the midbody of the corpus callosum. *Neurology* 45: 802–808.

Gibbons, F. X. 1990. Self-attention and behavior: A review and theoretical update. In *Advances in experimental social psychology,* ed. M. Zanna. Vol. 23, 249–303. San Diego, CA: Academic Press.

Gilbert, D. T. 1998. Ordinary personology. In *Handbook of social psychology,* 4th ed., eds. D. T. Gilbert, S. T. Fiske, and G. Lindzey. Vol. 1, 89–150. New York: Oxford University Press.

Gilbert, D. T., and J. Cooper. 1985. Social psychological strategies of self-deception. In *Self-deception and self-understanding,* ed. M. W. Martin, 75–94. Lawrence: University of Kansas Press.

Gilbert, D. T., R. P. Brown, E. C. Pinel, and T. D. Wilson. 2001. The illusion of external agency. *Journal of Personality and Social Psychology* 79: 690–700.

Ginet, C. 1986. Voluntary exertion of the body: A volitional account. *Theory and Decision* 20(3): 223–245.

Glass, D. C., and J. E. Singer. 1972. *Urban stress.* New York: Academic Press.

Gleaves, D. H. 1996. The sociocognitive model of dissociative identity disorder: A reexamination of the evidence. *Psychological Bulletin* 120: 42–59.

Godfrey, N. S. 1853. *Table-turning: the Devil's modern masterpiece, being the result of a course of experiments.* London: Partridge, Oakey.

Goffman, E. 1959. *The presentation of self in everyday life.* New York: Doubleday.

Goldman, A. I. 1970. *A theory of human action.* Princeton, NJ: Princeton University Press.

Gollwitzer, P. M. 1993. Goal achievement: The role of intentions. In *European review of social psychology,* eds. W. Stroebe and M. Hewstone. Vol. 4, 141–185. London: Wiley.

Gomes, G. 1998. The timing of conscious experience: A critical review and reinterpretation of Libet's research. *Consciousness and Cognition* 7: 559–595.

Gomez, C., E. D. Argandoña, R. G. Solier, J. C. Angulo, and M. Vàzquez. 1995. Timing and competition in networks representing ambiguous figures. *Brain and Cognition* 29: 103–114.

Goodman, F. D. 1972. *Speaking in tongues: A cross-cultural study of glossolalia.* Chicago: University of Chicago Press.

———. 1988. *How about demons? Possession and exorcism in the modern world.* Bloomington: Indiana University Press.

Gopnik, A. 1993. How we know our minds: The illusion of first-person knowledge of intentionality. *Behavioral and Brain Sciences* 16: 1–14.

Gopnik, A., and J. W. Astington. 1988. Children's understanding of representational change and its relation to the understanding of false belief and the appearance-reality distinction. *Child Development* 48: 26–37.

Gorassini, D. R. 1999. Hypnotic responding: A cognitive-behavioral analysis of self-deception. In *Clinical hypnosis and self-regulation: Cognitive-behavioral perspectives,* eds. I. Kirsch, A. Capafons, E. Cardena-Buelna, and S. Amigo, 73–103. Washington, DC: American Psychological Association.

Gorassini, D. R., and A. H. Perlini, 1988. Making suggested responses seem involuntary: Experience structuring by hypnotic and nonhypnotic subjects. *Journal of Research in Personality* 22: 213–231.

Gorman, B. J. 1999. Facilitated communication: Rejected in science, accepted in court—A case study and analysis of the use of FC evidence under Frye and Daubert. *Behavioral Sciences and the Law* 17: 517–541.

Goschke, T., and J. Kuhl. 1993. Representation of intentions: Persisting activation in memory. *Journal of Experimental Psychology: Learning, Memory, and Cognition* 19: 1211–1226.

Gotlib, I. H., and C. D. McCann. 1984. Construct accessibility and depression: An examination of cognitive and affective factors. *Journal of Personality and Social Psychology* 47: 427–439.

Gould, L. N. 1948. Verbal hallucinations and activity of vocal musculature. *American Journal of Psychiatry* 105: 367–372.

Graham, G., and G. L. Stephens. 1994. Mind and mine. In *Philosophical psychology,* eds. G. Graham and G. L. Stephens, 91–109. Cambridge, MA: MIT Press.

Grasset, J. 1910. *Marvels beyond science.* New York: Funk and Wagnalls.

Green, M. F., and M. Kinsbourne. 1989. Auditory hallucinations in schizophrenia: Does humming help? *Biological Psychiatry* 25: 633–635.

Greenwald, A. G. 1975. On the inconclusiveness of "crucial" cognitive tests of dissonance vs. self-perception theories. *Journal of Experimental Social Psychology* 11: 490–499.

————. 1982. Is anyone in charge? Personalysis versus the principle of personal unity. In *Psychological perspectives on the self,* ed. J. Suls. Vol. 1, 151–181. Hillsdale, NJ: Erlbaum.

Greenwald, A. G., and S. C. Draine. 1997. Do subliminal stimuli enter the mind unnoticed? Tests with a new method. In *Scientific approaches to consciousness,* eds. J. D. Cohen and J. W. Schooler, 83–108. Mahwah, NJ: Erlbaum.

Grice, H. P. 1975. Personal identity. In *Personal identity,* ed. J. Perry, 73–95. Berkeley: University of California Press.

Gross, N. C. 1998. Touched by angels? *The Jerusalem Report,* September 14.

Guthrie, S. E. 1993. *Faces in the clouds: A new theory of religion.* New York: Oxford University Press.

Haggard, P., and M. Eimer. 1999. On the relation between brain potentials and the awareness of voluntary movements, *Experimental Brain Research* 126: 128–133.

Haggard, P., and E. Magno. 1999. Localizing awareness of action with transcranial magnetic stimulation. *Experimental Brain Research* 127: 102–107.

Haggard, P., C. Newman, and E. Magno. 1999. On the perceived time of voluntary actions. *British Journal of Psychology* 90: 291–303.

Haidt, J. 2001. The moral emotions. In *Handbook of affective sciences,* eds. R. J. Davidson, K. Scherer, and H. H. Goldsmith. Oxford: Oxford University Press.

Haidt, J., and J. Rodin. 1999. Control and efficacy as interdisciplinary bridges. *Review of General Psychology* 3: 317–337.

Halperin, D. 1995. Memory and "consciousness" in an evolving Brazilian possession religion. *Anthropology of Consciousness* 6: 1–17.

Harnad, S. 1982. Consciousness: An afterthought. *Cognition and Brain Theory* 5: 29–47.

Harriman, P. L. 1942. The experimental production of some phenomena related to the multiple personality. *Journal of Abnormal and Social Psychology* 37: 244–255.

Hart, H. L. A. 1968. *Punishment and responsibility: Essays in the philosophy of law.* Oxford: Clarendon Press.

Harth, E. 1982. *Windows on the mind: Reflections on the physical basis of consciousness.* New York: Morrow.

Hartley, D. 1749. *Observations on man, his frame, his duty, and his expectations.* London: S. Richardson.

Hastorf, A. H., and H. Cantril. 1954. They saw a game: A case study. *Journal of Abnormal and Social Psychology* 49: 129–134.

Hebb, D. O. 1946. Emotion in man and animal: An analysis of the intuitive processes of recognition. *Psychological Review* 53: 88–106.

Heider, F. 1958. *The psychology of interpersonal relations.* New York: Wiley.

Heider, F., and M. Simmel. 1944. An experimental study of apparent behavior. *American Journal of Psychology* 57: 243–259.

Helmholtz, H. 1867. *Handbuch der physiologischen Optik.* Leipzig: Voss, 1925.

Henderson, W. R., and G. E. Smyth. 1948. Phantom limbs. *Journal of Neurological Neurosurgical Psychiatry* 11: 88–112.

Henninger, P. 1992. Conditional handedness: Handedness changes in multiple personality disordered subject reflect shift in hemispheric dominance. *Consciousness and Cognition* 1: 265–287.

Herman, C. P., and J. Polivy. 1993. Mental control of eating: Excitatory and inhibitory food thoughts. In *Handbook of mental control,* eds. D. M. Wegner and J. W. Pennebaker, 491–505. Englewood Cliffs, NJ: Prentice Hall.

Higgins, E. T., and G. King. 1981. Accessibility of social constructs: Information processing consequences of individual and contextual variability. In *Personality, cognition, and social interaction,* eds. N. Cantor and J. Kihlstrom, 69–121. Hillsdale, NJ: Erlbaum.

Highfield, R., and P. Carter. 1993. *The private lives of Albert Einstein.* London: Faber and Faber.

Hilgard, E. R. 1965. *Hypnotic susceptibility.* New York: Harcourt Brace and World.

———. 1986. *Divided consciousness: Multiple controls in human thought and action.* New York: Wiley.

Hilgard, E. R., and J. R. Hilgard. 1983. *Hypnosis in the relief of pain.* Rev. ed. Los Altos, CA: Kaufman.

Hilgard, E. R., A. H. Morgan, and H. Macdonald. 1975. Pain and dissociation in the cold pressor test: A study of hypnotic analgesia with "hidden reports" through automatic keypressing and automatic talking. *Journal of Abnormal Psychology* 84: 280–289.

Hirshoren, A., and J. Gregory. 1995. Further negative findings on facilitated communication. *Psychology in the Schools* 32: 109–13.

Hobson, A. 1988. *The dreaming brain.* New York: Basic Books.

Hodges, S., and D. M. Wegner. 1997. Automatic and controlled empathy. In *Empathic accuracy,* ed. W. J. Ickes, 311–339. New York: Guilford.

Hoffman, R. E. 1986. Verbal hallucinations and language production processes in schizophrenia. *Behavioral and Brain Sciences* 9: 503–548.

Hofstadter, D. R., and D. C. Dennett. 1981. *The mind's I: Fantasies and reflections on self and soul.* New York: Basic Books.

Holender, D. 1986. Semantic activation without conscious identification in dichotic listening, parafoveal vision, and visual masking: A survey and appraisal. *Behavioral and Brain Sciences* 9: 1–23.

Holmes, O. W. 1877. *Mechanism in thought and morals.* Boston: Osgood.

Home, D., and A. Robinson. 1995. Einstein and Tagore: Man, nature and mysticism. *Journal of Consciousness Studies* 2: 167–179.

Hook, S. 1965. *Determinism and freedom in the age of modern science.* New York: New York University Press.

Hughes, D. J. 1991. Blending with an other: An analysis of trance channeling in the United States. *Ethos* 19: 611–184.

Hull, C. L. 1933. *Hypnosis and suggestibility.* New York: Appleton-Century.

Hume, D. 1739. *A treatise of human nature,* ed. L. A. Selby-Bigge. London: Oxford University Press, 1888.

Humphreys, N., and D. C. Dennett. 1989. Speaking for our selves. *Raritan: A Quarterly Review* 9: 68–98.

Hunt, S. 1985. *Ouija: The most dangerous game.* New York: Harper and Row.

Hurskainen, A. 1989. The epidemiological aspect of spirit possession among the Maasai of Tanzania. In *Culture, experience, and pluralism: Essays on African ideas of illness and healing,* eds. A. Jacobson-Widding and D. Westerlund, 139–150. Stockholm, Sweden: Almqvist and Wiksell.

Huxley, T. H. 1874. On the hypothesis that animals are automata, and its history. In *Significant contributions to the history of psychology 1750–1920,* ed. D. N. Robinson. Washington, DC: University Publications of America, 1978.

———. 1910. *Methods and results.* New York: Appleton.

Ickes, W. J., M. L. Patterson, D. W. Rajecki, and S. Tanford. 1982. Behavioral and cognitive consequences of reciprocal versus compensatory responses to preinteraction expectancies. *Social Cognition* 1: 160–190.

Iglis, B. 1989. *Trance: A natural history of altered states of mind.* London: Grafton.

Ingvar, D. H. 1985. "Memory of the future": An essay on the temporal organization of conscious awareness. *Human Neurobiology* 4: 127–136.

———. 1994. The will of the brain: Cerebral correlates of willful acts. *Journal of Theoretical Biology* 171: 7–12.

Inouye, T., and A. Shimizu. 1970. The electromyographic study of verbal hallucination. *Journal of Nervous and Mental Disease* 151: 415–422.

Jackson, F. 1998. Epiphenomenal qualia. In *Consciousness and emotion in cognitive science,* eds. A. Clark and J. Toribio, 197–206. New York: Garland.

Jacobson, E. 1932. The electrophysiology of mental activities. *American Journal of Psychology* 44: 677–694.

Jacobson, J. W., J. A. Mulick, and A. A Schwartz. 1995. A history of facilitated communication: Science, pseudoscience, and antiscience. *American Psychologist* 50: 750–765.

James, W. 1889. Automatic writing. *Proceedings of the American Society for Psychical Research* 1: 558–564.

———. 1890. *The principles of psychology.* Vols. 1 and 2. New York: Dover Publications, 1950.

———. 1904. A case of automatic drawing. In *The works of William James: Essays in psychical research,* eds. F. H. Burkhardt, F. Bowers, and I. K. Skrupskelis, 220–228. Cambridge, MA: Harvard University Press, 1986.

———. 1910. *Pragmatism and other essays.* New York: Washington Square Press, 1963.

Janet, P. 1889. *L'automatisme psychologique*. Paris: F. Alcan.

Janis, I. L., and B. T. King. 1954. The influence of role playing on opinion change. *Journal of Abnormal and Social Psychology* 49: 211–218.

Jankovic, J. 1997. Phenomenology and classification of tics. *Neurologic Clinics* 15(2): 267–275.

Jastrow, J. 1906. *The subconscious*. Boston: Houghton-Mifflin.

———. 1935. *Wish and wisdom*. New York: Appleton-Century-Crofts.

Jastrow, J., and J. West. 1892. A study of involuntary movements. *American Journal of Psychology* 4: 398–407.

Jay, R. 1986. *Learned pigs and fireproof women*. New York: Villard.

Jaynes, J. 1976. *The origin of consciousness in the breakdown of the bicameral mind*. London: Allen Lane.

Jeannerod, M. 1995. Mental imagery in the motor context. *Neuropsychologia* 33: 1419–1432.

———. 1997. *The cognitive neuroscience of action*. Oxford: Blackwell.

Jenkins, H. M., and W. C. Ward. 1965. Judgments of contingency between responses and outcomes. *Psychological Monographs,* 79 (1, Whole No. 594).

Jensen, A. R. 1979. Outmoded theory or unconquered frontier? *Creative Science and Technology* 11: 16–29.

Johnson, J. T., K. H. Ogawa, A. Delforge, and D. Early. 1989. Causal primacy and comparative fault: The effect of position in a causal chain on judgments of legal responsibility. *Personality and Social Psychology Bulletin* 15: 61–174.

Johnson, M. K. 1988. Discriminating the origin of information. In *Delusional beliefs,* eds. T. F. Oltmanns and B. A. Maher, 34–65. New York: Wiley.

Johnson, M. K., M. A. Foley, and K. Leach. 1988. The consequences for memory of imagining in another person's voice. *Memory and Cognition* 16: 337–342.

Johnson, M. K., S. Hashtroudi, and D. S. Lindsay. 1993. Source monitoring. *Psychological Bulletin* 114: 3–28.

Johnson, M. K., and C. L. Raye. 1981. Reality monitoring. *Psychological Review* 88: 67–85.

Jones, E. E., D. E. Kanouse, H. H. Kelley, R. E. Nisbett, S. Valins, and B. Weiner, eds. 1972. *Attribution: Perceiving the causes of behavior*. Morristown, NJ: General Learning Press.

Jones, L. A. 1988. Motor illusions: What do they reveal about proprioception? *Psychological Bulletin* 103: 72–86.

Joseph, A. B. 1986. A hypergraphic syndrome of automatic writing, affective disorder, and temporal lobe epilepsy in two patients. *Journal of Clinical Psychiatry* 47: 255–257.

Kahan, T. L., and S. LaBerge, 1994. Lucid dreaming as metacognition: Implications for cognitive science. *Consciousness and Cognition* 3: 246–264.

Kampman, R. 1976. Hypnotically induced multiple personality: An experimental study. *International Journal of Clinical and Experimental Hypnosis* 24: 215–227.

Kanner, L. 1943. Autistic disturbance of affective conduct. *Nervous Child* 2: 217–250.

Kassin, S. M., and K. L. Kiechel. 1996. The social psychology of false confessions: Compliance, internalization, and confabulation. *Psychological Science* 7: 125–128.

Katz, J. 1988. *Seductions of crime.* New York: Basic Books.

Keasey, C. B. 1977. Young children's attribution of intentionality to themselves and others. *Child Development* 48: 261–264.

Keasey, C. B., and B. D. Sales. 1977. Children's conception of intentionality and the criminal law. In *Psychology in the legal process,* ed. B. D. Sales, 127–146. New York: Spectrum.

Keller, I., and H. Heckhausen. 1990. Readiness potentials preceding spontaneous motor acts: Voluntary vs. involuntary control. *Electroencephalography and Clinical Neurophysiology* 76: 351–361.

Kelley, H. H. 1972. Attribution in social interaction. In *Attribution: Perceiving the causes of behavior,* eds. E. E. Jones, D. E. Kanouse, H. H. Kelley, R. E. Nisbett, S. Valins, and B. Weiner, 1–26. Morristown, NJ: General Learning Press.

———. 1980. Magic tricks: The management of causal attributions. In *Perspectives on attribution research and theory: The Bielefeld symposium,* ed. D. Görlitz, 19–35. Cambridge, MA: Ballinger.

Kihlstrom, J. F. 1985. Hypnosis. *Annual Review of Psychology* 36: 385–418.

———. 1994. One hundred years of hysteria. In *Dissociation,* eds. S. J. Lynn and J. W. Rhue, 365–394. New York: Guildford.

Kihlstrom, J. F., and T. M. Barnhardt. 1993. The self-regulation of memory, for better and for worse, with and without hypnosis. In *Handbook of mental control,* eds. D. M. Wegner and J. W. Pennebaker, 88–125. Englewood Cliffs, N.J.: Prentice-Hall.

Kihlstrom, J. F., and E. Eich. 1994. Altering states of consciousness. In *Learning, remembering, believing: Enhancing human performance,* eds. D. Druckman and R. A. Bjork, 207–248. Washington, DC: National Academy Press.

Kihlstrom, J. F., and F. J. Evans. 1979. Memory retrieval processes during posthypnotic amnesia. In *Functional disorders of memory,* eds. J. F. Kihlstrom and F. J. Evans, 179–218. Hillsdale, NJ: Erlbaum.

Kihlstrom, J. F., and L. Wilson. 1984. Temporal organization of recall during posthypnotic amnesia. *Journal of Abnormal Psychology* 93: 200–206.

Kimble, G. A. 1964. Categories of learning and the problem of definition. In *Categories of human learning,* ed. A. W. Melton, 34–45. New York: Academic Press.

Kimble, G. A., and L. C. Perlmuter. 1970. The problem of volition. *Psychological Review* 77: 361–384.

King, B. J., and J. R. Council. 1998. Intentionality during hypnosis: An ironic process analysis. *International Journal of Clinical and Experimental Hypnosis* 46: 295–313.

Kinnunen, T., H. S. Zamansky, and M. L. Block. 1994. Is the hypnotized subject lying? *Journal of Abnormal Psychology* 103: 184–191.

Kinsbourne, M. 1997. What qualifies a representation for a role in consciousness? In *Scientific approaches to consciousness,* eds. J. D. Cohen and J. W. Schooler, 335–355. Mahwah, NJ: Erlbaum.

Kirkpatrick, J. 1985. Some Marquesan understandings of action and identity. In *Person, self, and experience: Exploring Pacific ethnopsychologies,* eds. J. D. Cohen and J. W. Schooler, 81–119. Berkeley: University of California Press.

Kirsch, I. 1998. Social psychological theories are not based on compliance: Setting the record straight. *American Journal of Clinical Hypnosis* 41: 155–158.

———. 1999. Clinical hypnosis as a nondeceptive placebo. In *Clinical hypnosis and self-regulation: Cognitive-behavioral perspectives,* eds. I. Kirsch, A. Capafons, E. Cardena-Buelna, and S. Amigo, 211–225. Washington, DC: American Psychological Association.

Kirsch, I., and S. J. Lynn. 1995. The altered state of hypnosis: Changes in the theoretical landscape. *American Psychologist* 50(10): 846–858.

———. 1997. Hypnotic involuntariness and the automaticity of everyday life. *American Journal of Clinical Hypnosis* 40: 329–348.

———. 1998. Social-cognitive alternatives to dissociation theories of hypnosis. *Review of General Psychology* 2: 66–80.

———. 1999. Hypnotic involuntariness and the automaticity of everyday life. In *Clinical hypnosis and self-regulation: Cognitive-behavioral perspectives,* eds. I. Kirsch, A. Capafons, E. Cardena-Buelna, and S. Amigo, 49–72. Washington, DC: American Psychological Association.

Klewe, L. 1993. An empirical evaluation of spelling boards as a means of communication for the multihandicapped. *Journal of Autism and Developmental Disorders* 23: 559–566.

Kluft, R. P. 1987. An update on multiple personality disorder. *Hospital and Community Psychiatry* 38: 363–373.

Koestler, A. 1964. *The act of creation.* New York: Macmillan.

Kornhuber, H. H., and L. Deecke 1965. Hirnpotentialandeerungen bei Wilkurbewegungen und passiv Bewegungen des Menschen: Bereitschaftspotential und reafferente Potentiale. *Pflugers Archiv fur Gesamte Psychologie* 284: 1–17.

Koutstaal, W. 1992. Skirting the abyss: A history of experimental explorations of automatic writing in psychology. *Journal of the History of the Behavioral Sciences* 28: 5–27.

Kreskin. 1991. *Secrets of the amazing Kreskin.* Buffalo, NY: Prometheus Books.

Kruglanski, A. W. 1975. The endogenous-exogenous partition in attribution theory. *Psychological Review* 82: 387–406.

Kruglanski, A. W., W. Alon, and T. Lewis 1972. Restrospective misattribution and task enjoyment. *Journal of Experimental Social Psychology* 8: 493–501.

Kruglanski, A. W., and M. Cohen, 1973. Attributed freedom and personal causation. *Journal of Personality and Social Psychology* 26: 245–250.

Kvavilashvili, L. 1992. Remembering intentions: A critical review of existing experimental paradigms. *Applied Cognitive Psychology* 6(6): 507–524.

Lajoie, Y., J. Paillard, N. Teasdale, C. Bard, M. Fleury, R. Forget, and Y. Lamarre. 1992. Mirror drawing in a deafferented patient and normal subjects: Visuoproprioceptive conflict. *Neurology* 42: 1104–1106.

Lambeck, M. 1981. *Human spirits: A cultural account of trance in Mayotte.* Cambridge, UK: Cambridge University Press.

———. 1988. Spirit possession/spirit succession: Aspects of social continuity among Malagasy speakers in Mayotte. *American Ethologist: The Journal of the American Ethological Society* 15: 710–731.

Lang, A. 1991. Patient perception of tics and other movement disorders. *Neurology* 41 (2, pt 1): 223–228.

Langer, E. J. 1975. The illusion of control. *Journal of Personality and Social Psychology* 32: 311–328.

———. 1983. *The psychology of control.* Beverly Hills, CA: Sage.

Langer, E. J., and J. Rodin. 1976. The effects of choice and enhanced personal responsibility for the aged: A field experiment. *Journal of Personality and Social Psychology* 34: 191–198.

Langer, E. J., and J. Roth. 1975. Heads I win, tails it's chance: The illusion of control as a function of the sequence of outcomes in a purely chance task. *Journal of Personality and Social Psychology* 32: 951–955.

Laplace, P. S. 1814. *A philosophical essay on probabilities,* trans F. W. Truscott and F. L. Emory. New York: Dover, 1951.

Latané, B., K. Williams, and S. Harkins. 1979. Many hands make light the work: The causes and consequences of social loafing. *Journal of Personality and Social Psychology* 37: 822–832.

Laurence, J., and C. Perry, 1983. Hypnotically created memory among high hypnotizable subjects. *Science* 222: 523–524.

———. 1988. *Hypnosis, will, and memory: A psycho-legal history.* New York: Guilford.

Laurendeau, M., and A. Pinard. 1962. *Causal thinking in the child.* New York: International Universities Press.

Leacock, S., and R. Leacock. 1972. *Spirits of the deep: A study of an Afro-Brazilian cult.* Garden City, NY: Doubleday Natural History Press.

Lee, R. B. 1966. The sociology of !Kung bushman trance performances. In *Trance and possession states,* ed. R. Prince, 35–148. Canada: l'Imprimerie Electra.

Lee, R. L. M. 1989. Self-presentation in Malaysian spirit séances: A dramaturgical perspective on altered states of consciousness in healing ceremonies. In

Altered states of consciousness and mental health: A cross-cultural perspective, ed. C. A. Ward. Vol. 12, 251–266. London: Sage.

Leiguarda, R., S. Starkstein, M. Nogues, and M. Berthier. 1993. Paroxysmal alien hand syndrome. *Journal of Neurology, Neurosurgery, and Psychiatry* 56: 788–792.

Leslie, A. M. 1994. Pretending and believing: Issues in the theory of ToMM. *Cognition* 50: 211–238.

Lévy-Bruhl, L. 1910. *How natives think.* Princeton, NJ: Princeton University Press, 1985. Originally published in French, *Les fonctions mentales dans les sociétés inférieures.* Paris: F. Alcan.

Lewin, K. 1951. *Field theory in social science: Selected theoretical papers.* New York: Harper and Row.

Lewis, H. B., and M. Franklin. 1944. An experimental study of the role of the ego in work. II. The significance of task-orientation in work. *Journal of Experimental Psychology* 34: 195–215.

Lewis, I. M. 1989. *Ecstatic religion: A study of shamanism and spirit possession.* 2d ed. London: Routledge.

Lex, B. 1976. Physiological aspects of ritual trance. *Journal of Altered States of Consciousness* 2: 109–122.

Lhermitte, F. 1983. Utilization behavior and its relation to lesions of the frontal lobes. *Brain* 106: 237–255.

———. 1986. Human autonomy and the frontal lobes. II. Patient behavior in complex social situations: The environmental dependency syndrome. *Annals of Neurology* 19: 335–343.

Libet, B. 1981. The experimental evidence for subjective referral of a sensory experience backward in time: Reply to P. S. Churchland. *Philosophy of Science* 48: 182–197.

———. 1985. Unconscious cerebral initiative and the role of conscious will in voluntary action. *The Behavioral and Brain Sciences* 8: 529–566.

———. 1992. The neural time-factor in perception, volition, and free will. *Revue de Métaphysique et de Morale* 97: 255–272.

———. 1993. *Neurophysiology of consciousness.* Boston: Birkhäuser.

Libet, B., C. A. Gleason, E. W. Wright, and D. K. Pearl. 1983. Time of conscious intention to act in relation to onset of cerebral activity (readiness-potential): The unconscious initiation of a freely voluntary act. *Brain* 106: 623–642.

Libet, B., E. W. Wright, and C. A. Gleason. 1982. Readiness potentials preceding unrestricted "spontaneous" vs. pre-planned voluntary acts. *Electroencephalography and Clinical Neurophysiology* 54: 322–335.

Lillard, A. 1998. Ethnopsychologies: Cultural variations in theories of mind. *Psychological Bulletin* 123: 3–32.

L'Illustration. 1953. 21(533): 305.

Linder, D. E., J. Cooper, and E. E. Jones. 1967. Decision freedom as a determinant of the role of incentive magnitude in attitude change. *Journal of Personality and Social Psychology* 6: 245–254.

Locke, J. 1690. *An essay concerning human understanding,* ed. P. H. Nidditch. Oxford: Oxford University Press, 1975.

Locke, R. G., and E. F. Kelly. 1985. A preliminary model of the cross-cultural analysis of altered states of consciousness. *Ethos* 13: 3–55.

Logan, G. D., and W. Cowan. 1984. On the ability to inhibit thought and action: A theory of an act of control. *Psychological Review* 91: 295–327.

Logan, M. H. 1993. New lines of inquiry on the illness of Susto. *Medical Anthropology* 15: 189–200.

Looft, W. R., and W. H. Bartz. 1969. Animism revived. *Psychological Bulletin* 71: 1–19.

Luria, A. R. 1961. *The role of private speech in the regulation of normal and abnormal behavior.* London: Pergamon.

———. 1966. *Higher cortical functions in man.* London: Tavistock.

Lynn, S. J. 1997. Automaticity and hypnosis: A sociocognitive account. *International Journal of Clinical and Experimental Hypnosis* 45: 239–250.

Lynn, S. J., J. W. Rhue, and J. R. Weekes. 1990. Hypnotic involuntariness: A social cognitive analysis. *Psychological Review* 97: 169–184.

Lynn, S. J., J. R. Weekes, C. L. Matyi, and V. Neufeld. 1988. Direct versus indirect suggestions, archaic involvement, and hypnotic experience. *Journal of Abnormal Psychology* 97: 296–301.

Maby, J. C., and T. B. Franklin. 1939. *The physics of the divining rod.* London: G. Bell.

Mach, E. 1906. *The analysis of sensations.* Rev. from the 5th German ed. New York: Dover, 1959.

MacKay, D. M. 1967. *Freedom of action in a mechanistic universe.* Eddington Memorial Lecture. London: Cambridge University Press.

Macrae, C. N., G. V. Bodenhausen, A. B. Milne, and R. L. Ford. 1997. On regulation of recollection: The intentional forgetting of stereotypical memories. *Journal of Personality and Social Psychology* 72: 709–719.

Macrae, C. N., G. V. Bodenhausen, A. B. Milne, and J. Jetten. 1994. Out of mind but back in sight: Stereotypes on the rebound. *Journal of Personality and Social Psychology* 67: 808–817.

Macrae, C. N., and L. Johnston. 1998. Help, I need somebody: Automatic action and inaction. *Social Cognition* 16: 400.

Macrae, J. 1987. *Therapeutic touch: A practical guide.* New York: Knopf.

Malenka, R. C., R. W. Angel, B. Hampton, and P. Berger. 1982. Impaired central error-correcting behavior in schizophrenia. *Archives of General Psychiatry* 39: 101–107.

Malle, B. F. 1999. How people explain behavior: A new theoretical framework. *Personality and Social Psychology Review* 3: 23–48.

Malle, B. F., and J. Knobe. 1997. The folk concept of intentionality. *Journal of Experimental Social Psychology* 33: 101–121.

Maquet, P., M. E. Faymonville, C. Degueldre, G. Delfiore, G. Franck, A. Luxen, and M. Lamy. 1999. Functional neuroanatomy of hypnotic state. *Biological Psychiatry* 45: 327–333.

Marcel, A. J. 1983. Conscious and unconscious perception: Experiments on visual masking and word recognition. *Cognitive Psychology* 15: 197–237.

———. 1988. Phenomenal experience and functionalism. In *Consciousness in contemporary science,* eds. A. J. Marcel and E. Bisiach, 121–158. New York: Oxford University Press.

Marsh, R. L., J. L. Hicks, and M. L. Bink. 1998. Activation of completed, uncompleted, and partially completed intentions. *Journal of Experimental Psychology: Learning, Memory, and Cognition* 24: 350–361.

Martin, L. L., and A. Tesser. 1989. Toward a motivational and structural theory of ruminative thought. In *Unintended thought,* eds. J. S. Uleman and J. A. Bargh, 306–326. New York: Guilford.

Marzollo, J., and W. Wick. 1992. *I spy.* New York: Scholastic.

Masson, J. M. 1984. *The assault on truth: Freud's suppression of the seduction theory.* New York: Farrar, Straus, Giroux.

Mates, J., T. Radil, U. Müller, and E. Pöppel. 1994. Temporal integration in sensorimotor synchronization. *Journal of Cognitive Neuroscience* 6: 332–340.

Matsumoto, D., and M. Lee. 1993. Consciousness, volition, and the neuropsychology of facial expressions of emotion. *Consciousness and Cognition* 2: 237–254.

Matthews, P. B. C. 1982. Where does Sherrington's "muscular sense" originate? Muscles, joints, corollary discharges? *Annual Review of Neuroscience* 5: 189–218.

Matthews, S. 1998. Personal identity, multiple personality disorder, and moral personhood. *Philosophical Psychology* 11: 67–88.

Mattison, H. 1855. *Spirit-rapping unveiled!* New York: J. C. Derby.

Matute, H. 1996. Illusion of control: Detecting response-outcome independence in analytic but not naturalistic conditions. *Psychological Science* 7: 289–293.

Mauss, M. 1902. *A general theory of magic,* trans. R. Brain. New York: W. W. Norton, 1972.

McArthur, L. Z., and D. L. Post. 1977. Figural emphasis in person perception. *Journal of Experimental Social Psychology* 13: 520–535.

McCloskey, D. I. 1978. Kinesthetic sensibility. *Physiological Review* 58: 763–820.

McCloskey, D. I., J. G. Colebatch, E. K. Potter, and D. Burke. 1983. Judgments about onset of rapid voluntary movements in man. *Journal of Neurophysiology* 49: 851–863.

McCloskey, D. I., M. J. Cross, R. Horner, and E. K. Potter. 1983. Sensory effects of pulling or vibrating exposed tendons in man. *Brain* 106, 21–37.

McClure, J. 1998. Discounting causes of behavior: Are two reasons better than one? *Journal of Personality and Social Psychology* 74: 7–20.

McConkey, K. M., A. J. Barnier, and P. W. Sheehan. 1998. Hypnosis and pseudomemory: Understanding the findings and their implications. In *Truth in memory*, eds. S. J. Lynn and K. M. McConkey, 227–259. New York: Guilford.

McGill, O. 1947. *The encyclopedia of genuine stage hypnotism*. Colon, MI: Abbott's Magic Novelty Co.

McGuire, P. K., G. M. S. Shah, and R. M. Murray. 1993. Increased blood flow in Broca's area during auditory hallucinations in schizophrenia. *Lancet* 342: 703–706.

Meacham, J. A. 1979. The role of verbal activity in remembering the goals of actions. In *The development of self-regulation through private speech*, ed. G. Zivin, 237–263. New York: Wiley.

Mead, M. 1932. An investigation of the thought of primitive children with special reference to animism. *Journal of the Royal Anthropological Institute* 62: 173–190.

Melden, A. I. 1961. *Free action*. London: Routledge and Kegan Paul.

Merikle, P. M., and S. Joordens. 1997. Measuring unconscious influences. In *Scientific approaches to consciousness*, eds. J. D. Cohen and J. W. Schooler, 109–123. Mahwah, NJ: Erlbaum.

Merton, P. A. 1948. The self-fulfilling prophecy. *Antioch Review* 8: 193–210.

———. 1964. Human position sense and sense of effort. *Symposium of the Society for Experimental Biology* 18: 387–400.

———. 1972. How we control the contraction of our muscles. *Scientific American* 226: 30–37.

Michotte, A. 1954. *The perception of causality*, trans. T. R. Miles and E. Miles. New York: Basic Books, 1963.

———. 1962. *Causalité, permanence et réalité phénoménales*. Louvain, Belgium: Publications Universitaires.

Milgram, S. 1974. *Obedience to authority*. New York: Harper and Row.

Mill, J. S. 1843. *A system of logic ratiocinative and inductive*. Toronto: University of Toronto Press, 1974.

Miller, A. G., A. K. Gordon, and A. M. Buddie. 1999. Accounting for evil and cruelty: Is to explain to condone? *Personality and Social Psychology Review* 3: 254–268.

Miller, D. T., and M. Ross. 1975. Self-serving biases in the attribution of causality: Fact or fiction? *Psychological Bulletin* 82: 213–225.

Miller, G. A., E. Galanter, and K. H. Pribram. 1960. *Plans and the structure of behavior*. New York: Holt.

Miller, M. E., and K. S. Bowers. 1993. Hypnotic analgesia and stress inoculation in the reduction of cold-pressor pain. *Journal of Abnormal Psychology* 102: 29–38.

Miller, S. D. 1989. Optical differences in cases of multiple personality disorder. *Journal of Nervous and Mental Disease* 177: 480–486.

Miller, S. D., and T. Blackburn et al. 1991. Optical differences in cases of multiple personality disorder: A second look. *Journal of Nervous and Mental Disease* 179: 132–135.

Milner A. D., and M. D. Rugg, eds. 1992. *The neuropsychology of consciousness*. London: Academic Press.

Minsky, M. 1985. *The society of mind*. New York: Simon and Schuster.

Mischel, W., and F. Mischel. 1958. Psychological aspects of spirit possession. *American Anthropologist* 60: 249–260.

Mitchell, S. W. 1872. *Injuries of nerves and their consequences*. London: Smith Elder.

Mlakar, J., J. Jensterle, and C. D. Frith. 1994. Central monitoring deficiency and schizophrenic symptoms. *Psychological Medicine* 24: 557–564.

Moll, A. 1889. *Hypnotism*. London: Walter Scott.

Monahan, J. 1973. Abolish the insanity defense? Not yet. *Rutgers Law Review* 26: 719–740.

Montee, B. B., R. G. Miltenberger, and D. Wittrock. 1995. An experimental analysis of facilitated communication. *Journal of Applied Behavior Analysis* 28: 189–200.

Morris, P. E. 1992. Prospective memory: Remembering to do things. In *Aspects of memory*, 2d ed., eds. M. Gruneberg and P. E. Morris. Vol. 1, 196–222. London: Routledge.

Morris, W. L., and D. M. Wegner. 2000. Disowning our unwanted thoughts: Thought suppression and introspective alienation. Poster presented at the American Psychological Society, Miami Beach, FL.

Moses, S. 2001. *Spirit teachings*. <http://www.spiritweb.org/SpiritTeachings>

Mühl, A. M. 1930. *Automatic writing*. Dresden, Germany: Steinkopff.

Mullen, B., J. G. Chapman, and S. Peaugh. 1989. Focus of attention in groups: A self-attention perspective. *Journal of Social Psychology* 129: 807–817.

Muraven, M., D. M. Tice, and R. F. Baumeister. 1998. Self-control as limited resource: Regulatory depletion patterns. *Journal of Personality and Social Psychology* 74: 774–789.

Nash, M. R. 1987. What, if anything, is regressed about hypnotic age regression? A review of the empirical literature. *Psychological Bulletin* 102: 42–52.

Neher, A. 1961. Auditory driving observed with scalp electrodes in normal subject. *Electroencephalography and Clinical Neurophysiology* 13: 449–51.

———. 1962. A physiological explanation of unusual behavior in ceremonies involving drums. *Human Biology* 4: 151–160.

Neisser, U. 1976. *Cognition and reality.* San Francisco: Freeman.

Nemeroff, C., and P. Rozin. 2000. The makings of the magical mind. In *Imagining the impossible: The development of magical, scientific, and religious thinking in contemporary society,* eds. K. Rosengren, C. Johnson, and P. L. Harris. New York: Cambridge University Press.

Newman, L. S., and R. F. Baumeister. 1996. Toward an explanation of the UFO abduction phenomenon: Hypnotic elaboration, extraterrestrial sadomasochism, and spurious memories. *Psychological Inquiry* 7: 99–126.

Nielson, T. I. 1963. Volition: A new experimental approach. *Scandinavian Journal of Psychology* 4: 215–230.

Nisbett, R. E., and L. E. Ross. 1980. *Human inference: Strategies and shortcomings of social judgment.* Englewood Cliffs, NJ: Prentice Hall.

Nisbett, R. E., and T. D. Wilson. 1977. Telling more than we can know: Verbal reports on mental processes. *Psychological Review* 84: 231–259.

Nissen, M. J., J. L. Ross, D. B. Willingham, T. B. MacKenzie, and D. L. Schacter. 1988. Memory and awareness in a patient with multiple personality disorder. *Brain and Cognition* 8: 21–38.

Noll, R. B. 1994. Hypnotherapy for warts in children and adolescents. *Developmental and Behavioral Pediatrics* 15: 170–173.

Nørretranders, T. 1998. *The user illusion: Cutting consciousness down to size.* New York: Viking.

Obeso, J. A., J. C. Rothwell, and C. D. Marsden. 1981. Simple tics in Gilles de la Tourette syndrome are not prefaced by a normal premovement EEG potential. *Journal of Neurology, Neurosurgery, and Psychiatry* 44: 735–738.

O'Brien, Terry. 2001. *Hypnosis in media.* <http://www.hypnosisinmedia.com/>.

Oesterreich, T. K. 1922. *Possession and exorcism,* trans. D. Ibberson. New York: Causeway, 1974.

Ofshe, R., and E. Watters. 1994. *Making monsters: False memories, psychotherapy, and sexual hysteria.* New York: Scribner.

Orlando, E. 2001. *The museum of talking boards.*
<http://www.museumoftalkingboards.com/>

Orne, M. T., and F. J. Evans. 1965. Social control in the psychological experiment: Antisocial behavior and hypnosis. *Journal of Personality and Social Psychology* 1: 189–200.

Owen, I. M. 1976. *Conjuring up Philip: An adventure in psychokinesis.* New York: Harper and Row.

Palfreman, J. 1993. Prisoners of silence. *Frontline.* Prod. D. Fanning. Boston: WGBH.

Passingham, R. E. 1993. *The frontal lobes and voluntary action.* Oxford: Oxford University Press.

Pearsall, R. 1972. *The table-rappers.* New York: St. Martin's.

Penfield, W. 1975. *The mystery of mind.* Princeton, NJ: Princeton University Press.

Penfield, W., and K. Welch. 1951. The supplementary motor area of the cerebral cortex. *Archives of Neurology and Psychiatry* 66: 289–317.

Perner, J. 1991a. On representing that: The asymmetry between belief and desire in children's theory of mind. In *Children's theories of mind,* eds. C. Moore and D. Frye. Hillsdale, NJ: Erlbaum.

———. 1991b. *Understanding the representational mind.* Cambridge, MA: MIT Press.

Perner, J., S. R. Leekam, and H. Wimmer. 1987. Three-year-olds' difficulty with false belief. *British Journal of Developmental Psychology* 5: 125–137.

Perry, C. 1992. Theorizing about hypnosis in either/or terms. *International Journal of Clinical and Experimental Hypnosis* 40: 238–252.

Perry, J. 1975. The problem of personal identity. In *Personal identity,* ed. J. Perry, 3–30. Berkeley, CA: University of California Press.

Perspectives. 1999. *Newsweek,* September 20, 21.

Peterson, C., S. F. Maier, and M. E. P. Seligman. 1993. *Learned helplessness.* New York: Oxford University Press.

Peterson, D., ed. 1982. *A mad people's history of madness.* Pittsburgh: University of Pittsburgh Press.

Pettinati, H. M. 1988. *Hypnosis and memory.* New York: Guilford.

Pfungst, O. 1911. *Clever Hans: The horse of Mr. Von Osten,* ed. R. Rosenthal. New York: Holt, Rinehart, and Winston, 1965.

Phillips, W., S. Baron-Cohen, and M. Rutter, M. 1998. Understanding intention in normal development and in autism. *British Journal of Developmental Psychology* 16: 337–348.

Piaget, J. 1927. *The child's conception of physical causality.* London: Routledge and Kegan Paul, 1951.

———. 1929. *The child's conception of the world.* London: Kegan Paul, Trench, Trubner.

———. 1932. *The moral judgement of the child.* London: Kegan Paul, Trench, Trubner.

Piaget, J., and B. Inhelder. 1948. *The child's conception of space.* New York: W. W. Norton.

Piccione, C., E. R. Hilgard, and P. G. Zimbardo. 1989. On the degree of stability of measured hypnotizability over a 25-year period. *Journal of Personality and Social Psychology* 56: 289–295.

Plutchik, R. 1980. *Emotion: A psychoevolutionary synthesis.* New York: Harper and Row.

Podmore, F. 1902. *Modern spiritualism.* London: Methuen.

Polley, G. A. 1995. A curve ball from the great beyond. *Harper's Magazine,* February, 35.

Pöppel, E. 1997. A hierarchical model of temporal perception. *Trends in Cognitive Sciences* 1: 56–61.

Porter, R., and R. Lemon. 1993. *Corticospinal function and voluntary movement.* New York: Oxford University Press.

Posey, T. B., and M. E. Losch. 1983. Auditory hallucinations of hearing voices in 375 normal subjects. *Imagination, Cognition and Personality* 3: 99–113.

Posner, M. I., and C. R. Snyder. 1975. Attention and cognitive control. In *Information processing and cognition,* ed. R. L. Solso, 55–85. Hillsdale, NJ: Erlbaum.

Poulin-Dubois, D., and T. R. Schultz. 1988. The development of the understanding of human behavior: From agency to intentionality. In *Developing theories of mind,* eds. J. W. Astington, P. L. Harris, and D. R. Olson, 109–125. New York: Cambridge University Press.

Povinelli, D. J. 1994. A theory of mind is in the head, not in the heart. *Behavioral and Brain Sciences* 17: 573–574.

———. 1999. Social understanding in chimpanzees: New evidence from a longitudinal approach. In *Developing theories of intention: Social understanding and self control,* eds. P. D. Zelazo, J. W. Astington, and D. R. Olson, 195–225. Mahwah, NJ: Erlbaum.

Powers, W. T. 1973. *Behavior: The control of perception.* Chicago: Aldine.

———. 1990. Control theory: A model of organisms. *System Dynamics Review* 6: 1–20.

Premack, D., and G. G. Woodruff. 1978. Does the chimpanzee have a theory of mind? *Behavioral and Brain Sciences* 1: 515–526.

Pressel, E. 1973. Umbanda in Sao Paulo: Religious innovation in a developing society. In *Religion, altered states of consciousness, and social change,* ed. E. Bourguignon, 264–318. Columbus: Ohio State University Press.

Price-Williams, D., and D. J. Hughes. 1994. Shamanism and altered states of consciousness. *Anthropology of Consciousness* 5: 1–15.

Prigatano, G. P., and D. L. Schacter. 1991. *Awareness of deficit after brain injury.* New York: Oxford University Press.

Prince, M. 1890. Some of the revelations of hypnotism: Post-hypnotic suggestion, automatic writing, and double personality. *Boston Medical and Surgical Journal* 122: 465.

———. 1906. *Dissociation of a personality.* New York: Longman, Green.

———. 1907. A symposium on the subconscious. *Journal of Abnormal Psychology* 2: 73.

Prinz, W. 1987. Ideo-motor action. In *Perspectives on perception and action,* eds. H. Heuer and A. F. Sanders, 47–76. Hillsdale, NJ: Erlbaum.

———. 1997. Explaining voluntary action: The role of mental content. In *Mindscapes: Philosophy, science, and the mind,* eds. M. Carrier and P. K. Machamer, 153–175. Konstanz, Germany: Universitätsverlag.

Putnam, F. W. 1989. *Diagnosis and treatment of multiple personality disorder.* New York: Guilford.

———. 1994. The switch process in multiple personality disorder and other state-change disorders. In *Psychological concepts and dissociative disorders,* eds. R. M. Klein and B. K. Doane, 283–304. Hillsdale, NJ: Erlbaum.

Putnam, F. W., J. J. Guroff, E. K. Silberman, L. Barban, and R. M. Post. 1986. The clinical phenomenology of multiple personality disorder: A review of 100 recent cases. *Journal of Clinical Psychiatry* 47: 285–293.

Radden, J. 1996. *Divided minds and successive selves: Ethical issues in disorders of identity and personality.* Cambridge, MA: MIT Press.

Rainville, P., R. K. Hofbauer, T. Paus, G. H. Duncan, M. C. Bushnell, and D. D. Price. 1999. Cerebral mechanisms of hypnotic induction and suggestion. *Journal of Cognitive Neuroscience* 11: 110–122.

Ramachandran, V. S., et al. 1996. Illusions of body image: What they reveal about human nature. In *The mind-brain continuum,* eds. R. Llinas and P. S. Churchland, 29–60. Cambridge, MA: MIT Press.

Ramachandran, V. S., and S. Blakeslee. 1998. *Phantoms in the brain.* New York: Morrow.

Ramachandran, V. S., and D. Rogers-Ramachandran. 1996. Synaesthesia in phantom limbs induced with mirrors. *Proceedings of the Royal Society, London* 263: 377–386.

Randi, J. 1982. *Flim flam! Psychics, ESP, unicorns, and other delusions.* Buffalo, NY: Prometheus Books.

Reason, J. 1984. Lapses of attention in everyday life. In *Varieties of attention,* eds. R. Parasuraman and D. R. Davies, 515–549. Orlando, FL: Academic Press.

Regal, R. A., J. R. Rooney, and T. Wandas. 1994. Facilitated communication: An experimental evaluation. *Journal of Autism and Developmental Disorders* 24: 345–355.

Richet, C. 1884. *L'homme et l'intelligence.* Paris: F. Alcan.

Rickers-Ovsiankina, M. 1937. Studies on the personality structure of schizophrenic individuals: II. Reaction to interrupted tasks. *Journal of General Psychology* 16: 179–196.

Ridall, K. 1988. *Channeling: How to reach out to your spirit guides.* New York: Bantam.

Rinn, W. E. 1984. The neuropsychology of facial expression: A review of the neurological and psychological mechanisms for producing facial expressions. *Psychological Bulletin* 95: 52–77.

Rizzolatti, G., L. Fadiga, V. Gallese, and L. Fogassi. 1996. Premotor cortex and the recognition of motor actions. *Cognitive Brain Research* 3: 131–141.

Roberts, J. 1970. *The Seth material.* New York: Prentice Hall.

Roberts, M. 1989. A linguistic "nay" to channeling. *Psychology Today,* October, 84–85.

Rode, G., Y. Rossetti, and D. Boisson. 1996. Inverse relationship between sensation of effort and muscular force during recovery from a pure motor hemiplegia: A single-case study. *Neuropsychologia* 34: 87–95.

Rodin, J., and E. J. Langer. 1977. Long-term effects of a control-relevant intervention with the institutional aged. *Journal of Personality and Social Psychology* 35: 897–902.

Roland, P. E. 1978. Sensory feedback to the cerebral cortex during voluntary movement in man. *Behavioral Brain Science* 1: 129–147.

Roman, S., and D. Packer. 1987. *Opening to channel: How to connect with your guide*. Tiburton, CA: Kramer.

Roob, A. 1997. *Alchemy and Mysticism*. London: Taschen.

Rosenthal, D. 1974. Voices from darkness: The evidentiary admissibility of sleep talk. *University of San Francisco Law Review* 30: 509–560.

Rosenthal, R., and L. Jacobson. 1968. *Pygmalion in the classroom: Teacher expectation and student intellectual development*. New York: Holt, Rinehart, and Winston.

Ross, C. A. 1988. Cognitive analysis of multiple personality disorder. *American Journal of Psychotherapy* 27: 229–239.

———. 1989. *Multiple personality disorder: Diagnosis, clinical features, and treatment*. New York: Wiley.

Ross, M., and R. F. Schulman. 1973. Increasing the salience of initial attitudes: Dissonance vs. self-perception theory. *Journal of Personality and Social Psychology* 28: 138–144.

Rossetti, Y. 1998. Implicit short-lived motor representations of space in brain damaged and healthy subjects. *Consciousness and Cognition* 7: 520–558.

Rotter, J. B. 1966. Generalized expectancies for internal versus external control of reinforcement. *Psychological Monographs* 80 (1, Whole No. 609).

Rouget, G. 1985. *Music and trance: A theory of the relations between music and possession*. Chicago: University of Chicago Press.

Rowland, L. W. 1939. Will hypnotized persons try to harm themselves or others? *Journal of Abnormal and Social Psychology* 34: 114–117.

Rozin, P., L. Millman, and C. Nemeroff. 1986. Operation of the laws of sympathetic magic in disgust and other domains. *Journal of Personality and Social Psychology* 50: 703–712.

Ruehle, B., and H. S. Zamansky. 1997. The experience of effortlessness in hypnosis: Perceived or real? *International Journal of Clinical and Experimental Hypnosis* 45: 144–157.

Russell, B. 1921. *The analysis of mind*. London: Allyn and Unwin.

Russell, S. J., and P. Norvig. 1995. *Artificial intelligence*. Englewood Cliffs, NJ: Prentice Hall.

Ryle, G. 1949. *The concept of mind*. London: Hutchinson.

Sacks, O. 1993/94. A neurologist's notebook: An anthropologist on Mars. *New Yorker,* December 27–January 3.

Samarin, W. J. 1972. *Tongues of men and angels.* New York: Macmillan.

Sanders, B., and J. A. Green. 1994. The factor structure of the dissociative experiences scale in college students. *Dissociation* 7: 23–34.

Sappington, A. A. 1990. Recent psychological approaches to the free will versus determinism issue. *Psychological Bulletin* 108: 19–29.

Sarbin, T. R. 1950. Contributions to role-taking theory: I. Hypnotic behavior. *Psychological Review* 255–270.

Sarbin, T. R., and V. L. Allen. 1968. Role theory. In *Handbook of social psychology,* 2d ed., eds. G. Lindzey and E. Aronson, 488–567. Reading, MA: Addison-Wesley.

Sarbin, T. R., and W. C. Coe. 1972. *Hypnosis: A social psychological analysis of influence communication.* New York: Holt, Rinehart, and Winston.

Sargent, E. 1869. *The despair of science.* Boston: Roberts.

Sartorius, N., R. Shapiro, and A. Jablensky. 1974. The international pilot study of schizophrenia. *Schizophrenia Bulletin* 1: 21–35.

Schank, R. C., and R. P. Abelson. 1977. *Scripts, plans, goals, and understanding.* Hillsdale, NJ: Erlbaum.

Scheerer, E. 1987. Muscle sense and innervation feelings: A chapter in the history of perception and action. In *Perspectives on perception and action,* eds. H. Heuer and A. F. Sanders, 171–194. Hillsdale, NJ: Erlbaum.

Scheier, M. F., and C. S. Carver. 1985. Optimism, coping, and health: Assessment and implications of generalized outcome expectancies. *Health Psychology* 4: 219–247.

Schenk, L., and D. Bear. 1981. Multiple personality and related dissociative phenomena in patients with temporal lobe epilepsy. *American Journal of Psychiatry* 138: 1311–1316.

Schlink, B. 1997. *The reader,* trans. C. B. Janeway. New York: Pantheon.

Schneider, K. 1959. *Clinical psychopathology.* New York: Grune and Stratton.

Schooler, J. W., D. Gerhard, and E. F. Loftus. 1986. Qualities of the unreal. *Journal of Experimental Psychology: Learning, Memory, and Cognition* 12: 171–181.

Schooler, J. W., and J. Melcher. 1995. The ineffability of insight. In *The creative cognition approach,* eds. S. M. Smith, T. B. Ward, and R. A. Finke, 97–133. Cambridge, MA: MIT Press.

Schopp, R. F. 1991. *Automatism, insanity, and the psychology of criminal responsibility: A philosophical inquiry.* Cambridge: Cambridge University Press.

Schreiber, F. R. 1974. *Sybil.* New York: Warner Books.

Schrenck-Notzing, F. von. 1902. *Kriminalpsychologische und psychopathologische Studien: Gesammelte Aufsätze aus den Gebieten der Psychopathia sexualis, der gerichtlichen Psychiatrie und der Suggestionslehre.* Leipzig: Verlag von Johann Ambrosius Barth.

Schubert, A., and D. Biklen. 1993. Issues of influence: Some concerns and suggestions. *Facilitated Communication Digest* 1: 11–12.

Schult, C. A. 1997. Intended actions and intentional states: Young children's understanding of the causes of human actions. *Dissertation Abstracts International. Section B: The Sciences and Engineering* 57(11-B): 7252.

Schultz, T. R. 1980. Development of the concept of intention. In *Development of cognition, affect, and social relations: The Minnesota symposia on child psychology,* ed. W. A. Collins, 131–164. Hillsdale, NJ: Erlbaum.

Schulz, R. 1976. Effects of control and predictability on the physical and psychological well-being of the institutionalized aged. *Journal of Personality and Social Psychology* 33: 563–573.

Searle, J. R. 1983. *Intentionality: An essay in the philosophy of mind.* New York: Cambridge University Press.

Seligman, M. E. P. 1975. *Helplessness: On depression, development, and death.* San Francisco: Freeman.

Shallice, T. 1988. *From neuropsychology to mental structure.* Cambridge: Cambridge University Press.

Sharp, L. 1990. Possessed and dispossessed youth: Spirit possession of school children in northwest Madagascar. In *Culture, medicine and psychiatry,* ed. B. J. Good. Vol. 14, 339–364. Dordrecht, Netherlands: Kluwer.

Sheehan, P. W. 1979. Hypnosis and the process of imagination. In *Hypnosis: Developments in research and new perspectives,* eds. E. Fromm and R. E. Shor, 381–411. Chicago: Aldine.

Sheehan, P. W., and M. T. Orne. 1968. Some comments on the nature of post-hypnotic behavior. *Journal of Nervous and Mental Disease* 146: 209–220.

Sherif, M. 1935. A study of some social factors in perception. *Archives of Psychology* 27: 1–60.

Shor, R. E., M. T. Orne, and E. C. Orne. 1962. *Harvard group scale of hypnotic susceptibility, form A.* Palo Alto, CA.: Consulting Psychologists Press.

Showalter, E. 1997. *Hystories: Hysterical epidemics and modern culture.* New York: Columbia University Press.

Sidis, B. 1906. *The psychology of suggestion.* New York: Appleton.

Siegel, B. 1995. Assessing allegations of sexual molestation made through facilitated communication. *Journal of Autism and Developmental Disorders* 25: 319–326.

Siegel, R. K. 1992. *Fire in the brain.* New York: Penguin.

Simeon, D., S. Gross, O. Guralnik, D. J. Stein, J. Schmeidler, and E. Hollander. 1997. Feeling unreal: 30 cases of DSM-III-R depersonalization disorder. *American Journal of Psychiatry* 154: 1107–1113.

Simpson, R. L., and B. S. Myles. 1995. Effectiveness of facilitated communication with children and youth with autism. *Journal of Special Education* 28: 424–439.

Skinner, B. F. 1953. *Science and human behavior.* New York: Macmillan.

———. 1971. *Beyond freedom and dignity.* New York: Knopf.

———. 1995. *Perceived control, motivation, and coping.* Thousand Oaks, CA: Sage.

Snyder, M. 1981. On the self-perpetuating nature of social stereotypes. In *Cognitive processes in stereotyping and intergroup behavior,* ed. D. L. Hamilton. Hillsdale, NJ: Erlbaum.

Snyder, M., and E. Ebbesen. 1972. Dissonance awareness: A test of dissonance theory versus self-perception theory. *Journal of Experimental Social Psychology* 8: 502–517.

Snyder, M. L., W. G. Stephan, and D. Rosenfield. 1978. Attributional egotism. In *New directions in attribution research,* eds. J. H. Harvey, W. Ickes, and R. F. Kidd. Vol. 2, 91–117. Hillsdale, NJ: Erlbaum.

Snyder, M. L., and W. Swann. 1978. Behavioral confirmation in social interaction: From social perception to social reality. *Journal of Experimental Social Psychology* 14: 148–162.

Sokolov, A. N. 1972. *Inner speech and thought.* New York: Plenum.

Solomons, L. M., and G. Stein. 1896. Normal motor automatisms. *Psychological Review* 3: 492–512.

Spanos, N. P. 1982. Hypnotic behavior: A cognitive, social psychological perspective. *Research Communications in Psychology, Psychiatry, and Behavior* 7: 199–213.

———. 1986. Hypnotic behavior: A social-psychological interpretation of amnesia, analgesia, and "trance logic." *Behavioral and Brain Sciences* 9: 449–502.

———. 1994. Multiple identity enactments and multiple personality disorder: A sociocognitive perspective. *Psychological Bulletin* 116: 143–165.

Spanos, N. P., W. P. Cross, M. Lepage, and M. Coristine. 1986. Glossolalia as learned behavior: An experimental demonstration. *Journal of Abnormal Psychology* 95: 21–23.

Spanos, N. P., and D. R. Gorassini. 1984. Structure of hypnotic test suggestions and attributions of responding involuntarily. *Journal of Personality and Social Psychology* 46: 688–696.

Spanos, N. P., and E. C. Hewitt. 1979. Glossolalia: A test of the "trance" and psychopathology hypotheses. *Journal of Abnormal Psychology* 88: 437–434.

———. 1980. The hidden observer in hypnotic analgesia: Discovery or experimental creation? *Journal of Personality and Social Psychology* 39: 1201–1214.

Spanos, N. P., and J. Katsanis. 1989. Effects of instructional set on attributions of nonvolition during hypnotic and nonhypnotic analgesia. *Journal of Personality and Social Psychology* 56: 182–188.

Spanos, N. P., R. J. Stenstrom, and J. C. Johnston. 1988. Hypnosis, placebo, and suggestion in the treatment of warts. *Psychosomatic Medicine* 50: 245–260.

Spelke, E. S., W. Hirst, and U. Neisser. 1976. Skills of divided attention. *Cognition* 4: 215–230.

Spellman, B. A. 1997. Crediting causality. *Journal of Experimental Psychology: General* 126: 323–348.

Spence, S. A. 1996. Free will in the light of neuropsychiatry. *Philosophy, Psychiatry, and Psychology* 3(2): 75–90.

Spence, S. A., D. J. Brooks, S. R. Hirsch, P. F. Liddle, J. Meehan, and P. M. Grasby. 1997. A PET study of voluntary movement in schizophrenic patients experiencing passivity phenomena (delusions of alien control). *Brain* 120: 1997–2011.

Sperry, R. W. 1950. Neural basis of the spontaneous optokinetic response produced by visual neural inversion. *Journal of Comparative Physiological Psychology* 45: 482–489.

———. 1961. Cerebral organization and behavior. *Science* 133: 1749–1757.

Spiegel, D. 1998. Social psychological theories cannot fully account for hypnosis: The record was never crooked. *American Journal of Clinical Hypnosis* 41: 158–161.

Spiegel, D., and E. Cardeña. 1991. Disintegrated experience: The dissociative disorders revisited. *Journal of Abnormal Psychology* 100: 366–378.

Spinoza, B. 1677. *The ethics*, trans. R. H. M. Elwes. London: Dover, 1883.

Spitz, H. H. 1997. *Nonconscious movements: From mystical messages to facilitated communication.* Mahwah, NJ: Erlbaum.

Stanislavski, C. 1936. *An actor prepares,* trans. E. R. Hapgood. New York: Theatre Arts Books.

Stay of execution for Weeks. 1999. *The Daily Progress,* September 2, A1, A7.

Steele, C. M., and J. Aronson. 1995. Stereotype threat and the intellectual test performance of African Americans. *Journal of Personality and Social Psychology* 69: 797–811.

Stein, G. 1898. Cultivated motor automatism: A study of character in its relation to attention. *Psychological Review* 5: 295–306.

———. 1933. *The autobiography of Alice B. Toklas.* London: John Lane.

Stern, J. A., M. Brown, A. Ulett, and I. Sletten. 1977. A comparison of hypnosis, acupuncture, morphine, valium, asprin, and placebo in the management of experimentally induced pain. In *Conceptual and investigative approaches to hypnosis and hypnotic phenomena,* ed. W. E. Edmonston. Annals of the New York Academy of Sciences No. 296, 175–193.

Stevenson, R. L. 1886. *The strange case of Dr. Jekyll and Mr. Hyde.* New York: Franklin Watts, 1967.

Stoller, P. 1995. *Embodying colonial memories: Spirit possession, power, and the Hauka in West Africa*. New York: Routledge.

Storms, M. D. 1973. Videotape and the attribution process: Reversing actors' and observers' points of view. *Journal of Personality and Social Psychology* 27: 165–175.

Stotland, E. 1969. Exploratory studies of empathy. In *Advances in experimental social psychology*, ed. L. Berkowitz. Vol. 4. New York: Academic Press.

Stratton, G. M. 1921. The control of another person by obscure signs. *Psychological Review* 28: 301–314.

Stuss, D. T. 1991. Disturbance of self-awareness after frontal system damage. In *Awareness of deficit after brain injury*, eds. G. P. Prigatano and D. L. Schacte, 63–83. New York: Oxford University Press.

Stuss, D. T., and D. F. Benson. 1986. *The frontal lobes*. New York: Raven Press.

———. 1987. The frontal lobes and control of cognition and memory. In *The frontal lobes revisited*, ed. E. Perelman, 141–158. New York: The IRBN Press.

Suler, H. J. 1999. The psychology of avatars and graphical space in multimedia chat communities. In *Psychology of cyberspace*. <http://www.rider.edu/users/suler/psycyber/psycyber.html>.

Surman, O. S., S. K. Gottlieb, T. P. Hackett, and E. L. Silverberg. 1973. Hypnosis in the treatment of warts. *Archives of General Psychiatry* 28: 439–441.

Sutcliffe, J. P. 1961. "Credulous" and "skeptical" views of hypnotic phenomena: Experiments in esthesia, hallucination, and delusion. *Journal of Abnormal and Social Psychology* 62: 189–200.

Sutcliffe, J. P., and J. Jones. 1962. Personal identity, multiple personality, and hypnosis. *International Journal of Clinical and Experimental Hypnosis* 10: 231–269.

Swann, W. B. 1999. *Resilient identities: Self-relationships and the construction of social reality*. New York: Basic Books.

Swann, W. B., B. W. Pelham, and D. C. Roberts. 1987. Causal chunking: Memory and interference in ongoing interaction. *Journal of Personality and Social Psychology* 53: 858–865.

Szechtman, H., E. Woody, K. S. Bowers, and C. Nahmias. 1998. Where the imaginal appears real: A positron emission tomography study of auditory hallucinations. *Proceedings of the National Academy of Sciences* 95: 1956–1960.

Szempruch, J., and J. W. Jacobson. 1993. Evaluating the facilitated communications of people with developmental disabilities. *Research in Developmental Disabilities* 14: 253–264.

Taylor, E. 1983. *William James on exceptional mental states*. Amherst: University of Massachusetts Press.

Taylor, M. 1999. *Imaginary companions and the children who create them*. New York: Oxford University Press.

Taylor, M., B. S. Cartwright, and S. M. Carlson. 1993. A developmental investigation of children's imaginary companions. *Developmental Psychology* 29: 276–285.

Taylor, M., B. M. Esbensen, and R. T. Bennett. 1994. Children's understanding of knowledge acquisition: The tendency for children to report that they have always known what they have just learned. *Child Development* 65: 1581–1604.

Taylor, S. E. 1989. *Positive illusions: Creative self-deception and the healthy mind.* New York: Basic Books.

Taylor, S. E., and L. G. Aspinwall. 1993. Coping with chronic illness. In *Handbook of stress: Theoretical and clinical aspects,* 2d ed., eds. L. Goldberger and S. Breznitz, 511–531. New York: Free Press.

Taylor, S. E., and J. D. Brown. 1988. Illusion and well-being: A social psychological perspective on mental health. *Psychological Bulletin* 103: 193–210.

Taylor, S. E., H. A. Wayment, and M. A. Collins. 1993. Positive illusions and affect regulation. In *Handbook of mental control,* eds. D. M. Wegner and J. W. Pennebaker, 325–343. Englewood Cliffs, NJ: Prentice-Hall.

Taylor, S. T., and S. E. Fiske. 1978. Salience, attention, and attribution: Top of the head phenomena. In *Advances in experimental social psychology,* ed. L. Berkowitz. Vol. 11, 250–283. New York: Academic Press.

Taylor, W. S., and M. F. Martin. 1944. Multiple personality. *Journal of Abnormal and Social Psychology* 39: 281–300.

Tellegen, A., and G. Atkinson. 1974. Openness to absorbing and self-altering experiences ("absorption"), a trait related to hypnotic susceptibility. *Journal of Abnormal Psychology* 83: 268–277.

Thigpen, C. H., and H. Cleckley. 1957. *The three faces of Eve.* New York: McGraw-Hill.

Thomason, S. G. 1989. "Entities" in the linguistic minefield. *Skeptical Inquirer* 13: 391–396.

Thompson, S. P. 1910. A physiological effect of an alternating magnetic field. *Proceedings of the Royal Society, London* 82: 396–398.

Thurber, J. 1960. Noted shipmates in Thurber's ark. *Life,* March 14, 104–108.

Tillman, J. G., M. R. Nash, and P. M. Lerner. 1994. Does trauma cause dissociative pathology? In *Dissociation: Clinical and theoretical perspectives,* eds. S. J. Lynn and J. W. Rhue, 395–414. New York: Guilford.

Tucker, M. A. 1897. Comparative observations on the involuntary movements of adults and children. *American Journal of Psychology* 8(3): 394–404.

Tulving, E. 1972. Episodic and semantic memory. In *Organization of memory,* eds. E. Tulving and W. Donaldson. New York: Academic Press.

———. 1985. Memory and consciousness. *Canadian Psychology* 26: 1–12.

———. 1999. On the uniqueness of episodic memory. In *Cognitive neuroscience of memory,* eds. L. G. Nilsson and H J. Markowitsch, 11–42. Seattle, WA: Hogrefe and Huber.

Turkle, S. 1995. *Life on the screen.* New York: Simon and Schuster.

Twachtman-Cullen, D. 1997. *A passion to believe: Autism and the facilitated communication phenomenon.* Boulder, CO: Westview.

Twain, M. 1906. *What is Man?* New York: Oxford University Press, 1996.

Uleman, J. S. 1989. A framework for thinking intentionally about unintended thoughts. In *Unintended thought.* eds. J. S. Uleman and J. A. Bargh, 425–449. New York: Guilford Press.

Vallacher, R. R., A. Nowak, J. Markus, and J. Strauss. 1998. Dynamics in the coordination of mind and action. In *Personal control in action: Cognitive and motivational mechanisms,* eds. M. Kofta, G. Weary, and G. Sedek, 27–59. New York: Plenum.

Vallacher, R. R., and D. M. Wegner. 1985. *A theory of action identification.* Hillsdale, NJ: Erlbaum.

———. 1987. What do people think they're doing? Action identification and human behavior. *Psychological Review* 94: 3–15.

———. 1989. Levels of personal agency: Individual variation in action identification. *Journal of Personality and Social Psychology* 57: 660–671.

Veith, I. 1970. *Hysteria.* Chicago: University of Chicago Press.

Velmans, M. 1991. Is human information processing conscious? *Behavioral and Brain Sciences* 14: 651–726.

Victor, J. S. 1993. *Satanic panic: The creation of a contemporary legend.* Chicago: Open Court.

Vinokur, A., and I. Ajzen. 1982. Relative importance of prior and immediate events: A causal primacy effect. *Journal of Personality and Social Psychology* 42: 820–829.

Vogt, E. Z., and R. Hyman. 1959. *Water witching U.S.A.* Chicago: University of Chicago Press.

Voltaire. 1752. *Voltaire's philosophical dictionary,* trans. H. I. Woolf. New York: Knopf, 1924.

von Holst, E. 1954. Relations between the central nervous system and the peripheral organs. *British Journal of Animal Behaviour* 2: 89–94.

Vygotsky, L. S. 1934. *Thought and language,* ed. and trans. E. Hanfmann and G. Vakar. Cambridge, MA: MIT Press. 1962.

Wadden, T. A., and C. H. Anderton. 1982. The clinical uses of hypnosis. *Psychological Bulletin* 91: 215–243.

Wafer, J. 1991. *Taste of blood.* Philadelphia: University of Pennsylvania Press.

Wagstaff, G. F. 1991. Compliance, belief, and semantics in hypnosis: A non-state sociocognitive perspective. In *Theories of hypnosis: Current models and perspectives,* eds. S. J. Lynn and J. W. Rhue, 362–396. New York: Guilford.

Washington, P. 1995. *Madame Blavatsky's baboon.* New York: Schocken.

Watts, F. N., F. P. McKenna, R. Sharrock, and L. Trezise. 1986. Colour naming of phobia-related words. *British Journal of Psychology* 77: 97–108.

Watzlawick, P., J. B. Beavin, and D. D. Jackson. 1967. *Pragmatics of human communication: A study of interactional patterns, pathologies, and paradoxes.* New York: W. W. Norton.

Weary, G., F. Gleicher, and K. Marsh. 1993. *Control motivation and social cognition.* New York: Springer-Verlag.

Wegner, D. M. 1982. *Intimate episodes.* Unpublished manuscript.

———. 1989. *White bears and other unwanted thoughts.* New York: Viking Penguin.

———. 1992. You can't always think what you want: Problems in the suppression of unwanted thoughts. In *Advances in experimental social psychology,* ed. M. Zanna. Vol. 5, 193–225. San Diego, CA: Academic Press.

———. 1994. Ironic processes of mental control. *Psychological Review* 101: 34–52.

———. 1997. Why the mind wanders. In *Scientific approaches to consciousness,* eds. J. D. Cohen and J. W. Schooler, 295–315. Mahwah, NJ: Erlbaum.

———. in press. Who is the controller of controlled processes? In *The new unconscious,* eds. R. Hassin, J. S. Uleman, and J. A. Bargh. New York: Oxford University Press.

Wegner, D. M., M. E. Ansfield, and D. Pilloff. 1998. The putt and the pendulum: Ironic effects of the mental control of movement. *Psychological Science* 9(3): 196–199.

Wegner, D. M., and J. A. Bargh. 1998. Control and automaticity in social life. In *Handbook of social psychology,* 4th ed., eds. D. T. Gilbert, S. T. Fiske, and G. Lindzey. Boston: McGraw-Hill.

Wegner, D. M., A. Broome, and S. J. Blumberg. 1997. Ironic effects of trying to relax under stress. *Behaviour Research and Therapy* 35: 11–21.

Wegner, D. M., and R. Erber. 1992. The hyperaccessibility of suppressed thoughts. *Journal of Personality and Social Psychology* 63: 903–912.

———. 1993. Social foundations of mental control. In *Handbook of mental control,* eds. D. M. Wegner and J. W. Pennebaker, 36–56. Englewood Cliffs, NJ: Prentice-Hall.

Wegner, D. M., R. Erber, and S. Zanakos. 1993. Ironic processes in the mental control of mood and mood-related thought. *Journal of Personality and Social Psychology* 65: 1093–1104.

Wegner, D. M., and V. A. Fuller. 2000. Clever hands: Action projection in facilitated communication. Unpublished manuscript.

Wegner, D. M., and D. T. Gilbert. 2000. Social psychology: The science of human experience. In *The message within: The role of subjective experience in social cognition and behavior,* eds. H. Bless and J. P. Forgas, 1–9. Philadelphia: Psychology Press.

Wegner, D. M., and T. Giuliano. 1980. Arousal-induced attention to self. *Journal of Personality and Social Psychology* 38: 719–726.

Wegner, D. M., T. Giuliano, and P. T. Hertel. 1985. Cognitive interdependence in close relationships. In *Compatible and incompatible relationships,* ed. W. J. Ickes, 253–276. New York: Springer-Verlag.

Wegner, D. M., and D. Schaefer. 1978. The concentration of responsibility: An objective self-awareness analysis of group size effects in helping situations. *Journal of Personality and Social Psychology* 36: 147–155.

Wegner, D. M., D. J. Schneider, S. Carter, and T. White. 1987. Paradoxical effects of thought suppression. *Journal of Personality and Social Psychology* 53: 5–13.

Wegner, D. M., and L. Smart. 1997. Deep cognitive activation: A new approach to the unconscious. *Journal of Consulting and Clinical Psychology* 65: 984–995.

Wegner, D. M., and R. R. Vallacher. 1980. *The self in social psychology.* New York: Oxford University Press.

———. 1986. Action identification. In *Handbook of motivation and cognition,* eds. E. T. Higgins and R. Sorrentino, 550–582. New York: Guilford.

Wegner, D. M., R. R. Vallacher, and M. Kelly. 1983. Identifications of the act of getting married. Cited in Vallacher and Wegner 1985.

Wegner, D. M., R. R. Vallacher, G. Macomber, R. Wood, and K. Arps. 1984. The emergence of action. *Journal of Personality and Social Psychology* 46: 269–279.

Wegner, D. M., and R. M. Wenzlaff. 1996. Mental control. In *Social psychology: Handbook of basic principles,* eds. E. T. Higgins and A. W. Kruglanski, 466–492. New York: Guilford.

Wegner, D. M., and T. Wheatley. 1999. Apparent mental causation: Sources of the experience of will. *American Psychologist* 54: 480–491.

Wegner, D. M., L. Winerman, and B. Sparrow. 2001. Action at a distance: Experienced control over the movements of others. Unpublished manuscript.

Weiner, B. 1974. *Achievement motivation and attribution theory.* Morristown, NJ: General Learning Press.

Weiskrantz, L. 1997. *Consciousness lost and found.* New York: Oxford University Press.

Weitzenhoffer, A. M., and E. R. Hilgard. 1962. *Stanford hypnotic susceptibility scale, Forms A and B.* Palo Alto, CA: Consulting Psychologists Press.

Welch, L. 1955. The relationship between conditioning and higher learning. *Journal of General Psychology* 53: 221–229.

Wellman, H. M. 1990. *The child's theory of mind.* Cambridge, MA: MIT Press.

Wellman, H. M., and S. A. Gelman. 1992. Cognitive development: Foundational theories of core domains. *Annual Review of Psychology* 43: 337–375.

Wenzlaff, R. M., and D. E. Bates. 1998. Unmasking a cognitive vulnerability to depression: How lapses in mental control reveal depressive thinking. *Journal of Personality and Social Psychology* 75: 1559–1571.

Wenzlaff, R. M., and D. M. Wegner, 2000. Thought suppression. *Annual Review of Psychology* 51: 59–91.

Werner, H. 1940. *Comparative psychology of mental development.* New York: Harper.

What is planchette? 1868. *Scientific American* 19(2): 17–18.

Wheeler, D. L., J. W. Jacobson, R. A. Paglieri, and A. A. Schwartz. 1993. An experimental assessment of facilitated communication. *Mental Retardation* 31: 49–60.

Whorf, B. L. 1956. Science and linguistics. In *Language, thought, and reality. Selected writings of Benjamin Lee Whorf,* ed. J. B. Carroll, 197–219. New York: Wiley.

Whyte, L. L. 1960. *The unconscious before Freud.* New York: Basic Books.

Wicklund, R. A., and J. W. Brehm. 1976. *Perspectives on cognitive dissonance.* Hillsdale, NJ: Erlbaum.

Wicklund, R. A., and P. Gollwitzer. 1982. *Symbolic self-completion.* Hillsdale, NJ: Erlbaum.

Wilkes, K. V. 1988. *Real people: Personal identity without thought experiments.* New York: Oxford University Press.

Wilson, T. D. 1985. Strangers to ourselves: The origins and accuracy of beliefs about one's own mental states. In *Attribution: Basic issues and applications,* eds. J. H. Harvey and G. Weary, 9–36. Orlando, FL: Academic Press.

Wilson, T. D., D. S. Dunn, J. A. Bybee, D. B. Hyman, and J. A. Rotondo. 1984. Effects of analyzing reasons on attitude-behavior consistency. *Journal of Personality and Social Psychology* 47: 5–16.

Wilson, T. D., S. Lindsay, and T. Y. Schooler. 2000. A model of dual attitudes. *Psychological Review* 107: 101–126.

Wilson, T. D., and J. W. Schooler. 1991. Thinking too much: Introspection can reduce the quality of preferences and decisions. *Journal of Personality and Social Psychology* 60: 181–192.

Wilson, T. D., and J. I. Stone. 1985. Limitations of self-knowledge: More on telling more than we can know. *Review of Personality and Social Psychology* 6: 167–183.

Wimmer, H., and J. Perner. 1983. Beliefs about beliefs: Representation and constraining function of wrong beliefs in young childrens' understanding of deception. *Cognition* 13: 103–128.

Winkleman, M. 1986. Trance states: A theoretical model and cross-cultural analysis. *Ethos* 14: 174–203.

Winter, A. 1998. *Mesmerized: Powers of the mind in Victorian Britain.* Chicago: University of Chicago Press.

Wittgenstein, L. 1974. *Philosophical grammar,* trans. A. Kenny, ed. R. Rhees. Oxford: Blackwell.

Woody, E. Z., and K. S. Bowers. 1994. A frontal assault on dissociated control. In *Dissociation: Clinical, theoretical, and research perspectives,* eds. S. J. Lynn and J. W. Rhue, 52–79. New York: Guilford.

Woolley, J. D. 2000. The development of beliefs about direct mental-physical causality in imagination, magic, and religion. In *Imagining the impossible: The development of magical, scientific, and religious thinking in children*, eds. K. Rosengren, C. Johnson, and P. L. Harris. New York: Cambridge University Press.

Wundt, W. 1912. *Lectures on human and animal psychology*, trans. J. E. Creighton and E. B. Titchener. London: Allyn and Unwin.

Yost, C. S. 1916. *Patience Worth: A psychic mystery*. New York: Holt, Rinehart, and Winston.

Young, M. E. 1995. On the origin of personal causal theories. *Psychonomic Bulletin and Review* 2: 83–104.

Young, P. C. 1948. Antisocial uses of hypnosis. In *Experimental hypnosis*, ed. L. M. LeCron, 376–409. New York: Macmillan.

Zajonc, R. B. 1980. Feeling and thinking: Preferences need no inferences. *American Psychologist* 35: 151–175.

Zeigarnik, B. 1927. On the recall of completed and incompleted tasks. *Psychologische Forschung* 9: 1–85.

Zelazo, P. D., J. W. Astington, and D. R. Olson. 1999. *Developing theories of intention: Social understanding and self-control*. Mahwah, NJ: Erlbaum.

Ziehen, T. 1899. *Introduction to physiological psychology*, trans. C. C. Van Liew and O. W. Beyer. New York: Macmillan.

Zimbardo, P. G. 1970. The human choice: Individuation, reason, and order versus deindividuation, impulse, and chaos. In *Nebraska symposium on motivation 1969*, 237–307. Lincoln: University of Nebraska Press.

Zivin, G. 1979. *The development of self-regulation through private speech*. New York: Wiley.

Zuzne, L., and W. H. Jones. 1989. *Anomalistic psychology: A study of magical thinking*. Hillsdale, NJ: Erlbaum.

Author Index

Subject Index